Helping Children and Adolescents with Chronic and Serious Medical Conditions

Helping Children and Adolescents with Chronic and Serious Medical Conditions

A Strengths-Based Approach

Nancy Boyd Webb, Editor

WILEY

JOHN WILEY & SONS, INC.

Library of Congress Cataloging-in-Publication Data:

Helping children and adolescents with chronic and serious medical conditions : a strengths-based approach/[edited by] Nancy Boyd Webb.
    p. cm.
    Includes bibliographical references and index.
    Summary: "Many practitioners lack the training to deal competently with acute and chronic health issues presented by their young clients and students. Providing an innovative inter-professional model, Helping Children and Adolescents with Chronic and Serious Medical Conditions provides a multi-disciplinary approach so that practitioners from a diverse range of helping fields, working in hospitals, out-patient clinics, agencies and schools, may be better equipped to foster children's resilience and build on their emotional strengths. This is a vital tool for a broad range of health care professionals, including social workers, school counselors, play therapists, nurses, and many others"–Provided by publisher.

    ISBN 978-0-470-37139-8 (pbk.)
    1. Child health services.   2. Teenagers–Medical care.   I. Webb, Nancy Boyd, 1932–
    RJ101.H43 2009
    362.198'92–dc22   2009028340

Printed in the United States of America

V10013545_083019

To all the children and youth who manage to carry on their lives despite serious health conditions . . .
and
to the professionals whose committed work with these youth contributes to their resiliency and determination to live their lives to the fullest

CONTENTS

Foreword

Barbara Sourkes, PhD

If kids are normal, not sick, they like to be treated special. But if kids have a disease, they want to be treated normal.
11-year-old child (Sourkes, 1995, p. 82)

I've had a closer relationship with my family than most other kids because I've needed them more these last years.
11-year-old child (Sourkes, 1995, p. 87)

These wise and incisive statements capture the essence of children's experience living with a serious medical condition. They long first and foremost to be seen as children, with the assurance that their identity remains larger than the "special" status of being a vulnerable patient. In fact, many of these children live a double life: They long for the normalcy of daily life and at the same time they live with the "abnormal" presence of illness (Sourkes et al., 2005, p. 370). From looking to feeling to *being* normal, the concept has implications for the child's sense of competence, coping, and self-esteem. The 11-year-old girl quoted in the epigraph continued: "Once you have a disease, people treat you as if you're not capable. Even though it's not true, it makes you feel really bad about yourself (Sourkes, 1995, p. 82).

Most of these children recognize the impact of their illness on the entire family, and instinctively reflect upon the child-in-the-family as a unit of its own. Each family has its own identity, strength, and vulnerability, and it is within this framework that the child struggles to withstand and integrate the illness. Children's ability to cope is greatly influenced by their family—the individual and collective responses of its members. Under optimal circumstances, "the interior of the family assumes a central role in preserving the . . . [child's] . . . psychological integrity" (Rait and Holland, 1986, p. 4).

The face of childhood illness is changing rapidly in the light of medical and scientific advances. Many diseases that were once uniformly fatal are now life-threatening in nature, with longer-term survival or even cure as an outcome. Chronic conditions that used to necessitate long-term hospitalization are now treated primarily on an outpatient basis. For those children who are facing death, hospice care has enabled many children to be at home for this last chapter. As a result of all these factors, children who are living with medical illnesses are far more visible in the community. It is therefore incumbent upon health and mental health professionals to broaden our concept of care to include the children's reintegration into that wider world.

The newly emerging interdisciplinary field of pediatric palliative care encompasses many of these children. Palliative care is defined as comprehensive care of children with life-threatening conditions (i.e., where prognosis is uncertain). It focuses on quality of life for the child and support for the family, including respite and bereavement care, if appropriate. Pediatric palliative care covers a much broader spectrum than the traditional and narrow definition that referred almost exclusively to the (imminently) dying child.

Helping Children and Adolescents with Chronic and Serious Medical Conditions is an important contribution to the evolving literature in psychosocial aspects of pediatric conditions. It is particularly timely given the increasing attention to the interaction between physical and mental health. Furthermore, children's psychological distress is now more often conceptualized as a symptom that must be addressed and can be ameliorated. Dr. Webb has assembled authors from a broad range of disciplines (including social work, psychology, pediatrics, nursing, chaplaincy, child life) and settings (hospital, clinic, hospice, home, school) to address ways to enhance the quality of these children's lives, as well as that of their families.

The opening section of the book provides the foundation for all that follows. Dr. Webb stresses from the outset that these children and families are facing extraordinary challenges and that an optimal clinical approach should focus on their strength and resilience rather than on pathology. Furthermore, the experience of these children and families must be viewed from an ecological perspective: As the child is embedded in the family, so the family is embedded within a social, cultural, and economic context. Access to care is a critical issue, and barriers within the current health care system render children and families even more vulnerable. Also addressed in this section is the impact of the illness on the healthy siblings. These children live the illness experience with the same intensity as the patient and parents; yet all too often their needs are underestimated or neglected in the dramatic focus on the ill child. In the words of a group of siblings, "Don't brothers and sisters count too?" (Sourkes et al., 2005, p. 371).

The following sections of this book present a multifaceted portrait of clinical approaches: practitioners from a variety of disciplines who treat children with a variety of medical conditions across a variety of settings. The reader is struck by both the unique and overlapping nature of these interventions, a reflection of the need for specialization within an integrated and seamless continuum of care for these children. The focus on school as a primary setting for care (along with the medical and home environment) reflects how profoundly school defines the "normal" structure of children's day-to-day lives. Its constancy can provide an anchor to the child who is coping with significant illness.

Helping Children and Adolescents with Chronic and Serious Medical Conditions provides a wellspring of knowledge, from the theoretical to the clinical. The many vignettes and transcriptions enrich immeasurably the reader's understanding of the interventions and their broader applicability. The focus on the experience of the professionals who work with these children—the challenges, the sadness, the triumphs—adds a rich dimension to the volume.

> *Thank you for giving me aliveness. Six-year-old child*
> *(Sourkes, 1995, p. 167)*

"Giving aliveness" to children whose lives are impacted by illness is the overarching goal for all of us. Dr. Webb and her colleagues have contributed significantly to that mission in the pages of this book.

References

Rait, D., & Holland, J. (1986). Pediatric cancer: Psychosocial issues and approaches. *Mediguide to Oncology,6.*

Sourkes, B. (1995). *Armfuls of time: The psychological experience of the child with a life-threatening illness.* Pittsburgh: University of Pittsburgh Press.

Sourkes, B., Frankel L., Brown, M., Contro, N., Benitz, W., Case, C., et al. (2005). Food, toys and love: Pediatric palliative care. *Current Problems in Pediatric and Adolescent Health Care, 35*(9), 345–392.

In my 30 years of clinical practice as a play therapist with children I often encountered young people who were grappling with physical health problems in addition to the emotional and psychological issues that had prompted their referral. I remember vividly one nine-year-old boy who was having a lot of difficulty dealing with his parents' high-conflict divorce and his need to adjust to a new stepparent and stepsiblings. One day when he was in my office describing to me his frustration at having to sleep in a stepbrother's room during a weekend visit and interact with this new sibling he didn't like, my client began to wheeze and gasp for air. I realized that he was having an asthma attack, but I had no idea what to do! His mother had dropped him off and would not return for another half hour. Fortunately, the boy pulled an inhaler out of his backpack and took some deep breaths, thereby relieving his symptoms. Although I had been working with this boy and his parents for more than a month, no one had ever informed me about his compromised health condition, and I immediately realized how the family stress over the divorce and remarriage was affecting his physical well-being. I also became aware that I had been remiss in not obtaining a health history when I took the boy's psychosocial history at intake, focused on detailed information about the family and about his academic and social adjustment. Unfortunately, this example is not unusual. Many children who are referred for help with their psychological difficulties also have accompanying health problems that interfere with their optimal adjustment in school, with peers, and within the family. Mental health practitioners must ask questions to learn about children's *physical and medical* as well as their emotional status.

This example, like many of the cases in this book, illustrates how even a potentially life-threatening condition such as asthma can take a backseat when a child and his or her therapist are focusing on family issues. The same example could have been used with a youngster with juvenile diabetes. Medical conditions that are not immediately evident can nonetheless have a *huge* impact on the child's quality of life, and it behooves therapists to be alert to a child's effort to ignore or minimize a serious health problem. In the case described here, it would have been incumbent on the therapist to have spoken directly to the boy about his medical status, about how he manages in school and after school, and to tell him that she wants to get updated information from his parents about it, since that could be important in her efforts to help him.

The intent of this book is to help practitioners better understand the stresses of children and adolescents, as well as their families, who must find a way to adjust to their youngsters' physical constraints related to their particular medical condition at the same time they are coping with other emotional pressures. It will serve as a resource for the various professions that work with medically compromised children and adolescents in settings such as hospitals, outpatient clinics, and schools. Because the content of the book focuses on the emotional component of illness for the youth and the family, it will help practitioners understand the impact of ongoing stress as it impacts the young person's usual developmental trajectory.

When acute or chronic health problems emerge in infancy, or later, they may seriously derail a child's developmental progression and create daunting problems for the young person and his or her family. This book illustrates the important collaborative role of social workers and other practitioners in helping such a chronically or acutely disabled young person and his or her family achieve the best quality of life possible under the reality of the specific circumstances. Grounded in a strengths-based perspective as it pertains to bio, psychosocial, developmental, and ecological factors. The book promotes ways to help the youth and the family focus on abilities and possibilities rather than on the limitations that accompany acute and chronic health conditions. The book will serve as a resource for social workers and practitioners in medical, school, and community settings where medically compromised children participate in educational and recreational programs and encounter health-related procedures. For example, most children who have asthma and diabetes attend school and engage to the best of their abilities in the regular routine, despite their need for medication, an inhaler, and/or other types of assistance. Children who are seriously disabled may require special education programs. Still other children with previously healthy backgrounds may suffer acute heath crises, such as accidents that require hospitalization, followed by periods of physical therapy and other remediation. Social workers, child life specialists, and school counselors often work together in these situations to facilitate the youth's optimal adjustment. This book highlights the separate and collaborative roles of these professionals on behalf of youth coping with serious health and medical challenges. The role of interdisciplinary collaboration is emphasized because professionals from different specialties must share the complex challenge of helping medically compromised children and adolescents at home, at school, and in the community, as well as in the hospital.

The book surveys the range of psychosocial, familial, and clinical services that social workers and other practitioners provide for children and adolescents and their families who are coping with various acute medical and health crises and ongoing conditions.

Part 1 provides an overview and theoretical framework for collaborative practice. Part 2 highlights the special contributions of practitioners in different settings who are specialists in the different areas that provide services to youths with acute and chronic medical conditions. The chapter authors in this section discuss the explicit role and contribution of their particular profession and its approach to helping. Chapters in Part 3 demonstrate the special challenges and issues that are associated with chronic medical conditions at various stages of the life cycle. Part 4 focuses on acute health crises and the need for interprofessional collaboration in work with the young person and the family. In order to fully understand this challenging helping task, the book's content reflects both general topics, such as dealing with ongoing stress, as well as very specific subjects, such as preparing a child for a surgical procedure. A strengths and empowerment philosophy integrates the various chapters with their unified emphasis on helping young people achieve optimal functioning, as outlined in Chapter 18.

This book will be an important resource in advanced college courses that train students to work with medically compromised children and adolescents in settings such as hospitals, outpatient clinics, and schools. At least three professions will find the book valuable as a required text in courses related to health, young people, and families. The professions are *social work, child life,* and *school psychology and counseling.* Pediatric nurses, pediatricians, and pastoral counselors will benefit from the content dealing with the emotional component of illness, and special education teachers will also appreciate this detailed focus on the young person's inner life and struggles to cope with various medical limitations.

The book covers basic information such as establishing relationships and helping clients accept restrictions while striving for as much healthy functioning as possible. It also deals with the unique situation of stress on the family system and the various stages of acceptance of a medical diagnosis, including the management of terminal illness. Cultural, ethical, and spiritual factors are emphasized as applicable to coping with life-and-death issues and to the numerous losses involved in medical situations.

As previously indicated, my interest in this topic grew from my outpatient child therapy practice, in which I encountered youths with medical conditions that were complicating their lives. My own medical experience at the time I initially proposed this book consisted of three different hospitalizations (two for childbirth and one for a broken ankle). It is ironic that in the six-month interval since I delivered the manuscript to the publisher I have had three additional hospitalizations. These have been for more serious conditions and have given me the opportunity to ponder how a young person might experience a hospitalization that potentially could change his or her life in a major way. My own sensitivity to this topic has increased manyfold as a result of my recent personal experience, and my hopes for the book have expanded as I have become more aware of its potential to reduce anxiety and increase adaptation. Hopefully, this will be a useful resource that will help practitioners more effectively help children and adolescents survive and thrive despite their serious medical conditions.

Nancy Boyd Webb

Acknowledgments

I am happy to take this opportunity to thank some of the people who have contributed to this book, although it probably never is possible to identify *all* the people, programs, and resources on whom the authors and I have drawn. An edited volume relies on the expertise of many individuals, and its value may be directly related to the different viewpoints and perspectives represented by the various chapter authors. Since this book is intended to demonstrate collaboration among different professionals, I am very grateful to this group of chapter authors who agreed to write about their specialized roles in helping medically compromised young people. My own circle of professional contacts has widened considerably as a result of working with this group of specialists, and, despite our different backgrounds, I became acutely aware of our unifying purpose in providing services to medically ill youth.

All of the authors cooperated in following my detailed chapter outline and completed the necessary revisions in a timely fashion. An edited book such as this moves at the pace of the slowest author, and although there were bumps along the way, we did manage to submit the edited manuscript within a reasonable time frame. I thank all the authors most genuinely for their willingness to share their specialized expertise for the overall good of the various helping professions that will rely on this book for information and guidance.

In addition I want to mention specifically my gratitude to the people at Maria Ferrerea Cancer Center in White Plains New York for their willingness to permit me to visit their outstanding program and to attend a staff meeting. The helpfulness of Rose Bartone, MSW, in facilitating this was especially appreciated.

All of the clinical cases used to illustrate various situations and interventions have been disguised. Some are composite cases, and others are used with signed permissions of parents who want their child's experiences to be used to help others. We are grateful to them.

On a personal level, I wish to thank my husband, Kempton, for his constant support and understanding. He transports my boxes of files, books, and office machines to my work places in Vermont and Florida, and he often responds to my request that he read a paragraph about which I want some independent input. He helps keep me grounded and happy.

This is my first experience working with the staff of John Wiley & Sons, and I have found them to be unfailingly responsive and professional in all our undertakings. I thank the dozens of individuals involved in the production process and look forward to having this book come into print so that it can add to the process of helping medically compromised children and youth.

Overview and Introduction: Theoretical Framework for Collaborative Practice

1

Part

When a Young Person's Health Becomes Problematic

Nancy Boyd Webb
Rose A. Bartone

1

Chapter

In the best of all possible worlds children would not develop serious health problems. We associate youth with vigor, energy, and well-being. Whereas all parents expect their children to acquire an occasional cold, earache, stomachache, or even a childhood disease such as chicken pox, they typically do not consider the likelihood that their child will develop a serious illness that has no cure and that will require continuous adaptation due to compromised bodily functioning. Similarly, young children, who are normally egocentric and bursting with feelings of strength and invulnerability, are even less likely to understand or accept the constraints of a serious illness or disability. The child thinks that older people sometimes get sick and have to go to the hospital, but not "kids like me." Therefore, the first challenge in working with medically compromised youth and their families is to help them deal with their initial fear, denial, and sense of unfairness in having to cope with all the pain and disruptions that accompany a serious health condition.

This book presents helping approaches to assist young people and their families handle in a positive manner the stresses involved in living with an illness or disability. Some conditions are evident at birth, and others may arise in early or later childhood or adolescence. The chapter authors discuss the multiplicity of factors that impact the coping ability of the child and family as they struggle to adapt to different acute and chronic health conditions, some of which may be life-threatening. Selected helping approaches that encourage positive attitudes and stimulate family and individual strengths are presented, together with developmental considerations that influence the patient, his or her siblings, and the parents.

Interprofessional Collaboration

Because helping a medically compromised child or adolescent inevitably involves input from a variety of professionals in different settings over many years, this book emphasizes the importance of interprofessional collaboration. Pediatricians, teachers, social workers, pastoral counselors, child life specialists, nurses, and many others typically are involved in any single health crisis. Part 2 of the book highlights the separate and collaborative roles of different professionals on behalf of youth who are coping with serious health and medical challenges. Each profession has its own focus, training, and language, but if children and families are to receive the best possible bio- psychosocial care it is imperative that all helpers be able to communicate with one another and acknowledge and appreciate their distinctive roles and contributions. This can be key to a positive outcome for the patient, the family, and the staff. We hope that the book will serve as a resource for social workers and other practitioners who counsel physically challenged children in medical, school, and community settings where they receive care and participate in various educational, recreational, and counseling programs.

The Incidence of Children's Health Conditions

Estimates indicate that between 10 and 15 percent of the children born in the United States have chronic health impairments of some kind. Many of these require lengthy and/or repeated hospitalizations and treatments that interfere with the child's usual activities (Clay, 2004; Phelps, 1998). In addition, several million children are admitted to hospital emergency rooms following severe and catastrophic injuries or illnesses. "Although many of their conditions [are] life-threatening, the large majority of clinically ill or disabled children survive to adulthood" (Perrin, 1989, p. xi).

A national survey of children's health (U.S. Department of Health and Human Services, 2005) collected data on more than 102,000 households in the United States with children under 18 years of age. Parents were asked to rate their child's health status in terms of five possibilities: excellent, very good, good, fair, or poor. The majority of parents (84.1 percent) reported that their children's health was excellent or very good. In contrast, the parents of 7.9 percent of children reported that their child currently had, or had had, at least one of a list of chronic health conditions that they ranked as moderate or severe. It is interesting that the percentages rose with the age of the child, from 4.4 percent among children from birth to age 5, to 9.1 percent among children ages 6 to 11, to 10 percent in the ages 12 to 17. Despite the many achievements of modern medicine, the fact remains that in the first decade of the twenty-first century a substantial number of children and their families continue to be burdened by serious health conditions.

The Most Frequent Pediatric Illnesses

According to Clay (2004), the most common high-incidence pediatric illnesses are the following:

- *Asthma*. Affects nearly 5 million children under the age of 18 in the United States.

- *Diabetes.* Occurs in about 15 to 20 children out of 100,000 under the age of 20 in the United States (Daneman & Frank, 1996).
- *Juvenile rheumatoid arthritis.* Estimated to affect nearly 200,000 children in the United States under the age of 18, with onset occurring as early as infancy and with most cases diagnosed between the ages of 1 and 4 (Cassidy & Petty, 1995).
- *Cancer.* May take the form of a blood cancer (e.g., leukemia or lymphoma), a solid tumor (e.g., neuroblastoma), or a brain tumor. Although all are being treated with increasing success, in some children the cancer is fatal.

Lower-Incidence Pediatric Medical Conditions

This list is selective and includes conditions that are not as frequent as those already mentioned but that also make physical demands on the child and require sensitive management in schools and other locales where the young person functions:

- *Heart conditions.* Congenital heart defects affect 8 to 10 children per 1,000; other conditions include heart murmurs and hypertension. Most congenital heart conditions are associated with other congenital conditions, such as Down syndrome (Clay, 2004, p. 26).
- *Seizure disorders, epilepsy.* About 40,000 cases a year are reported to begin in childhood; about 1 percent of the total population has epilepsy (Clay, 2004, p. 16).
- *Blood disorders.* Anemia, sickle cell disease, hemophilia.
- *Infectious diseases.* HIV, bacterial meningitis, hepatitis.

Other chronic and life-threatening conditions that are also frequently seen in children are cystic fibrosis, cerebral palsy, muscular dystrophy, blindness and hearing disorders, Down syndrome, and spina bifida. In order to be classified as *chronic,* the physical condition must be one that either actually does or is expected to (1) interfere with daily functioning more than three months a year or (2) cause hospitalization for more than one month a year (Wallander, Thompson, Alriksson-Schmidt, 2003).

These illnesses have certain elements in common that often become the focus of various psychosocial interventions. All require that the individual and family grieve and mourn the loss of good health in a young person's life. They also will necessitate various adjustments to the constraints of the disease or illness and adherence to the prescribed treatment regimen with ongoing follow-up. The responses of each young person will vary according to age- and illness-specific factors, but the pressures of stress and the need for adaptation lead to the development of anxiety and depression in many children (Auslander & Freedenthal, 2006).

This book presents counseling and therapy approaches to assist families in helping their children to achieve the best quality of life possible in their specific circumstance. We also discuss some ways to assist the young person to reconceptualize his or her illness as one that is a manageable challenge despite its restrictions. Different counseling methods are presented that involve the identification and utilization of the *strengths* of these young people and their families, in contrast to emphasizing the *limitations and problems* associated with an illness or disability. Clearly, certain hardships constitute part of the situation and cannot be ignored. However, the strengths-based philosophy emphasizes hope and possibility, and these attitudes significantly impact not only the child and family, but also the professionals who work with them. Clinicians are often intimately involved with their patients and families. Evidence-informed practices promise the greatest results for patients and families and also serve to bolster the clinicians' attitudes about their work. The next section reviews the central concepts on which this helping framework rests.

Theoretical Perspective for a Positive Helping Approach

Several interlocking perspectives form the basis for a helping philosophy that emphasizes a positive framework to be used by professionals who are working with medically challenged young people and their families. This guiding philosophy rests on concepts in the following models of helping:

- Ecological perspective
- Strengths perspective
- Crisis intervention to deal with stress and coping responses
- Individual and family resilience

Each of these interacting perspectives bolsters helping efforts that breathe a spirit of optimism and possibility into a situation that otherwise might be viewed as discouraging or even hopeless.

Ecological Perspective

Rooted in the work of Bronfenbrenner (1979), this concept has been widely adopted to recognize the many spheres of influence that impact any one individual's life. Each person is affected not only by his or her family and relatives, but also by peers, by the community, and by larger social and cultural influences. Furthermore, these interactive elements are bidirectional; in other words, children are influenced not only by their parents' attitudes about an illness, but the parents, in turn, are affected by the manner in which the child responds. In addition, the patient and the parents respond to the clinician by looking for clues or "hidden messages" in the practitioner's facial expression or tone of voice. The dynamics of this ecological person-in-situation relationship are not static, but evolving and ever changing.

Strengths Perspective

Introduced by Saleebey in 1992 and updated in 1997, this approach emphasizes assisting clients to "achieve their goals, realize their dreams, and shed the iron of their own inhibitions and misgivings" (Saleebey, 1997, p. 3). Such an inspirational philosophy becomes implemented through the following six statements of belief (adapted from Saleebey, 1997, pp. 12–15, as summarized by Openshaw, 2007, p. 67):

1. Every individual, group, family, and community has strengths.
2. Trauma, abuse, illness, and struggle may be injurious, but they also may be sources of challenge and opportunity.
3. We do not know the upper limits of anyone's capacity to grow and change; we must take the aspirations of individuals, groups, and communities seriously.
4. We best serve clients by collaborating with them.
5. Every environment is full of resources.
6. Caring, caretaking, and context are important.

As I read through these guiding principles I can't help but think that I would far prefer to be treated by someone who was following them in a hospital or clinic setting than by someone who was committed to a disease- or problem-focused medical model.

Crisis Intervention to Deal with Stress and Coping Responses

We all know how stress feels, and we realize that it can range in intensity from a slight irritation (e.g., being late for an appointment) to an overwhelming sense of anxiety (e.g., witnessing an automobile accident). Selye (1978) and Benson (2000) have written about the autonomic physiological changes in our bodies that occur in stressful circumstances. These often include increased heartbeat and changes in breathing and blood pressure that may be accompanied by either the impulse to get away from the situation (flight) or, alternatively, to fight it. Selye called this instinctive reaction the "fight or flight response" (Selye, 1978). People have different abilities to tolerate stress, based on their temperaments, the intensity of the particular stressful experience, and their past histories. Therefore, some people may respond with tears and depression when diagnosed with cancer, whereas other individuals may emphasize their strong intention to fight it. The diagnosis of an acute or chronic illness inevitably generates stress for anyone old enough to understand the terminology and its possible future course. When the stress response is acute, individuals may become so anxious that their functioning is impaired. In these situations, crisis intervention can be quite helpful initially in assisting young patients to employ some cognitive-behavioral strategies and expressive techniques to deal with their anxiety (Goodman, 2007). This will be discussed later.

However, young people have very different coping reactions depending on their level of cognitive development, the responses of family members, and even the expectations of their culture and social environment (Congress, 2004). Professional helpers must acknowledge and respect these variations in response and should subscribe to a philosophy of acceptance of individual differences, which sometimes includes the need to put aside and avoid expressing ones' personal feelings.

Individual and Family Resilience

Resilience has been defined as "the capacity to rebound from adversity strengthened and more resourceful" (Walsh, 2006, p. 4). As we think about the stresses of medical illness, we realize that this situation must be viewed through a systemic lens. According to Hauser (1999; quoted by Walsh, 2006, p. 12), "Resilience is woven in a web of relationships and experiences over the life course and across the generations." This statement clearly conveys the concept of a family ethos that might, for example, subscribe to the credo of never giving up. Certainly, parents and grandparents, both deliberately (in what they say) and indirectly (in their actions) convey to children and adolescents their views of acceptable and unacceptable methods of coping with adversity. Resilient families can somehow muster the strength to carry on even when all the cards seem to be stacked against them. Furthermore, family resilience involves not only how families survive, but also how they can "regenerate even in circumstances of overwhelming stress. It affirms the family potential for self-repair and growth out of crisis and challenge" (Walsh, 2006, p. 17). Although this concept may suggest a notion of "superfamilies," research suggests that with respect to *individual* behavior, children respond more positively when adults expect good behavior from them (Grusec, Goodnow, & Kuczynski, 2000). Probably the same dynamic would apply to families, thereby promoting their hardiness and resilience. A therapeutic model designed to support families of children with a chronic illness or disability includes the dynamics of hope, empowerment, reconnection, coping and resilience, and reframing (Morison, Bromfield, & Cameron, 2003).

The Language of Medical Conditions

Numerous terms have been used to refer to the physical status of people who have less-than-perfect bodies. Among these are the following:

- *Handicapped*
- *Physically impaired*

- *Hearing impaired*
- *Congenitally defective*
- *Disabled*
- *Chronically diseased*
- *Terminally ill*

All of these terms have very negative connotations and emphasize the deficits, losses, or disruptions created by the different conditions. A child who has more than one medical condition may be referred to as "multiply disabled." On the other hand, terminology that emphasizes what the child *can* do and that focuses on strengths rather than limitations, employs the much less pejorative expression "children with special needs" (Webb, 2003). It is ironic, however, that school programs refer to "children with disabilities" in conformity with the Americans with Disabilities Act (ADA) of 1990 in order to qualify for federal assistance (Friend, 2005). Therefore, we may need to change the language of the laws in order to make it more child-friendly and to encourage schools to use more positive terminology in identifying and planning programs for children who qualify for special education.

The Attribution of Meaning Related to a Medical Condition

It is natural for individuals and families to look for a reason behind the diagnosis of a medical condition and to want to know *why* it happened. A 14-year-old diagnosed with diabetes asks: "Did I get this because I gained too much weight and because I didn't follow the doctor's suggestion that I should exercise more?" His mother wonders if she should have taken more vitamins or somehow behaved differently during her pregnancy. A young child may also think that he or she did something bad to cause the illness and views the illness as a form of punishment. Adolescents may blame themselves or their family heritage by attributing the illness (correctly or not) to "bad genes" or to the fact that their family did something neglectful, such as avoiding regular medical checkups. Sometimes the patients or family members verbalize these questions, but more often they are silent and keep their worries unspoken for fear of creating more upset in the family.

All these uncertainties swirl around and reflect the overriding feeling that *this should not have happened to me or my child and that someone or something is to blame*. As mentioned, people may not admit their inner feelings, fears, and worries, but they nonetheless ponder them, and many become anxious and/or depressed trying to figure things out. Sometimes children who sense that their condition is serious wonder whether it means that they are going to die. This is especially true in the initial stage right after the diagnosis. It helps to permit these fears to be spoken, because unspoken fears have a way of escalating. The social worker and/or child life specialist can play a critical role in helping the child and parent deal openly with their fears. Chapter 2 discusses the emotional impact of a young person's illness on the entire family system.

When the illness is one that appears to be inherited, the responsible parent may feel burdened with guilt, even when he or she knows that it was not within his or her power to control the genes that were passed to the child. Sometimes adults who recall their own parents' responses years ago to a sibling's illness unconsciously try to avoid repeating a similar situation in their current family situation. This dynamic was poignantly demonstrated in a novel, *The Memory Keeper's Daughter* (Edwards, 2005), in which one of the main characters, a physician, had had a younger sister who was born with a "weak heart" and died when she was 12 years old. The man grew up acutely aware of his mother's terrible and ongoing grief over his sister's fragile condition during her childhood, which culminated in her eventual death. These memories of his mother's relentless pain proved to be a decisive factor many years later when the physician delivered his own twin babies in the middle of a snowstorm because he and his wife could not reach the hospital in time. When the man realized at the moment of birth that one of his twins had Down syndrome, all he could think about was wanting to protect his wife from suffering grief similar to that of his mother's. He therefore made a split-second decision to give the infant with Down syndrome to the attending nurse, with instructions that she was to place the child permanently in a nearby long-term-care facility. The doctor then told his wife that their female twin baby had died in childbirth and that he didn't want her to see the dead infant. The book graphically portrays how this well-intentioned lie and secret came to control the man and his marriage, as well as the nurse, who actually decided to keep the child and raise her as her own daughter.

The birth of a baby with a medically compromising condition creates many complicated realities for the parents, as illustrated in this book. Professionals who are involved with such families should be prepared to deal with different reactions in various family members and to remember these powerful dynamics:

- Grief responses are inevitable, although they may be denied and hidden.
- Parents are mourning the loss of their anticipated perfect baby.
- Guilt, blame, and shame may dominate the underlying feelings of sadness.
- Family members often are protective of each other and may avoid discussions that could be upsetting.
- Different people respond differently in situations of loss, and often spouses misunderstand the reactions of their partners.
- The pain of loss recurs sequentially and repeatedly over many years.

- Children pick up cues from family members, whether verbalized or unexpressed.

- Counseling and/or therapy can assist the individual and family cope with their confused and upsetting feelings.

Issues of Identity, Competency, and Future Life Planning

When a young person is born with a serious and disabling medical condition and/or when he or she develops a serious illness in childhood or adolescence, this factor often takes center stage and becomes magnified in the individual's own and his or her family's lives. The need for repeated visits to the doctor or hospital clinic annoyingly conflict with a youngster's wish to participate in after-school activities, and the doctor's treatment protocol can interfere with going to a friend's house for a sleepover or on a weekend overnight camping trip with the Scouts. A disability or illness "all too often sets (young people) apart and (may be) used to define (them) in ways that minimize their humanity" (Lavin, 2002). Thus, Johnny who used to be considered by his teacher as the boy with the charming smile, now becomes, in his teacher's perception, "the boy with cancer." The disease, illness, or disability becomes a major element of the affected young people's identity, and this may seriously affect their ability to view themselves as competent and capable despite the disability, and it may affect their view of a future with exciting possibilities. Sometimes their appearance changes due to treatments (e.g., hair loss) and they may not be able to attend school because of a compromised immune system. On the one hand, these children may miss their peers, and on the other, they may be relieved not to have to appear in public, because of discomfort about their appearance.

Of course, the ultimate meaning of a diagnosis to an individual depends on his or her age and ability to comprehend its seriousness. A classic study of children's awareness of their disease and its fatal potential (Bluebond-Langner, 1978) indicated that youngsters go through five stages of understanding, beginning with knowing the name of their disease and its seriousness, to the final realization that death is a possible outcome if the treatment plan doesn't work. Children who regularly attend hospital clinics and who see and make friends with other ill youngsters there may talk about and compare their symptoms with these peers. Many of them become very knowledgeable about their conditions, their treatments, and their prognoses. Increasingly, hospitals and clinics that treat such young people offer services such as specialized support groups, printed materials about specific illnesses, and lists of web sites that provide information and contact with others. This educational process is empowering to the patient and the family. The appendix of this book lists numerous resources.

Infertility as a side effect of treatment is a reality that adolescent cancer patients must face. Sexuality and reproductive rights are sensitive areas to address with both patients and their families. Adolescents are easily embarrassed and may be resistant to an open discussion on the topic. However, preserving the ability to reproduce is of paramount importance. Clinicians working with the families must be sensitive to the religious and cultural background of the families and provide support and education on this topic. An excellent web site dealing with this is http://www.fertilehope.org. Even after treatment, late and secondary effects of cancer may occur, and secondary cancers are always a possibility. In these instances, long-term loss and grief counseling should be made available.

Examples of Children's Responses to Serious Medical Conditions

The prize-winning photographer Jill Krementz has published two books that illustrate how children come to understand their different medical conditions (Krementz, 1992 and 1998). The books present timeless portraits of children and youth with different disabilities and medical conditions. Each book consists of in-depth interviews and photographs of the young people, who range in age from 6 to 16 and who have been diagnosed with a variety of conditions and disabilities. Many of these interviews (summarized here with the author's permission) touchingly convey and support the concept of different reactions in children's level of understanding and acceptance of an illness. For example, a 10-year-old girl reported her experience when her mother told her (when she was 7 years old) that she had diabetes. She said that she burst into tears because she was afraid that she was going to die. The girl stated that even after her parents convinced her that this was not going to happen, she nonetheless felt that her life was going to change completely (inevitably, she was right). This would have been a good time for clinical interventions such as support and review of the girl's continuing abilities: that is, recognition of what she *could* still do, rather than focusing on her fears of possible illness-related obstacles in her future.

Another child who was 15 years old and who had had cystic fibrosis all his life grappled with the meaning of his illness. He attached a religious purpose to being ill. This boy, who went to church every week, developed the belief that there had to be a reason for his illness. In an interview he stated as follows: "God didn't just draw my name out of a hat. There has to be a reason why I'm sick . . . . Sometimes I think that maybe he knew I'd have this [positive] attitude and he put me here so other kids who are sick can see me and say, 'Hey, you know, maybe he's right, maybe there *is* hope" (Krementz, 1989, p. 105).

Although the majority of the children interviewed in these two books (14 in one and 12 in the other) convey very positive can-do attitudes despite their serious illnesses and disabilities, a few admit to being depressed or even suicidal. This was the case with a 12-year-old boy who was born with a hole in his heart and who had a stroke during an operation soon after birth to repair his heart and who subsequently became paralyzed on one side of his body. This boy admitted to being very depressed at the limitations on his physical movements as he was growing up, and sometimes he felt that it was so bad he even wanted to kill himself. There is no indication that this boy had any counseling to help him; however, the youngster was somehow able to surmount those negative feelings, and he described how, at age 12, he gave a special presentation at school that included asking the audience try to tie one of their shoelaces and cut an orange with one hand so that they could begin to appreciate what it is like to live with paralysis on one side of their body! This same boy had taught himself how to deliver a one-handed serve in tennis, and at the conclusion of the interview he described his hope to learn to relax his spastic muscles through the use of biofeedback.

It was most impressive to me to notice in these very different personal histories how many of the young people managed to find a way to participate in sports despite their extensive disabilities. It seemed as if they were determined to prove that they *could* engage in physically challenging activities. In fact, while I was in the process of writing this chapter, the local newspaper reported the story of a 21-year-old South African man who had had both legs amputated below the knee when he was 11 months old and who was attempting to participate in the 2008 Beijing Olympics! His special prostheses ultimately served to disqualify him because they supposedly provided a mechanical advantage in running. Incredibly, this young man had previously participated in a variety of sports, including rugby and wrestling, and he had taken up running to recover from a rugby injury (*St. Petersburg Times*, 1/15/08).

As I reflected on this person's motivation and that of many of the disabled children in Krementz's two books, my psychotherapy-based diagnostic thinking made me label their behavior as "overcompensation" or "denial." However, from the strengths perspective, I realized that these young people were refusing to let their limitations define their lives. While that attitude will help them succeed in many life tasks, one wonders how long it will be necessary for them to continue to prove to themselves and others that they are capable. Playing rugby with a prosthesis must take a great toll on a person! Therefore, I believe that it is appropriate for the counselor or therapist to give the suggestion to such young people that they do not need to continue to demonstrate these physical feats unless they truly want to do so. In all likelihood each person has *many* capabilities, including cognitive, musical, and artistic, in addition to physical. It may be that because physically compromised or chronically ill young people have such a strong need to prove their *physical* abilities, they ignore or minimize some of their other strengths. Therefore, if I were working with such youngsters in a counseling situation, I might try to have them consider goals that would enlarge their life horizons beyond success in meeting physical challenges. For example, instead of encouraging the boy with the one-sided paralysis to spend hours trying to perfect his one-handed tennis serve, I could have gently suggested that he might want to explore other, related areas of achievement that would not require two-sided functioning and make such demands on him. For example, he might consider applying his interest in sports by using a computer with one hand to become a sportswriter or a reporter for a newspaper or magazine. Such occupations could build on his success and self-pride without the frustration of trying to force his body to continue to perform and excel. For young people and adults who want to challenge themselves physically, the Special Olympics fulfills this need and can be very gratifying. However, the reality is that few will be able to make a career of physical activity. Some may decide to become special education teachers and coaches to younger medically challenged youth, and in this position they can take pride in their role as mentors.

Clearly, the 26 children described in Krementz's two books do not comprise a valid research sample, and they may not be representative of young people who undergo similar life stresses. Nonetheless, their attitude of high motivation for personal achievement is commendable, as is their sincere interest in helping other people understand their illnesses. Positive attitudes such as these were labeled "posttraumatic growth" in a research study with 150 adolescent survivors of cancer and their mothers and fathers a year after treatment (Barakat, Alderfer, & Kazak, 2006). The majority reported positive changes in their views of self, their relationships with others, and plans for their future (p. 417). Therefore, although the diagnosis of cancer may be considered to be traumatic, posttraumatic growth (as well as distress) may characterize the responses of those involved. While we realize that not all ill or disabled youth receive optimal care, some, if not most, do. However, even with the best of care, some patients succumb to their illness and die. Even so, the majority of ill children survive until adulthood, and this book intends to guide professional counselors in helping those children and their families maintain hope and positive expectations for their futures.

Who Are the Helpers?

Professionals Involved with Ill or Disabled Children

Children and adolescents with medical conditions must interact with many adult professional helpers when they are admitted to hospitals and later receive follow-up care in clinics, rehabilitation, and school settings. Table 1.1 lists many of the various specialists who can have crucial roles in treating these youth. The accounts of the life experiences of the 26 young people in Krementz's books documents how difficult it can be for them to have to form relationships with so many different adults who have so much influence over their lives. Whereas this book is addressed to counselors, social workers, and those who provide psychosocial interventions,

Table 1.1   **Professionals Involved with Chronically Ill or Disabled Adolescents**

Physicians	Health Specialists	Counselors
Pediatricians	Nurses	Social workers
Hematologists, oncologists	Physical therapists	Child life specialists
Neurologists	Speech therapists	Pediatric psychologists
Radiologists	Occupational therapists	School counselors
Pediatric orthopedists	Nutritionists	Pastoral counselors
Rheumatologists	Prosthetists	Art therapists
Gynecologists	Pain management practitioners	Play therapists
Endocrinologists	Complementary medicine practitioners (e.g., reiki masters, yoga teachers, and massage therapists)	Music therapists
Metabolic disease specialists		Drama therapists
Geneticists		Dance therapists
Gastroenterologists		Coaches
Nephrologists		Sex therapists
Physiatrists		Educational tutors
Ophthalmologists		
Adolescent medicine specialists		
Psychiatrists		
Critical care specialists		
Developmental specialists		
Pulmonologists		
Urologists		
Otolaryngologists		
Dentists		

Table 1.1 illustrates the wide range of specialists who may be involved in any one young person's care. Despite my best attempts, the chart may not be all-inclusive.

Just imagine being five or six years old and having to deal with one-half or even a quarter of these people! Even parents may find this daunting. Certainly, this expectation could seem overwhelming to a young child, and the ongoing assistance of a parent would be critical in helping the child remain cooperative and willing to follow the various prescribed treatments. For an example of such a scenario, Table 1.2 shows possible specialists needed to care for children with spina bifida.

Another problem for children with spina bifida is that they may develop latex allergy from repeated exposures in the course of numerous operations and other procedures; even a pair of protective gloves or a tourniquet may cause breathing symptoms, hives, or unconsciousness.

Table 1.2 **Possible Specialists Required for Children Born with Spina Bifida**

Children born with spina bifida might see any of the following specialists

Physiatrist: To provide rehabilitation medicine, including bracing, physical therapy, and teaching specific exercises.

Neurologist: To prescribe and manage muscle relaxants for spasticity and to provide antiseizure medications.

Nephrologist: To manage recurrent urinary tract infections that may occur when children don't fully empty their bladders. This is referred to as *neurogenic bladder;* a complication after many infections may be kidney scarring. Also, decreased muscle tone in the abdomen and pelvis can lead to constipation and residual urine in the bladder. As these children get older, they must learn to perform self-catheterization in order to empty their bladders.

Older children who become sexually active may need counseling with a sex therapist on the topic of using latex condoms. A patient with a latex allergy would be advised to use a sheepskin condom underneath a latex condom. If the partner also has spina bifida, that person, in turn, would need to add a separate sheepskin condom as protection from latex exposure.

Because of the multiplicity of challenges, young people with spina bifida benefit greatly by affiliation with a "medical home," in which a primary care provider can synthesize and interpret the various recommendations into a care plan that clarifies the options available to the patient while also taking into account the patient's own expectations and wishes (Hom, 2008).

How Counselors Help: Various Helping Methods

Just as there are many helpers involved in any one case with an acutely or chronically ill child, there are numerous helping methods that may be used in counseling or therapy. Some of the methods depend on the background, training, and experience of the particular counselor. Other times, the nature of the services may depend on the staffing of a specific hospital or aftercare facility. Therefore, whereas we might agree that all hospitalized young people would benefit from some art or music therapy to help them express their feelings about their medical condition, many medical facilities do not have these trained specialists on staff. Fortunately, some professionals, such as social workers and child life therapists, have been trained to use art, play, and music as part of their counseling treatment.

Specific Helping Approaches

When medically compromised individuals develop mental health problems such as anxiety and depression, the use of crisis counseling, psychotherapy, and relaxation training have proven to be helpful (Auslander & Freedenthal, 2006). *Crisis counseling* is a short-term approach that focuses on anxieties, fears, and the various problems associated with a particular disability or illness. The goal of this intervention is to help people feel more in control over their situation. However, in view of the long-term adjustment necessary to deal with most illnesses and disabilities, crisis intervention alone may not be adequate, since it usually is limited to 10 to 12 weeks. Other forms of psychotherapy may be appropriate when anxieties persist over a longer period of time. These might take the form of individual, group, or family therapy and employ various methods to reduce stress and improve coping (see Chapters 6, 9, and 10). Relaxation training has been quite successful in helping children and adolescents cope with anxieties associated with receiving injections and other painful and stressful medical procedures. Child life specialists are trained specifically to help hospitalized children deal with such anxiety-producing situations (see Chapter 5). Again, the *modalities* of treatment (whether provided individually, in the family, or in group meetings) will depend on available services and the specific needs in each circumstance.

Summary

Acute and chronically ill youth and their families must deal with intense tension at the time of diagnosis as well as ongoing stresses when their illness or disability progresses and may require successive medical operations or other treatments. These young people must develop physical and psychological strategies to deal with both the physical pain and the emotional distress associated with their conditions. Professional counselors play an important role in reducing this anxiety, and this book is dedicated to presenting numerous helping approaches.

As discussed, the age and developmental level of the young people involved will determine how much they can comprehend about the future implications of their situation. The family and social/cultural environment of the child or adolescent will help or hinder his or her adaptation. Professional helpers have a critical role in assuring that this environment is supportive rather than dismissive or unfriendly. When such children attend school, most are very sensitive about how their peers will respond to them. Often, classmates do not understand the restrictions of a disability or medical condition, and sometimes they make fun of children who are different. This adds another layer of stress for the child or adolescent who already feels very isolated and alone because of his or her medical situation. Teachers and school counselors can use the situation to help sensitize other children about individual differences, even as they also seize every opportunity to help the ill or disabled student demonstrate his or her abilities. Sometimes, the hospital social worker visits the school to discuss disease-specific information with the school personnel so that they will be in a better position to help the young person when he or she returns to school.

An acutely or chronically ill child needs various kinds of help from many sources. This book describes the roles of different professionals in providing the emotional and psychological support to assist medically challenged young people and their families. We hope that it will become a resource for all who interact with these children and that they and their families will benefit from the strengths-based, collaborative approach advocated here.

Appendix: Medical Resources

Web site of Medical Specialists: http://www.webmd.com/a-to-z guides/ medical-specialists-medical-specialists.

Chabner, D. (2003). *Medical terminology. A short course.* Philadelphia: W.B Saunders.

Steiner, S.S. (2002). *Quick medical terminology. A self-teaching guide.* Hoboken, NJ: Wiley.

References

Auslander, W., & Freedenthal, S. (2006). Social work and chronic disease. Diabetes, heart disease, and HIV/AIDS. In S. Gehlert, & T. A. Browne (Eds.), *Handbook of health social work* (pp. 532–567). Hoboken, NJ: Wiley.

Barakat, L. P., Alderfer, M. A., & Kazak, A. E. (2006). Posttraumatic growth in adolescent survivors of cancer and their mothers and fathers. *Journal of Pediatric Psychology, 31*(4), 413–419.

Benson, H. (2000). *The relaxation response.* New York: HarperCollins.

Bluebond-Langer, M. (1978). *The private worlds of dying children.* Princeton, NJ: Princeton University Press.

Bronfenbrenner, U. (1979). *The ecology of human development.* Cambridge, MA: Harvard University Press.

Cassidy, J., & Petty, R. (1995). *Textbook of pediatric rheumatology* (3rd ed.). Philadelphia: Saunders.

Clay, D. L. (2004). *Helping schoolchildren with chronic health conditions: A practical guide.* New York: Guilford Press.

Congress, E. P. (2004). Cultural and ethical issues in working with culturally diverse patients and their families. The use of the culturagram to promote culturally competent practice in health care settings. *Social Work in Health Care, 30*(3/4), 249–262.

Daneman, D., & Frank, M. (1996). The student with diabetes mellitus. In R. H. A. Haslam, & P. J. Valletutti (Eds.), *Medical problems in the classroom. The teacher's role in diagnosis and management* (pp. 97–114). Austin, TX: Pro-Ed.

Edwards, K. (2005). *The memory keeper's daughter.* New York: Viking/Penguin.

Friend, M. (2005). *Special education. Contemporary perspectives for school professionals.* Boston, MA: Allyn & Bacon.

Goodman, R. (2007). Living beyond the crisis of childhood cancer. In N. B. Webb (Ed.), *Play therapy with children in crisis. Individual, group, and family treatment* (pp. 197–227). New York: Guilford Press.

Grusec, J. E., Goodnow, J. J., & Kuczynski, L. (2000). New directions in analyses of parenting contributions to children's acquisitions of values. *Child Development, 71*, 205–211.

Hauser, S. T. (1999). Understanding resilient outcomes. Adolescent lives across time and generations. *Journal of Research on Adolescence, 9*(1), 1–24.

Hom, C. (2008). Personal communication, February 20, 2008.

Krementz, J. (1989). *How it feels to fight for your life.* New York: Simon & Schuster.

Krementz, J. (1992). *How it feels to live with a physical disability.* New York: Simon & Schuster.

Lavin, C. (2002). Disenfranchised grief and individuals with developmental disabilities. In K. J. Doka (Ed.), *Disenfranchised grief. New directions, challenges, and strategies for practice* (pp. 307–322). Champaign, IL: Research Press.

Morison, J. E., Bromfield, L. M., & Cameron, H. J. (2003). A therapeutic model for supporting families of children with a chronic illness or disability, *Child and Adolescent Mental Health,* 8: 3, 125–130.

Openshaw, L. (2007). *Social work in schools: Principles and practice.* New York: Guilford Press.

Perrin, J. M. (1989). Foreword. *How it feels to fight for your life* (p. xi). New York: Simon & Schuster.

Phelps, L. (1998). *Health-related disorders in children and adolescents: A guidebook for understanding and educating.* Washington, DC: American Psychological Association.

Saleebey, D. (Ed.). (1997). *The strengths perspective in social work practice* (2nd ed.). New York: Longman.

Selye, H. (1978). *The stress of life.* New York: McGraw Hill.

Times wires (2008, January 15). "Advantage" disqualifies amputee from Olympics. *St. Petersburg Times,* p. 1. Author.

U.S. Department of Health and Human Services. (2003). *The health and well-being of children: A portrait of states and the nation.* Rockville, MD: Author.

Wallander, J. L., Thompson, R. J., Alriksson-Schmidt, A. Psychosocial adjustment of children with chronic physical conditions. In M. C. Roberts (Ed.), *Handbook of pediatric psychology* (3rd ed., pp. 141–15). New York: Guilford Press.

Walsh, F. (2006). *Strengthening family resilience* (2nd ed.). New York: Guilford Press.

Webb, N. B. (2003). (Ed.). *Social work practice with children* (2nd ed.). New York: Guilford Press.

The Emotional Impact of a Young Person's Illness on the Family

Cindy Dell Clark

Introduction

Although biomedical diagnosis places its clinical attention on a separated, individual child through physical tests and probing, each child experiences illness through the connective tissue of family and culture. How the child copes emotionally with illness depends very much on how the family comes to terms with the stressors and losses implicit to a child's condition. Nor can the family's emotional response be considered as a distinct issue from the way illness fits into the commonalities of a social milieu. Disease is largely a matter of shared interpretation. If all of society's children and adults stuttered, for instance, stuttering would not be considered a handicapping behavior. The way a family adjusts to a child's illness and its emotional challenges rests on how the members of the family jointly regard and categorize illness within their shared social circumstances.

Families act in concert when facing the strains brought by illness. This is why it is often proposed that families (not individual young persons) should be the unit of assessment and intervention in childhood illness. *Family systems theory* is an increasingly prevalent framework used by scholars to study members' responses to illness. Family systems theory, a school of thought closely aligned with family therapy, holds that a family is itself a social system, a kind of living organism in which the members operate in a dynamic, reciprocal relationship that makes the whole (the family) greater than the sum or its parts (each member). Applied to illness, family systems theory focuses on how families use adaptive behaviors and resources to cope with stressors (Barakat & Kazak, 1999). Sources of stress vary from family to family, from disease to disease, or based on other factors such as a child's developmental age, social class, family makeup (e.g., single parents versus married parents), marital harmony, or culture/ethnicity. Strains such as financial or time burdens, worries about the future, problems with carrying out a treatment regimen, loss of privacy, and the onus of medical decisions are just some of the stressors that affected families face.

Chapter 2

Adaptability is a term used to refer to a family's capacity to adjust or change in response to illness stressors. The systemic functioning of the family, which dynamically shapes how adaptation takes place, can sometimes be at odds with the particular dictates of medical treatment. Families may selectively embrace forms of pediatric medical treatment that fit with maintaining a "normal life" for family and child (Prout, 1996) while neglecting to administer treatments that disrupt family routines and shared family meanings (Potts & Reagan, 2004).

Implicitly, adaptation is a matter of partaking in coordinated systems of meaning. The sense and significance made of illness by family members are essential to comprehend, as the next section addresses, in order to trace how the aberrant claims of disease have emotional impact.

Stages of Coping: The Role of Meaning

Having a shared sense of meaning, a common way of conveying significance to events, persons, and things, is part of what binds a family group together. Persons in a family tend to understand one another's allusions and jokes and reactions. Family worlds pivot on certain taken-for-granted tenets of assumed reality. Families reinforce these tenets through routines, rituals, narratives, gestures, and expressions of feelings. Children learn about their family's ways through stories told around and about them, through family rituals shared, and through such routines as leave-taking, waking, sleeping, preparing and having meals, and so on. Shared routines and significances convey a steady-state stability or equilibrium within a family system, a synchronized balance of givens. Members operate and respond emotionally based on the shared assumptions that are constructed. That which disrupts shared significance constitutes an immanent crisis, most likely causing emotional disjunction.

Childhood illness is such a crisis. Illness ruptures prior meanings because it renders the stricken child out of sorts with a taken-for-granted, expected reality, in the process displacing how a family construes significance. The dynamic balance by which family members operate is disturbed. A sense of disorganization and upheaval often comes into the family, jarring parent, siblings, and the ill child. Family members may feel disconnected. Role transformations may be launched. While events vary from family to family (and vary, too, by disease), in all cases the malady compels affective, social, and cognitive accommodation. In other words, somehow the family must adjust for the rupture. "Normal" as it once was gives way, and the breach must be filled with "a new kind of normal," a phrase taken from a mother experienced in navigating childhood disorder.

Family members themselves have explained the illness trajectory in a way that implies fractured significance. An obvious instance is the very idea that children with an illness are not as children "should" be. The notion of illness offends parental wishes for a whole and normal child, an expectation for children that even expectant parents assume prenatally.

Upon diagnosis of a living child's condition, intense feelings of grief, anger, and/or helplessness befall parents. One mother of a child with juvenile arthritis mustered a way to describe the crisis of meaning and emotion when her child became ill: "You go through feelings of anger or sometimes sadness; you go through the whole thing. The first year was just dreadful, it was a tempest. Nothing seemed to fit, everything was in turmoil; you are so emotional" (Jerrett, 1994, p. 1053).

The family crisis of significance during illness has been said to be threefold: (1) *appraisal* (corresponding to the sensing and defining of the health situation when illness strikes); (2) *coping* (renegotiating ways of thinking, feeling, and being to adjust for the illness-related challenges); and (3) *adjustment* (living compatibly with a revised sense of reality) (Patterson & Garwick, 1994).

Along similar lines, a model applied to families with children has been proposed by Clarke-Steffen (1993). Based on her research with families affected by childhood cancer, Clarke-Steffen's trajectory of stages matches well with a range of investigations on differing pediatric conditions. The four-stage model designated by Clarke-Steffen taps into a prevailing pattern found in diverse disorders and possibly in diverse national contexts. The stages likewise correspond well with how families have described firsthand their process of adjustment. These are the stages:

Stage one. First clue Familial reality is threatened or fractured by the first indications of illness.

Stage two. Limbo The undone reality leads to a period of reacting to the diagnosis, along with facing preoccupying issues of not knowing, uncertainty, and/or vulnerability.

Stage three. Reconstructing meaning Family members adopt strategies to reconstruct their habits and outlook through a remaking of reality and through new information, new priorities, new outlooks, reorganized roles and routines, and/or managing the therapeutic program.

Stage four. New normal The family operates with a new disposition and shared outlook, one that incorporates needed medical regimens and accepts the implicated uncertainties. There is a quality of normality to this modified, shared set of meanings and routines, even though they differ from what was "normal" before the child's illness.

Note that this ordering of stages may not always be neat and delineated in practice, which Clarke-Steffen recognizes. Families differ in the mix of behaviors at any particular stage. Stages two and three tend to overlap, in time, with stages three and four, so that stage-associated behaviors and sentiments are not entirely set apart. Death or other complications may intervene to stop the progression of stages. In some instances, families may not fully transition through the four stages, but may remain largely at one or another stage due to the unique circumstances of their family system or situation (e.g., if the weight of stressors on the family outweighs the available coping resources). Finally, the trajectory is not necessarily predictable, because disease can be capricious. Whether or not one anticipates it, there can be a relapse of symptoms, raising new ambivalences and disruptions, perhaps leading a family to cycle back.

Despite the complexities in practice, however, the Clarke-Steffen model maps out a relevant, if rough, pathway of families' responses to pediatric illness, potentially extending to diverse cultural settings. Emotional reaction shades the dilemmas at each stage of the model, as can be seen in these adapted examples from the United States (diabetes) and Taiwan (epilepsy).

American Families with Insulin-Dependent Diabetes (Clark, 2003)

Lethargy, dehydration and thirst, frequent urination or bed-wetting, extreme hunger, irritability, and other physical symptoms in the child can signal the onset of childhood diabetes. These are among the *first clues* for a family, who must adapt to the vagaries of the condition. Another *first clue,* salient to many parents, takes place when the child is treated in a medical facility where a diagnosis is pronounced (backed up by medical tests). The diagnosis, like the hospitalization that usually follows the diagnosis, is a distinct clue to parents that the child's health status can no longer be interpreted as before. These clues have emotional implications, especially anxiety and a sense of turmoil. Recalling such a time, a maternal informant became teary-eyed and aroused as she reflected, in hindsight, upon the "clue" of diagnosis: "She [the doctor] said he's dehydrated. I'm going to do a blood test . . . . She caught the diabetes right away." As often takes place, this mother's child was hospitalized while the parents received training about how to care for their child (how to dose insulin, give shots, do blood tests, plan meals, handle exercise, etc.). The training, a sort of rite of passage for the parents, cast aside denial and served as an emotional call to action. Clearly, this early stage posed a looming pressure for this family (and others), as they began to learn about procedures for treating a child's diabetic condition.

The ambivalence of the *limbo* stage comes with the full realization of responsibility among the family members of a young diabetes sufferer, as the parents must take on the role of caring for a child with round-the-clock, intrusive medical needs (starting with blood tests, insulin injections, monitoring, and addressing emergencies). Family routines and emotions are off balance. One mother aptly called her child's time in the hospital her "last normal weekend" since the family's entire worldview was dashed apart upon diagnosis and hospitalization. At this point, "things as usual," even everyday habits, are undone. Treatment obligations force parents to wrestle with the staggering idea that, as one mother said, "your child's health depends on you." The message implied is that the parents have the burden of being responsible for their child's survival in a profound way. Concurrently, the family's way of being is upset and in a state of limbo.

Reconstructing meaning extends across the first year of caring for a diabetic son or daughter, as families come to grips with a thoroughly reordered daily life. This first year of caregiving (sometimes called the "honeymoon" phase by diabetes care specialists) is an apprenticeship (under professional guidance) evoking a mixture of approach and avoidance by family members. Extended families have to recognize, even if reluctantly, that this new way of life is not a passing fluke. In many ways, the sick child's required inpatient stay makes it socially undeniable to those around the immediate family that this is a formidable, serious adjustment, no minor matter. Bit by bit, reality comes to be reframed as parents face their new roles and responsibilities. During the first year following hospitalization, the specific issues of treating diabetes put stress on the family with a myriad of emotionally taxing adjustments—from how to draw blood from a child at sleepovers to how the treatment routine influences activities and eating times to whether the parents will find a qualified babysitter.

New normal, in a family with a diabetic child, refers to a new equilibrium in the family with greater emotional acceptance—in which there are assumptions and habitual behaviors that have come to be shared, ones consistent with managing diabetes. The repetitive acts involved in treatment have themselves become meaning-rich routines that give family life a shared significance. The family, at this stage, now anticipates diabetic treatments as an inherent part of mundane life. Consider some examples of behaviors taken in stride: Some fathers stay at jobs they dislike in order to be sure the condition of diabetes is covered by insurance. Some mothers rise in the middle of the night to check a child's blood sugar levels and avoid dangerous "lows." Siblings settle for sugar-free birthday cakes, and don't tease when the child with diabetes has to give up Halloween candy after a night of trick-or-treating. To the outsider, together these actions appear extraordinary. But within the family, these coordinated actions become routine, taken in stride, mere strands in the web of family life. Treating diabetes day in and day out (doing blood tests and insulin injections), parents often become so attuned with the child's rhythms that they serve as human substitutes for a child's nonfunctioning pancreas (a kind of human "remote control," doing what the pancreas would normally do automatically). Diabetes is a remarkable example of families' abilities to remake the significance of their daily world into a remarkably transformed version of normal life. Resilience is taken in stride in the *new normal* stage.

Taiwanese Families with Childhood Epilepsy (Mu, 2008)

A typical *first clue* discovered by a Taiwanese family with an epileptic child likely would be one or more seizures, according to Mu's research. Seizures are traumatizing experiences during which parents (and children) are startled, nervous, or even panicked. Imagining the worst, parents are prone to worry that the seizing child could have brain damage or even die. Although the child is suffering, the parents at this stage are not really equipped to help. One mother commented about the anxiety of a seizure, "It is very scary, if that happens. We do not know what we can do. I am highly stressed." Finding out the diagnosis of epilepsy is also a clue, one that dramatically disrupts a family's assumptions. Emotional pain at the lack of a healthy child, and the hurt of stigmatization, replace previous expectations of a child's good health. The dismay of possible stigma may cause families to avoid discussing epilepsy altogether, thus preventing disclosure of the diagnosis to friends or relatives. As one parent admitted, "We do not talk about it. Because families and my parents think he has a 'fever' seizure. Actually, I have not discussed this with my family. All my family members avoid this topic."

A sense of *limbo*, of dislocation, follows in the next stage. As parents struggle with administering medication and trying to trace the connection between medicine and the child's unstable condition, they are worried and concerned for the child's emotional well-being. By and large, the child's situation is sensed to be out of control and at risk at this stage. Parents become relatively more relaxed if the child's condition improves, but worries still abound. "At night, I cannot sleep well and I will get up to check him around four times," remarked one mother. Her husband added, "It is really a burden. It is difficult to put into words. It's just like you are tense and you cannot relax at all. Just like waiting for a war, very nervous."

As part of *reconstructing meaning*, parents adjust in roles and identity as they gain experience as caretakers of an epileptic child. Motivated to gain information to aid their roles as caregivers, they begin to question and learn from physicians' visits and to grapple with the treatment process. They learn about side effects of prescribed medications, and they apply what they learn, for example, by warning a teacher if a drug's side effects might influence learning. They gather information about epilepsy from relevant sources, including other parents. Another turning point is the parent's emerging willingness to address the consequences of the culturally prevalent stigmatization of epilepsy. This means that a certain portion of parents prefer to coach a child on how to hide the illness from others, whereas other parents openly assist a child in disclosing the illness at school. Navigating the issue of competent caretaking and dealing with stigma is laced with affective highs (efficacy) and lows (frustration, embarrassment, and anxiety).

The *new normal* stage comes gradually out of the struggles preceding it, as the family develops a new equilibrium or balance based on a remade system of meaning. As parents and children perceive that epilepsy can be well controlled with treatment and that the child with epilepsy indeed can enter the mainstream, integrating the needed modifications becomes a way of life. Because of the stigma of epilepsy in Taiwan, the achievement of a *new normal* stage may not apply to every extended relative, but for the diabetic child's immediate family, the modified routines come to be taken in stride. As one mother described the changes set into motion by her son's epileptic condition, those in the family's inner circle (if not the older generation) have come to regard the current routine as an established fact of life: "After he became ill, we, our lives, and our lifestyle changed somewhat. The path of our life has to fit his needs. If we go out, we bring him along because [his grandmother] doesn't know how to give him medicine."

For both diabetes and epilepsy, borrowing from this pair of studies done in different countries, the stages by which families come to terms with illness are a matter of common meanings (routinized in family habits and rituals) and shared truths (that transform under stress). Emotional challenges to parents are not independent of this jointly enacted family process. In some sense, both the anguish and the resilience of families are tied to how families construct a shared system of actions and significations.

Losses and Grief

Chronic illness in the United States is more common than acute illness. Still, loss is a pervasive feature of illness generally, in fatal and nonfatal illnesses alike. Losses are more often than not multiple. When a child is diagnosed with chronic illness, for example, not only does the parent lose a healthy child, but many times a certain lifestyle, a sense of freedom, support systems (e.g., child care), confidence (including self-confidence about being able to protect the child), and perhaps even the assumption that the child will live (Lowes & Lyne, 2000). The multiplicity of losses also applies when a child dies. The death of a child is excruciating in its impact on parents, an emotional amputation that attacks a parent's being. The double-edged pain of bereavement reflects the irony of a relationship that, in emotional terms, can be neither retrieved nor cut. As Brice (1991) has written, the intense grief after a child's death involves too much contradiction to be reduced to simple terms. A mother losing a child can feel as if her life is "stopped," yet she is juggling many activities all the same. She may want to "get over" the loss, yet doesn't relish "forgetting" her child. She might feel angry that her child has been taken from her, yet have no one to blame. Life ceases to make sense, even as the hunger for explanations is enormous.

Grief is the term for the emotional response to intense loss, assumed to be a process rather than a specific emotion. Indeed, a cavalcade of feelings can characterize grief, in combinations that vary over time and over people. Shock, anger, guilt, blame, anxiety, insecurity, sadness, despair, preoccupation, sleeping problems, changes of appetite, or illness can occur as reactions to bereavement. The experience of bereavement or mourning can occur in response to *death or physical loss*, but also in response to *symbolic losses* in which intangible aspects (safety, freedom, normality, etc.) are severed. Both sorts of loss happen to the family members of ill children, whether those children suffer from acute or chronic illnesses.

Grief has no standard formulation. Even within one family experiencing a loss, the open emotional expression of one spouse may be at odds with the partner's reserve (Worden & Monahan, 1993). Losses that co-occur, happening at once to the same family, can change the nature of bereavement, such as a child becoming ill in the midst of a family divorce or a relative's death (Webb, 1993, p. 97). In the case of chronic illness, parents may experience loss anew when children enter new points of development (e.g., youngsters with Tourette's syndrome who are beginning school and facing stigma about their tics).

It is often assumed that grief is worked through (so-called grief work) and reaches a point of resolution or resolve when it ceases to be burdensome. In this view, the mental suffering eventually abates through acceptance and equilibration.

Among theorists of grieving, there are two schools of thought about the trajectory of grief.

> *Stages-of-grief approach.* Grief, according to this approach, occurs in phases, as it is worked through, and comes to a truncated resolution. The best-known version of this phased model of grieving is the theory of Elisabeth Kübler-Ross, whose theorized stages have been widely applied to catastrophic and chronic loss. The stages are as follows:
>
> 1. *Denial* ("Everything's fine. This isn't really happening.")
> 2. *Anger* ("This is so unfair!")
> 3. *Bargaining* ("I'll do anything if I can have another month.")
> 4. *Depression* ("There's no point anymore.")
> 5. *Acceptance* ("What will be will be, and we'll manage.")
>
> *Chronic-sorrow approach.* Many scholars (including from the field of nursing) have been critical of the phase or stage approach to grieving. The ubiquitous idea that grief is a process that comes to completion, and that this is a prerequisite to resuming normal life, is questioned under this approach. Rather than viewing grief as having resolute boundaries, Lindgren (1992) found that confronting loss and sadness is a recurring, not finite, experience. As such, Lindgren has supported the concept of *chronic sorrow,* a phrase coined by Olshansky (1962) to describe the suffering of parents caring for a mentally defective child. Olshansky observed that parents' grieving was lifelong rather than ever being fully resolved. Lifelong sorrow does not imply unrelenting sadness, but rather sadness that can recur in remitting patterns. Studies have used the notion of *chronic sorrow* to explain parental reactions when raising cognitively impaired children, children with orthopedic disabilities, children with Down syndrome, children with diabetes, and other conditions.

The contrast between *stage-based grieving* as opposed to *chronic sorrow* reminds us of the value of longitudinal research conducted over time with families of ill children. By following families systematically over time, the degree of affective closure families can ultimately gain (over the multiple losses accompanying a child's condition or death) would be brought into more dynamic focus. This might help to sort out the place for stage theory versus chronic sorrow (or some combination of both) in explaining bereavement and grief.

Adaptation in the Short Term and Long Term

To be a family with pediatric illness and to maintain some sort of equilibrium requires stamina and adaptability. Families are not home free once they initially reach a reintegrated sense of what is normal; the challenges don't necessarily stay at bay, but can be turbulent and unsettling. Juvenile cancer, for example, is less often fatal than it once was. But over time, childhood cancer can leave stresses (to be discussed) and the cancer can recur. In short, a family's "career" in giving care to an ill child is not scripted, nor can it cleanly end with "retirement" after a particular time. Rather, dealing with a pediatric disorder is an unpredictable process in large part, fraught with ongoing restructuring of relationships and presumptions.

Examples to bear in mind are families who care for children with cerebral palsy who are more than 10 years into the process of dealing with the condition, yet still facing daunting problems. After a decade or more of caring for a child with cerebral palsy, research suggests, the strain on these parents is such that parental health is at risk. The risk is more intense in the event of extreme caregiving demands or when dealing with behavioral provocations (Raina et al., 2005).

Cancer, like some other conditions, can morph or bring added tribulations over the long run. Surviving childhood cancer has been documented to leave a formidable trail of long-term consequences. Emotionally, family members of a young cancer survivor often have nagging anxiety that the threatening disease could come back. Recurring levels of posttraumatic stress are associated with long-term survival, too, estimated to affect more than 10 percent of mothers of young survivors. Young adult survivors of juvenile cancer incur PTSD symptoms in one-fifth of cases (Hobbie et al., 2000).

One of the trials for families of children with chronic illness is managing the treatment regimen day in and day out, year in and year out. Physician's orders are often challenging to implement, especially if the regimen is time-draining, complicated, accompanied by perceived side effects, viewed as ineffective, or simply aversive. At times, the concern for doing what is medically correct can lead to ignoring other concerns in the family, such as when the parents of a child with cystic fibrosis are so intent on the issues of adequate food intake for the ill child that they neglect the other aspects of dinnertime, such as conversation across the table (Fiese, 2006). If the symptoms of a child's illness abate, family adherence may fall by the wayside, despite the physician's instructions and explanation of sustained medical necessity. In managing adherence, physicians often overlook the known central role played by a family's cohesion and well-being. Families without persistent conflict, families who possess positive ways of coping and positive feedback, and families without an undue amount of parental control are more successful over time in maintaining an illness regimen (LeBlanc et al., 2003).

Although coping with child illness can be a grueling marathon, some families do demonstrate success and resilience, especially in cohesive, integrated families. Families appear to be resilient when their members have aligned outlooks and connectedness (LeBlanc et al., 2003).

Research into family interaction in households with a pediatric illness has shown that particular sorts of expressive practices enhance a family's sense of coherence and identity and, in turn, strengthen adjustment. Two examples are stories and ritual (Fiese, 2006; Fiese & Wamboldt, 2000). Listening to and telling stories have benefits as a healing strategy and a means to link parents and children. Family stories can connect present issues to past family events, helping to mesh and situate the present and past. Narratives are commonly known to help patients interpret and come to terms with health conditions (Kleinman, 1988; Mattingly & Garro, 2000). Sharing stories facilitates a family in making difficult circumstances graspable and able to be shared. The following story, told by a diabetic eight-year-old as her mother listened and smiled in appreciation, forms an apt example. The story reframed a frightening event (a girl's hypoglycemic crisis) from a more lighthearted angle, such that the event could be laughed about together, within the family (Clark 2003, p.132).

> *I had dark circles around my eyes and I was very pale. And [my mother] said, um, she gave me some Life Savers and glucose tablets, and then I was fine for a couple of minutes. . . . My mom went to call the ambulance because [my blood sugar was] really low, and then my dad was giving me red Life Savers [to raise blood sugar] and I was coughing, like spitting them up. And the [medical] guy with the walkie-talkie was coming along, and he said 'She's spitting up blood! She's spitting up blood!' [Laughs heartily along with her mother at the medic's mistaking red Life Savers in her saliva for blood.] He thought I was spitting up blood!*

In this narrative, which the mother enjoyed as audience, a shared truth is implied. The truth asserts that an emergency is also an occasion for laughter and may not always be as dire or somber as others suppose. Sharing a story is a way these family members turned the situation toward a lighter meaning, perhaps reassuring themselves.

Family rituals touch upon emotions and symbolic significance just as stories do. Rituals seem to safeguard overall family well-being, when families adapt their rituals to circumstances at hand. Rituals are models for coherent family interaction. In a classic investigation of family ritual, it was found that families who were able to maintain shared rituals despite paternal alcoholism protected offspring from some of the harmful effects of the addictive parent. More recent studies have examined the benefit brought by ritual in the circumstance of pediatric illness. Ongoing maintenance of shared family rituals has been shown to have anxiety-reducing effects (Fiese & Wamboldt, 2000).

Rituals, in that they involve interacting family members, are truly a family affair. If rituals become a part of treatment for an illness, they can serve to reinforce shared meaning and highlight the significance of treatment. As one example, a five-year-old boy with diabetes practiced a ritual of singing "Alleluia" from Handel's *Messiah* upon receiving an insulin injection, which might be thought of as a distraction that conveyed reframed, positive joy about the treatment. This ritual was conceived and recommended by the boy's father and then incorporated into injections given by every one of the boy's caregivers: his dad, his mom, and even his day care provider (Clark, 2003). In another family, a mother and her five-year-old boy shared pretend play during each insulin injection, jointly imagining that the syringe with its demarcated lines of measurement was a zebra. In pretense, the mother spoke as if the syringe were a zebra "kissing" the boy when she injected, a way of ritually marking the notion that this act had an affectionate intent. The boy, as part of the same interaction, was invited to hit or dismantle the syringe (as a bad, hurtful zebra) since the "kiss" was physically painful. A ritual centering on a pretend zebra allowed each family member to express contrasting meanings about injections, be they loving (to mother) or hurtful (to son). The interplay preserved a coordinated togetherness of mother and son in which each person gave voice to heartfelt concerns, meshed in play. Rituals like these contribute to family coherence, supporting resilience within a family even when facing the upsetting demands of illness.

Family Members: Siblings

Raising any child calls for extensive time and energy, and the demands are especially pronounced when parents are caretakers of a critically or chronically ill child. But parental energy and time are not infinite resources. The question has been raised regarding whether healthy brothers or sisters of ill children are negatively affected by getting short shrift of parental attention. Reports have found that healthy siblings are at risk for adjustment difficulties, but the record is not unequivocal. Some studies have reported negative consequences (such as depression, isolation, and behavioral issues). Yet other studies have uncovered positive consequences for healthy siblings of ill children, such as greater empathy, patience, and family cohesion (Van Riper, 2003). In one investigation of healthy siblings of diabetic youth, it was found that siblings both benefited (with high levels of behavioral competence) and were penalized (by anxiety and low self-concept) (Hollidge, 2001).

Although the record of research is mixed regarding healthy siblings of ill children, interesting insights have emerged when researchers have taken the approach that healthy siblings are coordinated actors within a family context rather than treating each youngster as an autonomous individual to be studied in isolation. Healthy siblings operate as active members of a family. They endeavor to participate to support family cohesion in the midst of strain. In a study conducted by Roberta Woodgate (2006) of healthy siblings related to children with cancer, a nine-year-old girl explained that part of family unity meant recognizing the parent needed greater time with the sick child. "I think that some kids would get jealous because their brother or sister gets more attention than them and they want the attention. Well I'm not jealous 'cause I know that Ann needs the help and that my mom and dad have to take care of her." In view of the family situation, in other words, the need for parents to devote their attention to the sick member was understandable to siblings, even if this simultaneously led to feelings of isolation. Healthy siblings wanted to pitch in and help, and their willingness to endure feeling "left out" essentially allowed them to play their part in relation to the family. The healthy sibling's sadness that went with seeing a brother or sister so sick, though, often remained unacknowledged by parents who had (as another child put it) "other things to worry about." Ironically, then, healthy siblings suffered isolation and unsupported stress as a way for them to scaffold the family balancing act.

Siblings of children with cystic fibrosis typically find themselves in a situation where parental attention may not be adequate. Communication between these healthy children and their parents can involve attempts by a youngster to protect overwhelmed parents from upset, discomfort, or pain, in short, to contain the intrusion upon family functioning (Bluebond-Langner, 1996). Healthy siblings may have questions that are never asked and concerns that are never expressed in order to make sure the family is not overloaded. It would seem that children act to preserve families amidst a situation of being overwhelmed.

If siblings suffer privately from unacknowledged stress and inattention, this is not interpreted by them as a selfish loss, but rather a means to actively coordinate with the family dynamics. The healthy sibling does his or her part by laying low.

To address the entailed stress and isolation, hospitals and camps have organized support groups and getaways specifically for healthy brothers and sisters of ill children. A national organization dedicated to the needs of such siblings, SuperSibs, has numerous programs that advance supportive communication, such as a call-in phone arrangement that connects siblings to trained peers (who have been in a similar situation). Camps and support group sessions are well-placed interventions for siblings' communicative needs.

Summary

Although medical diagnosis is pronounced upon a singular individual, coping with illness is a family endeavor. Siblings make way for parents' needs as care providers, albeit while risking the pains of isolation and sadness. Parents lead the way in overturning former ways of doing things and facing multiple losses to be grieved. In time, the family learns a "new normal" existence in which treatment and lack of certainty are part of an ordinary course of experiences. Shared patterns of interaction, including stories and rituals, can help to sustain the resilience and flexibility needed over time.

Stress, challenge, and emotional strain seem to be expected forces working on families whose children have chronic or acute disorders. The adversities likely are inevitable. But they underscore the way in which family coherence—sustained by the epoxy of mutual, acted-upon meanings—brings resilience.

References

Barakat, L., & Kazak, A. (1999). Family issues. In R. T. Brown (Ed.), *Cognitive aspects of chronic illness in children*. New York: Guilford Press.

Bluebond-Langner, M. (1996). *In the shadow of illness: Parents and siblings of the chronically ill child*. Princeton: Princeton University Press.

Brice, C. (1991). Paradoxes of maternal mourning. *Psychiatry, 54*, 1–12.

Clark, C. D. (2003). *In sickness and in play: Children coping with chronic illness*. New Brunswick, NJ: Rutgers University Press.

Clarke-Steffen, L. (1993). A model of the family transition to living with childhood cancer. *Cancer Practice, 1*(4), 285–292.

Fiese, B. H. (1997). Family context in pediatric psychology from a transactional perspective: Family rituals and stories as an example. *Journal of Pediatric Psychology, 22*(2), 183–196.

Fiese, B. H. (2006). *Family routines and rituals*. New Haven: Yale University Press.

Fiese, B. H., & Wamboldt, F. (2000). Family routines, rituals, and asthma management: A proposal for family-based strategies to increase treatment adherence. *Family, Systems and Health, 18*(4), 405–418.

Hobbie, W. L., Stuber, M. L., Meeske, K., Wissler, K., Rourke, M. T., Ruccione, K., et al. (2000). Symptoms of posttraumatic stress in young adult survivors of childhood cancer. *Journal of Clinical Oncology, 18*(25), 4060–4066.

Hollidge, C. (2001). Psychological adjustment of siblings to a child with diabetes. *Health and Social Work, 26*(1), 15–25.

Jerrett, M. (1994). Parents' experience of coming to know the care of a chronically ill child. *Journal of Advanced Nursing, 19*, 1050–1056.

Kleinman, A. (1988). *The illness narratives: Suffering, healing and the human condition*. New York: Basic Books.

Kübler-Ross, E. (1973). *On death and dying*. London: Tavistock.

LeBlanc, L. A., Goldsmith, T., & Patel, D. R. (2003). Behavioral aspects of chronic illness in children and adolescents. *Pediatric Clinics of North America, 50*, 859–878.

Lindgren, C., Burke, M., Hainsworth, M., & Eakes, G. (1992). Chronic sorrow: A lifespan concept. *Scholarly Inquiry for Nursing Practice, 6*(1), 2–42.

Lowes, L., & Lyne, P. (2000). Chronic sorrow in parents of children with newly diagnosed diabetes: A review of the literature and discussion of the implications for nursing practice. *Journal of Advanced Nursing, 32*(1), 41–48.

Mattingly, C., & Garro, L. C. (Eds.). (2000). *Narrative and the cultural construction of illness and healing.* Berkeley: University of California Press.

Mu, P. F. (2008). Transition experience of parents caring of children with epilepsy: A phenomenological study. *International Journal of Nursing Studies, 45,* 543–551.

Olshansky, S. (1962). Chronic sorrow: A response to having a mentally defective child. *Social Casework, 43,* 190–193.

Patterson, J. M., & Garwick, A. W. (1994). The impact of chronic illness on families: A family systems perspective. *Annals of Behavioral Medicine, 16*(2), 131–142.

Potts, A. L., & Reagan, C. B. (2004). Thinking outside the inhaler: Potential barriers to controlled asthma in children. *Journal of Pharmacy Practice, 17*(3), 211–220.

Prout, A. (1996). Actor-network theory, technology and medical sociology: An illustrative analysis of the metered dose inhaler. *Sociology of Health and Illness, 18*(2), 198–219.

Raina, P., O'Donnell, M., Rosenbaum, P., Brehaut, J., Walter, S. D., Russell, D., et al. (2005). The health and well-being of caregivers of children with cerebral palsy. *Pediatrics, 115,* e626–e636.

Van Riper, M. (2003). The sibling experience of living with childhood chronic illness and disability. *Annual Review of Nursing Research, 21,* 279–302.

Webb, N. B. (1993). Complicated grief—dual losses of godfather's death and parents' separation. *Helping bereaved children: A handbook for practitioners.* New York: Guilford Press.

Woodgate, R. (2006). Sibling experiences with childhood cancer. *Cancer Nursing, 29*(5), 406–414.

Worden, J. W., & Monahan, J. R. (1993). Caring for bereaved parents. In A. Armstrong-Dailey & S. Z. Goltzer (Eds.), *Hospice care for children.* New York: Oxford University Press.

The Economic, Social, and Cultural Context of Health Care

Virginia Rondero Hernandez

3
Chapter

A day does not go by without a headline or sound bite about health care. We are told that health care costs are soaring, that segments of the population go uninsured, and that employee health care benefits are being reduced or eliminated. These discussions are filled with concerns about the future, but they are also pertinent to the present. Numerous national and state studies acknowledge that the well-being of our nation hinges on the health of our nation's people. There is specific concern about the children. Not only do they represent the future, but ignoring their health care needs can compromise their educational preparedness, occupational pursuits, and longevity. Of special concern are children and youth with chronic and acute health care needs. Their health and well-being are already compromised by physical, developmental, emotional, or behavioral limitations. Restricted access to health care services, inadequate health insurance coverage, and unresponsive health care systems exacerbate these limitations and can threaten the viability and potential of these children and youth.

In order for social workers and other health care practitioners to address the complexities of health care today and help optimize care for children and youth with chronic and acute health care needs, they must be sensitized to economic, social, and cultural influences that impede access to care and must be able to identify the inherent strengths of families in order to enhance client outcomes. This chapter focuses on major issues that influence the provision and delivery of health care services to children and youth with acute and chronic illnesses and, identifies the role of social work practice, advocacy, research, and policy in addressing the care needs of this special population.

Estimates of Prevalence and Need

National data reflect that 16.2 percent, or 11.7 million children, ages 0 to 17 in the United States have special health care needs (Chevarley,

2006) related to chronic physical, developmental, behavioral, and emotional conditions that require health care services beyond those of a child without these types of conditions.[1,2]

Asthma is one of the most highly reported chronic conditions reflected in parent survey and national expenditure data, followed by allergies, attention-deficit disorders, and anxiety or mood disorders (U.S. Department of Health and Human Services Health Resources and Services Administration Maternal and Child Health Bureau, 2008b). (See Table 3.1.) Youth ages 12 to 17 have a higher number of special health care needs compared to younger children, and more boys than girls are affected by such needs (Chevarley, 2006).

The health care needs of children with chronic and acute conditions range from preventive care to acute care requiring hospitalizations, and a range of health services may be needed to manage the child's condition and optimize his or her abilities and general development. (See Table 3.2.) It is understandable, therefore, that caring for a child with chronic physical, developmental, behavioral, or emotional conditions places disproportionate demands on a family. Of the 21.8 percent of parents who reported caring for a child with special health needs, more than one-third spent 4 to 11 hours a week providing or arranging care for their child (e.g., direct care, medical care, therapies), and one-fifth of all families who care for a child with special health care needs experience financial burdens (U.S. Department of Health and Human Services Health Resources and Services Administration Maternal and Child Health Bureau, 2008b).

Although children with special health care needs represent a small portion of children who need health care, they account for 41 percent of all health care expenditures made for children in the United States (Chevarley, 2006). The average medical expense for children with special health care needs in 2000 was three times higher ($2,497.84) than for children without a chronic condition ($803.12) (Chevarley, p. 3). These disproportionate costs have been attributed to complex care needs and hospitalization costs (Neff, 2007). The cost of prescription drugs (and home health care) for children with special health care needs also outstrips that of children without special health care needs by six to one (Neff), and in some instances, families do not buy them because of limited income (Children's Defense Fund, 2005). In addition, the health care needs of children with chronic conditions change with age. Younger children require home health care, durable medical equipment, and hearing

---

[1] This definition is utilized for the Medical Expenditures Survey (Chevarley, 2006). It is based on the work of McPherson et al., 1998, and Bethel et al., 2002. It does not expressly relate to children who experience acute health conditions, although it is widely acknowledged that children with chronic conditions often experience episodes of acute illness (Neff, 2007).

[2] By definition, acute illness is of short duration, lasting three months or less, and is not serious enough to have an impact on a child's behavior (U.S. Department of Health and Human Services, 2007).

aids, whereas older children require more mental health care, eyeglasses or vision care, and mobility aids (U.S. Department of Health and Human Services Health Resources and Services Administration Maternal and Child Health Bureau, 2008b).

Even under optimal circumstances, the care needs of children with chronic or acute conditions are not always fully addressed. More than one out of six households surveyed in 2005 to 2006 reported that their children did not receive at least one needed health care service (i.e., preventive care, mental health care, and therapies) during the previous 12 months because of financial barriers, limited access to providers, and competing demands on families' time (U.S. Department of Health and Human Services Health Resources and Services Administration Maternal and Child Health Bureau, 2008b).

Indicators of Access to Quality Care

Access to quality care is key in addressing the health care needs of children with chronic or acute health conditions. Quality care for this population occurs when they (1) have access to health insurance coverage, (2) are actually enrolled in a health insurance plan, (3) have access to covered services and care, (4) have a consistent source of primary care, and (5) can access referral services (Simpson & Dougherty, 2007). These elements are reflected in the following six "core outcomes" established by the Maternal and Child Health Bureau to measure the nation's progress in creating systems of care for children with special health care needs:

- Families of children and youth with special health care needs partner in decision making at all levels and are satisfied with the services they receive.
- Children and youth with special health care needs receive coordinated ongoing comprehensive care within a medical home.
- Families of children with special health care needs have adequate private and/or public insurance to pay for the services they need.
- Children are screened early and continuously for special health care needs.
- Community-based services for children and youth with special health care needs are organized so families can use them easily.
- Youth with special health care needs receive the services necessary to make transitions to all aspects of adult life, including adult health care, work, and independence (U.S. Department of Health and Human Services Health Resources and Services Administration Maternal and Child Health Bureau, 2008b).

These definitions reflect an ideal care situation for children with chronic and acute health conditions. However, pervasive economic, social, and cultural influences can compromise access to quality of care for children with special health care needs in very specific ways.

What Influences Access to Quality Care?

According to the 2007 National Healthcare Disparities Report (Agency for Healthcare Research and Quality, 2008), access to quality care involves more than just having health insurance. It is composed of three discrete and essential steps: (1) obtaining entry into a health care system, (2) being able to access the location where the needed services are offered, and (3) engaging with a health care practitioner who addresses the needs of the patient and shares a mutual relationship based on sound communication and trust with the patient. Access to quality care is also influenced by larger, macrolevel forces that can translate into barriers to care. Common barriers to health care access include cost of care, societal stigma, fragmented organization of services, shame, discrimination, racism, mistrust, patient-provider communication, literacy levels, language differences, and cultural differences (Agency for Healthcare Research and Quality, 2008). Racial and ethnic minorities and persons from low educational and income levels are particularly affected by access barriers and, as a result, experience higher morbidity and mortality rates in almost every disease category (Syme, 2008).

The study of health disparities and access issues has helped to affirm what social workers have intuitively held to be true—health is a biopsychosocial experience (Zimmerman & Dabelko, 2007); the social environment is host to numerous influences that negatively affect health and health behaviors (Office of Behavioral and Social Sciences Research, 2007); and using an ecological perspective can help to leverage possible points of intervention designed to improve the public health (MacIntyre & Ellaway, 2000). It is incumbent upon social workers and other health care practitioners to be thoroughly familiar with economic, social, and cultural factors that influence access in order to develop appropriate approaches to facilitate access to quality care.

Financing Health Care

The economics of funding health care is a macrolevel influence that must be thoroughly understood and considered when working with children with chronic and acute conditions and their families. According to the Centers for Medicare and Medicaid Services (CMMS) (2007a), health care expenditures comprised 16 percent of the gross domestic product. During 2007, the cost of health care grew 6.7 percent, to $2.1 trillion dollars, and the average expenditure per person averaged $7,026 (CMMS, 2007a). More than two-thirds (67.9 percent) of these expenditures were subsidized by private plan insurance, followed by government-sponsored plans

(27.3 percent) such as Medicare, Medicaid, State Children's Health Insurance Program (SCHIP), and military health care (DeNavas-Walt, Proctor, & Smith, 2007). The remainder of the population (15.8 percent) had no health insurance at all (DeNavas-Walt et al.).[3]

In 2006, 11.7 percent of the U.S. child population, or 9 million children, were uninsured (DeNavas-Walt et al., 2007; Perlino, 2007; American Academy of Pediatrics, 2008a). This percentage was nearly double (19.3 percent) among children who lived in poverty (DeNavas-Walt et al.). Although SCHIP programs have helped to reduce the number of children without health insurance, the proposed expansion of SCHIP coverage will reach only 25 percent of children who are uninsured (Perlino, 2007). In the meantime, children without health insurance will most likely continue to use emergency rooms as a primary care source, a costly experience for both families and taxpayers.

For those who are insured, children represent a group for which the least amount of expenditures is made. In 2004, children accounted for 26 percent of the population; however, only 13 percent of all personal health care expenditures were made for children ages 0 to 18 (Centers for Medicare & Medicaid Services, 2008a). Annual expenditures in 2004 for adults ages 65 and older averaged $14,797, which was 5.6 times higher than the amount spent for children. The average annual expenditure for working age adults was $4,511, almost double the $2,650, on average, that was spent for children (CMMS, 2008a).

Although children incur a smaller proportion of overall health care costs, a higher proportion of costs are spent on children with special health care needs. Neff (2007) reports that while children with special health care needs comprise 14 percent of all children in the United States, they account for 40 to 60 percent of total health care costs for children. Compared to children without chronic or acute conditions, the average expenses for children with special health care needs are five times higher for inpatient hospital care, two times higher for physician services, and seven times higher for nonphysician services; and prescriptions are needed five times more often (Neff). Costs can soar exponentially when children experience catastrophic conditions (metastatic cancer, traumatic injury, multiple congenital disorders, etc.) that require lengthy hospitalizations, specialty care, and outpatient care.

Health insurance provides access to quality care. It is critical, therefore, for social workers and health care practitioners to have a basic understanding of health insurance programs in order to facilitate access to care and to work toward reducing barriers for children who are uninsured or underinsured.

---

[3] The total percentages cited exceed 100 percent, as estimates by type of coverage are not mutually exclusive; people can be covered by more than one type of health insurance during the year (DeNavas-Walt et al., 2007).

Private Insurance Programs

In 2006, more than two-thirds (68.5 percent) of people in the United States were covered by a privately funded health insurance (DeNavas-Walt et al., 2007). Private insurance programs are largely funded through employment. In 2007, 54 percent of health care expenditures were paid for by private plans (Kaiser Family Foundation, 2008). Private insurance can also be funded through direct purchase plans, which covered 9.1 percent of Americans in 2006 (DeNavas-Walt et al., 2007). The availability of employer-sponsored health insurance is highly related to the type of employment held and whether benefits are offered at all. Those who earned higher incomes were more likely to be covered by employer-based plans compared to those who earned lower incomes. In 2006, 92 percent of employees who were at or above 400 percent of the federal poverty level[4] were covered by employer-sponsored health insurance, whereas only 30 percent of employees (the working poor) who were at or below 100 percent of the FPL had employer-based coverage (Kaiser Family Foundation, 2008). Although employers contribute the majority of dollars for health insurance coverage, these contributions have been shrinking. In 2000, 69 percent of employers offered health care benefits; only 60 percent did so in 2007 (Kaiser Family Foundation).

Government Insurance Programs

Medicaid, SCHIP, and military health care cover the health care costs of a substantial number of children.[5] However, current statistics indicate that more needs to be done in order to provide coverage for all children. To inform practitioners about the unique aspects of these programs, a description of each, along with the services provided, follows.

Medicaid is jointly funded by federal and state governments, is administered by county governments in conjunction with the state, and is considered the "payer of last resort" (Hoffman, Klees, & Curtis, 2007). Eligibility is determined by both income level and categorical need. Eligible participants include children and adolescents under age 19 whose family incomes are at or below 133 percent of the federal poverty level ($21,200 for a family of four in 2008), pregnant women who meet this

---

[4] Each year the federal government releases an official income level for poverty and establishes federal poverty guidelines to determine families' eligibility for federal or state assistance. Poverty thresholds or levels are also established and range from 100 percent (poverty level) to 400 percent above poverty level. In 2008, a family of four residing in the 48 contiguous states and earning $21,200 or less was considered to be living in poverty (U.S. Department of Health and Human Services, 2008).

[5] Medicare provides health coverage to children with end-stage renal disease for hemodialysis treatment, kidney transplantation, and other costs associated with kidney disease (National Kidney Foundation, 2008). The proportion of costs covered by Medicare for children is minimal, however, compared to costs paid for adults (Centers for Medicare & Medicaid Services, 2007b).

same income criteria, infants born to Medicaid-eligible women, recipients of Supplemental Security Income (SSI), children receiving adoption or foster care services under Title IV-E of the Social Security Act, specially protected groups at risk of losing SSI or Social Security benefits, and certain Medicare beneficiaries (Hoffman et al., 2007).

Under current regulations, states can also offer Medicaid coverage using more liberal criteria to cover certain classes of children, persons who are aged, blind, or disabled, certain working-and-disabled persons not eligible for SSI, and other persons determined to be medically needy (Hoffman et al., 2007). Services funded by Medicaid include inpatient and outpatient services, pregnancy-related services, services of physicians and approved practitioners, skilled nursing and home health care, vaccines, laboratory services, and services received through the Early Periodic Screening, Diagnostic, and Treatment (EPSDT) program, as well as optional diagnostic, clinical, prescription, rehabilitation, hospice, and case management services determined necessary by a state (Hoffman et al., 2007). The Medicaid program provided health coverage to at least 29.2 million children under 19 years of age in 2007 (Centers for Medicare & Medicaid Services, 2007b), but proportionately, Medicaid pays more for adults than it does for children. In 2006, expenditures on adults were five times higher than they were for children (Wise, 2007).

SCHIP is a partnership between federal and state governments to fund health insurance coverage to uninsured children who are not eligible for Medicaid, who are under the age of 19, and whose families are at or below 200 percent of the federal poverty level (American Association of Pediatrics Committee on Child Health Financing, 2007). SCHIP was legislated by the Balanced Budget Act of 1997, a bipartisan compromise engineered by Senator Edward Kennedy and signed into law by President Bill Clinton in 1997 for a 10-year period. SCHIP funds states to provide health coverage to families with children in one of three ways: (1) as independent SCHIP programs operated separately and apart from Medicaid, (2) as an expansion of a state's Medicaid program, or (3) as a combined program whereby the federal government matches SCHIP expenditures at rates higher than Medicaid (Perlino, 2007). SCHIP is currently credited for expanding enrollment of child health insurance coverage from fewer than 1 million children in 1997 to an estimated 6.2 million children in 2005 (Rosenbach et al., 2007). Other positive outcomes include identification of children eligible for Medicaid but not receiving it, and enrollment retention rates as high as 75 percent or more across the United States (Rosenbach et al., 2007). Not only has SCHIP helped to reduce the rate of uninsured children, it also has helped to reduce health disparities experienced by child minority populations (Perlino, 2007).

SCHIP, however, has its detractors. Although SCHIP has demonstrated its effectiveness in reducing the rate of uninsured children and increasing access to health care services, critics accuse the program of crowding out competition with private insurance companies and of expanding the government's role in health care (Cannon, 2007). These arguments helped to delay the reauthorization of SCHIP in 2007, when legislation to fund the program was set to expire. After two failed House resolutions to expand the SCHIP program, President Bush signed a compromise bill to extend SCHIP legislation in its original form into 2009.

Title V funds, established by the Social Security Act of 1935, is one of the oldest public health programs in the nation and was intended to create federal-state partnerships to improve maternal and child care and promote care for children with special health care needs (U.S. Department of Health and Human Services Health Resources and Services Administration Maternal and Child Health Bureau, 2008a). Title V currently is administered by the Maternal and Child Health Bureau, and funds are used by states to support statewide maternal and child health programs, including programs for children with special health care needs.

Title V funds can also be used to purchase direct services to children with extraordinary medical needs, disabilities, and chronic health conditions not covered by Medicaid, SCHIP, private insurance, or third-party payers. Increasingly, states have used Title V funds to fulfill federal mandates for systems of care that are family-centered, comprehensive, community-based, and culturally and linguistically competent. This has prompted critics to question the wisdom of expending Title V monies to build systems instead of providing direct services to children with chronic and acute conditions, who are typically underserved to begin with (Neff, 2007).

Military health care provides coverage for children of men and women in the U.S. armed forces. This coverage may be complemented by other programs available to military personnel, including TRICARE, a component of the military health system managed through the U.S. Department of Defense and federal and state health insurance programs. TRICARE is available to dependent children through an HMO, a PPO, or a standard plan (formerly known as CHAMPUS), which allows participants to see authorized nonnetwork providers (Specialized Training of Military Parents [STOMP], 2003b; TRICARE Management Activity, 2008b). The TRICARE Enhanced Care Health Option (ECHO) offers up to $2,500 in cash benefits to families who care for a child with a mental or physical disability to help pay for assistive devices, durable medical equipment, respite care, and other medical and rehabilitative services (STOMP, 2003b; TRICARE Management Activity, 2008a). When coverage from military health care sources is not enough to address the needs of dependent children with special needs, military families may be eligible for federal and state health care programs if they meet eligibility criteria (Military HOMEFRONT U.S. Department of Defense, 2008). Dependent children of veterans who are permanently and totally disabled may also be eligible for CHAMPVA, which is administered by the U.S. Department of Veterans Affairs (Medicare Interactive U.S., 2008).

Out-of-Pocket Costs

Even if a child has insurance, it does not cover out-of-pocket expenses for premiums, deductibles, co-payments, and items not covered by a plan.

The logic behind out-of-pocket costs is that they encourage people to make more efficient and better decisions about their health (Kaiser Family Foundation, 2006a). However, these costs can quickly become a financial burden to families who care for a child with special health care needs. In 2000, families caring for a child with special health care needs spent 10.4 percent of their family income on out-of-pocket costs, compared to 3.7 percent of families with children who did not have these types of care needs (Chevarley, 2006). Costs for prescriptions, therapeutic services, dental services, over-the-counter drugs, and medical devices not covered by plan become the financial responsibility of families, who must come up with the money to pay for them. At least 20 percent of parents with children with special health care needs surveyed in 2005 to 2006 reported that they paid more than $1,000 a year in out-of-pocket expenditures (not including premiums), and families who were not enrolled in Medicaid or SCHIP paid higher amounts of out-of-pocket expenditures (Chevarley, 2006; U.S. Department of Health and Human Services Health Resources and Services Administration Maternal and Child Health Bureau, 2008b).

If past trends are any indication, out-of-pocket costs will continue to rise over time. Research comparing types of out-of-pocket expenses paid by the families of children with chronic and acute illnesses revealed a 38.2 percent increase in out-of-pocket expenditures from 1999 to 2001 and a 51.0 percent increase for children with more complex health care needs (Neff, 2007). The cost of prescription drugs averaged 25.5 percent of all costs borne by families in 2001, and the costs for prescriptions increased by 56.3 percent, even though the use of pharmaceuticals increased by only 8.1 percent between 1999 and 2001 (Neff, 2007). The unrelenting rise in out-of-pocket costs for children with chronic and acute illnesses clearly demonstrates how the burden of care for a child with special health care needs is made heavier—and heavier still by an outdated assumption that out-of-pocket costs "encourage" families to make more efficient and better decisions about their child's health.

Managed Care

Managed care was legislated into being by the Health Maintenance Organization Act of 1973 and is used by private and government insurance programs as a strategy to control for health care costs (Mitka, 1998). Current debates over managed care rest on two opposing viewpoints: (1) It is an efficient strategy for containing costs and ensuring access to quality care; and (2) it actually contributes to administrative costs and restricts access to coverage and patient choice. Public opinions about managed care are generally negative (e.g., decreased time that doctors spend with patients, greater difficulties in securing the services of specialists, decreased quality of care, and insignificant cost savings) (Kaiser Family Foundation, 2006b). Regardless of the public's opinions, managed care is now a permanent feature of most health care plans and is unlikely to disappear. In order to prepare parents for the realities of managed care, advocates for children with special health care needs have initiated a consumer-driven movement to educate parents about their legal rights and options if costs are denied (National Center on Financing for Children with Special Health Care Needs, 2004; American Academy of Pediatrics Medical Home Initiatives for Children with Special Needs, 2008; Family Voices, 2008).

The reality is that insurance program criteria (e.g., preexisting conditions, insurance limits, restrictive clauses), cost-containment strategies, and the unavailability of services may ultimately trump access to quality care. However, it is important for social workers and other health care practitioners to remember that facilitators reflect strengths, or what is working well for a child and family, and barriers are indicators of where possible macrolevel and microlevel interventions can take place. This perspective is especially critical when it comes to assessing social and culture influences that affect access to quality care.

Social and Cultural Considerations

Recent science about the social determinants of health has helped to establish what social workers and some health care practitioners have long believed to be true—the social environment is host to a number of biological, psychological, and social factors that influence human health and the human condition. Brunner & Marmot (2002) propose that individuals are born into a specific social structure and, as a result, respond to the influences of the social environment to which they are exposed. Their social environment is composed of material (poverty, quality of medical care, etc.), psychosocial (e.g., stressors, physical and/or mental illness), and behavioral (health habits, diet, physical activity, etc.) pathways that converge to determine one's health outcomes, specifically, well-being, morbidity, or mortality. Poverty, class inequalities, social stigma and isolation, and cultural and linguistic differences are principle influences of these pathways.

Poverty

In 2006, families of 17.4 percent of U.S. children (12.8 million) lived at or below the federal poverty level ($20,000 for a family of four) (DeNavas-Walt et al., 2007). Of these children, 40 percent experienced extreme forms of poverty (50 percent below the federal poverty level) (Annie E. Casey Foundation, 2008). Whereas children represented 24.9 percent of the total population in 2006, they represented 35.2 percent of people in poverty (DeNavas-Walt et al.). Poverty has long been associated with a number of negative outcomes on the health and well-being of children, and its effects comprise one of the strongest social determinants of child health and well-being. Although children with chronic or acute conditions in low-income families are more likely to be eligible for government insurance programs and less likely to have medical expenses (Chevarley, 2006), they must nonetheless find the resources for co-pays on medical visits and prescription medications, as well as other expenses not covered by insurance (U.S. Department of Health and Human Services Health Resources and Services Administration Maternal and Child Health Bureau, 2008b).

Class Inequalities

Inequalities in income and wealth are associated with adverse child health outcomes. Increases in poverty, single-parent households, housing costs, and food insecurity affect one's ability to secure and maintain access to quality health care and contribute to the occurrence of health disparities among children (Wise, 2004). Syme (2008) assigns " . . . higher rates of illness and death from virtually every disease . . . " to racial and social class inequalities, suggesting that " . . . deprived circumstances experienced by people in disadvantaged positions result in a cumulative toll on health and well-being that is reproduced in successive generations over the years" (p. 436). Leading researchers in the field of epidemiology continue to forge the link between class inequality and health as a way of demonstrating how social forces compromise the nation's health and vulnerable populations (e.g., children with special health care needs) (Kawachi, 2000). Recent research clearly demonstrates the relationship between social status and a series of variables that influence health beliefs, health behaviors, and health outcomes (Brunner & Marmot, 2006).

Social Stigma and Isolation

The societal stigma and isolation associated with health conditions is well documented and felt by children and parents alike (Sobo, 2007). The story of Ryan White, who contracted HIV during a blood transfusion to treat hemophilia, epitomizes what can occur when need intersects with fear and ignorance. Ryan confronted the stigma of AIDS head-on when he attempted to return to school following his diagnosis (High Noon Communications, n.d.). Social stigma and the subsequent isolation experienced by children with special health care needs can have profound effects. More than one-fourth of parents responding to the National Survey of Children with Special Health Care Needs reported ongoing emotional, behavioral, or developmental problems associated with their child's health condition (U.S. Department of Health and Human Services Health Resources and Services Administration Maternal and Child Health Bureau, 2008b). Parents may also feel stigmatized when their child is diagnosed with a chronic or acute disorder. Since it is easy to internalize feeling different and being treated differently, Sobo proposes that stigma management be integrated into developmental and physical care plans across the life of a child. This would entail *culture work*, which reframes a child's condition in a more positive manner, *and social work*, which involves developing social support networks around families (Sobo, p. 220). Stigma management prepares children, adolescents, and their families for the reality of social and cultural responses to chronic and acute health conditions, strengthens their coping skills, and prepares them to educate others about the realities of their conditions.

Cultural and Linguistic Differences

The racial and ethnic diversity of the United States is expanding at an exponential rate. One-third of the U.S. population was composed of ethnic minorities in 2000, and that will grow to one-half by 2050 (Agency for Healthcare Research and Quality, 2008). It appears, however, that the health care system in general falls short of being able to relate to these populations in a culturally competent manner. Members of minority groups report difficulties relating to their health care providers because of cultural and linguistic differences (Agency for Healthcare Research and Quality, 2008; Mead, 2008). Culturally based beliefs and attitudes may run counter to current medical science, and perceptions of need or cure may not match those of care providers, leading to cultural misunderstandings (Losier, Taylor, & Fernandez, 2005; Agency for Healthcare Research and Quality, 2008). Language barriers also compromise physician-patient communication (Agency for Healthcare Research and Quality, 2008; Mead, 2008), and using family members or nonprofessionals to translate health information can jeopardize patient care if information is translated inaccurately or incompletely (Rondero Hernandez, Selber & Tijerina, 2006).

Current literature on cultural competence in health care reflects that culturally competent interventions positively affect health services' utilization, satisfaction, and patient education (Fortier & Bishop, 2003). Interpreter services also have been found to have a positive effect on patient satisfaction and comprehension and improved health care delivery (e.g., increases in the amount of time spent with patients, reduction in diagnostic testing disparities among non-English-speaking patients, higher clinic return rates, and increases in primary care services utilization) (Fortier & Bishop). Knowledge of cultural beliefs, language preferences, and acculturation levels are important to understand in order to effectively communicate and interact with persons from different cultural backgrounds and to uncover inherent strengths of families (Bailey, Correa, & Rodriguez, 1999).

Knowledge of social determinants, socioeconomic inequities, and cultural barriers to care equip practitioners from all disciplines to address macrolevel influences that affect children with special health care needs. There is no place where this type of thinking and action is needed more than in the area of health disparities.

Health Disparities: The Perfect Storm of Policy, Practice, and Need

By definition, health disparities are population-specific and occur when there are gaps in the level of health and access to care based on gender, race, ethnicity, educational level, income, disability, geographic location, sexual orientation, and linguistic differences (U.S. Department of Health and Human Services, 2000). They usually are related to lack of health insurance, not having a usual source of care (e.g., primary physician), and patient perceptions of need (Agency for Healthcare Research and Quality, 2008; National Partnership for Action to End Health Disparities, 2008). Regardless of their origin, health disparities typically translate into a disproportionate rate of disease for specific populations, poorer health outcomes, and/or unequal access to health care services.

Child health disparities are especially worrisome because they affect the health and well-being of specific groups more profoundly. Donovan & Rose (2005) reported that 14.4 infant deaths were reported for every 1,000 live births for African Americans in 2006 compared to 5.8 infant deaths per 1,000 live births for whites during the same year. Child health disparities extend across a number of health condition categories, including early childhood vaccinations, dental care, hospital admissions for pediatric asthma, and health insurance coverage; and children from low-income groups received less timely care for illness and injury (Agency for Healthcare Research and Quality, 2008). Child health disparities also extend to children and youth with special health care needs. Families of color were more likely to report unmet needs in the areas of health services and support services, more difficulties obtaining specialty care, not having a primary practitioner to follow their children's case, and fewer incidences of receiving family-centered care (Betz, 2005).

It is now widely accepted that access to health care is especially limited for children of color and children who live in poverty (Betz, 2005; National Partnership for Action to End Health Disparities, 2008; Willis, 2002). Comprehending the effects of health disparities requires practitioners to incorporate a multisystemic perspective into their clinical practice to envision and distinguish the various economic, social, and cultural influences that facilitate and strengthen children and families and identify strategies to reduce barriers to health care access, funding, and services.

Strategies for Facilitating Access to Quality Care

The manner in which health care is delivered to children with chronic and acute care needs and their families has been widely discussed in the literature. These discussions have historically been framed around fragmented service systems, the unresponsiveness of health care systems, the difficulties in navigating through these systems, and the "centeredness" of care. Following are responses to these long-standing concerns, most of which are the outcomes of partnerships between parents and providers and all of which are intended to facilitate the delivery of care and services to children with chronic and acute conditions.

Family-Centered Care

The term *family-centered care* was first used to describe an approach that places an emphasis on the family unit as opposed to the individual patient. The family-centered approach has been described as both a conceptual and philosophical approach (Dunst, 1997). It is conceptual in that it "recognize[s] the facts that the family is an important source of influence affecting the physical and emotional well-being of family members," and it is philosophical because it " . . . evolved from the fact that more traditional professionally centered intervention practices often usurped families' rightful role to be meaningfully involved in important decisions . . . " related to their children's care (Dunst, p. 75). Family-centered care is an outcome of the consumer and family support movement initiated in the 1960s (Johnson, 2000). These movements advocated for children with special needs and were supported by national leaders such as former U.S. surgeon general C. Everett Koop, parents, researchers, and countless other advocates in health care, education, and social services (Allen & Petr, 1998). These movements were responsible for promoting several landmark legislation and policy changes, including the passage of Public Law 94-142, the Education for All Handicapped Children Act, which codified the principles of "least restrictive environment" and parental involvement in individual education plans (IEPs), the Katie Beckett Waiver,[6] and the Mental Health Amendments of 1990 (PL 101-63), which called for the construction of family-centered systems of care (Johnson).

Family-centered care, as it is currently defined, involves two essential elements—informed family choice and a family strengths perspective (Allen & Petr, 1998). Family-centered care prompted a "paradigm shift" in the professional community (Regan, Curtin, & Vorderer, 2006) that (1) redefined the role of parent from passive observer to active participant, (2) required effective communication and collaboration skills on the part of providers, (3) encouraged professionals to build on family strengths, and (4) promoted parent-provider partnerships and interprofessional collaboration (Allen & Petr; Johnson, 2000; Graves, 2007; Sobo, 2007). Over time, family-centered care has become a "best practice" in the fields of health, mental health, and education and is now taught as essential content in medical training programs, which sometimes includes presentations and field-based activities taught by parents themselves (Hanson & Randall, 2007; A. M. Johnson, Yoder, & Richardson-Nassif, 2006). Family-centered care is now considered a dimension of the "medical home" model (American Academy of Pediatrics, 2008c).

---

[6] Katie Beckett was comatose and ventilator-dependent. She required hospitalization to receive the care she needed. Katie's mother believed her daughter could receive equivalent and less expensive care at home if Katie qualified for Medicaid. However, the family's income exceeded the allowable limits to qualify. Katie's mother and advocates successfully lobbied for change in Medicaid regulations that now extend coverage for home-based services, thereby circumventing the need to be institutionalized (Specialized Training of Military Parents (STOMP), 2003a).

Medical Home

The "medical home" is a national initiative and model of delivering primary care to children with special needs. It has been defined as a "continuous, comprehensive, family-centered, coordinated, compassionate, and culturally effective" way of delivering services to a child and family by a primary care physician who (1) knows them, (2) is able to develop a partnership of mutual responsibility and trust with them, and (3) can manage and facilitate all aspects of pediatric care (American Academy of Pediatrics Medical Home Initiatives for Children with Special Needs Project Advisory Committee, 2002). Currently, federal and state agencies are offering data, block grants, and training opportunities to support a national mentoring effort that offers states the technical assistance and coaching needed to increase access to medical homes by 2010 (American Academy of Pediatrics, 2008d). The medical home is a long-overdue response to the historical challenges patients and parents have encountered navigating through complex health care systems in order to qualify for and secure needed services (McCarthy & Stough, 1999; Zimmerman & Dabelko, 2007). It also is a response to the ongoing need for case coordination that parents and advocates describe as essential in order for children with special health care needs to reach their maximum potential (Sobo, 2007; U.S. Department of Health and Human Services Health Resources and Services Administration Maternal and Child Health Bureau, 2008b).

Noncategorical Approach

The noncategorical approach is the outcome of historical discussion regarding whom to include in the category of children with special needs and where to focus initial interventions (Sobo & Kurtin, 2007). First and foremost, it focuses on the needs of the child and the consequences provoked by the condition rather than on the pathology of the condition.[7] The model, shown in Figure 3.1, assumes a parent's perspective and specifies the tasks and skills a parent needs to acquire in order to manage the health care needs of a child with chronic illness or disability (Sobo, 2007).

There are three components of the model: (1) initial classification or diagnosis, (2) care coordination, and (3) stigma management. These components are not discrete. They interact over the lifetime of the child. This model assumes that early and clear diagnosis, coordinated care, and dealing effectively with cultural beliefs and social stigma will empower parents with knowledge and skills that will benefit their children over

---

[7] Sobo (2007) states the noncategorical model is more relevant for parents of children with disabilities and health conditions that are not life threatening. She also notes that this model does not accommodate the complications associated with death and dying. However, aspects of the model may pertain to children with acute care needs, especially during the recovery and rehabilitation phases of care.

Figure 3.1

Noncategorical model of parental coping.

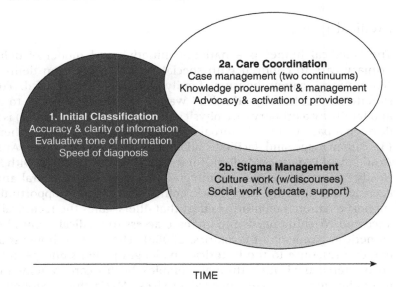

time. It also assumes that purposeful collaboration between parents and providers will accelerate the speed at which parents are able to navigate through health care systems, advance knowledge through mutual sharing of perspectives between parents and providers, and, ultimately, influence social policies and system improvements that serve children with special health care needs more effectively and more compassionately. The non-categorical model advocates for a "context of providing nonjudgmental, family-centered, case-managed care" (Sobo, 2007, p. 224) and offers specific recommendations to providers based on the values of (1) appreciation, acknowledgment, and service to the child and family, (2) informing, empowering, and communicating effectively with parents, and (3) engaging parents' perspectives about their child's condition and advocating for improved policies and programs for accessing quality care (Sobo, p. 225). Many of these recommendations coincide with those made by medical educators who advocate for greater parental involvement in the education of future practitioners and joint research with parents (Graves, 2007; Hanson & Randall, 2007; A. M. Johnson, Yoder, & Richardson-Nassif, 2006; Uding, Sety, & Kieckhefer, 2007).

The three strategies featured—family-centered care, the medical home, and the noncategorical model—share several things in common. The family system is acknowledged as the primary system of care and an authority about the needs of the child. Partnerships between parents and providers are valued, as are the perspectives of parents, and rest on the principles of communication and collaboration. Parents have a role in decisions made on behalf of the child, and a trust-filled relationship between provider and parent is essential in order to effectively broker a partnership that endures over the life span of the child.

Summary

One in five American households report caring for at least one child with special health care needs (U.S. Department of Health and Human Services Health Resources and Services Administration Maternal and Child Health Bureau, 2008b). In order for families to adequately care for their children, they must have access to quality care. Macrolevel economic, social, and cultural influences can enhance or impede access to quality care and affect a family's ability to manage costs and cope with care demands. Current literature reflects poverty and class inequalities that reduce access to quality care, as do social stigma and culturally insensitive behaviors (Syme, Lefkowitz, & Kivimae Krimgold, 2002; Wise, 2007; Syme, 2008; Agency for Healthcare Research and Quality, 2008). Inequities and insensitivities are now recognized as contributing factors in the development of health disparities (Agency for Healthcare Research and Quality, 2008; Mead, 2008), and current efforts to address them focus on the reduction of individual-level, environmental- and community-level, and system-level barriers (National Partnership for Action to End Health Disparities, 2008). Although the needs of children with special health care needs in the United States are still not addressed in a comprehensive manner, progressive efforts by family members, providers, and advocates over the past four decades have resulted in broader access to quality care for this population than ever before.

Conclusion

Large and sometimes pervasive economic, social, and cultural influences may be difficult to detect at times. However, they often have profound effects on our young clients and their families. Incorporating a multisystemic perspective into one's clinical practice can help a practitioner distinguish these influences more readily. A multisystemic perspective can also generate innovative strategies (i.e., family-centered care, the medical home, and noncategorical approaches). Insight about the complex interactions between human beings and their social environments, about the role of facilitators and barriers in health care access, and about the importance of cultural and language in clinical settings can also strengthen and enrich the work of practitioners and better prepare them for interprofessional and intersystem collaborations where the goal is the same—to assist and preserve families while building on their inherent strengths and expertise regarding the needs of their children.

References

Agency for Healthcare Research and Quality. (2008). *2007 National Healthcare Disparities Report*. Retrieved May 21, 2008, from http://www.ahrq.gov/qual/nhdr07/Chap3.htm#barrriers.

Allen, R., & Petr, C. G. (1998). Rethinking family-centered practice. *American Journal of Orthopsychiatry, 68*(1), 4–15.

American Academy of Pediatrics. (2008a). Access to care, Medicaid, and the State Children's Health Insurance Program (SCHIP). Retrieved June 9, 2008, from http://www.aap.org/advocacy.html.

American Academy of Pediatrics. (2008c). Medical home talking points: Final version.

American Academy of Pediatrics. (2008d). The National Center for Medical Home Initiatives for Special Needs Children. Retrieved May 21, 2008, from http://www.medicalhomeinfo.org/.

American Academy of Pediatrics Medical Home Initiatives for Children with Special Needs. (2008). Health insurance/managed care tools. Retrieved August 5, 2008, from http://www.medicalhomeinfo.org/tools/insur.html.

American Academy of Pediatrics Medical Home Initiatives for Children with Special Needs Project Advisory Committee. (2002). The medical home. *Pediatrics, 110*(1), 184–186.

American Association of Pediatrics Committee on Child Health Financing. (2007). State Children's Health Insurance Program achievements, challenges, and policy recommendations. *Pediatrics* (119), 1224–1228.

Annie E. Casey Foundation. (2008). Kids Count Data Book 2008. Baltimore, MD. Document Number ISSN 1060–9814.

Bailey, D. B., Correa, V., & Rodriguez, P. (1999). Narrating self and disability: Latino mothers' construction of identities vis-à-vis their child with special needs. *Exceptional Children, 65*(4), 481–495.

Bethel, C. D., Read, D., Stein, R. E., Blumberg, S. J., Wells, N., & Newacheck, P. W. (2002). Identifying children with special health care needs: Development and evaluation of a short screening instrument. *Ambulatory Pediatrics, 2*(1).

Betz, C. L. (2005). Health care disparities of children and youth: A pediatric nursing concern. *Journal of Pediatric Nursing, 20*(6), 399–401.

Brunner, E., & Marmot, M. (2006). Social organization, stress, and health. In M. Marmot & R. G. Wilkinson (Eds.), *Social determinants of health* (2nd ed.). New York: Oxford University Press.

Cannon, M. (2007). *Sinking SCHIP: A first step in stopping the growth of government health programs* (pp. 1–14). Washington, DC: Cato Institute.

Centers for Medicare & Medicaid Services. (2007a). Research, statistics, data & systems: Data compendium (2007 ed.). Retrieved June 12, 2008, from http://www.cms.hhs.gov/DataCompendium/.

Centers for Medicare & Medicaid Services. (2007b). Medicare enrollment by state, age, group, and entitlement, 2003. Retrieved June 12, 2008, from http://www.cms.hhs.gov/MedicareEnrpts/.

Centers for Medicare & Medicaid Services. (2008a). National health expenditures data: Health expenditures by age. Retrieved July 30, 2008, from http://www.cms.hhs.gov/NationalHealthExpendData/04_NationalHealthAccountsAgePHC.asp#TopOfPage.

Chevarley, F. M. (2006). Utilization and Expenditures for Children with Special Health Care Needs. Research Findings No. 24. Retrieved July 21, 2008, from http://www.meps.ahrq.govrf24rf24.pdf.

Children's Defense Fund. (2005). The State of America's Children 2005. Washington, DC.

DeNavas-Walt, C., Proctor, B. D., & Smith, J. (2007). *Income, Poverty, and Health Insurance Coverage in the United States: 2006.* Washington, DC. (U.S. Government Printing Office. Document Number: P60-233).

Donovan, E. F., & Rose, B. (2005). Use of evidence to reduce child health disparities on the U.S.: An introduction to this issue of Public Health Reports. *Public Health Reports, 120,* 366–369.

Dunst, C. J. (1997). Conceptual and empirical foundations of family-centered practice: Opportunities for psychological practice. In R. J. Illback, C. T. Cobb, & H. M. J. Jr. (Eds.), *Integrated services for children and families: Opportunities for psychological practice* (pp. 75–91). Washington, DC: American Psychological Association.

Family Voices. (2008). Financing health care: Insurance, managed care, medicaid, and other programs. Retrieved August 1, 2008, from http://www.family-voices.org/pub/index.php?topic=hcf.

Fortier, J. P., & Bishop, D. (2003). Setting the Agenda for Research on *Cultural Competence in Health Care: Final Report.* Retrieved July 25, 2008, from http://www.ahrq.gov/research/cultural.htm#Context.

Graves, K. N. (2007). Family empowerment as a mediator between family-centered systems of care and changes in child functioning: Identifying an important mechanism of change. *Journal of Child and Family Studies, 16*(4), 556–566.

Hanson, J. L., & Randall, V. F. (2007). Perspectives: Advancing a partnership: Patients, families, and medical educators. *Teaching & Learning in Medicine, 19*(2), 191–197.

High Noon Communications. (n.d.). www.ryanwhite.com. Retrieved August 2, 2008, from www.ryanwhite.com.

Hoffman, E. D., Klees, B. S., & Curtis, C. A. (2007). *Brief Summaries of Medicare & Medicaid: Title XVIII and Title XIX of the Social Security Act as of November 1, 2007.* Retrieved June 20, 2008, from http://www.cms.hhs.gov/MedicareProgram RatesStats/02_SummaryMedicareMedicaid.asp.

Johnson, B. H. (2000). Family-centered care: Four decades of progress. *Families, Systems & Health: The Journal of Collaborative Family HealthCare, 18*(2), 137–156.

Johnson, A. M., Yoder, J., & Richardson-Nassif, K. (2006). Using families as faculty in teaching medical students family-centered care: What are students learning? *Teaching & Learning in Medicine, 18*(3), 222–225.

Kaiser Family Foundation. (2006a). Distribution of out-of-pocket spending for health care services: May 2006. Retrieved July 31, 2008, from http://www.kff.org/insurance/snapshot/chcm050206oth.cfm.

Kaiser Family Foundation. (2006b). The public, managed care, and consumer protections. Retrieved August 1, 2008, from http://www.kff.org/spotlight/managedcare/upload/Spotlight_Jan06_ManagedCare.pdf.

Kaiser Family Foundation. (2008). Health insurance/costs. Retrieved July 31, 2008, from http://www.kff.org/insurance/index.cfm.

Kawachi, I. (2000). Income inequality and health. In L. F. Berkman & I. Kawachi (Eds.), *Social epidemiology.* New York, NY: Oxford University Press.

Losier, A., Taylor, B., & Fernandez, C. V. (2005). Use of alternative therapies by patients presenting to a pediatric emergency department. *Journal of Emergency Medicine, 28*(3), 267–271.

MacIntyre, S., & Ellaway, A. (2000). Ecological approaches: Rediscovering the role of the physical and social environment. In L. F. Berkman & I. Kawachi (Eds.), *Socio epidemiology.* New York: Oxford University Press.

McCarthy, M. G., & Stough, L. M. (1999). The qualifying game: A search for services by individuals with disabilities. *Education and Training in Mental Retardation and Developmental Disabilities, 34*(4), 485–498.

McPherson, M., Arango, P., Fox, H., Lauver, C., McManus, M. A., Newacheck, P. M., et al. (1998). A new definition of children with special health care needs. *Pediatrics (1 Pt. 1), 102,* 137–140.

Mead, H., Cartwright-Smith, L., Jones, K., Ramos, C., Woods, K., & Siegel, B. (2008). Racial and ethnic disparities in U.S. health care: A chartbook. New York: Commonwealth Fund.

Medicare Interactive U.S. (2008). What services does the Department of Veterans Affairs (VA) cover? Retrieved June 13, 2008, from http://www.medicare-rights.org/.

Military HOMEFRONT. U.S. Department of Defense. (2008). Federal Medical Care Programs. Retrieved June 13, 2008, from http://www.militaryhomefront.dod .mil/portal/page/mhf/MHF/MHF_DETAIL_1?section_id=20.40.500.570.0.0. 0.0.0&current_id=20.40.500.570.500.60.120.0.0.

Mitka, M. (1998). A quarter century of health maintenance. *Journal of the American Medical Association, 280*(24), 2059–2060.

National Center on Financing for Children with Special Health Care Needs. (2004). Financing and reimbursement strategies in managed care: Glossary of terms. Retrieved August 1, 2008, from http://cshcnfinance.ichp.ufl.edu/.

National Kidney Foundation. (2008). ESRD Medicare guidelines. Retrieved June 11, 2008, from http://www.kidney.org/.

National Partnership for Action to End Health Disparities. (2008). A strategic framework for improving racial/ethnic minority health and eliminating racial/ethnic health disparities. Retrieved June 13, 2008, from http://www. omhrc.gov/npa/templates/content.aspx?ID=78&lvl=1&lvlID=13.

Neff, J. M. (2007). Matters of finance: How do we pay for the care of children with special health care needs? In E. J. Sobo & P. S. Kurtin (Eds.), *Optimizing care for young children with special health care needs: Knowledge and strategies for navigating the system.* Baltimore, MD: Paul H. Brookes Publishing Co.

Office of Behavioral and Social Sciences Research. (2007). *The contributions of behavioral and social sciences research to improving the health of the nation: A prospectus for the future.* Retrieved May 1, 2008, from http://obssr.od.nih.gov/ Content/Strategic_Planning/Strategic+Plan_2007/ObssrIndex.htm.

Perlino, C. M. (2007). *Reauthorization of the State Children's Health Insurance Program (SCHIP): A key step to covering all kids, American Public Health Association Issues Brief* (pp. 1–10). Washington, DC: American Public Health Association.

Regan, K. M., Curtin, C., & Vorderer, L. (2006). Paradigm shifts in inpatient psychiatric care of children: Approaching child- and family-centered care. *Journal of Child & Adolescent Psychiatric Nursing, 19*(1), 29–40.

Rondero Hernandez, V., Selber, K., & Tijerina, M. (2006). Visioning family-centered care in genetics: What parents and providers have to say. *Journal of Genetic Counseling, 15*(5).

Rosenbach, M., Irvin, C., Merrill, A., Shulman, S., Czajka, J., Trenholm, C., et al. (2007). *National evaluation of the State Children's Health Insurance Program: A decade of expanding coverage and improving access: Final report.* Princeton, NJ. (Mathematica Policy Research, Inc. Contract No.: 500-96-0016(03) MPR Reference No.: 8644–103).

Simpson, L. A., & Dougherty, D. (2007). Accessing quality care for children with special health care needs: The future of policy and research. In E. J. Sobo & P. S. Kurtin (Eds.), *Optimizing care for young children with special health care needs.* Baltimore, MD: Paul H. Brookes Publishing Co.

Sobo, E. J. (2007). Mastering the health care system for children with special health care needs. In E. J. Sobo & P. S. Kurtin (Eds.), *Optimizing care for young children with special health care needs.* Baltimore, MD: Paul H. Brookes Publishing Co.

Sobo, E. J., & Kurtin, P. S. (Eds.). (2007). *Optimizing care for young children with special health care needs: Knowledge and strategies for navigating the system.* Baltimore, MD: Paul H. Brookes Publishing Co.

Specialized Training of Military Parents (STOMP). (2003a). Fact Sheet #4 Medicaid. Retrieved June 13, 2008, from http://www.stompproject.org/down/materials/fs4.pdf.

Specialized Training of Military Parents (STOMP). (2003b). Publications. Retrieved June 13, 2008, from http://www.stompproject.org/publications.asp.

Syme, L. (2008). Reducing racial and social-class inequalities in health: The need for a new approach. *Health Affairs, 27*(2), 456–459.

Syme, L., Lefkowitz, B., & Kivimae Krimgold, B. (2002). Incorporating socioeconomic factors into U.S. health policy: Addressing the barriers. *Health Affairs, 21*(2), 113.

TRICARE Management Activity. (2008a). Enhanced Care Health Option (ECHO). Retrieved June 13, 2008, from http://tricare.mil/mybenefit/home/LifeEvents/SpecialNeeds/ECHO?plan=TRICARE+Prime&status=Active+Duty+Service+Member&zipCode=13602&country=United+States.

TRICARE Management Activity. (2008b). What is TRICARE? Retrieved June 13, 2008, from http://tricare.mil/mybenefit/home/overview/WhatIsTRICARE?

Uding, N., Sety, M., & Kieckhefer, G. M. (2007). Family involvement in health care research: The "building on family strengths" case study. *Families, Systems & Health: The Journal of Collaborative Family HealthCare, 25*(3), 307–322.

U.S. Department of Health and Human Services. (2007). Data definitions. Retrieved August 2, 2008, from http://www.cdc.gov/nchs/datawh/nchsdefs/healthcondition.htm#acute.

U.S. Department of Health and Human Services. (2008). The 2008 HHS federal poverty guidelines. Retrieved July 31, 2008, from http://aspe.hhs.gov/poverty/08Poverty.shtml.

U.S. Department of Health and Human Services Health Resources and Services Administration Maternal and Child Health Bureau. (2008a). Maternal and Child Health Bureau: Timeline. Retrieved July 21, 2008, from http://mchb.hrsa.gov/timeline/.

U.S. Department of Health and Human Services Health Resources and Services Administration Maternal and Child Health Bureau. (2008b). *The National Survey of Children with Special Health Care Needs Chartbook 2005–2006.* Retrieved June 2, 2008, from http://mchb.hrsa.gov/cshcn05/.

U.S. Department of Health and Human Services. (2000). *Healthy People 2010: Understanding and Improving Health.* 2nd ed. Retrieved July 30, 2008, from http://www.healthypeople.gov/Document/html/uih/uih_2.htm.

Willis, D. J. (2002). Introduction to the special issues: Economic, health and mental health disparities among ethnic minority children and families. *Society of Pediatric Psychology, 27*(4), 309–314.

Wise, P. H. (2004). The transformation of child health in the United States. *Health Affairs, 23*(5), 9–25.

Wise, P. H. (2007). Childhood epidemiology and policy change. Stanford, CA: Center for Policy, Outcomes and Prevention.

Zimmerman, J., & Dabelko, H. I. (2007). Collaborative models of patient care: New opportunities for hospital social workers. *Social Work in Health, 44*(4), 33–47.

Helping Approaches of Practitioners in Different Settings

Part

A Behavioral Pediatrician's Perspective on Helping Children Recover from Traumatic Medical Experiences

Joan Lovett

Introduction

Illness, injury, and medical procedures can be distressing and overwhelming. They pose a particular challenge for children who are too young to understand what is happening, who have limited ability to express their concerns, and who are not capable of participating in decision making about their care. Medical experiences can be traumatizing and may interfere with a child's normal social, emotional, and cognitive development. Clinicians who recognize the signs and symptoms associated with medical trauma can help children recover from its potentially debilitating effects.

What Is Trauma?

Trauma refers to overwhelming experiences that undermine a person's sense of safety and well-being and leave the victim with distorted, negative beliefs about self and the world. Trauma can result from exposure to clearly tragic events, such as violent crimes or natural disasters. Trauma may also arise from relatively minor events, such as criticism by a teacher, bullying by peers, or the birth of a sibling. Both catastrophic and minor trauma can result in feelings of helplessness or powerlessness, distorted beliefs about self, and loss of trust.

Some children and adults who experience potentially traumatizing events do not develop posttraumatic stress disorder. The risk of developing posttraumatic symptoms following exposure to a traumatic experience varies, generally depending on characteristics of the child, characteristics of the event, and characteristics of the family and social system (Webb, 2007).

What Is Medical Trauma?

In this chapter, the term medical trauma refers to any overwhelming experience that is related to illness, injury, or medical treatment. Medical experiences inherently have the potential for being traumatic. The experiences of illness, pain, loss of control, violation of integrity through intrusive medical procedures, separation from parents and other family members, and parental distress are difficult for children. In combination, these experiences can overwhelm a child and result in feelings of helplessness and loss of trust in self and others.

Trauma sometimes cannot be prevented. Even lifesaving medical interventions, provided competently and tenderly by excellent professionals, can be traumatizing.

For children, traumatic medical memories may forge behavioral and personality problems that interfere with normal development and with the formation of healthy relationships. Distressing memories of medical experiences may prevent an individual from seeking or receiving necessary medical care as an adult.

This chapter discusses factors that can make a medical experience traumatic for a child, posttraumatic symptoms that can arise from medical trauma, how the symptoms can interfere with normal child development, what the clinician needs to know in order to help the traumatized child, and the role of behavioral pediatricians in the treatment of medical trauma. The chapter includes a case example of a boy who became fearful of going to the hospital after a medical procedure.

Similarities of Medical Trauma to Other Trauma

Medical trauma has many similarities to other kinds of trauma. Typically, children who have been traumatized tend to have distorted, negative beliefs about themselves (e.g., "I'm bad," "Whatever happened is my fault," "I'm not lovable," "I'm not important," "I don't deserve good things," "I can't tolerate it if things don't go the way I want," "I can't tolerate anything going wrong," or "I am in danger if I'm not in control"). Children may develop behaviors of protest and avoidance that indicate their belief that anything that reminds them of the traumatic event, even medical care, is dangerous. Negative and distorted thoughts can circulate repeatedly, distracting children from their important tasks of learning, playing, and relating to others.

Posttraumatic symptoms may occur immediately after medical trauma or may be delayed for a year or more. Sometimes symptoms do not arise until the child encounters a subsequent illness, injury, or medical encounter. Delayed symptoms can be confusing, especially if symptoms like separation anxiety, school refusal, or anxiety about sleep do not immediately suggest medical trauma. Sometimes it is not obvious that trauma is involved. A history of previous medical intervention or injury should raise suspicions of medical trauma.

Factors That Can Make a Medical Experience Traumatic for a Child

Helplessness and Vulnerability

A child undergoing any type of medical procedure has very little, if any, say about what is being done to him or her. In addition, physical restraint by adults or a restraining "papoose" used to hold a child still during a medical procedure, renders the child physically powerless. This sense of helplessness contributes to the development of medical trauma. A perceived threat to physical well-being, caused by illness, injury, or medical intervention can be traumatic.

Having experienced a loss of control and actual helplessness in a previous medical situation, traumatized children may regard themselves as ineffectual or incapable in other areas of their lives. Children who develop a sense of helplessness and vulnerability following trauma may be fearful and reluctant to engage in developmentally appropriate activities. Presuming ineffectiveness, they may adopt a "why try?" attitude that makes them reluctant to experiment or learn. They may shun independent activities and need help with routine self-care activities that they had previously mastered. They may develop fears and separation anxiety that interfere with normal sleep, school activities, or relationships with peers.

Discomfort and Pain

Physical discomfort and pain that accompany illness or injury, as well as under-medication for medical procedures, may be traumatizing. Occasionally, anesthesia wears off during surgery, and the resulting post-traumatic symptoms may include nightmares or fear of lights.

Hospitalized infants and children are subjected to many painful procedures. They are routinely poked with a needle to draw blood and for insertion of intravenous lines for delivering fluids or medication. Because young patients' veins are so tiny, it can take several pokes to successfully insert a needle. Critically ill infants may be subjected to repeated heel sticks, nasogastric tube insertion, central line insertion, suctioning, enemas, endotracheal intubation, and other invasive procedures. Some infants in neonatal intensive care units are subjected to more than 50 procedures per day (McClain & Kain, 2005).

Medical procedures children experience are often more painful than those performed on their adult counterparts. Until recently, even surgery on neonates was performed with paralytics, but with minimal or no analgesia. It was believed that infants did not really feel pain, and even if they did feel pain, they would not remember it. We now know that this is not so (McClain & Kain, 2005; AAP, 2006).

Today we know that the neurotransmitters and structures required for pain sensation as well as structures needed for long-term memory are developed adequately in the neonate and have the potential to affect long-term outcomes. Studies indicate that poorly controlled acute pain may lead to heightened pain sensitivity, or *hyperalgesia*, altered pain perception, and possibly a predilection to chronic pain states. Surgical procedures without pain relief are certainly traumatic—and the memory of pain is stored in the body long after the healing of physical wounds is complete (McClain & Kain, 2005).

Doctors now realize that lifesaving care in the neonatal intensive care unit (NICU) is intrusive and painful, and, from the infant's perspective, the pain of lifesaving care is indistinguishable from the pain of abuse (Gardener, Barland, Meremstein, & Lubchenco, 1993).

Confusion

Another factor central to medical trauma is the confusion related to experiences of medical intervention. In part, this confusion arises from children's developmental limitations. Young children are developmentally unable to comprehend that a painful or frightening medical procedure can be helpful. Children may not be able to articulate their distress and confusion, but we can imagine that they might wonder: "Why would someone hurt me when I am already in pain?" "How can something help if it hurts?" "Who is doing this to me, and why?" "What did I do to cause this?" Also, illness and injury that are sudden, unexpected, and difficult to understand are inherently confusing.

Another source of confusion is the effect of narcotic pain medications and premedication for surgery. Children sometimes experience confusion as well as nausea or dizziness as they emerge from general anesthetic following surgery. It is useful for children to be told that the medicine is making them feel weird and/or nauseated, that this is expected, and that they will feel normal again soon.

According to a study conducted at Great Ormand Street Children's Hospital in London, about one-third of children who have been treated in the pediatric intensive care unit (PICU) have delusional memories or hallucinations. The timing of the hallucinations appeared to coincide with the period during which they were being weaned off the sedatives commonly prescribed in the PICU (benzodiazepines and opiates), and children were five times as likely to report having had delusions or hallucinations if they had been prescribed opiates and benzodiazepines for more than two days. These children who reported delusions and hallucinations had a significantly higher score on the posttraumatic stress screening test than others (American Thoracic Society, 2008).

Confusion, like pain, becomes a visceral memory. The common practice of under-medication of pain in the pediatric population contributes to the confusion and trauma of medical interventions.

Confusion can interfere with attachment and trust. When parents are absent during medical procedures, the child is more likely to be frightened and may feel abandoned. Parents are encouraged to be with their children and hold them and comfort them during painful medical procedures. While this practice is usually reassuring to the child, it can also be confusing for children when their parents acquiesce to painful procedures.

Special Considerations

Parental Distress

Parents' reactions to a child's illness, injury, or medical condition are always important. Parents whose child is ill or injured are sometimes in a state of shock and may themselves develop posttraumatic symptoms. Parents usually believe that they are responsible for protecting their child and keeping him or her safe. When their child is born with a congenital defect or becomes seriously ill or injured, it is not unusual for parents to feel guilty or inadequate in caring for their child. These feelings may interfere with a parent's ability to bond with their child. Some parents of ill, injured, or disabled children may become resentful or depressed when the child's problems interfere with family functioning, deplete finances, or interrupt work schedules. The parents may not be able to provide the care and support their child needs.

Parents whose child has been ill, injured, or has experienced medical trauma may be reluctant to trust that their compromised child will ever be healthy and resilient. This lack of confidence in the child's potential for recovery can be transmitted to the child, further diminishing his or her self-confidence.

Children turn to their parents or caregivers for reassurance and emotional connection. However, it can be difficult for distressed parents to provide effective reassurance. Children often internalize their parents' distress. Seeing parents act frightened, extremely sad, or concerned can cause children to assume that they caused the upset and that they are in danger. Furthermore, when parents' reassurances don't match with their distressed demeanor, children don't know how to gauge their own emotional response.

The clinician must decide whether the child's recovery will help resolve the parent's trauma or whether the parents need therapy first so that they can be emotionally available and supportive to their child. A referral for support of parents may be more effective than direct services to the child. This referral should be made tactfully so as not to increase the parents' sense of inadequacy or guilt.

Parents' individual therapy can help them gain skills or develop useful beliefs, such as "I can cope with my child's medical problems, be his advocate, and give him love and emotional support," "I am a good parent, even though my child has these problems," I can trust my child can heal from this," "I can talk with doctors to advocate for my child."

Complicating Factors

Many factors can complicate the healing process. Multiple events, illness, injury or death of other family members, ongoing uncertainty or disability, unavailability of parents, and family financial problems are all major stresses. The medical social worker or child life practitioner may need to work with a team of professionals and may need to reassure the child that other caring adults are taking care of their parents. It should not be the responsibility of injured or ill children to take care of their parents or their parents' feelings. As described in Chapter 1, the clinician may work together with other professionals to serve and support the child and family to strengthen their personal resources for coping with ongoing stress.

Uncertainty of Outcome

Sometimes a child's diagnosis and prognosis are unknown, or the diagnosed condition will require undetermined or distressing interventions. Medical trauma may become complex and multifaceted. It is valuable for the child and family to learn stress-reduction strategies and to have ongoing support as they face upcoming challenges.

Literal Interpretation of Language

Traumatized children tend to interpret language very literally. In cases of medical trauma, the words "bad" and "hurt" may be particularly significant. Traumatized children can confuse feeling bad (from physical pain or emotional distress) with being bad (in the sense of being a bad person). They may even believe that illness and painful procedures are punishments for something they have done wrong.

The word *hurt* in the English language can be problematic. It can be used as a noun, an adjective, an active verb, or a passive verb. "I hurt myself" has a different meaning from "I got hurt." "I hurt myself" implies purposeful self-injury, whereas "I got hurt" implies accidental harm. Traumatized children may feel confused and uncertain about whether they are responsible for their situation, no matter whether it is accidental or whether someone else is to blame. Often, at the time of an accident or injury, someone may say, "Oh, you hurt yourself." In a posttraumatic state, children may interpret this statement as meaning that they literally actively did something to injure themselves.

How Can Posttraumatic Symptoms from Medical Trauma Interfere with Normal Child Development?

Anxiety

Anxiety may manifest as avoidance of medical visits, doctors, medical treatment, or any other experience reminding the child of the traumatic medical experiences. Fear may also appear in the form of separation anxiety, insomnia, and nightmares. The hyper-vigilance resulting from anxiety can interfere with concentration and the ability to stay on task, making it difficult for a child to do well in school. Sometimes even relaxation can trigger anxiety if the relaxation reminds the child of being anesthetized or if the child perceives relaxation as a precursor to pain.

Confusion may be a trigger for anxiety. Since confusion is a necessary part of learning, the child who has been traumatized may have trouble performing in school or trying new and unfamiliar activities. Academic subjects, like math, are intrinsically confusing until they have been practiced and understood. Adding anxiety to the confusion may hinder the process of learning.

Unexpected, sudden, or new experiences may trigger anxiety in a child who has experienced sudden illness or injury or who has had frightening medical procedures without preparation. This fear of new experiences can prevent a child from trying new things.

Children who have experienced pain may be afraid of touch, even if it is gentle and loving. This avoidance of touch is called *sensory aversion*. Children who have had oral surgery or procedures like intubation or nasogastric tube insertion may be diagnosed with "oral sensory aversion." These symptoms may be regarded as developmental or neurological or a sign of a sensory processing disorder, although the symptoms are actually posttraumatic responses. Some children who have experienced severe oral trauma may even refuse to eat and require a gastrostomy tube for years.

Children who have experienced medical trauma may have anxiety triggered by bright lights, mechanical noises, having clothes pulled over their head, medicinal smells or flavors, or anything else that reminds them of their traumatic experience. Once aware of the effects of trauma, it is usually not difficult to trace the root of the symptom to the medical experience that provoked it.

Sleep Disturbances and Nightmares

Children who have been traumatized may have difficulty falling asleep, staying asleep, and sleeping soundly. They often have nightmares or night terrors. The children and their families may become sleep-deprived, further compromising their ability to function during the day.

Dissociation

Children who have been severely traumatized may dissociate when they feel physically or emotionally unsafe. Dissociation during a painful medical procedure is adaptive and helpful. Dissociation is a type of psychic hiding in which being conscious and aware is too painful to bear. The child may appear dazed or blank or display inappropriate affect. A child who continues to experience dissociation long after painful medical experiences is unavailable for relationships, play, or learning.

Attachment and Trust Issues

A secure base of attachment is the foundation of a child's emotional well-being. Medical trauma can interfere with a child's relationship with parents, other family members, and medical personnel. Disturbed attachment can undermine the sense of physical and emotional confidence that is so important in meeting new developmental milestones.

Developmental Considerations

Developmental regression can be a sign of trauma. Children who may have mastered falling asleep independently may be unable to sleep without a parent present. Children who have been toilet trained may begin bed-wetting or daytime wetting. Those who have become somewhat independent and able to dress and feed themselves may begin to feel unable to do these tasks. A child who normally speaks fluently may revert to baby talk. These symptoms may occur transiently with any stress, but they are cause for attention if the symptoms persist and interfere with normal development.

Extreme Behavior

Children tend to respond to stress by increasing the frequency and intensity of their coping strategies. Young children who have tantrums to express anger when they don't get what they want or when they perceive something as unfair may develop more frequent and more intense tantrums, even if the triggering event is minor. When parents ask friends or their doctor about the symptoms, they may get reassurance that the child's behavior is developmentally appropriate. Young children may have temper tantrums, difficulty sleeping, or toileting inconsistency. An individual child's intensity and frequency of response to minor provocation helps distinguish a normal behavior from a posttraumatic stress response.

Children who have been traumatized can become rigid about schedules and become extremely upset when something unexpected happens. They may not be able to tolerate a change of plans or something not going their way. They can be reluctant to try anything new. Traumatized children can be obsessed with fairness and become very upset when they lose a game or perceive injustice of any kind. They can become excessively controlling. They can have emotional outbursts over minor incidents. These extreme behaviors can interfere with family and peer relationships and other social interactions.

Changes in Play

Traumatized children often reenact their trauma through play. Post-traumatic play is repetitive, without resolution (Terr, 1983). Children who lose their ability for creative play do not have full access to their problem-solving capability. This loss of flexibility can make it difficult for the child to get along in social situations.

Somatic Symptoms

Children who have experienced medical trauma may later develop head-aches, stomachaches, and anxiety, sometimes with a racing heart, a lump in the throat, or difficulty breathing. These somatic symptoms may lead the child to the doctor's office—necessitating more diagnostic procedures.

A careful history, physical exam, and lab work may be needed to evaluate somatic symptoms. A stomachache can be an indication of stress, constipation, a reaction to a medication, or something more serious. Somatic symptoms that are ongoing, such as stomachaches associated with irritable bowel syndrome or acid-reflux, may require both medical and psychological intervention. It is important to plan an intervention that will address both medical and psychological conditions, as they can create an undesirable feedback loop. For example, abdominal pain can cause anxiety in a traumatized child, which then further exacerbates the abdominal pain.

What Does the Clinician Need to Know to Help a Traumatized Child?

1. Details of the traumatic event
    A clinician who works to help children overcome traumatic memories of medical problems must be prepared to offer develop-mentally appropriate explanations for medical experiences. Famil-iarity with issues pertaining to medical trauma helps the clinician provide effective therapy for children. This knowledge allows the clinician to teach the child how the interventions are meant to help.
    Early childhood trauma is stored "frame by frame," or as a series of events. Knowing the sequence of upsetting events in detail allows the clinician to address the many fragments of the child's memories, whenever the child is ready to revisit these.

2. Information about the child's medical situation

The clinician must know about the child's medical diagnoses, past and anticipated medical course, effects and side effects of medications, procedures, and prognosis.

3. Posttraumatic symptoms

The clinician must be familiar with the child's behaviors, his or her somatic or physical symptoms, and medical history in order to understand the cause of the trauma and to outline treatment goals.

4. Developmental considerations

The clinician needs to be aware of the behavior range that is normal for a child of this age, the child's cognitive level and understanding of the situation, the developmental milestones the child has already achieved, and any regressive behaviors exhibited by the child.

5. Parental and family functioning

The clinician must evaluate the family situation, determine whether anyone else in the family needs help, and organize appropriate support while helping the child recover from medical trauma.

The Role of a Behavioral Pediatrician

When a child has persistent anxieties or puzzling behaviors that interfere with normal social development and family functioning, it is appropriate to consider an evaluation by a professional who has experience helping stressed, anxious, or traumatized children. The title of that professional may vary and can include behavioral pediatricians, psychiatrists, psychologists, clinical social workers, and therapists who offer a variety of approaches for managing traumatic symptoms. Even within these categories, there is no single standard of evaluation or treatment.

Psychiatrists, behavioral and developmental pediatricians, and pediatricians are the only practitioners qualified to prescribe medication for children. They are also qualified to evaluate children to determine whether symptoms like irritability, fatigue, change in eating habits, or bed-wetting are due to organic problems or whether they have emotional roots.

As a behavioral pediatrician, I begin my evaluations by meeting with parents alone to take a careful medical and developmental history. I listen to their concerns and ask what they would like to have go easier or better for their child and their family. We outline treatment goals. At the next visit, I meet with the parents and their child, and I observe the child's way of relating to his or her parents, to me, and to the toys in my room. I begin to develop a relationship with the child and help him or her feel safe, comfortable, and appreciated in my office.

During the next visit, I meet the child with one parent or alone. I continue to assess the child's behavior and pay close attention to the child's themes of play, and I work with the parent and child to identify a goal—such as being able to play at other children's houses or being able to have pleasant dreams—that the child may want.

I use a variety of modalities to address medical trauma. Depending on the situation, I may use eye movement desensitization and reprocessing (EMDR) or incorporate EMDR into play, artwork, games, puppetry, narrative, role playing, as well as therapy involving parents.

Eye movement desensitization and reprocessing is a method for treating trauma, stress, and anxiety. *Desensitization* refers to the process of taking the emotional charge off of a memory. *Reprocessing* refers to the process of changing a distorted, negative belief to a belief that is true and useful. For example, a child who has been hospitalized may feel very upset remembering being held down for a medical procedure. EMDR can help to turn the upsetting memory into a neutral one. The child may have come away from the medical experience believing that he or she is powerless, helpless, unable to tolerate not being the one in charge, and unable to trust doctors and nurses. EMDR can be helpful in restoring the child's sense of confidence and trust in professional help.

Only clinicians who have received specialty training in EMDR can use it safely. There is additional information about EMDR in the appendix of this book.

Case of Daniel, Age 9

Children's understanding of a medical situation changes with age and their level of maturity. The following case underscores the value of identifying the developmental concerns of the child at the time of a medically traumatic event. Seven-year-old Daniel was born with a congenital eye condition that required several eye examinations under general anesthesia. Daniel was four-years-old when he had his last hospitalization, and he was very fearful of going to the hospital again. This case is presented here with the parents' written permission.

In this case, EMDR offered the unique opportunity to address the physical sensations associated with the uncomfortable and traumatic medical experience, as well as reducing or eliminating the distress triggered by reminders of the medical events. Play therapy allowed the possibility of working metaphorically with particularly sensitive and complex issues. EMDR, integrated into play and storytelling, facilitated the progression from negative, distorted self-assessments to positive, dynamic beliefs that are essential for a child's growth and development. Artwork and imaginative interweaves facilitated trauma resolution. EMDR, along with a reframing of the trauma by adults important to the child, contributed to a coherent, cohesive story that helped the child integrate his experience into his life story.

Therapeutic decisions

I viewed the memory of Daniel's hospitalization at age 4 as a "critical incident trauma." It was complicated by the fact that both Daniel and his parents were apprehensive about what the ophthalmologist might find when he examined Daniel's eye.

Initially, it was not clear exactly what was most upsetting to Daniel about the event—the separation from his parents when he was wheeled into the operating room, the smell of the anesthesia, nausea from anesthesia, or something else. In working with Daniel, I wanted to be sure to empower him

(continued)

with information and choices. Traumatic memories feel as though they are current and present. One goal of our work was to help Daniel regard the past experience as over.

I involved Daniel's parents in helping him regain his sense of confidence. Parents who are present during therapy with their child usually feel that they, too, have benefited. I asked one of Daniel's parents to sit beside him and the other to read Daniel's story of what happened when he went to the hospital. I began EMDR to take the upsetting charge off of the memory and to provide the information Daniel needed to develop a positive view of himself and his hospital experience.

While Daniel was recalling the memory of seeing the operating room, I asked him about that experience, "Now you know it was just an eye appointment, but what did you think when you were four-years-old?" Daniel responded, "I thought I was going somewhere. Like to a haunted house or something." Now I knew one source of confusion and anxiety for Daniel. It makes sense that a four-year-old would think that a hospital is a haunted house. The hospital is a strange place with lots of lights, where the people are "covered in white and wear masks" and where medicine tastes bad and makes you feel "sad and confused."

Next, I asked Daniel to remember how the medicine tasted. He agreed to draw a picture of the medicine. Daniel's picture was a glass with green scribbling in it. "Yuck," Daniel exclaimed as he remembered the taste. I asked, "If you could use your imagination to make it taste really yummy, what kind of taste would cover up the yucky taste?" Daniel replied, "Candy canes." I asked, "Okay—can you imagine taking that medicine and turning it into candy canes? You have such a good imagination. Is it peppermint flavor? Would you draw a picture to show me?"

Daniel smiled as he drew a picture of a candy cane.

Follow-up

Daniel came back with his parents for a final visit after having the eye exam under general anesthesia. He had handled the hospital visit and medical procedure well. His father asked him, "How did the medicine taste this time?" Daniel calmly replied, "Bitter." After EMDR, Daniel was able to be matter-of-fact about his experience.

Comments

Daniel was seven-years-old when he came for treatment of anxiety stemming from a medical experience and four-years-old when he had the traumatic experience at the hospital. The memory of his traumatic experience as a four-year-old was "stuck" in his body as confusion from the anesthesia and from lack of understanding. His four-year-old self thought that the hospital was a haunted house. By understanding the confusing aspects of his experience in a new way and reframing the meaning, and by processing the stuck physical sensations, he was able to resolve the trauma.

The therapy included storytelling, EMDR with cognitive interweaves or educational interweaves, imaginative interweaves, artwork, and parental involvement. All therapy was focused on helping the child believe the positive cognitions, "I'm safe now." These changes from fear to calm and from passive voice to active indicate that Daniel overcame his trauma.

Summary

Children who have experienced medical trauma may present with fear of anticipated medical procedures, such as Daniel did. They may present with unusual symptoms following a hospitalization. They may have generalized anxiety. The reason for a child's posttraumatic symptoms may be obscure, but a history of medical problems is notable.

Medical trauma is complex and always consists of a series of events. Medical interventions usually involve physical pain or discomfort (from the illness, injury, and/or intervention), as well as feelings of helplessness, fear, uncertainty, confusion, shame, and guilt. Medical trauma affects parents and other family members. It is important for the therapist to recognize and consider the needs of the whole family system.

Treatment of medical trauma may include the standard EMDR protocol for an older child or teen, but young children do not form a single consolidated memory of medical trauma. Children who experience preverbal trauma usually do not have conscious memory of the traumatic events. The clinician can work by installing positive cognitions and desensitizing layers of trauma as they emerge. The clinician who works with children must be versatile! A hallmark symptom of posttraumatic stress disorder is avoidance of traumatic reminders, and children may be unable or unwilling to focus on memories of their traumatic experiences. In order to meet the special needs of children who suffer from medical trauma, the clinician must be familiar with the details of the child's illness or injury, the sequence of events, the medical procedures the child has experienced and anticipates, the prognosis, and the effects and side effects of medications. The therapist must be able to integrate EMDR with play, sand trays, and/or storytelling to highlight strengths, to offer educational interweaves, and to desensitize and reprocess distressing memories.

Narrative (i.e., storytelling) is a useful way to help children understand the series of events that happened to them. A story can be constructed following the principles of EMDR: Begin with a safe place, detail the upsetting targets to desensitize and reprocess, provide trauma reframing and resolution, and end the story with positive cognitions. I find that engaging a parent in the child's treatment, calling on the parent to assist the therapist in writing a healing narrative for their child, and teaching the parents skills for helping their child cope and be comforted in times of distress may all obviate the need for parental psychotherapy.

Resolution of trauma will help a child be more flexible in a variety of situations, more able to comfort himself or herself and be more emotionally stable even in stressful situations. The child will become more compassionate toward himself and others. He will become appropriately trusting. He will be free to develop and explore and learn and play and love.

References

American Academy of Pediatrics. (November 2006). Policy Statement, 118: 5, 2006–2277.

American Thoracic Society. Haunted by hallucinations: Children in the pediatric ICU traumatized by delusions. *Science Daily*, 2008, May 1, May 25, from http://www.sciencedaily.com/releases/2008/05/080501062745.htm.

Gardener, S. L., Barland, K. R., Meremstein, S. L., & Lubchenco, L. O. (1993). The neonate and the environment: Impact on development. In G. B. Meremstein

& S. L. Gardener (Eds.), *Handbook of neonatal intensive care* (3rd ed., pp. 564–608). St. Louis, MO: Mosby Year Book.

Greenwald, R. (1999). *Eye movement desensitization reprocessing in child and adolescent psychotherapy*. Northvale, NJ: Jason Aronson Inc.

Lovett, J. (1999) *Small wonders: Healing childhood trauma with EMDR*. New York: Free Press.

McClain, B. C., & Kain, Z. N.(April 2005). Procedural pain in neonates: New millennium. *Pediatrics, 115*(4), 1073–1075.

McClain, B. C., & Kain, Z. N.(April 2005). Prevention and management of pain in the neonate: An update. *Pediatrics, 115*(4), 1073–1075.

Morris-Smith, J.(Ed.). (2002). EMDR: Clinical application with children: Association of child psychology and psychiatry, Occasional Paper No. 19.

Shapiro, Francine. *Eye movement desensitization and reprocessing: Basic principles, protocols, and procedures*. New York: Guilford Press, 2001.

Terr, L. C. (1983). Play therapy and psychic trauma: A preliminary report. In C. E. Schaefer & K. J. O'Connor (Eds.), *Handbook of play therapy* (pp. 308–319). New York: Guilford Press.

Tinker, Robert, and Wilson, Sandra. *Through the eyes of a child*. New York: Norton Press, 1999.

Webb, N. B. (Ed.). (2007). *Play therapy with children in crisis* (3rd ed.). New York: Guilford Press.

Child Life Practice in Hospitals

Deborah Vilas

Introduction: What Is Child Life?

"A child life specialist is a professional who is [specifically] trained to help children and their families understand and manage challenging life events and stressful healthcare experiences. Child life specialists are skilled in providing developmental, educational, and therapeutic interventions for children and their families under stress. Child life specialists support growth and development while recognizing family strengths and individuality, and respecting different methods of coping" (Child Life Council, 2007). Child life is relatively new on the radar of mental health services for children. Emma Plank created the earliest child life program in 1955 at Cleveland City Hospital. The profession grew with the initial guidance of the Association for Children in Hospitals (ACCH), and it continues to grow with the support and standards set by the Child Life Council (CLC). The CLC consists of over 500 programs in hospitals throughout the United States, Canada, and other countries around the world, such as England, Romania, Israel, and Japan (Vilas, 2006).

Specialists come from a variety of fields, such as art therapy, social work, and education. They can enter the field after either undergraduate or graduate training. Certified Child Life Specialists (CCLS) hold either a bachelor's or master's degree, with an academic background that includes courses in human growth and development, education, psychology, and counseling. There are 37 colleges and universities that offer graduate or undergraduate degrees in child life. Specialists are required to complete a 480-hour internship program and a rigorous application and examination process. The CLC oversees the administration of the certification process (Child Life Council, 2007).

Following is a list of the typical roles and functions of the child life specialist (referred to as "specialist" throughout this chapter). The chapter describes each of these roles and functions, giving practical examples of many. We take a closer look at procedural prep and support, play and expressive therapies, interdisciplinary collaboration, management of pain and distress, end-of-life support, advocacy, special events, and school reentry.

Typical Roles and Functions of the Child Life Specialist

- Prepare children and caregivers for procedures using developmentally appropriate language, play, and medical instruments.
- Teach children and caregivers coping skills (e.g., therapeutic positioning for comfort, refocusing of attention, deep breathing, guided imagery) to help them cope with procedures, pain, and anxiety.
- Provide hands-on support to children and caregivers during procedures through modeling, empathic responses, and coaching.
- Provide developmentally appropriate activities and an environment to support ongoing development of children while hospitalized.
- Provide opportunities for mastery through child-centered play and medical play pre- and postprocedure.
- Provide support to siblings of ill children through preparation, therapeutic activities, support groups, and consulting with parents.
- Provide support to well children of ill parents through preparation, therapeutic activities, support groups, and consulting with parents.
- Collaborate with other disciplines (including medicine, social work, chaplaincy, art therapy, music therapy, pet therapy, etc.) to provide holistic, family-centered care to the patient and family.
- Provide in-service training to medical staff on child development and techniques for meeting the unique needs of children.
- Provide interventions that assist in the management of pain and distress.
- Provide end-of-life support to patients and families through therapeutic activities and bereavement services.
- Advocate for children and families within the medical system.
- Advocate for children and caregivers with special needs.
- Coordinate special events.
- Assist with the process of school reentry.

Preparing Children and Their Families for Procedures

In a medical environment, the child life specialist is often the only member of the interdisciplinary team who has the time and expertise to focus on the emotional and developmental needs of the child regarding preparation. The challenges of managed care have made the specialist's role an even more vital variable in preventing and mitigating trauma for children and families.

Studies have shown that children who are prepared for procedures such as surgery have lower anxiety, use less pain medication, void sooner after surgery, and have a shorter hospital stay. Families who partnered with a child life specialist "did significantly better than control children and parents on measures of emotional distress, coping during procedures, and adjustment during hospitalization, the post-hospital period, and recovery" (Committee on Hospital Care, 2003).

Specialists must often convince parents of the efficacy of preparation, as some caregivers' instincts are to protect their child from medical information that they fear will upset the child. It is sad but true that sometimes a child will arrive for day surgery having been told that he or she is actually going to attend a birthday party. When the child realizes the truth, there may be irrevocable damage done to the bond of trust between that child and the parent. Therefore, it is essential to prepare the parent to prepare the child.

Optimal preparation occurs in advance of a procedure, giving the patient ample time to play or talk through any questions or concerns, but not so far in advance that the child either forgets or has too much time to become overly anxious. In settings such as emergency rooms, the specialist may have mere moments to prepare a child for any number of procedures. Some child life programs have preadmission tours and surgical preparation available to children and families scheduled for elective surgery. These programs provide hands-on, experiential, developmentally appropriate information for children and their caregivers.

Children are prepared for procedures from the routine to the more complex and invasive. Specialists use directive medical play to alert children to what they will experience, focusing on the child's five senses and exactly what the child will encounter (see Figure 5.1 below). The child is introduced to medical equipment (e.g., stethoscopes, syringes, alcohol swabs, anesthesia masks, EEG leads, tourniquets), and procedures are demonstrated on plain cloth dolls or more intricate dolls designed for this purpose (http://www.legacyproductsinc.com/).

Figure 5.1

Educator using MediKin™ with implanted port adapter to explain medical treatment procedure.

Source: Photo provided by LegacyProductsInc. com ©2009 Legacy Products. Reprinted with permission.

The child is encouraged to be an active participant in this type of medical play. Photographs of what the child will see in an operating room and during diagnostic tests (e.g., MRIs, CT scans, X-rays) are shown to the child and caregiver, along with developmentally appropriate explanations for what the child will encounter. Specialists can use the Internet to download and demonstrate audio recordings of the sounds that an MRI machine makes. Miniature models of CT scanners and other diagnostic machines are available for a child to explore and use with a doll.

Child life specialists are flexible in their approach with each child. Although there are certain parameters and expectations regarding how a child at a given developmental level will respond to preparation, it is understood that each child is an individual and that responses to preparation and the hospital experience will vary tremendously. Specialists know that they must be tuned in to the child's most subtle reactions and be able to vary their approach accordingly. One preschool-age girl, "Gracie," interrupted a specialist's demonstration of a urinary catheterization on a doll, exclaiming, "I'm going to go roller skate now!" She returned on her own moments later and was able to tolerate the rest of the preparation. Gracie was also able to tolerate the actual procedure well, both at the radiology unit and six months later in an unfamiliar emergency room. When children are partners in their treatment, they can feel a sense of mastery and pride. This particular girl had suffered from a phobia of doctors and hospitals. Following her catheterization, she proudly told her dad that she'd gotten through it, "without even a whimper."

Some children are more comfortable with pretend medical equipment, while others gravitate toward exploring the actual instruments. Some want detailed information, while others are overwhelmed by it. Specialists understand that some children are verbal learners, and others are more visual or kinesthetic. If medical equipment can be left for the child to play with in a nonthreatening manner, the comfort level with the medical environment increases. Gracie was given the catheter to blow bubbles with in the bathtub.

Specialists prefer to engage the child with a nonmedical play activity first in order to build rapport and obtain some developmental and temperamental data prior to proceeding with the medically based instruction. The child can be given a cloth doll and markers with which to decorate it. During this activity, the specialist can determine simple developmental milestones and discover which words the child uses for certain body parts. This comes in handy when the preparation ensues, as the specialist can use the child's language when describing the medical procedure. Sometimes children will project their emotions freely onto the doll and inform the specialist that the doll is "afraid of getting a shot."

Another vital component of procedural preparation involves assessing the child's coping strategies (and the caregiver's!), supporting these strategies, and modeling and practicing new coping strategies with the family. These strategies incorporate appropriate choices, such as whose lap the child will sit on, whose hand the child will hold, whether he or she wishes to watch the procedure, which distraction toy or book the child might enjoy, as well as deep breathing and other self-calming techniques (e.g., guided imagery). Other supportive strategies include instructing the parent on therapeutic positioning for comfort. Studies have shown that children who are forced to lie down during procedures are more likely to experience distress and helplessness (Sparks, Setlik, & Luhman, 2007). Parents and children can be empowered when a specialist models more humane ways to help a child remain upright and still during procedures such as IV insertions, blood draws, injections, and ear checks.

Procedural Support

Preparing a child and family for a procedure is one step toward a family-centered, holistic approach to minimizing trauma. Another piece of the puzzle involves supporting a child and caregiver through the procedure itself. There are a wide range of procedures that a child may encounter in a hospital setting, including suturing, setting a broken bone, having a central line (catheter) placed in an artery, or undergoing surgery. Diagnostic procedures also may be required, including MRIs, CT scans, X-rays, biopsies, and spinal taps. While the medical team focuses on accomplishing the procedure in a timely and accurate manner, the child life specialist acts as an advocate for the child's emotional well-being. The specialist must assess the child and parents' coping styles and support that style, encouraging parent participation and acting as a bridge between the family and the medical staff. Specialists know the importance of parental presence and support when a child must face a painful or frightening procedure (Boie, Moore, Brummett, & Nelson, 1999; Bru, Carmody, Donahue-Sword, & Bookbinder, 1993).

However, a parent's presence may not be enough if the parent is at a loss for what to do to support the child in the face of pain and possible physical restraint.

Therefore, another task of the specialist is to act as a stage director or coach. To function optimally as a support for their child, parents need to know what to expect as much as the child does. Informing the parents, in lay terms, what is about to happen as the procedure unfolds gives them a sense of control and empowerment. It is helpful for parents to know what will be done to the child, and also to be able to anticipate certain behaviors from their child. Parents, often disempowered by the medical environment, may feel like strangers in a new and confusing culture. If they do not speak the primary language spoken in the hospital, they are at an even greater disadvantage. Through educating and encouraging parent participation, specialists are supporting the family system by recognizing that the parents are the child's most important support in this time of crisis (Committee on Hospital Care, 2003).

Parents may be encouraged to hold children on their lap, and they will be coached regarding how to position and hold their children in a safe and comforting manner (Sparks, Setlik, & Luhman, 2007). If the child must lie down, the parent can be at the head of the examining table, providing physical touch, eye contact, a soothing voice or singing. If the specialist has had time to prepare the family, the parent can take the role of narrator, informing the child of each step of the procedure. When children know what is coming next, without judgment from the adults present, they can often tolerate the proceedings in a calmer manner. When young children undergo an IV insertion, it is not uncommon for them to begin shrieking the minute they feel the tourniquet or alcohol swab touching their skin. Parents and medical staff often respond with disbelief, defensiveness, and irritation: "I haven't even done anything yet! There's nothing to be afraid of!" This will escalate the child's distress and distrust. Informed parents can act much like sports announcers, giving a blow-by-blow account of what their children will experience through their senses: "First, the nurse is going to roll up your sleeve and put the tourniquet around your arm. It's like a big rubber band that'll give your arm a squeeze to help the nurse see your veins better. Now the nurse is going to clean your skin with an alcohol swab, and that will feel cool and wet." Sometimes, small details and inside information can be very important variables in how well children tolerate a procedure. Finding out whether the child is right- or left-handed before inserting an IV can make a difference in the child's ability to play comfortably afterward. If the child is very sensitive to sensory input, asking the nurse to place gauze underneath the tourniquet can make it more bearable. Knowing that the needle does not stay in the child's vein once the IV catheter has been placed can be extremely comforting to children and adults. Specialists often know important details that need to be conveyed, and if they are able to share the information and turn this role over to the parents, it empowers the parents and supports the bonds between children and their caregivers.

Specialists can encourage parents to help children refocus their attention during a procedure by providing distraction through blowing bubbles, reading an *I Spy* book (Marzollo & Wick, 1996), or supporting deep breathing and guided imagery. At times, a parent is asked by the medical staff to take an active role in restraining the child. The specialist can coach the parent and provide empathic responses to both caregiver and child, as this can be very upsetting to the whole family. Parents, with the best of intentions, may try to control a child's reactions and behavior with admonitions, punishment, threats, or bribes. They may feel embarrassed that their child is struggling or crying out. The specialist can normalize the child's behavior by reassuring parents about what is common behavior in children of this age and developmental stage.

Play and Expressive Therapies

The previous section describes a clinical and medically based model for intervention. Child life specialists also play a role beyond the medical experience by providing a safe and developmentally appropriate balance to the hospitalization. They provide expressive arts modalities and opportunities for developmentally appropriate play, both in a playroom and at the bedside. Many programs also include a space set aside for adolescents, as the discipline recognizes their needs for privacy and socialization apart from younger children.

Playrooms provide space and materials for individual exploration as well as for group sessions that offer opportunities for socialization and normalization. The group activities can be medically focused or can be less structured and make use of art as a form of expression. Sometimes, the medical and artistic aspects are combined when medical implements are used to create art. For example, medical gauze, tape, gloves, masks, tongue depressors, and the like can be used to create collages or sculptures. Syringes can be used for painting or to frost cupcakes. Surgical face masks can be decorated with feathers and sequins. Casting material can be used to make finger puppets. Groups can also gather around projects that encourage the expression and discussion of emotions. Building three-dimensional volcanoes that actually explode, and talking about what makes kids feel like exploding, is one example of this (Cabe, 1999). One hospital that treated pediatric oncology patients had an "Explorers" group that met weekly to do hands-on science exploration. This group was for school-age children whose natural curiosity about their own environment and experiences in the hospital formed the basis for the group. As all play is therapeutic, group activities don't always have to have a specific goal that is medically driven in order to be successful. Sometimes, just an old-fashioned game of bingo, or an interactive party game like Pictionary or Guesstures, can be exactly what a child needs to just be a kid.

For young children, dramatic play and fantasy play are a crucial medium to work through their feelings about the hospital. Having a medical play corner in the playroom, or in the midst of a clinic setting, is beneficial in many ways. (Table 5.1 lists many props that can be used in medical role-playing.) While medical play may be directive to *prepare* a child for a procedure, the opportunity to approach and explore the medical equipment on their own *following* a procedure also gives children invaluable opportunities for mastery. An example of this occurred when a four-year-old boy approached a specialist during daily visits to the pediatric oncology clinic for chemotherapy. He would eagerly request the "baby stuff," indicating a baby doll and medical kit. The boy would stake out a corner in the clinic, don a surgical mask and gloves, and enact upon the doll his own daily ritual of having the dressing changed on his "tubie." One day, he looked solemnly at the specialist as he put on his mask and gloves, and declared, "Doctors are never scared." This was his time each day to be in charge and feel brave in order to counterbalance the fears he faced on a continual basis.

We all know that play is the primary language of all children. For children who are young, language-delayed, disabled, or just learning the English language, play becomes even more vital as a form of communication. Hospitals can be overwhelming to children, and the children may

Table 5.1 **Typical Medical Supplies Used in Medical Play**

Reusable Medical Equipment	Disposable Medical Equipment	Toys and Props
Syringes (without needles)	Disposable surgical gloves (nonlatex, as many kids have latex allergies)	Play medical kit with pretend stethoscope, otoscope, thermometer, reflex hammer, etc.
Angiocath IV starters (syringe with needle that inserts IV catheter and then pops back into syringe casing)	Surgical mask	Toy microscope and slides
IV tubing	Alcohol pads	Blank cloth dolls in ethnically appropriate skin tones or Medkin teaching mannequins (by Legacy Products http://www.legacyproductsinc.com/)
Empty saline bags that attach to tubing and IV	Medical tape	A play telephone (for paging doctors and contacting the labs for results)
Tourniquet	Band-Aids (lots of these!)	Playmobile ambulance and hospital sets
Professional stethoscope	Tegaderm (transparent plastic bandages that cover IVs)	Miniature wooden MRI, CT scan, and X-ray machines on which child can manipulate dolls or stuffed animals to prepare for procedures (http://www.colestoyblog.com/2008/02/scan-it-operation-checkpoint-toy-x-ray.html)
Pill cups	Gauze pads	Puppets or dolls representing doctors and nurses (http://www.letusteachkids.com/puppets/people.htm; http://www.thepuppetstore.com/Doctor_Black_Puppet_p/gl1105b.htm)
Bedpans (for art projects and expressive techniques)	EEG leads and stickers	MRI scanner sounds (http://www.lodestone.co.uk/faqscansounds.htm)
Finger-stick lancets (very sharp, so supervise carefully)	Casting plaster gauze (comes in rolls) for making plaster casts on dolls or finger puppets)	
Catheter tubing and lubricant	Tongue depressors	
Tubes used for blood collection		
Surgical scissors, clamp, needle, and thread (for amputation simulations)		

*Medical supplies can be purchased over the Internet or in surgical supply stores and some pharmacies.

respond by withdrawing from hospital personnel. Child-centered play, which asks nothing of the child, can be an invaluable bridge for the specialist, building rapport and trust so that more directive interventions can take place when needed. Play therapists such as Virginia Axline (Axline, 1993) and Garry Landreth (Landreth, 2002) have led the way for the child-centered approach, which is highly applicable and adaptable to a child life specialist's needs and goals. Verbally tracking a child's play behavior, narrating the medical procedures as they occur, providing empathic responses to a child's expressions of emotions, and refraining from asking the child questions are all aspects of a child-centered approach that are directly applicable to the hospital environment. In the spirit of meeting children where they are, approaching young children through the use of parallel play builds rapport and trust in an environment that may feel hostile or overwhelming to children. One specialist recalls a real "aha" moment when she was asked to approach a young child who was in an intensive care unit. He was not eating or talking, and the medical staff was very focused on pressuring the child to cooperate. The specialist did not necessarily share the goals of the medical staff, but knew that her own goals of providing emotional outlets through play would complement the medical goals and support the child where he was in the process. The specialist entered the room, did not make eye contact with the child, set up a toy garage and miniature cars close to the bed, and began to play quietly, making car noises and moving the cars about. Within moments, the child was sitting up in bed watching the specialist intently. He then reached for the toy cars, stating emphatically, "No, not that one, the red one!" It was a normative moment in an alien and pressured situation, giving the child an alternative way to control his environment other than by refusing to eat.

Play can be a family affair as well, supporting siblings and parents through unthinkable traumas. One such family had arrived in the United States after fleeing the Serbo-Croatian war in the early 1990s. They had lost their home and their jobs, along with many relatives and friends who had died in the war. As if that weren't enough, their five-year-old son, "Serge" (a pseudonym), had been diagnosed with a malignant tumor on his foot and was about to undergo an amputation. The specialist involved with the family used dramatic medical play to prepare the whole family for the amputation. She arrived in the patient's room with two sets of surgical garb (gowns, booties, hats, masks, and gloves), surgical tools, and a cloth doll.

She invited Serge and his 10-year-old brother, "Dejan" (a pseudonym) to join her in performing surgery on the doll. Dejan was eager to participate, but Serge wasn't so sure, so it was agreed that Dejan would be the surgeon in charge and that Serge would watch and assist should he feel comfortable. With costumes and props, and with Dejan and his parents acting as English translators, the surgery proceeded. The IV was placed, the anesthesia administered to the doll, and the foot was removed from the doll using surgical scissors, followed by suturing with needle and thread, as well as bandaging. Serge joined in when he was ready, and worked with his brother to enact this difficult scenario. Many questions came up during the procedure, and the specialist was able to answer them, offering information about what the surgery and recovery would entail while at the same time exploring the boys' concerns and fantasies about what would occur.

It is difficult and painful for adults to imagine this sort of play. The alternative, however, is to avoid telling children the truth, which results in them waking up after surgery with a part of themselves missing and no way to talk about it or understand what has happened. Siblings, too, are often unintentionally shunted aside as parents struggle with their own feelings of fear and despair. These opportunities for family play give the siblings important information, offer an outlet for the expression of feelings and concerns, and, as in this case, empower them to feel a vital part of the family's experience.

In addition to the play and expressive therapies described here, well-funded child life programs often hire art therapists, music therapists, dance, yoga, or movement therapists, and massage therapists to work alongside the child life specialists to add their own expertise. Some departments also have pet therapy programs available to children, the benefits of which are enormous.

Collaboration with Other Disciplines: Nurses, Medical Doctors, Social Workers, Chaplains, and Psychiatrists

Child life specialists interact daily with the other disciplines within the hospital. They attend medical rounds with doctors and nurses, where patients are discussed and treatment plans forged. They attend psychosocial rounds with social workers, psychiatrists, and chaplains, where the needs of families and children are addressed. Specialists meet with nurses individually to gather information about the children in their care, so that they can be alerted to scheduled procedures and specific needs of patients. Specialists work side by side with the medical teams in clinics, emergency rooms, treatment rooms, and operating rooms.

Beyond daily interactions, child life specialists also collaborate with other disciplines to work on certain programs, projects, and groups. Specialists often team up with social workers to run support groups of many different kinds. Parent groups, sibling groups, medical play groups, and teen groups are all examples of either short-term or ongoing groups that child life specialists may help to run. The groups may be created to address recreational, respite, socialization, or psychoeducational needs of children and families.

Specialists often observe children at play and in interaction with their families and thus may witness behaviors and signs that indicate the need for interventions of a nonmedical nature. Child life personnel are in the perfect position to make referrals for mental health services, developmental support (occupational therapy, speech and language therapy), early intervention, special education, and social services.

Management of Pain and Distress

Child life specialists are a vital component in a child's ability to manage pain and distress while in the hospital. Some of the examples mentioned earlier, such as procedural preparation and support and post-procedural play, all help children manage their pain and their emotions. One method of assisting children with pain management is the use of progressive relaxation and guided imagery to help children learn to help themselves (Kuttner, 1998). Children as young as the age of five are able to learn and practice these techniques to help them cope with procedures, treatments, and post-operative pain. One such technique involves having children imagine a "switch" that is located in their brain and that can be used to "turn down" both pain and anxiety (Kuttner, 2006). The techniques can be learned through a guided imagery session in which children are asked to envision this switch and describe its size, its shape, its color, and so on. They can even draw it or make it out of clay to make the image more concrete. Then, when the time comes, they can take a few deep, relaxing breaths, locate the switch in their mind, and turn it down to decrease their pain and anxiety.

Another way to manage distress is the adaptation of Neil Cabe's use of balloons to express and process feelings of anger (Cabe, 1999). "Jonah" had been waiting in the clinic for a CT scan. He hadn't eaten that day due to the pending procedure, and after he had been waiting several hours he got news that the test would be delayed by at least another hour. He was very frustrated, and his anxiety level was increasing as well. The specialist used balloons to help him "blow away his worries" by inflating the balloons. They then played catch, keep-away, and keep-the-balloons-in-the-air, all of which brought down Jonah's anxiety and helped him fill the waiting time as well. When latex is an issue, nonlatex rubber gloves can be used instead of balloons for this activity.

Specialists may sometimes have to advocate for a patient experiencing chronic pain, as well as to sensitize medical staff to the challenges children in pain face. For children with sickle cell disease, who have repeated hospitalizations when they are in crisis, medical staff may sometimes begin to question whether a child is actually in pain. This can be invalidating and shaming to the child, and the specialist may need to work with the child and staff to establish trust and communication so that the pain is adequately addressed and managed.

Death and Dying

Child life specialists are an active part of all aspects of a child's treatment and hospitalization, and therefore they will be part of helping families cope with loss and death as well. Most hospitals have protocols for what ensues following a child's death, and some of these practices are set in place and begin prior to the actual death. Specialists play an important role in preparing siblings to visit their dying brother or sister in the intensive care unit, preparing them for what they will see and hear while they are there and letting them know that even if their sibling can't speak to them, he or she can hear whatever they have to say. Specialists also work with children of parents who are dying, providing them with the same preparation and support. They act as consultants to parents as well, letting them know about how children of various developmental stages might react to the dying process and the death of a loved one. This information is a crucial step in parents being able to provide the optimal support for surviving children. Specialists can also provide suggested reading and make referrals to mental health providers.

Specialists work with children and families to honor and memorialize the deceased loved one by making memory boxes, plaster handprints, and videos. Because of the unique bond that specialists often form with parents, they are often present when a child is removed from artificial life support. One child life intern accompanied a family to the hospital's morgue to view their six-month-old infant. Specialists organize and carry out memorial services within the hospital in collaboration with other disciplines. These services may be specifically for staff members who cope with numerous deaths throughout the year, or they may be carried out with the needs of families of the diseased in mind.

Advocacy

Advocacy is a three-pronged concept for child life specialists, and it can feel like a full-time job in and of itself. Specialists have to advocate on several levels on a daily basis. The first level involves advocating for the family within the medical culture of the hospital. This was described briefly earlier in this chapter. It can also involve the specialist's need to request an interpreter when families do not speak English or to inform families of their rights as parents and of the child's patient rights. Many hospitals promote the concept of family-centered care, an approach that considers the family as important members of the decision-making team in caring for pediatric patients (Community Gateway, 2008; Academy of Pediatrics, 2003; PBS, 2006). Child life specialists are often staunch advocates for this approach, informing parents of their rights and reminding medical personnel of the importance of family input.

One way a specialist models family-centered care is to advocate for parental presence during procedures and the administration of anesthesia. The medical team's comfort level with parental presence during procedures varies widely. Some institutions have policies that encourage and scaffold a parent's presence. Others do not, and whether a caregiver is allowed to remain at a child's side is up to the individual doctor attending to the patient. The specialists' knowledge of child development makes them keenly aware of the vulnerability of certain developmental stages and temperament styles to separation anxiety and anxiety around strangers.

Specialists also often need to advocate for the use of pain medication in very young children and the use of numbing medicines during IV placements. In neonatal intensive care units, specialists advocate for skin-to-skin contact between parents and infants, as well as optimal environments regarding noise levels, positioning of infants, and accommodations so that parents can spend nights by their infant's side.

The second level of advocacy involves promoting the child's developmental and emotional needs within the family system, providing psychoeducational information to families and supporting them in their parenting skills and care of the child. This type of advocacy, however, must be tempered with the knowledge of and appreciation for the parent's role as expert in the care of the child. Specialists must approach families with a genuine and deep respect for their style of parenting and coping, augmenting that style with helpful information about child development and the particulars of how children react to the hospital experience. Specialists must maintain awareness that their training is culturally bound and that it may or may not fit with the culture of a particular family they are servicing. This is paramount to providing family-centered care.

The third level of advocacy is sometimes the most challenging for specialists, and it can often seem like an uphill battle. Child life is, like social work, a guest profession in a host environment, meaning that the medical environment is the majority culture, and psychosocial services play second fiddle to the medical services as a rule of thumb. But child life faces another challenge. Social work has been around for more than a hundred years, and everyone knows what it is and what the role of a social worker is in the hospital setting. In contrast, many people have never even heard of child life as a specialty, and medical personnel within the hospital setting are no exception. Some medical staff welcome the partnership with specialists, and others are not always informed or on board with the role of child life. The most advanced hospitals, and the ones that invest in family-centered care as part of their philosophy and mission statements, are more likely to take full advantage of child life expertise. One public hospital in a large city houses a child abuse detection, prevention, and treatment clinic. The doctors who run this program will not medically examine a child for sexual abuse without the presence and involvement of a child life specialist, both to prepare the child and to support the child through the exam. Other hospitals may not even have a child life program, or they may view their child life program as purely recreationally based. It is a challenge for specialists to advocate for children and families in the medical environment if they are seen as babysitters or as people who merely hand out crayons. Child life programs often designate "Child Life Month" as a time during the year when they offer programs and activities to promote hospital-wide awareness, but day-to-day visibility and integration into the medical team is a year-round goal.

Special Events

Child life departments host many special events on the pediatric wards of their hospitals. With a focus on family-centered care comes an understanding of the importance of holidays and milestones in the lives of children and families. Specialists are often in charge of scheduling, planning, coordinating, and executing special meals and parties on holidays, and they must take into consideration the many holidays celebrated by the various cultures that make up their patient census. They are called upon to manage the onslaught of donations, celebrity visitors, and eager volunteers who come out of the woodwork to bring holiday cheer to children. They are also responsible for giving tours to potential donors. These responsibilities can sometimes conflict with the specialists' priorities of patient care, but they are a vital part of any program.

Holidays aren't the only meaningful occasions that need to be marked in a child's life. When children live with chronic or life-threatening diseases such as cancer, some of their typical developmental milestones or rites of passage, such as a prom at school, may be missed due to hospitalization. One hospital that specializes in cancer treatment hosts an annual prom in its playroom, underwritten by donors. It is a special time for kids who would otherwise miss their own rite of passage or who may not feel comfortable attending a school prom or dance due to hair loss and other bodily changes brought on by their illness and treatment. One specialist recalls a particular prom where two teens on the unit were romantically involved. The specialist enlisted volunteers to decorate a bed on wheels to look like a limo and picked up both the boy and the girl and brought them in style to the prom, chauffeuring them down the halls to the celebration.

Child life departments also coordinate individual celebrations such as the recognition of birthdays or an "end of treatment" party for a patient who has undergone rigorous treatment.

School Reentry

Although the majority of child life interventions take place within the hospital walls, specialists are well aware that the children's lives continue long after they leave the hospital and that a return to school is one of the main environments that they will be encountering. School reentry can be a challenge for children who cope with chronic or serious illnesses that require them to miss a lot of school, for those who attend school when they've experienced visible bodily changes, and for those who must attend to the management of their illness while at school. Children with asthma, diabetes, sickle cell anemia, HIV/AIDS, and cancer, as well as many other illnesses and disabilities, are included in this category.

Specialists can be an instrumental force in helping a child reacclimate to school and cope with the many challenges of keeping up and fitting in. Specialists can alert the teacher and school staff to normal developmental behaviors that might occur in children who have been hospitalized, and they can give teachers valuable information about how to support the child and the whole class. Specialists encourage teachers to do the following, as befits the situation:

- Consult with a local child life specialist.
- Invite a child life specialist to visit your class.
- Invite a child life specialist to provide an in-service for your staff.
- Research the child's health issue on the Internet.
- Have a hospital corner in your early childhood classroom, and prepare a modified one for school-age children. Include play medical kits, dolls, and some real items (alcohol swabs, bandages, syringes without needles, etc.).
- Collaborate with the child and family to coordinate a class or school presentation.
- Maintain contact with the child when he or she is hospitalized. Work with hospital-based teachers to keep the child caught up.
- Involve peers in maintaining contact and in welcoming the child back.
- Ask the child how he or she would like to deal with questions peers may have.
- Deal with young children's questions honestly and simply.
- Don't correct or direct medical dramatic play. Instead, respond and reflect empathically.
- Brainstorm and role-play with peers prior to the child's return about how they might best support the child.

Summary

Children and families cope better with support from child life specialists. Their presence and interventions can make the difference between coping well and being traumatized by the hospital experience. The Child Life Council or the child life department at your local hospital can be wonderful partners in the holistic treatment of children.

References

American Academy of Pediatrics. (2003). Family-centered care and the pediatrician's role: Committee on hospital care. In *Pediatrics 112*(3) 691–696.

Axline, V.(1947, 1993). *Play therapy*. Canada: Ballantine Books.

Boie, E. T., Moore, G. P., Brummett, C., & Nelson, D. R. (1999). Do parents want to be present during invasive procedures performed on their children in the emergency department? A survey of 400 parents. *Annuals of Emergency Medicine, 34*, 70–74.

Bru, G., Carmody, S., Donahue-Sword, B., & Bookbinder, M. (1993). Parental visitation in the post-anesthesia unit: A means to lessen anxiety. *Children's Health Care, 22*, 217–226.

Cabe, N. (1999). *Taming dragons: Play therapy for anger management* [VHS/DVD recording]. Northfield, OH: Cabe, Inc.

Child Life Council. (2002). *Official documents of the Child Life Council*. Rockville, MD: Child Life Council, Inc.

Child Life Council, Inc. (2007). The child life profession. Retrieved May 20, 2008, from www.childlife.org.

Committee on Hospital Care. (2003). Institute for family centered care policy statement. *American Academy of Pediatrics*. *112*(3), 691–696.

Kuttner, L. (2006). *A child in pain: How to help, what to do*. Vancouver, BC, CANADA: Hartley & Marks Publishers.

Kuttner, L. (1998). *No fears, no tears—13 years later* [VHS/DVD recording]. Fanlight Productions.

Landreth, G. (2002). *Play therapy: The art of relationship*. New York: Brunner-Routledge.

Marzollo, J., & Wick, W. (1996). *I spy spooky night*. New York: Scholastic—Cartwheel Books.

Sparks, L., Setlik, J., & Luhman, J. (December 2007). Parental holding and positioning to decrease IV distress in young children: A randomized control trial. *Journal of Pediatric Nursing, 22*(6), 440–447.

Thompson, R. H., & Stanford, G. (1981). *Child life in hospitals: Theory and practice*. Springfield, IL: Charles C. Thomas.

Vilas, D.(June 2006). Learning how to play: The development of a course on play techniques for child life specialists. *Play Therapy, 1*(2), 32–35.

Working with Families of Medically Challenged Youth

Jennifer Baggerly

6
Chapter

The purpose of this chapter is to increase understanding of the following five factors: (1) the role of counselors and play therapists in working with families of youth with medical challenges, (2) family members' stress and coping strategies, (3) assessments for family members, (4) filial therapy for parents, and (5) support for siblings.

The Role of Counselors and Play Therapists

Team Approach

When multiple professionals collaborate in offering strengths-based comprehensive wraparound services to the families of youth with medical challenges (YMC), a synergy of hope and possibilities uplifts the family to optimal functioning (Anderson, Loughlin, Goldberg, & Laffel, 2001; Drotar, 2001). Divisiveness between professionals and families fades away. Each family member is valued; their unique role is respected; their strengths are recognized; and support is given. A multidisciplinary team approach helps the family effectively adapt to medical challenges; increases their ability to use community resources; increases YMC's medical treatment compliance, emotional well-being, and academic performance; and decreases hospitalizations (Sayger, Bowersox, & Steinberg, 1996). According to Bradley-Klug, Grier, and Ax (2006), "The key to preventing further difficulties for a child with chronic illness is education and collaboration for all who are involved" (p. 864).

Contribution of Counselors and Play Therapists

Counselors offer unique therapeutic skills of individual, group, family, and crisis counseling to families of YMC. Counselors have four specific tasks at initial diagnosis and three specific tasks after the initial diagnosis. First, when the diagnosis is presented to the family, counselors can provide crisis counseling skills to help family members manage their emotions, develop accurate cognition, and accept the medical treatment plan and prognosis (Sayger et al., 1996). Second, counselors can identify immediate needs such as information, medical resources, support groups, and financial assistance (Sayger et al., 1996). Then they can educate parents about community resources (e.g., American Cancer Society, Juvenile Diabetes Foundation, Pediatric AIDS Foundation) and their legal rights (e.g., Individuals with Disabilities Education Act and Rehabilitation Act of 1973). Third, counselors can help family members develop active coping strategies to manage stress. Fourth, counselors can implement assessment interviews and instruments to identify strengths, stress levels, and clinical symptoms.

After receiving the diagnosis, counselors can provide family counseling to decrease the occurrence of maladaptive family patterns such as enmeshment, triangulation, rigidity, and overprotectiveness (Sayger et al., 1996). Counselors can also provide solution-focused brief therapy, as described by Lloyd and Dallos (2006), as well as person-centered therapy and cognitive behavioral therapy at varying stages of the family's adjustment process (Livneh & Antonak, 2005). Finally, counselors can coordinate periodic team meetings to share information, clarify roles and expectations, agree upon interventions, and provide support (Sayger et al., 1996).

Play therapists can add their specialization by providing (1) filial therapy for parents to improve the parent-child bond, as described later in the chapter, and (2) play therapy for siblings to resolve emotional or behavioral problems and increase self-esteem and self-responsibility. For further discussion on contributions of play therapists, see Chapter 10. In order for counselors and play therapists to be effective, it is important to begin with an understanding of the unique stress experienced by families of YMC as well as coping strategies.

Stress and Coping

Stress

When a youth has a medical challenge, each family member and the entire family system is impacted (Sayger et al., 1996). Parents of YMC experience extraordinary stress due to many unique demands on several levels. First, their daily routine may be significantly altered by frequent doctors' appointments, medication needs, special diets, disrupted sleep patterns, and the uncertainty and unpredictability of the medical condition (Livneh & Antonak, 2005; Sayger et al., 1996). Second, emotional and psychological challenges occur due to grieving over lost dreams; chronic sorrow from the constant reminders of loss; stressed family relationships; altered family goals; emotional and behavioral problems of their children, such as mood swings and excessive lethargy from medications; and witnessing their children's pain from medical conditions and interventions (Bradley-Klug et al., 2006; Nabors & Lehmkuhl, 2004; Sayger et al., 1996). Third, community contact may be hindered due to prejudice and discrimination, limited numbers of child care providers trained in caring for YMC, and feelings of social isolation (Lynch & Morley, 1995). Finally, finances may be diminished because of extensive medical costs and lost wages or unemployment due to the need to manage numerous medical matters.

The stress from medical challenges can impact the family system by creating enmeshment between the primary caretaker and the YMC, alienation of other family members due to feelings of neglect, overprotectiveness of the child leading to separation anxiety, rigidity in routines, and unresolved conflict (Nabors & Lehmkuhl, 2004; Sayger et al., 1996). Dysfunctional family patterns may worsen the youth's medical condition. For example, a child may have more asthma attacks when parents are arguing. The child may realize that parents will stop arguing during the asthma attacks, so the child chooses not to comply with the medical regime in an attempt to control the parents' arguments (Sayger et al., 1996).

Siblings of YMC experience their own unique difficulties, including behavioral and emotional distress, hindered social acceptance, and adjustment problems (Labay & Walco, 2004). Specifically, siblings of YMC are likely to experience overidentification, embarrassment, guilt, isolation, loneliness, loss, resentment, increased responsibilities, and pressure to achieve (Meyer & Vadasy, 2008). Siblings' emotional needs are often overlooked by their parents and professionals, and their questions are often left unanswered (Kaffenberger, 2006).

Coping

Coping has been described as our efforts to manage excessive demands and the emotions they generate (Lazarus, Lazarus, & Campos, 2006). Coping effectiveness can range from intentional, active coping to reactive, passive coping. Coping effectiveness depends on how family members appraise both the situation and their ability to handle it (Gal, 2003; Lazarus et al., 2006). Family members' appraisal is determined by antecedents such as familiarity with the medical condition; support systems; age, health, and personalities of family members; and ideologies (e.g., religion and sense of meaning) (Lazarus et al., 2006).

Authority figures such as doctors, educators, and mental health professionals can positively or negatively influence family members' appraisal of the situation and their ability to cope effectively (Gal, 2003; Lazarus et al., 2006). Families will have a more favorable appraisal and thus more effective coping if authority figures present information in a calm, supportive, and empowering manner and make referrals to support groups that provide relational opportunities. In addition, authority figures can reassure parents that "children with chronic conditions and their families do not differ substantially from healthy children in terms of disease-specific personality patterns or prevalence of severe emotional disorders" (Shuman & La Greca, 1999, p. 289). This information may help family members contain their fears and provide hope for a positive future.

Counselors need to encourage parents and siblings to activate the typical strategies they use to cope with stress in their lives and then help them develop additional coping strategies. One model that can guide the facilitation of coping strategies is the BASIC Ph (i.e., beliefs, affect, social, imagination, cognition, and physical) (Lahad, 1997). *Beliefs* entail attitudes, values, and meaning. Coping strategies related to beliefs may include prayer or scripture readings, cultural rituals, and works of hope, such as planning a fund-raising event. *Affect*, or emotional expression coping strategies include the use of bibliotherapy, counseling, play therapy, art therapy, and metaphors. *Social* coping strategies include being involved in social support systems, classroom meetings, teams, family gatherings, and role-playing situations. *Imagination* encompasses creativity and symbols. Coping strategies related to imagination include the use of psychodrama, guided imagery, creative games, and as-if symbols. *Cognition* coping strategies include reading, reappraisal or reframing, problem solving, and stress inoculation. *Physical* coping strategies include aerobic exercise, movement activity, games, and relaxation techniques. Additional coping strategies specific to families of YMC are assertiveness, problem-solving methods, stigma management, and time management (Livneh & Antonak, 2005).

Research on coping has shown that the difference between people who cope effectively and those who do not is that the former use higher amounts of coping strategies and resources (Lynch & Morley, 1995). These researchers also found that mothers were able to buffer stress via nutrition, interpersonal support, and psychoeducational interventions that explained disabilities and taught behavior management techniques (Lynch & Morley, 1995). Hence, counselors should encourage family members to seek support groups and use coping strategies frequently.

Assessments

Family Assessment Interview

Since each family is unique, counselors should conduct a family assessment interview to ascertain family strengths, natural supports, and potential resources. In addition, it is helpful for the counselor to identify numerous aspects of family structure, such as (1) each family member's characteristics, functions, and roles; (2) its cultural and ethnic belief systems; (3) family interaction patterns on the enmeshment-to-disengagement and chaotic-to-rigid continuums; (4) use of open or closed communication patterns; (5) life-cycle stage; (6) social-environmental context, such as status of federal budgets and school policies; and (7) each member's grieving style (Becvar & Becvar, 1993; Lynch & Morley, 1995;

Olson, 1986). Identification of difficulties in these areas will guide the counselor in treatment planning.

Since some family members may feel self-conscious if negative family patterns are identified, counselors could inform parents that family difficulties are usually due to an overstressed system rather than faulty people (Lynch & Morley, 1995). Children's medical challenges often exacerbate negative family patterns that were manageable before the medical challenge occurred. Thus, a positive reframe may be that the family now has reason and opportunity to develop new positive family patterns. Another helpful reminder is that a *healthy functioning family* is not composed of perfect family members but rather consists of family members that are connected, flexible, committed, have positive communication patterns, enjoy activities together, and use positive coping skills to deal with crises (Maynard & Olson, 1987; Stinnett, 1998).

Assessment Instruments

In addition to the family assessment interview, counselors may use standardized assessments for parents and children. General assessments that could be used to measure stress and symptoms in parents include the *Parenting Stress Index*, third edition (Abidin, 1995); *Symptom Checklist-90*, revised (Derogatis, 1983); *Beck Depression Inventory-II* (Beck, Steer, & Brown, 1996); and the *Beck Anxiety Inventory* (Beck & Steer, 1993). For children, general assessment instruments that could be used to measure their symptoms are the *Child Behavior Checklist* (Achenbach, 1994), *Children's Depression Inventory* (Kovacs, 2003), and *Revised Children's Manifest Anxiety Scale* (Reynolds & Richmond, 1985).

There are a few assessment instruments specifically related to *families* of youth with medical challenges. The *Questionnaire on Resources and Stress* (Holroyd, 1987) consists of 285 self-administered true/false questions designed to identify the resources and stress in families with a member who is chronically ill or disabled. This assessment may help counselors prioritize families' needs (Holroyd, 1987). The *Psychosocial Adjustment to Illness Scale* (Derogatis & Lopez, 1983) is a 46-question semi-structured interview and a 46-question self-report form designed to determine a patient's or family member's overall adjustment, assets, and liabilities, in addition to the unique aspects of the individual's adjustment to illness. *The Reactions to Impairment and Disability Inventory* (Livneh & Antonak, 1990) is a 60-item self-report scale that measures eight psychosocial reactions: shock, anxiety, denial, depression, internalized anger, externalized hostility, acknowledgment, and adjustment. This assessment will help counselors identify the grieving cycle stage that a parent is experiencing due to their child's medical condition. Other assessments specific to particular medical conditions (cancer, diabetes, arthritis, etc.) are listed by Livneh and Antonak (2005).

Data from the family interview and assessment instruments will help counselors determine whether parents and/or children may benefit from counseling. Lynch and Morley (1995, p. 215) suggest that a risk-factor profile for families who might benefit from counseling could include the following:

- Low number of coping strategies
- Lack of movement in the grief and loss process
- Financial problems
- Marital dissatisfaction
- Lack of social networks
- Lack of extended family support
- Overinvolved family orientation style
- Paternal physical absence
- High levels of certain maternal perceptions (e.g., feeling burdened, embarrassed, old, fearful of the future, on guard, fearful of what others say, and resentful of people with nondisabled children)
- A family with a child under age 3 who has a disability and whose mother works fulltime

Cultural Considerations

Prior to providing interventions in a family's home or the community setting, counselors should become knowledgeable about the family's cultural and ethnic customs and beliefs (Webb, 2001). For example, it is the custom in some cultures (e.g., Puerto Rican and Mexican) to spend considerable time talking in the home while drinking coffee in order to make a personal connection before discussing family problems or private matters such as medical conditions (Zayas, Canino, & Suárez, 2001). In contrast, families who are refugees or immigrants may prefer to meet in an office building due to previous experiences of feeling persecuted by officials who came to their home. Counselors can consult literature (Webb, 2001) or cultural informants to learn about the culture's typical family structure (e.g., some cultures prefer that questions be directed to the father); perceptions of the medical condition (e.g., some may consider it a family shame); and child rearing values (e.g., whether permissive, democratic, or authoritarian).

Using Filial Therapy to Assist Parents

Filial Therapy Description

Filial therapy is "a unique approach used by professionals trained in play therapy to train parents to be therapeutic agents with their own children through a format of didactic instruction, demonstration play sessions, required at-home laboratory play sessions, and supervision in a supportive atmosphere" (Landreth & Bratton, 2006, p. 11). In 1964, Bernard and Louise Guerney developed this approach because they believed the parent-child relationship is usually the most important relationship in the child's life. "If a child were to experience the phenomena of expression, insight, and adult acceptance in the presence of this powerful person [the parent], it would result in a greater effect, leading to greater gains for the child than if experienced in the presence of a therapist" (Guerney, 2000, p. 3). In the 1980s, Garry Landreth reformatted filial therapy into a 10-session model, now termed Child Parent Relationship Therapy (CPRT; Landreth & Bratton, 2006). A detailed CPRT treatment manual complete with parent handouts on a CD-ROM has been developed (Bratton, Landreth, Kellam, & Blackard, 2006).

Over 33 studies with more than 800 subjects have been conducted on the effectiveness of filial therapy, and it is now considered to be an evidence-based approach (Baggerly, 2009; Landreth & Bratton, 2006). A meta-analysis of 93 individual play therapy and filial therapy studies conducted between 1953 and 2000 found that filial therapy by parents had a larger treatment effect ($d = 1.15$) than did play therapy by therapists ($d = .73$) (Bratton, Ray, Rhine, & Jones, 2005). This finding indicates the viability of filial therapy by parents is an effective treatment approach.

Furthermore, several research studies specific to parents of YMC have demonstrated that filial therapy helps parents and their children. Tew, Landreth, Joiner, and Solt (2002) found that parents of chronically ill children who participated in filial therapy significantly increased their acceptance toward their child; decreased parenting stress; and decreased children's behavior problems, anxiety, and depression when compared to a control group. Beckloff's (1998) study with parents of children with spectrum pervasive development disorders demonstrated that filial therapy significantly improved their acceptance of their children's need for autonomy compared to a control group. In a quantitative collective case study of filial therapy with seven parents who had a child with a life-threatening illness, Steen (2005) found that parents increased their confidence in parenting, increased their tolerance of their children's struggle with emotional and physical pain, and increased their ability to empower their children. The children in this study showed increased confidence, increased cooperation in the medical setting, and increased communication with medical staff and parents about emotions and personal concerns.

Rationale for Child Parent Relationship Therapy

There are numerous benefits for providing CPRT for parents of YMC. First, it strengthens an appropriate bond between parent and child by focusing on the relationship rather than on medical and behavioral problems. Second, CPRT helps parents focus on the uniqueness of their child. When parents receive the diagnosis of their child's medical challenges, either at birth or later in life, their mental images of a "perfect" child are often disrupted (Lynch & Morley, 1995). CPRT encourages parents to identify unique, delightful aspects of their children that they may have overlooked. Third, it addresses Rodin, Craven, and Littlefield's (1991) three-phase treatment approach for medically impaired individuals by (1) encouraging expression of feelings via the skill of reflecting feelings, (2) facilitating personal meaning via the process of play, and (3) promoting mastery of emotional experiences via encouragement and setting therapeutic limits. Fourth, CPRT provides a support group format, which is particularly helpful to parents in decreasing isolation and reducing stress (Lynch & Morley, 1995).

Examples of Child Parent Relationship Therapy

Filial therapy with parents of YMC is demonstrated through the following example of two parents who attended a community clinic for CPRT. The names and information are disguised to preserve confidentiality. "Ann" was a 45-year-old mother of a 10-year-old daughter, "Adrian," who has mild cerebral palsy and has exhibited aggression toward her mother. Ann reported Adrian frequently hit her when she did not get what she wanted, was too dependent on her parents, provoked others, and was frequently irritable. "Bob" was a 35-year-old father of a 6-year-old son, "Billy," who has asthma and attention-deficit/hyperactivity disorder. Bob reported that Billy gave him "attitude," annoyed him while he was working on the computer, threw objects if he did not receive help when requested, and was resistant to baths and bedtime. Both parents stated they wanted to decrease their children's behavior problems and improve their communication with their children.

During session 1, the play therapist followed the CPRT treatment manual by providing an overview of training objectives and essential concepts such as focusing on strengths and the relationship rather than on the problem, viewing play as the natural language of children, responding rather than reacting to children, and reflecting feelings (Bratton et al., 2006). During group introductions, both parents expressed frustration and dissatisfaction with their children. The play therapist reflected their feelings, facilitated connection between parents, and instilled hope through the process. Table 6.1 shows the results.

Table 6.1 CPRT Session One Transcript

Content/Transcript	Rationale/Analysis
Ann: "I am so tired of Adrian ordering me around. She can walk with crutches but screams if I don't get her a drink ASAP, so I have to do it to keep the peace."	Indication of possible enmeshment and role reversal in which the child is in control.
CR: "You are *really* frustrated and want to find ways to help her be more independent. Bob, do you also have moments of frustration?"	Reflection of feeling to role-model empathy. Solution-focused comment toward desired outcome. Linking with other parent to increase group cohesion.
Bob: "Yes, Billy drives me crazy while I'm on the computer. I finally lock him out of my room. He won't even go to bed until 10:30 p.m.!"	Indication of possible disengagement and chaotic environment.
CR: "You are not only frustrated but perhaps angry with him as well. You'd prefer to put him to bed earlier. One benefit of CPRT is that it will help return control to you as parent and help your child develop self-control."	Reflection of underlying feeling without judgment. Made statement in the positive while reinforcing the responsibility for bedtime belongs to the parent. Instilled hope and confidence that program will provide desired outcome.

Table 6.2 CPRT Session Two Transcript

Content/Transcript	Rationale/Analysis
Ann: "Adrian won't know how to use some of those toys. I'll probably have to show her how each toy works."	Further indication of enmeshment and lack of confidence in the child's ability.
CR: "You're worried that she'll become frustrated, but the play session is a time for her to discover for herself so she'll develop self-confidence. Your new role will be to make statements about what she is doing and reflect her feelings through the process, even when she struggles. We might be surprised at how the dynamics will change."	Reflection of feeling to role-model empathy. Confined the new skill to just the play session rather than all the time. Identified end goal of self-confidence for the child. Redirected mom to her new role and skills. Refocused her on looking for change.
Bob: "Well, I don't think Billy will play at all with the toys. He'll probably throw them at me or try to run away. It probably won't work."	Further indication of chaotic environment and disengagement between father and son.
CR: "You also have hesitation, which is quite understandable when we start something new. Throwing toys at you and running away are times we do set therapeutic limits by acknowledging the feeling [I know you are mad], communicating the limit [toys are not for throwing or our time is not over], and targeting an alternative [you can choose to play with the toys or throw the paper at the wall]. Try that and see what happens."	Normalized feeling. Provided needed skill of setting therapeutic limits. Focused on finding out what happens.

During session 2, the play therapist reviewed homework, in which parents were asked to notice a physical characteristic of their child; explained and demonstrated basic play session principles, such as allowing the child to lead the play and tracking play behavior; and discussed toys needed for at-home play sessions (Bratton et al., 2006). Both parents seemed hesitant to allow the child to lead their play for different reasons. Table 6.2 describes this session.

Table 6.3 CPRT Session Three Transcript

Content/Transcript	Rationale/Analysis
Ann: "I still don't see how just playing with Adrian will help her demanding behavior."	Parents often refocus on a child's behavior when they lack confidence in their ability to improve the relationship.
Bob: "With Billy, I think this playtime may just make him and me more frustrated."	
CR: "You both feel unsure. Remember our principle of focusing on the donut [strengths and relationship] and not on the hole [deficits]. The playtime will strengthen your relationship and understanding of your child. I have faith that you are both going to start seeing improvement soon. You can borrow my faith in the process until you see that it works!"	Refocused on guiding principle and purpose for the play process. Provided confidence in the process and encouragement.

(continued)

In session 3, the therapist reviewed play session do's (e.g., let the child lead; verbally track child's play; encourage child's effort) and don'ts (e.g., don't criticize any behavior; don't ask leading questions; don't be passive) (Bratton et al., 2006). Then the parents viewed a live demonstration and practiced their new skills with each other. Both parents were visibly nervous and lacked confidence in their skills and the process. Consequently, they expressed their anxiety through numerous questions, as shown in Table 6.3.

Table 6.4   CPRT Session Four Transcript

Content/Transcript	Rationale/Analysis
Ann: "Right off the bat, I asked Adrian if she needed help opening the doctor's kit, even though I knew I wasn't suppose to ask any questions."	Frustration with self but evidence that she was aware of the need to encourage rather than rescue her daughter.
CR: "Your awareness that she needed time to try and encouragement through the process shows that you are learning!"	Role-modeled encouragement.
Bob: "Oops! I also asked a question when I asked, 'How can you solve that problem?'"	Awareness of the need to allow the child to take the lead.
CR: "You also are aware and thus learning to let Billy take the lead. I'll rewind the tape and stop it right before you asked the question. Then you can make the statement that you would like to make next time."	Encouraged his learning process. Provided opportunity to practice new skill with focus on future improvement.

Table 6.5   CPRT Session Ten Transcript

Content/Transcript	Rationale/Analysis
Ann: "These play sessions have helped me realize that Adrian really can do things in her own time. Yesterday, she not only got her own drink, she even brought me one! Of course, some spilled on the floor, but I just said 'Sometimes accidents happen' and let her choose to clean it up before or after her TV show."	Indication that parent is less overprotective and more flexible. She appreciates her child's capability.
CR: "You are not only proud of her. You are proud of yourself. You look much happier and less stressed."	Reflected feelings. Provided encouragement for the change in her.
Bob: "I've even started to enjoy Billy more since the play sessions started. When I give him choices, he is much more cooperative with taking his medicine and going to bed. Last night, I said, 'Do you want to take your medicine before or after we play a computer game for 10 minutes?' He took it after, but I still put him to bed by 9:00 p.m."	Indication that he is more emotionally engaged with his son and has established a routine that will benefit his son's health.
CR: "You are also happier and less stressed. You mastered choice giving, and you feel closer to Billy! I bet Billy feels closer to you as well."	Reflected feelings. Provided encouragement. Emphasized the relationship.

In session 4, both parents described their surprise at how excited their children were about their home play sessions. For example, Bob said "I was freaked out that Billy was not going to want to play, but he actually enjoys it." As the group reviewed each of their videotaped play sessions, both parents recognized several mistakes, but the therapist encouraged their efforts and highlighted their strengths. Then the therapeutic limit setting was reviewed and practiced (Bratton et al., 2006), as shown in Table 6.4.

In sessions 5 through 9, the therapist used the first part of the sessions to provide feedback on the parents' videotapes of their weekly home play sessions. During the second part of the sessions, the group reviewed and practiced one skill, such as choice giving, self-esteem building, encouragement, and managing children outside the play session (Bratton et al., 2006). During session 10, the therapist encouraged parents to continue conducting play sessions after the formal group sessions ended, reviewed guiding principles, recommended parenting books, and discussed improvements seen in each parent and child. By this time, each parent expressed satisfaction with the play process, described how their relationship with their children had improved, appreciated their children's uniqueness and strengths, reported decreased behavior problems, and acknowledged that they had improved their own attitude and self-control, as reflected in Table 6.5.

As illustrated in the case study, CPRT can help parents make needed changes in their attitudes and behavior toward their children, which in turn helps their children make needed changes in their own attitudes and behavior. Overall, CPRT can promote the health of YMC by improving the parent-child relationship, decreasing parent and child stress, and improving children's behavior and medical compliance. When working with parents of YMC, it is recommended that therapists add time for parents to discuss management of medical symptoms, realistic expectations (given the medical conditions), environmental adjustments, and helpful resources (Sayger et al., 1996; VanFleet, 2000).

Helping Siblings Deal with a Disabled Brother or Sister: Support Groups and Play Therapy

Support Groups

Siblings of YMC benefit from a playful, supportive group atmosphere where they can share the wonderful and difficult aspects of having a sibling with medical challenges (Meyer & Vadasy, 2008). Johnson (1997) suggests the following goals for counseling siblings of children with medical conditions: "(1) Validate the healthy children's feelings about their sick brother or sister; (2) normalize the experience; (3) provide direct information about the illness and treatment; (4) facilitate open communication among family members; (5) encourage involvement with their brother or sister with the medical condition; (6) identify positive aspects of the experience; and (7) cultivate age-appropriate coping strategies" (p. 421). Meyer and Vadasy (2008) also encourage emphasizing positive opportunities of having a sibling with a disability,

Table 6.6　**Sibling Support Group Session 1 Transcript**

Content/Transcript	Rationale/Analysis
CR: "Some children who have a brother with Down Syndrome feel embarrassed or mad, and others feel okay or even proud. What feelings do both of you have about your brothers?"	Attempt to normalize negative feelings without implying they should have them. Providing opportunity to talk about feelings.
KT: "I feel okay most of the time. But sometimes my friends call him 'retard' and I get mad and embarrassed."	Siblings are often bullied by peers and internalize cognitive distortions and negative feelings.
ST: "Me too. I feel like punching those mean kids."	Siblings frequently lack skills in how to respond to bullies.
CR: "You both feel angry that they make fun of your brother. You also feel embarrassed, as if you or your brother did something wrong."	Reflection of feelings. Identifying cognitive distortion of "it is wrong to be different."
KT: "Yes, I hate it when they tease him. It's not my brother's fault he is that way."	Child begins to externalize negative feelings and beliefs.
CR: "Yes, you know it is wrong when kids are prejudiced and bully you and your brother. It's normal to feel angry about that. You also know you and your brother didn't do anything wrong. He's just different, and that's okay. Let's play a game of coming up with the 'Top Ten Best Responses' when people say mean things."	Clarify that prejudice and bullying are wrong. Normalize feelings. Correct cognitive distortion. Promote acceptance of disability. Use game to develop assertiveness skills.

which include developing maturity, social competence, insight, tolerance, pride, vocational opportunities, advocacy, and loyalty. A sibling group with these goals may help siblings resolve fears and concerns, develop greater insight, and gain social support (Livneh & Antonak, 2005). For example, consider the dialogue, as shown in Table 6.6, that occurred between a counselor (CR), 8-year-old Katelyn (KT), and 10-year-old Stephen (ST), who both have a brother with Down syndrome.

Play Therapy

For siblings who are experiencing behavioral, emotional, or psychological problems, play therapy may be needed in addition to sibling support groups. Research studies have found that play therapy significantly decreased classroom and social behavior problems of special education children (Fall, Navelski, & Welch, 2002); increased diabetes adaptation in children with diabetes (Jones & Landreth, 2002); and significantly improved ADHD symptoms, anxiety/withdrawal, and learning disabilities in children with ADHD (Ray, Schottelkorb, & Tsai, 2007). Research studies still need to be conducted on the effectiveness of play therapy with siblings of YMC.

According to Landreth (2002), *child-centered play therapy* (CCPT) is defined as "a dynamic interpersonal relationship between a child and a therapist trained in play therapy procedures who provides selected play materials and facilitates the development of a safe relationship for the child to fully express and explore self (feelings, thoughts, experiences, and behaviors) through play, the child's natural medium of communication, for optimal growth and development" (p.16). Standard CCPT procedures include allowing the child to lead the play, tracking the child's play behavior, reflecting feelings and content, returning responsibility, encouraging, building self-esteem, facilitating understanding, and therapeutic limit setting (Landreth, 2002). Group CCPT provides the additional benefit of a social process in which children help each other assume responsibility in interpersonal relationships (Landreth, 2002). For siblings of YMC, group CCPT may also be able to help correct distorted cognitions and decrease anxiety.

Consider the group play therapy case reenacted in Table 6.7. Two 7-year-old boys each had a sibling with asthma. Chris presented with

Table 6.7 Group CCPT Transcript

Content/Transcript	Rationale/Analysis
Chris: [Playing with dolls in dollhouse.] "Oh no, the little girl can't find her inhaler. She's going to die!"	A common fear of siblings of YMC is death of their sibling. Chris's anxiety hinders his problem-solving processes.
PT: "Chris, she's really scared. She doesn't know what to do and needs help from someone."	Reflection of feeling validates his experience. Identification of need facilitates problem-solving process.
Dan: [Playing with toy soldiers in a different section of the room.] "Emergency. Let me through!" [Knocks down other dolls.]	Group PT allows children to give and receive help. Dan's aggression may be related to his misconception that he must be overly tough to control potential threats.
PT. "Dan, you wanted to help in a hurry, even if it meant knocking down and maybe hurting others."	Acknowledging his motive of behavior as well as negative consequences promotes his insight and prompts alternative positive behavior.
Chris: "Stop hitting the people. You made it worse! Go call 911 now."	Peers are often effective in helping other children modify behaviors in exchange for social acceptance.
PT. "Chris, you're telling Dan you don't like that. You knew what to do in an emergency."	Reinforced Chris's assertiveness and modulated conflict. Built his self-esteem by recognizing the knowledge he did possess.
Dan: "Okay. Just sit down and breathe slowly while I call 911. Then I'll get the backup inhaler mom put in the bathroom."	Group play therapy allowed Dan to exercise self-control and immediately improve his behavior to be more helpful.
PT: "Dan, you also knew what to do to help the kid with asthma. You both worked together to solve the crisis! You should both feel proud and relieved.	Built Dan's self-esteem. Linked group members together to build group cohesion. Reinforced problem solving. Reflected feelings to increase awareness of decreased anxiety.

generalized anxiety and obsessions with death. Dan presented with behavior problems of hitting his sister and other children at school.

Summary

Counselors and play therapists are an important part of the treatment for YMC. They offer unique therapeutic processes and skills in helping parents and siblings decrease stress, increase coping skills, improve the family system, resolve emotional and psychological symptoms, and improve their relationships with the YMC and others. When parents, siblings, and the family system improve their functioning, the YMC will receive more support and may improve his or her attitudes and behaviors, which may lead to a more stable health condition.

References

Abidin, R. (1995). *Parenting Stress Index* (3rd ed.) Odessa, FL: Psychological Assessment Resources Inc.

Achenbach, T. M. (1994). *Child Behavior Checklist*. Burlington, VT: University of Vermont Department of Psychiatry.

Anderson, B., Loughlin, C., Goldberg, E., & Laffel, F. (2001). Comprehensive, family-focused outpatient care for very young children living with chronic disease: Lessons learned from a program in pediatric diabetes. *Child Serv. Soc. Policy, Res., Pract. 4*, 235–250.

Baggerly, J. (2009). Play therapy research: History and current empirical support. In A. Drewes, *Effectively blending play therapy and cognitive behavioral therapy: A convergent approach* (pp. 97–116). Hoboken, NJ: Wiley.

Beck, A. T., & Steer, R. A. (1993). *Beck Anxiety Inventory*. San Antonio, TX: The Psychological Corporation.

Beck, A. T., Steer, R. A., & Brown, G. K. (1996). *Beck Depression Inventory-II*. San Antonio, TX: The Psychological Corporation.

Beckloff, D. R. (1998). Filial therapy with parents of children with spectrum pervasive development disorders (Doctoral dissertation, University of North Texas, 1997). *Dissertation Abstracts International, B, 58*(11), 6224.

Becvar, D. S., & Becvar, R. J. (2006). *Family therapy: A systematic integration* (6th ed.). Boston: Allyn & Bacon.

Bradley-Klug, K., Grier, E. C., & Ax, E. E. (2006). Chronic illness. In G. G. Bear & K. M. Minke (Eds.), *Children's needs III: Development, prevention, and intervention* (pp. 857–869). Washington, DC: National Association of School Psychologists.

Bratton, S. C., Landreth, G., Kellam, T., & Blackard, S. (2006). *Child Parent Relationship Therapy (CPRT) Treatment Manual: A 10-Session Filial Therapy Model for Training Parents*. New York: Taylor & Francis.

Bratton, S. C., Ray, D., Rhine, T., & Jones, L. (2005). The efficacy of play therapy with children: A meta-analytic review of the outcome research. *Professional Psychology: Research and Practice, 36*(4), 376–390.

Derogatis, L. (1983). *Symptom Checklist-90* (Rev. ed.). Minnetonka, MN: NCS Assessments.

Derogatis, L. R., & Lopez, M. C. (1983). *Test manual for psychosocial adjustment to illness scale*. Towsen, MD: Clinical Psychometric Research.

Drotar, D. (2001). Promoting comprehensive care for children with chronic health conditions and their families: Introduction to the special issue. *Child Serv. Soc. Policy, Res., Pract. 4,* 157–163.

Fall, M., Navelski, L. F., & Welch, K. K. (2002). Outcomes of a play intervention for children identified for special education services. *International Journal of Play Therapy, 11*(2), pp. 91–106.

Gal, R. (2003). *Acute Stress Model.* Zikhron Ya'akov, Israel: Carmel Institute for Social Studies.

Guerney, L. (2000). Filial therapy into the 21st century. *International Journal of Play Therapy, 9*(2), 1–18.

Holroyd, J. (1987). *Test manual for the questionnaire on resources and stress for families with chronically ill or handicapped members.* Brandon, VT: Clinical Psychology.

Johnson, L. S. (1997). Developmental strategies for counseling the child who has a parent or sibling with cancer. *Journal of Counseling and Development, 75,* 417–427.

Jones, E., & Landreth, G. (2002). The efficacy of intensive individual play therapy for chronically ill children. *International Journal of Play Therapy, 11*(1), 117–140.

Kaffenberger, C. J. (2006). School reentry for students with a chronic illness: A role for professional school counselors. *Professional School Counseling, 9*(3), 223–230.

Kovacs, M. (2003). *Children's Depression Inventory.* North Tonawanda, New York: Multi-Health Systems, Inc.

Labay, L. E., & Walco, G. A. (2004). Brief report: Empathy and psychological adjustment in siblings of children with cancer. *Journal of Pediatric Psychology, 29,* 309–314.

Lahad, M. (1997). BASIC Ph: The story of coping resources. In M. Lahad & A. Cohen (Eds.), *Community Stress Prevention* (Vols. 1 & 2, pp. 117–145). Kiryat Shemona, Israel: Community Stress Prevention Center.

Landreth, G. L. (2002). *Play therapy: The art of the relationship* (2nd ed.). New York: Brunner-Routledge.

Landreth, G. L., & Bratton, S. C. (2006). *Child Parent Relationship Therapy (CPRT): A 10-Session Filial Therapy Model.* New York: Taylor & Francis Group.

Lazarus, R. S., Lazarus, B., & Campos, J. J. (2006). Emotions and interpersonal relationships: Toward a person-centered conceptualization of emotions and coping. *Journal of Personality, 74*(1), 9–46.

Livneh, H., & Antonak, R. F. (1990). Reactions to disability: An empirical investigation of their nature and structure. *Journal of Applied Rehabilitation Counseling, 21*(4), 13–21.

Livneh, H., & Antonak, R. (2005). Psychosocial adaptation to chronic illness and disability: A primer for counselors. *Journal of Counseling & Development, 83*(1), 12–20.

Lloyd, H., & Dallos, R. (2006). Solution-focused brief therapy with families who have a child with intellectual disabilities: A description of the content of initial sessions and the process. *Clinical Child Psychology and Psychiatry, 11*(3), 367–386.

Lynch, R. T., & Morley, K. L. (1995). Adaptation to pediatric physical disability within the family system: A conceptual model for counseling families. *The Family Journal: Counseling and Therapy for Couples and Families, 3,* 207–217.

Maynard, P. E., & Olson, D. H. (1987). Circumplex model of family systems: A treatment tool in family counseling. *Journal of Counseling & Development, 65,* 502–504.

Meyer, D., & Vadasy, P. (2008). *Sibshops: Workshops for siblings of children with special needs* (Rev. ed.). Baltimore, MD: Brookes Publishing.

Nabors, L. A., & Lehmkuhl, H. D. (2004). Children with chronic medical conditions: Recommendations for school mental health clinicians. *Journal of Developmental and Physical Disabilities, 16*(1), 1–15.

Olson, D. H. (1986). Circumplex model VII: Validation studies and FACES III. *Family Process, 25,* 337–351.

Ray, D., Schottelkorb, A., & Tsai, M. (2007). Play therapy with children exhibiting symptoms of Attention Deficit Hyperactivity Disorder. *International Journal of Play Therapy, 16*(2), 95–111.

Reynolds, C. R., & Richmond, B. O. (1985). *Revised Children's Manifest Anxiety Scale.* Los Angeles: Western Psychological Services.

Rodin, G., Craven, J., & Littlefield, C. (1991). *Depression in the medically ill: An integrated approach.* New York: Brunner/Mazel.

Sayger, T. V., Bowersox, M. P., & Steinberg, E. B. (1996). Family therapy and the treatment of chronic illness in a multidisciplinary world. *The Family Journal: Counseling and Therapy for Couples and Families, 4*(1), 12–21.

Shuman, W. B., & La Greca, A. M. (1999). Social correlates of chronic illness. In R. T. Brown (Ed.), *Cognitive aspects of chronic illness in children* (pp. 289–311), New York: Guilford Press.

Steen, R. L. (2005). Adapting filial therapy for families who have a child with a life-threatening illness (Doctoral dissertation, University of North Texas, 2004). *Dissertation Abstracts International, B, 65*(08), 4306.

Stinnett, N. (1998). *Good families.* New York: Doubleday.

Tew, K., Landreth, G., Joiner, K., & Solt, M. (2002). Filial therapy with parents of chronically ill children. *International Journal for Play Therapy, 11*(1) 79–100.

VanFleet, R. (2000). Short-term play therapy for families with chronic illness. In H. G. Kaduson & C. E. Schaeffer (Eds.), *Short-term play therapy for children* (pp. 175–193). New York: Guilford Press.

Webb, N. B. (2001). *Culturally diverse parent-child and family relationships: A guide for social workers and other practitioners.* New York: Columbia University Press.

Zayas, L. H., Canino, I., & Suárez, Z. (2001). Parenting in mainland Puerto Rican families. In N. B. Webb (Ed.) *Culturally diverse parent-child and family relationships: A guide for social workers and other practitioners* (pp. 133–156). New York: Columbia University Press.

School-Based Interventions for Children and Youth with Medical Conditions

Suzanne C. Griffith and
Rosemary Doyle

7
Chapter

Introduction

Schools play a central role in a young person's life. Being away from school due to an acute or chronic illness deprives children of peer socialization as well as the educational structure that is a part of their normal life (Kaffenberger, 2006). While almost all children like time away from the work and routine of school, a return to school is a sign that their life may return to some normalcy (Bessell, 2001).

Approximately 20 percent of children have chronic illness (ranges from 10 to 30 percent appear in the literature), and for at least one-third of these, the illness is severe enough to interfere with schooling (Clay, 2004). Some of these children would not have survived the disease or the treatment ordeal decades earlier, or they would have stayed in the hospital long term (Bessell, 2001). Now, they may be out of school for an initial period of hospitalization and then discharged to recuperate at home, but they may have to come and go repeatedly for doctor appointments, rehospitalizations, and treatments. Such irregularities in attendance require more flexibility from schools than established policies often allow (Kaffenberger, 2006). Yet the research is unequivocal that a successful transition back to the schools can have long-term benefits across all developmental areas for the child (e.g., Bessell, 2001; Kliebenstein & Broome, 2002; Prevatt, Heffer, & Lowe, 2000).

The literature on the need for quick and smooth reintegration of the child into the school highlights the crucial role and importance of having a central person, a liaison, who coordinates the school's response. Kaffenberger (2004, 2006) makes a strong case for the school counselor as having ideal preparation to assume that role. The purpose of this chapter is to focus on the school counselor's role, as part of a school response team, in providing interventions and support to the child with ongoing medical issues.

School reentry is a complex process (Shaw & McCabe, 2007) made more complex by the decentralization of health care and the uniqueness of each case and school. When absence from school for surgery and/or treatment are known ahead, then a coordinated response can be initiated and under way long before the child returns to school (Kaffen-berger, 2006). The school counselor, as the designated contact, can stay in touch with the family and the child and can work to keep communication open and the school as an active partner. Setting up or activating a school response (or school crisis) team is a first step in this process (Prevatt et al., 2000).

Legal and Ethical Considerations

Open communication is necessary for the child's safe and successful return (Mukherjee, Lightfoot, & Sloper, 2001). But one of the trickier responsi-bilities of the school counselor is working with confidentiality restraints versus the need-to-know issues (Stone, 2005). Parents, and to some extent the student who is ill, have a right to decide how much information to share with the school, according to the Family Educational Rights and Privacy Act (FERPA, 1974). For parents, especially during the initial stages of diagnosis and when coming to grips with the issues, talking to school staff means acknowledging not only to themselves but to the community that their son or daughter has an illness (Kliebenstein & Broome, 2002). Depending on the severity and prognosis, there may be other adjustments to make before the family can take this public step; so, initially, the parents may share minimally (Boekaert & Röder, 1999). It is important for the school counselor to understand what the family is going through and to reach out with support and patience in order to build the necessary communication lines instrumental to the child's successful return. By discussing with the family whom they would like to inform and how they would like to inform them, the counselor can help parents feel that they have control over the sharing of information (Cohen, 1999). This may reduce some stress and improve the family's response (Aldwin, 2007; Bessell, 2001).

On the other side is the school's need to know in order to prepare for the child's return (Clay, 2004). Information concerning the diagnosis and how it will or might affect the student allows the school team to plan possible educational adjustments (Prevatt et al., 2000). The school coun-selor must work with the family to obtain releases to talk with medical personnel so that accurate information is shared (Clay, 2004; HIPPA, 1996). When members of the medical team are made part of the specific school response team, this allows for clearer and ongoing communication and planning. Medical personnel and hospital staff do not need to be physically present, but can take part in discussions and planning by speakerphone and other technologies.

Families often assume that a school nurse will be the contact, as he or she would be the person most involved and most able to translate the medical information into educational needs (Kliebenstein & Broome, 2000). But school districts often require the nurse to move around among buildings, in more of a supervisory role, meaning the nurse is not readily available to assist with adjustment, even though he or she can still be part of the team. The family may question whether anyone at the school can understand their child's medical needs and how to respond in case of an emergency (Boekaert & Röder, 1999). Again, by discussing with the family the importance of open but judicious communications between the medical team, the family, and the school, the counselor may be able to assure the family that the school *is* a supportive partner. Additionally, the school counselor is often put in charge of an in-service training (and ongoing ones, as needed) for all staff and for arranging medical training for some staff when needed. This can be worked out with the help of the child's medical team (Kliebenstein & Broome, 2002).

Once the school counselor knows more about the condition and how long the child may be absent from school, he or she can initiate interventions (Kaffenberger, 2006). As more information is gained, the school counselor can become more knowledgeable about the illness, plan appropriate educational supports, and develop information for the rest of the school, per the family's wishes (Prevatt et al., 2000). If siblings are in the school, there is the additional need for discussing how the sibling(s) may want to handle the sharing of information (Johnson, 1997). Information shared at this stage may change as the family and student adjust and as treatment progresses. Remaining flexible is essential for a supportive environment (Shaw & McCabe, 2007). Undoubtedly, school personnel and students may be curious and ask questions. Working out with the family how to respond and using discretion over what others need to know (versus what they *want* to know) is an important way to ensure a trusting relationship (Cohen, 1999).

Children may decide for themselves how much to tell their friends (Sartain, Clarke, & Heyman, 2000), and, given the multiple social networks available, it is possible that the child with the illness will share information that is greater than or different from what the parents prefer to share or is contradictory to what they have shared (Shiu, 2001). Misinformation can be a problem, and sorting through and clarifying the mix of information becomes an ongoing task of the liaison or school counselor (Shaw & McCabe, 2007).

Years ago, children's hospital stays for recuperation were often lengthy. Nowadays, children are released earlier and expected to return as needed (Granville, 2008). Some school policies do not start homebound instruction until after a consecutive two-week absence or longer and do not allow for a varied attendance schedule (Kaffenberger, 2006). A quick response by the school can lead to an initial Section 504 Plan (Clay, 2004), which can maintain the student's accessibility to a free and appropriate education. Section 504 is much broader than the Individuals with Disabilities Education Act (IDEA, 1990) since it focuses more on *accessibility* to education rather than a diagnosed disability that interferes with learning. Clay also points out that sometimes IDEA (or the newer Individuals with Disabilities Improvement Act [IDEIA], 2004) is appropriate under Other Health Impaired (OHI) problems or actual learning and/or emotional problems that may develop and compromise the child's ability to learn (e.g., traumatic brain injury (TBI), spinal meningitis, radiation). In such cases, referral for at-risk or a multidisciplinary team evaluation may proceed. However, it takes time to move through the required steps, and initiating a 504 plan can start the school response process and does not infer major interference with the child's learning process, other than accommodations for equal access (Shaw & McCabe, 2007; Shiu, 2001).

Social and Emotional Adjustments

The diagnosis of an acute or chronic illness can be a life-changing experience for all involved; it literally shakes the ground under the youth and family (Boekaert & Röder, 1999; Huegel, 1998; Lightfoot, Wright, & Sloper, 1998). Children report feeling that they are not and never will be like any of the other kids (Johnson, 1997). The same applies to the family: they can feel besieged (Cohen, 1999; Kliebenstein & Broome, 2002) and allow the illness to become their central focus. According to Cohen, it is important to *put the illness in its place* and regain a balance that lets all members move forward. Research shows that the reaction to the illness can have a major impact on its progression (Aldwin, 2007; Boekaert & Röder, 1999) and that achieving a more balanced response can positively influence the progression. However, the research is equivocal on the development of socioemotional disturbance (Shiu, 2001). Some children with certain diseases or illnesses in some studies appear to develop psychological issues related to their condition and experiences, but the research also shows that there is room for positive interventions that allow for healthier adjustment (Hayman, Mahon, & Turner, 2002). Family and parental variables, the child's self-concept and intelligence, and life stress are better predictors of the child's adjustment than the severity of the illness (Shiu, 2001). Parental distress impacts not only the child's ability to cope but also the siblings' behavioral responses (Johnson, 1999).

Therefore it is in everyone's interest for the family to function and cope well with this new reality (Cohen, 1999). The school counselor plays a major role in making the reentry and ongoing integration into the school a positive experience (Kaffenberger, 2004). This requires coordinated and collaborative services and support among the three main groups: family, medical team, and school team. While each school district and even each school building can be different in its organization and personnel available, the school team might well include an administrator or principal, social worker, school psychologist, child's teacher(s), and school counselor (Kaffenberger, 2006).

Using best practices, the team members work out several important steps: First they designate a coordinator and then decide who will consult with the family; next they involve the medical team, coordinate direct services to the student, educate school personnel, and inform classmates (Prevatt et al., 2000; Shaw & McCabe, 2007). After consulting with the family and gaining appropriate releases, several of these actions unfold simultaneously. While these steps appear straightforward and informational, there is a need for sensitivity: Preparing staff and students for a student's reentry needs to be done without pity or exaggeration (Mukherjee et al., 2000). Not everyone will be comfortable due to misperceptions, previous experiences, or required adjustments on their part. The educational process of the school community can require group (large and small) and individual work with staff as well as with students (Kaffenberger, 2004).

The school counselor, along with the team, sets the tone, answers questions, and responds to concerns in a manner that models a positive, caring response to the family crisis. Three major issues impact a student's reintegration and adjustment: attitude of the family, attitude of the school personnel, and attitude of peers and other students (Shaw & McCabe, 2007). From an ecological perspective (Bronfenbrenner, 1979), one can image a series of nesting circles (see Figure 7.1), with the child as the focal point surrounded by parents and siblings and, a little farther out, school, peers, medical team, and community. The interaction of these players is dynamic: The illness changes the relationships, and reentry requires new and intense interactions among the players (Kliebenstein & Broome, 2002). The coordinator and school team need to consider how the illness might impact the various players. The more proactive the school team (as well as family and medical team), the better the chances for the child's resiliency to surface (Bessell, 2001; Cohen, 1999).

Acute or chronically ill young persons may be active participants in discussions, if they want this. They can often understand more than they can verbalize and have fears and concerns over the decisions being made (Lightfoot et al., 1998). Overprotecting (by parent or teacher) is not beneficial for the student's mental health and can send the wrong message to peers (Cohen, 1999). Yet teachers often voice concerns over

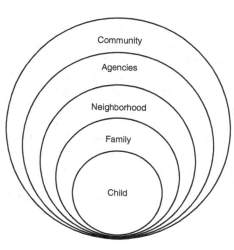

Community System includes:
• Community settings
• Community organizations
• Spiritual community
• School system
• Medical system
Agencies include:
• School contacts of the child/sibling/parents
• Doctors and nurses involved with the child/family
• Community contacts of the child/siblings/parents
• Faith-based contacts of the child/family
Neighborhood includes:
• Close family friends
• Extended family members
Family includes:
• Parents
• Siblings
• Others in the home
Child—with chronic/acute Illness

Concept adapted from Urie Bronfenbrenner's
Ecological Model of Child Development (1979).

Figure 7.1

Dynamic interaction and interrelationship.

how much to push or expect from the child. Research that specifically elicits children's views (e.g., Bessell, 2001; Sartain et al., 2000) indicates that students want to be active participants in their reentry and that they appreciate it when teachers take steps to include them in activities and when those teachers believe them when they talk of their ailments and the effects of drugs.

Teachers, peers, and siblings in school need to also be active participants (Mukherjee et al., 2000; Shaw & McCabe, 2007). The reentering child or adolescent is both eager and anxious about returning. Absences often take a major toll on academics, friendships, and social status. Treatments, time away, and medications can directly affect motivation, attention, energy levels, and physical activity. Even with ongoing or intermittent homebound instruction, it can be difficult for the student to stay current and comprehend the educational material. Returning to school can require more time out of class for tutoring, resting, medication, and/or therapy, which can add to feeling stigmatized and different (Shiu, 2001). If team members anticipate potential teasing and harassment, social isolation, misunderstanding of the medical condition, and the potential for academic delays, they can take steps to minimize the impact. It may be possible to utilize new technologies available in schools (e.g., school portals, ITV, online classes) for the student to take part in classes. Once the child returns, the teachers may need support to set up new routines, accommodations, and additional adjustments. Listening and responding to children's questions and concerns can help to build a positive attitude.

The counselor can also arrange for ongoing social contacts during absences: Having the young person's friends stay in touch can be a preventive step against a reaction toward isolation. Technology can also assist classmates by appropriate (and limited) use of social networking, IM, and cell phone; and when personal contact is not possible, the family or school can post updates on the Web to provide information about the student's progress and conditions (Drotar et al., 2006; Shaw & McCabe, 2008).

Upon the child's return to school, the counselor can arrange small-group support activities, peer tutoring and study groups, and classroom presentations by the student, parent, and/or medical team that tactfully present accurate information about the condition as well as an appreciation for the courage and stamina it takes for the student to get through treatment. While some academic problems can develop directly from the illness or treatment (Clay, 2004; Kaffenberger, 2006), many problems arise from secondary causes, such as the high number of absences. Students report that recommendations from the school that they be retained a grade or placed in special education were especially demoralizing and compounded their feelings of being different (Bessell, 2001; Lightfoot et al., 1998; Shiu, 2001). The following case study models many of these points.

The Case: Dani, age 13

In this case, a combination of play therapy and cognitive behavior therapy were used during the initial diagnosis, treatment, and remission of Dani's acute lymphoblastic leukemia (ALL), which she had developed as a five-year-old kindergarten student. The therapist, Mrs. Doyle, was a K–8 school counselor with training in both approaches and years of experience working with children and adolescents.

Background Information

This case took place in a rural community in an elementary and middle school, combined in one building, with 350 students. As a result, Dani's counselor was able to follow her progress through the seven years of this case. Dani's family consisted of an older sister, Katie, age 9; a younger brother, Kevin, age 4; her parents, Jim and Mary Therese Brown; and an extended family in the immediate area.

Dani was diagnosed in the fall of her kindergarten year. She had been enrolled in the 4K program for four days a week the previous school year and was a well-liked, friendly girl who had good relationships with the rest of her classmates. She had presented to her family physician with a resistant ear infection since the beginning of the summer, with enlarged lymph nodes. As her symptoms worsened and initial testing revealed problems with her white blood cell count, Dani's physician referred her to a pediatric oncologist in a larger community 50 miles away, who then referred her to a large pediatric cancer center four hours away. Dani's mother, Mary Therese, recounts the next few weeks as "the most terrifying, confusing, and horrible weeks of my life." Dani's siblings were well cared for by their paternal grandparents, but Mary Therese recalls wrenching guilt at being separated from them so often, especially when Dani's care and treatments were taking place so far from home. Dani's father worked in an industry that required his presence at work, with only minimal time off; therefore, during Dani's hospitalizations and long-distance travel, the care was left to Mary Therese, who took a long-term leave from her job.

Dani's treatments involved chemotherapy, surgeries to place intrathecal ports, and hospitalizations when she had fevers and possible infections. The treatments and diagnostic tests were at times painful, and Dani and her mother were often away from home for extended periods of time. The treatments were successful, with remission occurring in the first stages of treatment.

The school's response was an important part of the family's recovery plan. Because the community was small, rural, and had few resources to offer the family, the school became an important partner in the overall response, including fund-raisers that took place at the school (the largest building in the community). The family asked the counselor to serve as the liaison who would coordinate the school's response for all the children in the family. In turn, the counselor looked to a university counseling department and nearby hospital grief center to bolster her own resources.

The school also had a well-established crisis response plan and trained staff, but it had not been organized to address the needs of a chronically ill child who survived a life-threatening illness and needed a transition plan for school reentry. The school counselor reviewed the research and concluded that her role should be based on best practices, as identified by Prevatt et al. (2000) and later summarized by Kaffenberger, (2006), which consist of six features: (1) Identify a school-based or medical team coordinator of services; (2) provide direct services to the student; (3) consult with the family; (4) educate school personnel; (5) provide information to classmates; (6) involve the medical team.

The existing crisis plan at the school identified team members whose responsibility became to develop a team response to Dani's medical crisis. The team consisted of the school counselor, principal, all the teachers who had Dani and her siblings in class, the elementary special education teacher, school secretary, and the part-time school psychologist. The family also asked that their minister be included in the team. At times, one of Dani's parents or grandparents would attend team meetings. The school did not have a nurse on staff, but a county nurse provided services one-half day a week; although she was

(continued)

included as a team member, she was often only able to participate by phone. The medical team that provided Dani's care was also available only by phone, e-mail, or fax.

One helpful "partner" was a web site (CaringBridge) that friends and family could log on to for the most up-to-date information about Dani's care and progress. They could also use it to send her and her family messages of support and caring throughout the long recovery. The family could choose what information to post about Dani. Anything they posted was public information and not considered confidential. This site enabled the team to concentrate on their primary task of coordinating school-based educational services to the children.

Initial Team Response and Planning

The first news of Dani's illness was delivered by her mother to the school secretary, who took the calls for school absences. Dani had been out again for an ear infection, and this call was to inform the school that Dani would be seeing a specialist and might be out for an extended period. The school secretary was a member of the crisis team and recognized that this issue might require a response. She suggested talking to the counselor as soon as the mother knew more.

Two days later, the family's worst fears were confirmed: a diagnosis of ALL. This began a whirlwind of treatment decisions and plans. Mary Therese called Mrs. Doyle from the physician's office, gave her the news, and asked that she check in with Katie's teacher to make sure her daughter was okay. She also asked Mrs. Doyle for advice on how to handle talking with the children. This was the first of many requests that sent the school counselor on a fact-finding search. Her first call was to a hospital-based grief support program that the school had a long-term relationship with from crisis team training and previous school crises. Mrs. Doyle knew that this program ran support groups for siblings of children with cancer and for parents of critically ill children. The advice from the grief support center was to tell the children about their sister's illness in words that they could understand, not to hide the diagnosis from their other children. The center said that it was critical to make time for the other two children and to not fall into the trap of allowing the siblings to become invisible during the expected focus of family time and resources on the child with cancer. It was especially important for Katie to be an individual and not to become the "reporter" of her sister's progress to the school community.

One of the first tasks for Mrs. Doyle was to get the information about the diagnosis to the school staff. An all-staff meeting was convened the following morning. As in most small communities, the news of Dani's illness had already spread, and many staff members needed clarification on the actual details of her case. Using the information approved by the parents, the details were shared with staff. Because the school district had experience with crisis preparedness, the outline of the meeting was familiar to staff. First the known details were discussed, then the expectation of confidentiality was stressed, and finally the focus on the students or staff that may be in need of special care or counseling services was shared. The members of the crisis team, discussed previously, had met for an hour earlier that morning and had made plans to discuss Dani's illness with her classmates and with her sister's classmates.

Because Mrs. Doyle delivers developmental guidance lessons in every classroom, the children were familiar with her, so she and each classroom teacher led a discussion in the kindergarten and fourth-grade classrooms to explain Dani's illness. Special emphasis was placed on the nature of cancer, that it is not "catching" and no one needed to fear for his or her own health. They also focused on the body's strengths in fighting illness and reviewed good health practices to empower the children to see the possibilities of a good outcome for Dani. The school guidance program has a philosophy of fostering resiliency in all of the students through a schoolwide program that focuses on one's strengths and building supportive relationships between students and staff. Group and individual counseling techniques, utilized by the counselor, focused on wellness and building a good self-concept in the children.

Session 1

This session, recounted in Table 7.1, was the first between the counselor and Dani when Dani reentered school after an eight-week absence, during which a homebound instructor had met with Dani at home.

Table 7.1   Session 1

Session Content	Rationale/Analysis
Dani: "I missed you, too, and I want to stay in school all day today." C: "You would like to stay all day today?"	Counselor wants to welcome Dani, and Dani's statement actually brings up an issue that has her family concerned. Dani is scheduled for *half days* until her doctors feel she is ready for longer days, but Dani is insisting that she stay as long as the other students.
C: "While you are here, what would you like to do?" D: "Play with your toys, okay?" [Dani proceeds to pick a small family of dogs to play with in the dollhouse.]	Hoping to resolve the issue of staying all day through projective play and encouraging problem solving and empowerment. I know Dani has been resistant to a lot of the decisions that have been made for her but she is good-natured and usually does what she needs to do. At the same time, she needs a place to feel powerful and make her own decisions.
D: "We had a dog at the hospital . . . her name was Scout and she visited and you could pet her and tell her stuff." C: "How cool. Does that dog look like Scout?"	Glad to hear Dani is so ready to talk about the hospital, which, according to her mother, is the source of a lot of her fear. She cries inconsolably when she has to spend time there. Her mother has worked with the hospital team to console her while she is there, and they have been in contact with the school team about this issue.
D: "Sort of, but Scout is bigger and fluffier. You be one of the puppies, okay?" C: "Okay."	We proceeded to play and Dani led us to run through the house and then we pretended the house was a hospital, but "a really nice one that gave you a lot of candy." I resisted the impulse to bring the conversation around to any obvious questions about the hospital and instead let Dani lead the way.
D: "Puppy, you need to come over here." C: "I am happy over here, I don't want to."	
D: "I am your mom, you have to listen." C: "Okay, Mom, I am coming."	We then played with the "people" who lived in the house/hospital and all ended up having a party where we all slept in the same bed and ate candy. I thought by refusing to come to "my mom" dog, it would give Dani an opening to deal with her issues with not wanting to do what her own mother wanted. She did not seem inclined to go in that direction and instead seemed happy to put together a party, which seemed to be a scenario she would enjoy at the hospital. The hospital's use of a therapy dog was a big hit with Dani.

(continued)

Table 7.1 **Continued**

Session Content	Rationale/Analysis
C: "Well, it is time to go back to class, Dani, and then your Mom is coming to pick you up. Would you like to go home after lunch or before lunch?" D: After lunch, and I want to sit with my friends.	I had talked with her mother about giving her some choice about when she went home. Our school discipline policy is based on a popular model that helps give students some choices about their activities while retaining our responsibility to set clear boundaries.

This session focused on feelings and utilized an assortment of toys that were available in the counselor's office.

Second Year of Dani's Journey

In the spring of Dani's kindergarten year, she was in remission, as was expected by her treatment team. We were told that 95 percent of children with Dani's type of ALL went on to a first remission. In late summer before her first-grade year, Dani's 504 team met to discuss the changes we needed to make and to decide if in fact she needed a plan. Initially, when Dani was first diagnosed, the team had met to discuss her educational needs. The obvious question was whether she needed to be referred to the school psychologist to determine whether she met the criteria to be offered services under IDEA. She met the criteria under Other Health Impairment (OHI), but her parents were resistant to the idea of Dani being designated a "special education student." They felt that she would be needlessly labeled, then recover quickly and not need any services as soon as she was in remission. The IEP team readily accepted the parents' preference and instead wrote a 504 plan to make sure Dani's educational needs would be met. The advantage of this plan in the minds of the parents was that it recognized the transitory nature of her illness, and, based on the treatments she was receiving, they felt she would not have any long-term effects on her ability to learn.

It was important for us as a team to honor the parents' wishes, and therefore we did not focus on the negative possibilities that could happen but rather on their daughter's strengths. As a result, in reviewing Dani's accomplishments in kindergarten with the help of her homebound instructor, we felt she was at grade level, and we planned to reevaluate her progress quarterly while she was in first grade. We had the advantage of using a progress monitoring system for all of our students, so Dani would not feel different or singled out. In the next few years Dani's family continued to do well, and her 504 plan was discontinued in second grade.

Cancer-Free and Starting Sixth Grade

The clinical team that provided Dani's care while she was sick followed a model called *long-term follow-up care* (LTFU). Children with ALL are heterogeneous, and their need for follow-up varies broadly. Survivorship starting in childhood challenges stakeholders to work out new responses across the life span (Landier, 2007).

Dani's parents were diligent in her follow-up care and were Dani's best advocates. Dani started to develop very bad headaches the summer before middle school and then, as middle school progressed, started to fail her math class. Her parents discussed these changes with members of the treatment team, who were aware of the treatment's long-term effects. Dani had so many headaches and stayed home so often that she was in danger of being truant. The principal arranged for a conference with Dani's parents to put a plan together to address her school attendance. Unfortunately, the principal was new to the district and did not have the information that would have helped him make an informed decision. The result was a meeting that did not go well, and for the first time since Dani's diagnosis, the family felt that

Dani's needs were not being addressed. The parents felt that the principal thought that they were "giving in" to a child who just wanted to stay home, especially on days when she had math tests.

When Mrs. Brown contacted Mrs. Doyle, she was very frustrated. She asked that the same kind of team that helped when her daughter was diagnosed be convened and that the new issues be addressed. While the new assessments began, Dani met with her counselor again. This had not been happening because Dani had expressed a desire "to be like everyone else," and she had not felt the need to talk about her experiences as a young child. But as her struggles emerged in sixth grade, Dani asked to see her. The results are recounted in Table 7.2.

Table 7.2 **Middle School Sessions**

Counselor: "Dani, I am glad to see you today. Make yourself comfortable and catch me up on your life."	I want to start where Dani is comfortable, listen to her words, her images, and develop a sense of her processing of what has been happening. Her tone, breathing, and facial expressions match her words.
Dani: "Well, I am really freaking out because the stupid principal wants my parents to go to jail for letting me stay home. I have these horrible headaches and I can't come to school on the bus because it makes my head hurt and my sister is always late and I have to wait for her to drive me so then I'm late [takes a breath] and so I am not really very happy."	As I listen to Dani I notice that she seems increasingly distressed, her hands are trembling, and she is ready to cry and shrinks into the chair.
C: Wow, it sounds like you are really upset. Tell me more."	
D: "Well, you know that I get these really bad headaches and I think Mr. Loftus [the principal] thinks I am faking it and my math teacher keeps saying I have the ability to do better, but I don't think so, because I feel like I forget everything he says." [She is breathing quickly and her eyes start to fill with tears.]	It is important to really listen to her and also observe her affect. From my point of view, she seems to be a very anxious young woman. I want her to get in touch with what is happening and how her physical body is feeling. I have also talked with her mother, who has described her daughter as sleeping less, eating less, and very clingy. I suspect that Dani is both anxious and depressed. Dani is exhibiting some classic thinking errors. She is "snowballing" her problems in math and creating a future in which she fails school and has to give up on college. She is "catastrophizing" by thinking that her memory is failing her and will continue to. I am also suspicious about her concerns about her health and so I ask her some questions about that.
C: "Dani, what is happening in your body right now?"	
D: "I feel sick and my head is really starting to hurt."	
C: "What thoughts are in your head right now?"	
D: "I think I am going crazy and I can't go to math because I am going to flunk and then I will flunk sixth grade and then I won't get to go to college."	
C: "Dani, those are some big fears. Tell me more about the thoughts that you are having?"	
D: "I think my headaches mean there is something wrong with my brain. My friends think I could have cancer again. That is not what I felt like when I was little—my head never hurt back then."	It is interesting that Dani mentions her friends' fears. She has a close group of friends who have been together since they were in kindergarten and may have memories of Dani as a child with cancer. But Dani seems more worried about her
C: "Do you worry about the cancer coming back?"	

(continued)

Table 7.2 continued

D: "Not now, but I am worried that what if it comes back when I go to college? Who will take care of me?"

cancer recurring when she is older. Are her fears an exaggeration of normal developmental worries that all adolescents go through?

C: "Would you like to work with me on reducing some of these thoughts and getting your headaches better when you are in school?"

D: "Yes, that means you believe me—that I am not making this up."

C: "Yes, I really believe you, and I want to help you take charge and feel better."

D: "I am sick of these problems, and I want to feel better and stop worrying all the time."

C: "I have some ideas that might work. Do you want to try an experiment?"

D: "Yes."

C: "I want you to keep track of the thoughts going through your head when you are worried. And also what other feelings come up as well as the worried feeling."

D: "That's it?"

C: "Yes—keep track on this log sheet."
[Counselor hands her a template (Table 7.4) with columns to record the situation, her thoughts, and associated feelings.]

Her anxiety may be more about the future than the here and now, but her headaches seem to be brought on by the stress of not doing well in school.

This technique is quite common in CBT, and I wanted to get Dani involved in her solving her own problems, giving her a sense of accomplishment and self-control. Her mother was working with her physician to identify what was behind her severe headaches. The physician diagnosed the headaches as migraines, most likely related to her fluctuating hormone levels and stress and not related to her previous cancer treatments.

The Team Collaborates Anew

After our sessions started, the team met to discuss Dani's new challenges. Her medical team made arrangements for a psychological evaluation by a psychologist familiar with the cognitive and emotional effects of Dani's treatments. At the second team meeting, we had just received the psychological evaluation: Dani was diagnosed with an anxiety disorder, NOS, and some impairment was noted in her short-term memory.

However, the meeting was not without controversy. The recent testing by a special education teacher did not show a short-term memory issue. She felt that since Dani was already receiving accommodations as part of our "at-risk program," a 504 plan was not needed. She questioned whether Dani's concerns reached the threshold that a 504 demands. The psychologist from the medical team was on speakerphone, attending the meeting long-distance. He discussed the very real memory deficits Dani was experiencing as an effect of her treatments for leukemia and that this and the headaches would continue to interfere. This was useful information and helped us come to an agreement that Dani did need a new 504 plan to address these issues. Accommodations included steps to lower Dani's level of anxiety related to math. She was able to work with a tutor and had the choice to take her math tests in a quieter environment with no time limits. Dani was involved in the planning for the accommodations. Counseling with the school counselor to decrease and manage her anxiety was also included, as summarized in Table 7.3.

Table 7.3 Next Session

C: "Were you able to keep track of your thoughts this past week?" D: "Yes, it was like doing an experiment, and I had fun."	This assignment is a very typical one I use with students who are anxious and/or depressed.
Counselor: "Dani, I see from your 'homework' from our last session that you have identified some negative thoughts that keep coming back and that lead to some negative feelings." Dani: "Yeah, I was surprised at how mean I can be to myself. And how often I think about getting cancer again."	Dani seems open to doing the work she needs to do to take control of her thoughts and increasing her feelings of competence and happiness.
C: "I notice you have your iPod with you. Let's use it as a prop to help with something called *thought stopping*." D: "Sure." C: "One way you can help yourself stop thinking the negative things that keep popping into your head is to imagine your iPod is playing the same bad song that you hate over and over and louder and louder in your head." D: "Sounds horrible. I would turn it off." C: "Exactly! When the automatic thoughts come, try to imagine yourself turning down the volume and then choosing another song—one that you really like and that helps you feel better."	This a new version of the old "tapes in your head" exercise. I want her to use the thought-stopping technique and then help Dani replace those thoughts with some positive affirmation. To make it more fun, I am inviting some of her friends to participate in a small group and all work together on their own messages. Participation in a group will also help Dani understand that she is not alone in having difficulties with grades, anxiety, or depression. I also work with Dani on relaxation and visualizations to use when she feels her body tensing, and encourage her to play her positive-self tapes.

Table 7.4 Template for Recording Situations, Thoughts, and Associated Feelings

Date	Situation	Thoughts	Feelings

Dani continued in counseling with Mrs. Doyle and was able to reduce her focus on the negative and to correct her thinking errors, and she began to experience relief from her headaches. She was able to talk more openly with her family about her fears. She learned to problem-solve and began to feel more capable in her life. Dani told her mother she was glad she had a "normal" reason for her headaches, and she has been on effective medications to help control the pain.

Summary

Reintegration does not mean just ensuring the quick return to school, but also adaptations that facilitate reconnecting in positive ways and that provide the necessary academic, social, and emotional interventions for all involved. The school counselor can take positive, responsive steps from the initial indication that a child is acutely ill or has a potentially chronic illness. Steps may be taken to form a response team that from the start works to ensure a supportive connection with the family, opens communication channels with multiple players, and has as its goal the eventual return of the student to the school community. The school counselor, by training and position in the school, can take a leadership role in coordinating support while the child is out and then with the reintegration process. Once the child returns, the counselor can provide supportive counseling to the student individually and in small groups and to siblings and friends. Consulting with teachers about their comfort in making adaptations, accommodations, and any extra tasks required is also quite within the school counselor's normal role. Reaching outside of the school, the counselor can check in with the family to make sure that they are tied into community supports and to hear their sense of how the child and siblings are doing. Consultation with the medical team may also continue for the long term and provide regular two- or three-way updates (Landier, 2007). The number of children with acute and chronic illnesses who are recovering and returning to school, or who are entering school initially, will continue to rise. It is important for schools to work out methods of response that encourage respect and support for the child and that build resiliency and a positive climate for adaptation.

References

Aldwin, C. M. (2007). *Stress, coping and development: An integrative perspective* (2nd ed.). NY: Guilford Press.

Bessell, A. (2001). Children surviving cancer: Psychosocial adjustment, quality of life, and school experiences. *Exceptional Children, 67*(3), 345–359.

Boekaert, M., & Röder, I. (1999). Stress, coping, and adjustment in children with a chronic disease: A review of the literature. *Disability and Rehabilitation, 21*(7), 311–337.

Bronfenbrenner, U. (1979). *The ecology of human development: Experiments by nature and design.* Cambridge, MA: Harvard University Press.

CaringBridge. Downloaded June 15, 2008, from http://www.caringbridge.org/.

Clay, D. L. (2004). *Helping school children with chronic health conditions: A practical guide.* New York: Guilford Press.

Cohen, M. S. (1999). Families coping with childhood chronic illness: A research review. *Families, Systems & Health, 17*(2), 149–264.

Drotar, D., Greenley, R., Hoff, A., Johnson, C., Lewandowski, S., Moore, M.,et al. (2006). Summary of issues and challenges in the use of new technologies or clinical care and with children and adolescents with chronic illness. *Children's Health Care, 34*(1), 91–102.

Family Educational Rights and Privacy Act (FERPA), 20 U.S.C. § 1232g; 34 CFR Part 99 (2008), http://www.ed.gov/policy/gen/guid/fpco/ferpa/index.html.

Granville, S. (2008, June 29). *Understanding pediatric chronic illness.* Paper presented at the American School Counselor Association Conference, Atlanta, GA.

Hayman, L. L., Mahon, M. M., & Turner, J. R. (Eds.). (2002). *Chronic illness in children: An evidence-based approach.* New York: Springer Publishing Company, Inc.

Health Insurance Portability and Accountability Act (HIPAA), Pub. L. No. 104-191 262 and 42, U.S.C. 1320 *et seq.* (1996).

Huegel, K. (1998). *Young people and chronic illness: True stories, help, and hope.* Minneapolis, MN: Free Spirit Publishing.

Individuals with Disabilities Education Act (IDEA), Pub. L. No. 101-476 (1990).

Individuals with Disabilities Education Improvement Act (IDEIA), Pub. L. No. 108-446, 118 Stat. 2647 (2004).

Johnson, L. S. (1997). Developmental strategies for counseling the child whose parent or sibling has cancer. *Journal of Counseling and Development, 75,* 417–427.

Kaffenberger, C. J. (2004). School reentry for students with a chronic illness. In B. T. Erford (Ed.), *Professional school counseling: A handbook of theories, programs, and practices* (pp. 691–691). Austin, Texas: Pro-Ed/CAPS Press.

Kaffenberger, C. J. (2006). School reentry for students with a chronic illness: A role for professional school counselors. *Professional School Counseling, 9*(3), 223–230.

Kliebenstein, M. A., & Broome, M. E. (2002). School reentry for the child with chronic illness: Parent and school personnel perceptions. *Pediatric Nursing, 26* (6), 579–582.

Landier, W. (2007) *Children's Oncology Group Long-Term Follow-Up Program Resource Guide. Children's Oncology Group.* Downloaded June 15, 2008, from http://www.survivorshipguidelines.org/.

Lightfoot, J., Wright, S., & Sloper, P. (1998). Supporting pupils in mainstream school with an illness or disability: Young peoples' views. *Child: Care, Health & Development, 25*(4), 267–283.

Mukherjee, S., Lightfoot, J., & Sloper, P. (2000). The inclusion of pupils with a chronic health condition in mainstream school: What does it mean for teachers? *Educational Research, 42*(1), 59–72.

Prevatt, F. F., Heffer, R. W., & Lowe, P. A. (2000). A review of school reintegration programs for children with cancer. *Journal of School Psychology, 38*(5), 447–467.

Sartain, S., Clarke, C., & Heyman, R. (2000). Hearing the voices of children with chronic illness. *Journal of Advanced Nursing, 32*(4), 913–921.

Section 504 of the Rehabilitation Act, 29 U.S.C. § 794 (1973).

Shaw, S. R., & McCabe, P. S. (2007). Hospital-to-school transitions for children with chronic illness: Meeting the new challenges of an evolving health care system. *Psychology in the Schools, 45*(1), 74–87.

Shiu, S. (2001). Issues in the education of students with chronic illness. International Journal of Disability. *Development and Education, (48)*3, 269–281.

Stone, C. (2005). *Ethics and law: School counseling principles.* Alexandria, VA: American School Counselor Association.

Students with chronic illnesses: Guidance for families, schools, and students [Special report]. (2003). *Journal of School Health, 73*(4), 131–132. Also available online at www.nhlbi.nih.gov/public/lung/asthma/guidfam.htm.

School Social Work Interventions for Medically Compromised Youth and Families

Linda Openshaw

8

Chapter

Children whose medical conditions cause continual absences from school are at risk for falling behind in classes and failing. School social workers help prevent the medically at-risk child from failing by providing a supportive link between the child, the school, and the community.

Effective intervention from a school social worker in the context of the daily school experience may consist of collaborating, consulting, developing behavior plans, and training others to work with difficult children (Frey & George-Nichols, 2003).

The basic tasks of the school social worker consist of:

- *Consultation* with others in the school system as a member of a team
- *Assessment* applied to a variety of different roles in direct service, in consultation, and in program development
- *Direct intervention* with children and parents in individual, group, and family modalities
- *Program development* (Constable et al., 1999)

The theoretical framework underlying school social work interventions for medically at-risk children includes an accurate assessment of the medically at-risk child's situation, consultation and collaboration with professionals both within and outside the school system, and direct interventions that build upon both school and community support.

Direct intervention with medically at-risk children should utilize theories that are evidence-based as effective, designed to improve the interactions between the child and the various systems around the child (the ecosystem), and focus on the child's strengths. This approach utilizes the resources and strengths of the medically at-risk child, the school system, and the community.

When addressing client problems through the strengths perspective, everything a social worker does "will be predicated, in some way, on helping to discover and embellish, explore and exploit clients' strengths and resources in the service of assisting them to achieve their goals, realize their dreams, and shed the irons of their own inhibitions and misgivings" (Saleebey, 1997, p. 3). Accordingly, the school social work standards of the National Association of Social Workers mandate that "[s]chool social work services shall be extended to students in ways that build students' individual strengths and offer students maximum opportunity to participate in the planning and direction of their own learning experiences (NASW, 2002, Standard 5).

The strengths-based approach should consider the personal resiliency characteristics of each child and the protective factors that contribute to the child's ability to thrive. In a supportive environment, the capacity for resilience generally develops over time. Hence, resilient children usually come from supportive environments (Egeland, Carlson, & Sroufe, 1993).

Review of Literature: Models of Service

Homelessness, poverty, living with stress, and trauma put the health of a child or adolescent at risk. Many children who are abused or placed in foster care experience both mental and physical health problems. In one study of children in foster care, the children tended to be lighter and shorter than normal, 12 percent of the children required an antibiotic at the time of entry into foster care, and more than half of the children required urgent or nonurgent referrals for medical care. A scant 12 percent of the children studied required only routine follow-up care (Chernoff, Combs-Orme, Risley-Curtiss, & Heisler, 1994).

Homelessness and poverty adversely affect the health of children and adolescents and their access to health care. Health consequences associated with living in transitory shelters, such as malnutrition, asthma, infections, and possible high lead exposure, hinder a child's development. When children are homeless, their transience prevents them from receiving consistent support from a school social worker, school district, or medical doctor. In many cases, children move just as services have begun. Consequently, the children of homeless families do not receive the consistent, ongoing support from schools that would prevent absences resulting from poor health. Instead, they fail and drop out of school.

To bring health services to disadvantaged children and to cut down on school absences, some school systems have established school-based health centers. The St. Paul, Minnesota Maternal, and Infant Care Project, which began in 1973, was the first comprehensive health care program within a school building (Harold & Harold, 1993). The project was designed to help with "prenatal, postpartum, and infant care to low-income, high-risk populations" (Harold & Harold, 1993, p. 66).

School-based health services have expanded their scope to offer a wide range of assistance, including "primary health care, health education, and mental health counseling" (Balassone, Bell, & Peterfreund, 1991, p. 162). However, some school-based health programs target specific student groups or specific health needs or risks, such as children with asthma or youthful drug users (Basen-Engquist et al., 1997). School-based health programs utilize social workers in both the development of the program and as an important part of the school-based health team (Stock et al., 1997).

School-based health programs frequently target the prevention of obesity and physical problems that come as a result of inactivity. These programs teach students about activity and exercise, develop behavioral and motor skills for lifelong activity, and encourage physical activity away from formal classes (Andersen, Crespo, Bartlett, Cheskin, & Pratt, 1998).

Many school districts provide health care programs for teen mothers. These programs, which are often self-sufficient and frequently utilize school social workers, are typically housed at an alternative school. Many of these programs allow the children of teen mothers to come to school so teen parents can learn how to care for their children properly.

In general, most current school-based health programs:

- are located on school grounds;
- attempt to become an essential part of the school;
- use a multidisciplinary team of providers, such as physicians, nurses, physician assistants, social workers, drug and alcohol counselors, and other health professionals;
- provide a wide range of services to meet the physical and behavioral health needs of children and adolescents;
- provide services through a health care provider, such as a hospital, department of health, or medical practice;
- require written parental consent before children enroll in the program; and
- have an advisory board of community representatives, parents, youth, and family organizations that plans and provides oversight (National Assembly on School-Based Health Care, 2008).

Many school-based health centers are classified as Medicaid providers. As the number of school-linked services and school-based health centers in the schools increases, more schools and other organizations offering health services in the schools are claiming Medicaid dollars (Hare 1996; Farrow & Joe, 1992). Many "states have established a credentialing or licensing process to ensure that school-based health centers seeking public grant funds and Medicaid reimbursement will adhere to quality standards consistent with health care industry practice" (National Assembly on School-Based Health Care, 2001, p. 4).

The school social worker links medically at-risk children and their families with medical and school personnel to ensure that the child's educational and health needs are respected. School social workers must be able to "promote collaboration among community health and mental health service providers and facilitate student access to these services" (NASW, 2002, Standard 26). School social workers work in collaboration with these service providers, who are located at or linked with school sites, to ensure that the services promote student educational success (NASW, 2002, Standard 40).

Theoretical Framework and Service Model

Consultation and Collaboration

Consultation in the context of the school involves seeking the expertise of another professional within the school team, family, or community in order to serve clients most effectively. Collaboration occurs when two or more people work together to serve a given client. "As leaders and members of interdisciplinary teams and coalitions, school social workers . . . work collaboratively to mobilize the resources of local education agencies and communities to meet the needs of students and families" (NASW 2002, Standard 9). Through consultation and collaboration, school social workers are able to seek advice and use the expertise of other professionals to ensure full and appropriate service to students with medical problems.

Collaboration with School District Personnel
Intraorganizational collaboration occurs when teachers, social workers, school psychologists, nurses, and volunteers contribute information about their areas of expertise and provide direction about which strategies promote the best results for students (Anderson-Butcher & Ashton, 2004). Students benefit when all of the helping professionals of the school community coordinate with each other.

The school social worker, school psychologist, school guidance counselor, and school nurse historically have been the primary helping professionals concentrating on the health component of the learning process (Caruso, 2000). Special education teachers also may help medically at-risk students understand their schoolwork and receive special help when needed.

The Individuals with Disabilities Education Improvement Act of 2004 (IDEIA, 2004) has had a strong impact on the role of the school social worker and other educators as they provide special education services to students. IDEIA ensures the rights of students with disabilities to a free public education that meets their unique needs. It is necessary for school social workers to understand IDEIA to perform their jobs effectively (NASW, 2002, Standard 22). The school social worker must assist teachers and administrators to meet their obligations under the law to both normal and disabled students.

The case examples in this chapter are based on real students or composites of student problems. Names and other identifying information have been changed to protect the confidentiality of the child and family.

Kinzy was a 14-year-old ninth-grade student who entered high school a couple of months late because she had undergone surgery over the summer for a brain tumor. She was still receiving radiation treatment when school started. At her mother's request, Kinzy was placed in a special education resource class to give her extra help with her school assignments. Kinzy was often sick at school and depressed. She was very frail and had limited energy. The resource teacher and school social worker coordinated with Kinzy's other teachers so that on days when Kinzy was quite ill, she could stay in the resource classroom and do her work there rather than having to walk around the building to her classes. At the suggestion of the social worker, the resource teacher's aide would often go to the cafeteria and bring Kinzy's lunch to the resource classroom so she could rest and relax during lunchtime rather than stand in line at the cafeteria.

On days when Kinzy was not able to attend her classes, the social worker arranged to have her teachers send her work to the resource teacher and visit with Kinzy during their free periods. Students also provided friendship and support. The school social worker coordinated these activities and services and also let Kinzy's mother know when Kinzy was having a hard time. This helped the mother to keep Kinzy's doctor informed and also helped the mother know which days she needed to pick up Kinzy after school rather than have her ride the school bus home.

The collaboration between teachers, aides, and the school social worker allowed Kinzy to attend school and remain current with her schoolwork. The school social worker utilized the school system and Kinzy's strength and desire to overcome her illness to help her succeed.

Collaboration with Visiting Teachers and Homebound Programs

Homebound programs provide students who experience severe physical problems, serious illness, or behavioral difficulties with academic instruction at home from public school teachers. Students who receive home or hospital visits from teachers typically have had recent surgery or another significant medical treatment, have rapidly changing medical conditions or very limited stamina, or have disabilities that make them medically fragile (Friend, 2005, p. 73). Homebound programs are usually short term (three to six weeks), but visiting teachers occasionally work with the same student for an entire school year.

School social workers can be instrumental in linking medically at-risk students to homebound and visiting teacher programs. Once the student is linked to the program, the school social worker helps coordinate services by collecting student textbooks and assignments from the teachers and apprising school personnel about the child's condition.

Interprofessional Collaboration

Interprofessional collaboration takes place when two or more people from different professions work together to help a child and his or her family (Lawson, Adelman, Anderson-Butcher, Barkdull, Briar-Lawson, Butcher, 1999; Lawson & Barkdull, 2000). School social workers must collaborate with medical personnel when children have extended absences for medical reasons. In assessing the child's situation, the school social worker must obtain parental consent before viewing the child's medical records or talking to the child's doctor. Medical doctors have the most thorough

Case of Carol, Age 16

Carol, a 16-year-old eleventh-grader, had developed cancer and had to undergo surgery, then chemotherapy and radiation. She was unable to attend school during her ongoing treatment. During most of that time, she was incapacitated. She also lost her hair. Carol's mother asked the school to help Carol continue with her studies during this time. As a result, Carol was assigned to work with the school social worker, who coordinated efforts with the homebound program. Carol also was assigned a homebound visiting teacher to coordinate with her regular education teachers.

The social worker arranged to have Carol's teachers leave her assignments in the school social worker's office. The homebound teacher came to the school weekly, picked up the assignments, and delivered them to Carol's home. Two days per week, the homebound teacher reviewed Carol's homework with her and made sure that Carol knew what was being covered in her classes. The homebound teacher brought Carol's homework back to school and discussed Carol's progress with her teachers every other week. The teacher did this for three months, after which Carol returned to school.

Carol was able to keep up with her classes while she was away from school. When she returned, she was placed in the special education resource classroom for two class periods each day for extra tutoring and support. She also attended her academic classes, which were American history, English, chemistry, and algebra.

She lacked confidence when she first returned to school because she was wearing a wig and did not feel physically strong. The school social worker met with her two times per week to provide supportive counseling. Carol used the resource teacher and school social worker for support until she felt she was able to resume the regular pace of high school and advance toward graduation.

Case of Mark, Age 6

Mark, age 6, was diagnosed with leukemia during the spring of his kindergarten year. He received chemotherapy during the summer, and his doctor said he was ready to return to first grade in the fall but that his treatment might leave him susceptible to other illnesses and that he would tire easily. In response to Mark's condition, the school social worker collaborated with the school nurse, Mark's doctor, his parents, and his first-grade teacher to formulate a health plan for him at school.

The teacher was asked to watch for signs of weariness. When Mark seemed tired, the teacher would call the social worker, who would take Mark to her office to rest. The social worker would call Mark's mother if he needed to go home. He was allowed to go home whenever he felt too tired to participate at school. Mark's doctor recommended that the teacher and students should use extra precautions to cut down on germs and the spread of bacteria in the classroom, because Mark had a reduced ability to fight off illness. The teacher worked with the students in Mark's classroom to keep their desks and supplies clean. The students cleaned their desks daily and used liquid sanitizer on their hands throughout the day to keep the room germ-free. A homebound teacher worked with Mark's regular first-grade teacher whenever he was home for an extended period of time so that he would not fall behind.

Mark's parents wanted to be sure that he would know how to handle difficult questions regarding his illness from other students. Mark rehearsed his answers with his parents so that if other children asked him if he was going to die, he would say "no" emphatically. This was not difficult for him because he had a positive outlook and believed he would get well.

knowledge about a child's diagnosis, treatment regimen, and prognosis. The information that doctors can provide is invaluable and should be provided through a letter or direct contact with a school social worker, school nurse, counselor, or member of the school administrative team.

The coordination between the school, the homebound teacher, and the home helped Mark during his first months after returning to school and kept him on track with his first-grade curriculum. Through the collaborative efforts of a child's doctor, school social workers, homebound programs, and the child's teachers at school, a child can continue to progress in school in spite of illness.

Interprofessional collaboration is particularly valuable in assisting students who are HIV-positive or who have AIDS.

Hannah, an eight-year-old third-grade student, had been HIV-positive since birth. During her third-grade year, she began to experience a series of illnesses. Hannah's doctor recommended that her parents call the school social worker seeking support. After consulting with Hannah's parents to determine which school personnel should be involved, the school social worker arranged a meeting with the school nurse, assistant principal, and Hannah's teacher to create a school health plan. The team wrote a school health plan for Hannah that identified and addressed potential problems at school. The team decided that the school social worker and school nurse would coordinate services with Hannah's doctor and family to ensure that her privacy was protected. The medical doctor discussed Hannah's diagnosis with the school nurse and made suggestions about how the school could help Hannah. The school staff worked as a team to implement Hannah's health care plan and to ensure that confidentiality was maintained.

Hannah's Health Care Plan

Hannah's illness makes it difficult for her body to fight off infectious diseases. It can infect and damage part of her body's defenses. Her illness consumes her energy, and she is frequently tired at school. Her illness cannot be transmitted to others through casual contact, but through direct contact with blood or body fluids.

1. **Problem:** Hannah requires daily medication.
   Goal: To provide for Hannah's medication.
   Action: (1) Hannah's parents will sign a medical permission form giving the nurse permission to dispense Hannah's medications. (2) The medications will be sent in a prescription bottle with orders from a physician regarding how they are to be dispensed. (3) Hannah will receive her medication from the school nurse twice during the school day.
2. **Problem:** Hannah becomes exhausted easily.
   Goal: To prevent exhaustion.
   Action: (1) Allow Hannah to rest in the school nurse's office when she feels tired. (2) Go home if the exhaustion continues after resting for one hour.
3. **Problem:** There is the potential for opportunistic infection because of Hannah's impaired immune system.
   Goal: To protect others from exposure to HIV and limit Hannah's exposure to disease.
   Action: (1) Cover Hannah's sores, cuts, or skin lesions. (2) Ensure immediate cleanup and sanitation of any area where Hannah discharges bodily fluids. (3) Keep Hannah away from bacteria by wiping off her desk at the beginning of the day and washing her hands on a regular basis.
4. **Problem:** Hannah needs emotional support.
   Goal: To provide emotional support at school.

(continued)

> **Action:** (1) The school social worker will provide weekly counseling. (2) Hannah will visit the social worker if she is overwhelmed.
> 5. **Problem:** There is stigma attached to HIV.
>   **Goal:** To protect Hannah's privacy.
>   **Action:** (1) The team members will not disclose Hannah's medical condition except to those who are allowed by law to know of it. (2) Hannah's medical records will be protected.

The intervention with Hannah is an example of how interprofessional collaboration between school personnel and medical doctors can assist students who are medically at risk.

Community Collaboration

Community collaboration involves "all community stakeholders that are committed to improving children's learning and healthy development" (Anderson-Butcher & Ashton, 2004, p. 45). There are many community resources to assist with medical problems. Before school social workers can coordinate services with other agencies in the community, they must make themselves knowledgeable about the services that are available. As part of this "asset inventory" of community resources and services, the social worker must determine where there are gaps and overlaps in services. During these inventories "collaborative strategies are explored across agencies to meet the needs of youths who are receiving multiple services. An asset inventory takes into account the findings from the needs assessment and recognizes, for example, the importance of extended family members and 'informal helpers' in ethnic minority communities" (Caruso, 2000, p. 111).

School social workers are instrumental in connecting children who are medically at risk with agencies that can help them. In their capacity as resource brokers, school social workers are strategically positioned to sustain community and school social services partnerships (Caruso, 2000). When connections are built between service delivery programs, the resulting collaboration between professionals on co-occurring needs and issues makes the professionals' jobs easier (Anderson-Butcher & Ashton, 2004).

Case of Pam, Age 13

Pam, a 13-year-old eighth-grade student, was diagnosed with diabetes. Her doctor had referred her to a dietician to help her learn how to eat appropriately in order to keep the condition under control. As a result, she did not often miss school because of her diabetes. However, one of her teachers saw her crying in class one day and referred her to the school social worker. The social worker determined that Pam was depressed and felt isolated because of her diabetes. The social worker obtained parental permission to refer Pam to a local hospital that sponsored a weekly diabetes support group.

Pam attended several sessions, and, although she was younger than many of the participants, she developed a connection to them. This support group helped her cope with her condition and learn how to accept it. The collaboration with community resources provided ongoing support that was not available within the school system for a student with diabetes.

Assessment

Assessment is the gathering of relevant information about a problem as a first step to solving it and as preparation for intervention at any level of practice (Kirst-Ashman & Hull, 2002). School social workers must "incorporate assessments in developing and implementing intervention and evaluation plans that enhance students' abilities to benefit from educational experiences" (NASW, 2002, Standard 13). School social workers contribute an essential dimension to the assessment of students through the ecological perspective, which necessarily considers the child's family and neighborhood (NASW, 2002, Standard 12).

It is essential for social workers to know about risk and protective factors for the child, parents, and family, and also about those of the environment (Davies, 2004). These factors should be identified and included in every assessment by the social worker. A complete assessment includes information from collateral sources, including the child's doctor. However, the Health Insurance Portability and Accountability Act of 1996 (HIPAA) protects the privacy of individuals' health information through nationwide standards that govern how the information can be used and disclosed. Generally, an entity governed by HIPAA cannot use or disclose protected health information for any purpose other than treatment, payment, or health care unless the individual authorizes it. Therefore, in order to obtain information from the student's doctor, the school social worker must obtain a release from the student's parents (unless the student is age 18 or older, in which case the student may provide the release).

Likewise, school personnel are limited in the information they can disclose to those outside the school system by the Family Education Rights and Privacy Act (FERPA) (20 U.S.C.A. § 1232g). FERPA protects the privacy of student education records. Parents or eligible students over the age of 18 must sign a release of information for schools to be allowed to release educational records.

School social workers should consult with the parents or guardians of medically at-risk children in order to obtain complete assessment and diagnostic information about the child's medical problems. It is often the school social worker who visits the home to assess the child's situation, after which the social worker can provide information about the child to the school district and provide the child and parents with information from the school. Coordination between the school and home can keep the child from worrying about school and help the parents support the child through the school system.

Parental support is critical in coordinating school services for medically at-risk children. Parental support includes providing school supplies, helping with assignments, and assisting the child with needed research at the library or with other community resources. Parents also provide support by making arrangements for visiting teachers to visit the home and by being present during those visits.

With the help of collateral sources, a school social worker can provide other school personnel with a thorough assessment of the medically at-risk child. A thorough assessment provides the foundation for planning the right intervention. The planning process involves prioritizing the problems, evaluating the level or intervention for each need, setting goals and objectives, and formalizing a contract (Kirst-Ashman & Hull, 2002).

Direct Intervention

Direct intervention is provided by school social workers to children and parents in individual, group, and family modalities. "School social workers . . . help empower students and their families to gain access to and effectively use formal and informal community resources" (NASW, 2002, Standard 6). The school social worker should help the student and parents prioritize the most pressing need and plan the intervention accordingly. When no program for intervention exists, the school social worker should participate in developing one.

School social workers often assist in the implementation and delivery of services to students with special needs. They must "be able to select and apply empirically validated or promising prevention and intervention methods to enhance students' education experiences" (NASW, 2002, Standard 23). The social worker's services include assessment, early identification, and direct services. Empirically validated or evidence-based interventions are mandatory, particularly in cases where school districts are compensated by Medicaid for the school social work intervention. School social workers must be able to validate the effectiveness of the intervention and show that the correct intervention strategy was applied through the use of pre- and posttests.

Case of Matthew, Age 14

Matthew was a 14-year-old ninth-grade student. He had lost the use of his legs when he fell out of a tree during the summer between eighth and ninth grades. He was in a wheelchair and extremely angry about his physical losses. He would ram his wheelchair into walls, ride into the street, and often leave school and ride through the park that was near the school. The school administration referred him to the school social worker after his parents asked the school for help with his behavior.

The school social worker's assessment was that Matthew was in the anger stage of the grief process over his physical losses. He also was extremely depressed and suicidal. The school social worker did research on the appropriate interventions for loss, depression, and acceptance of Matthew's changed physical capacities. Matthew and the social worker prioritized his problems and determined that he needed assistance with the depression and grief first. The school social worker contacted Matthew's parents to discuss the possibility of working with a psychiatrist to provide medication and support for Matthew's depression and suicidal ideation.

The school social worker met with Matthew each morning to assess his mood, build upon his strengths, and offer him support at school. The social worker helped set up peer tutoring for classes in which Matthew was struggling. The school social worker used graphs to help Matthew measure his growth and accept his physical limitations by keeping track of the number of times he wanted to hurt himself. These numbers decreased steadily.

Matthew's strengths were his intelligence, his physical strength, and his sense of humor. The school social worker helped him see that he had retained his personality. The school social worker also helped link him to weight training at school, where he received encouragement from the coaches. The support of the coaches was instrumental in his acceptance of his physical limitations.

The school social worker's intervention helped Matthew focus on his strengths and measure the changes he was making in accepting himself. The collaborative effort of parents, psychiatrist, school social worker, coaches, and students enabled Matthew to get through the depression, accept his physical condition, and find worth in himself again.

Program Development

Medically at-risk students and their families often are unaware that they can request special services. As a result, they frequently fail to do so. School social workers should advocate for parental and student rights, whether for students in special education or those with medical needs who do not qualify for special education. Sometimes, social workers must do so by using district resources in new and creative ways.

The principal of an alternative school was aware that there were frequent requests for funds to meet both staff and student needs throughout the school year. He also knew that the funds available to him through the school district were insufficient to meet all of these needs. He installed vending machines in the faculty break room, and, whenever school funds were not available, he used the profits to help send teachers and staff members to conferences, provide student services, and purchase school supplies for needy students.

When principals do not have extra funds, school social workers can look for grants to help provide funding for students with special needs. If there are limited district resources to help meet the needs of students, the school social worker must be creative in looking for funds. To address an overwhelming need for social work services, for example, the social worker can seek a grant to pay stipends for social work interns whose field placements are in the school district. In addition to providing extra services, the interns will give the social work profession more visibility in the district.

Challenges

Obstacles

School social workers who deal with medically at-risk students face a lack of resources within some schools and communities. This is particularly true in rural communities. Where there is a lack of school and community resources, school social workers must be creative in serving students and their families.

In addition to limited resources, another obstacle that school social workers face with medically at-risk students is that others within the school system do not understand the social worker's role or the skills and services the social worker can offer. Because the social work profession is practiced in a wide range of venues, it is often unclear to those who are not social workers how best to use social workers in host systems, such as the public schools.

School social workers who have been in a particular school district for a long time or who work in only one or two schools are relatively well known and visible in their schools. Those who don't must do some of their own public relations with school administrators, other school district personnel, parents, and community agencies to promote the use of social workers in the schools.

Many states are cutting funding for extra programs, such as social work services, in the schools and putting those funds into programs connected with state-mandated competency exams. Consequently, the social work profession needs to advocate for itself with state legislatures to convince them to provide social work services in the schools. To succeed, social workers must present information to state legislators about the role school social workers can play in helping students succeed in school, which includes succeeding on state competency exams.

School social workers do not receive specific training on all of the wide variety of medical issues they may face within the school system. Accordingly, in working with a student who is medically at risk, it often is necessary for the social worker to become self-educated about the student's medical diagnosis and the best evidence-based treatment to use to help the student adjust to his or her medical disorder and to meet the student's needs at school.

Once a school social worker has become educated about a child's particular medical problem, he or she can help the child by educating other school personnel about the best approaches to use with the child. School social workers also can educate teachers and administrators about the prevalence of teen suicide, the warning signs of suicide, and what behaviors constitute a major depressive episode so they can be on the lookout for behavior changes in students. Likewise, school social workers must help the school community understand the needs of medically at-risk children and advocate for those needs to be met by the school system.

Proposed Ideal Treatment

The ideal treatment model has been presented in this chapter. It begins with the availability of a school social worker to intervene on behalf of medically at-risk children. This intervention begins with a thorough strengths-based assessment. The intervention also involves collaboration between professionals both within and outside the school system. Direct services are provided through individual and group counseling.

Program development is necessary when the school district does not have the programs students need. In this case, the social worker should seek support from the community, either to create programs in the schools or to offer needed services when they are available outside the school.

The best person to coordinate student services for the student who is medically at risk is the employee who oversees social work services within the school district. The director of social work services can also help publicize the diverse role and expertise offered by school social workers. Where a pupil service department is not led by a social worker, which is often the case, the administrator may not fully understand the range of social work services. In these situations, social workers should advocate for the profession by educating administrators.

Strains and Satisfaction from the Work

School social work is frequently rewarding. "School social workers receive a lot of recognition and reinforcement for fixing kids, because this is what is expected of them by teachers and administrators" (Dupper & Evans, 1996, p. 190). It also is very rewarding to see medically at-risk children receive services that will improve their lives and put them on the road to recovery. However, when school social workers do not receive needed resources or cooperation from the student or family, it can be frustrating. Over time, continued frustration often leads to burnout and compassion fatigue.

School social workers must face the frustration of knowing that their interventions cannot always change everything that is wrong in a child's world. Intervention may alleviate the student's problems at school, but a host of other problems lie outside the classroom door. School social workers must accept the fact that their interventions may be limited to school-related problems. In spite of social work's unique ecological perspective, school social workers do not have influence over all of the systems in a child's life and thus cannot always affect the home situation or community surroundings to meet all the needs of each child.

Hope for the Future

Medically at-risk children can thrive within the school system when they are provided with the right service plan or school health plan that is coordinated by a school social worker. School social workers are skilled professionals who can address the needs of medically at-risk children on many levels and help them stay connected to the school and keep current with their schoolwork despite their medical problems.

By collaborating with service providers both within and outside the school system, the school social worker can help the student and family members utilize resources that will help them accept and work to resolve the student's medical problems.

References

Anderson-Butcher, D., & Ashton, D. (2004). Innovative models of collaboration to serve children, youths, families, and communities. *Children & Schools*, *26*(1), 39–53.

Andersen, R. E., Crespo, C. J., Bartlett, S. J., Cheskin, L. J., & Pratt, M. (1998). Relationship of physical activity and television watching with body weight and level of fitness among children. *JAMA*, *279*(12), 938–942.

Balassone, M. L., Bell, M., & Peterfreund, N. (1991). School-based clinics: An update for social workers. *Social Work in Education*, *13*(3), 162–175.

Basen-Engquist, K., Parcel, G. S., Harris, R., Kirby, D., Coyle, K., Banspach, S., et al. (1997). The safer choices project: Methodological issues in school-based health promotion intervention. *Journal of School Health*, *67*(9), 365–371.

Caruso, N. (2000). Lessons learned in a city-school social services partnership. *Social Work in Education*, *22*(2), 108–115.

Chernoff, R., Combs-Orme, T., Risley-Curtiss, & Heisler, A. (1994). Assessing the health status of children entering foster care. *Pediatrics*, *93*(4), 594–601.

Constable, R., Kuzmickaite, D., Harrison, W. D., & Volkmann, L. (1999). The emergent role of the school social worker in Indiana. *School Social Work Journal*, *24*(1), 1–14.

Davies, D. (2004). *Child development: A practitioner's guide*. New York: Guilford Press.

Dupper, D. R., & Evans, S. (1996). From Band-Aids and putting out fires to prevention: School social work practice approaches for the new century. *Social Work in Education*, *96*(3), 187–192.

Egeland, B., Carlson, E., & Sroufe, L. A. (1993). Resilience as process. *Development and Psychopathology*, *5*, 517–528.

Farrow, F., & Joe, T. (1992). Financing school-linked, integrated services. *Future of Children*, *2*(1), 56–67.

The Family Education Rights and Privacy Act (FERPA), 20 U.S.C.A. § 1232g; 34 CFR Part 99 (2008).

Frey, A., & George-Nichols, N. (2003). Intervention practices for students with emotional and behavioral disorders: Using research to inform school social work practice. *Children & Schools*, *25*(2), 97–104.

Friend, M. (2005). *Special education: Contemporary perspectives for school professionals*. Boston: Allyn & Bacon.

Hare, I. (1995). School-linked services. In R. L. Edwards (Ed.), *Encyclopedia of social work* (19th ed., *3*, pp. 2100–2109). Washington, DC: NASW Press.

Hare, I. (1996). Regulating school social work practice into the 21st century. *Social Work in Education*, *18*(4), 250–258.

Harold, R. D., & Harold, N. B. (1993). School-based clinics: A response to the physical and mental health needs of adolescents. *Health & Social Work*, *18*(1), 65–74.

The Health Insurance Portability and Accountability Act of 1996, 42 U.S.C. § 1301, *et seq.* (1996).

Individuals with Disabilities Education Improvement Act of 2004, 20 U.S.C. § 1400, *et seq.* (2004).

Kirst-Ashman, K., & Hull, G. H., Jr. (2002). *Understanding generalist practice* (3rd ed.). Pacific Grove, CA: Brooks/Cole Thomson Learning.

Lawson, H. A., Adelman, H., Anderson-Butcher, S., Barkdull, C., Briar-Lawson, K., Butcher, T. L., & Vogel, M. B. (1999). *Developing caring school communities for children and youth: The facilitator's guide.* Jefferson City: Missouri Department of Elementary and Secondary Education.

Lawson, H. A., & Barkdull, C. (2000). Gaining the collaborative advantage and promoting systems and cross-systems change. In A. Sallee, K. Briar-Lawson, & H. A. Lawson (Eds.), *New Century Practice with Child Welfare Families* (pp. 245–270). Las Cruces, NM: Eddie Bowers.

National Assembly on School-Based Health Care. Retrieved February 18, 2008, from http://www.nasbhc.org/site/cjsJPKWPFJrH/b.2561553/k.B21.

National Assembly on School-Based Health Care. (2001). Partners in access: *School-based health centers and Medicaid: Policies & practices.* p. 4. Retrieved February 18, 2008, from http://www.nasbhc.org/site/cjsJPKWPFJrH/b.2561553/k.B21.

National Association of Social Workers (NASW). (2002). *NASW standards for school social work services.* Washington, DC: Author.

Saleebey, D. (Ed.). (1997). *The strengths perspective in social work practice* (2nd ed.) New York: Longman.

Stock, M. R., Morse, E. V., Simon, P. M., Zeanah, P. D., Pratt, J. M., & Sterne, S. (1997). Barriers to school-based health care programs. *Health and Social Work, 22*(4), 274–281.

Strengths-Based Group Work with Children

Ariel Allena Botta

9

Chapter

Group work is a cost effective, efficient, powerful and meaningful way to support children and families who are coping with medical illness. This chapter provides a description of the unique and important role of the medical social worker as a group worker. Additionally, it provides a theoretical framework to guide strengths-based group work practice. Finally, a case presentation and vignettes are provided to illustrate the remarkable journey of one child's group experience over the course of four years. This story illustrates how much these resilient children can heal and thrive over time within the sanctuary of a supportive group and, as groups act as microcosms of the world, ultimately in other important areas of their lives.

Collaborative Role of the Medical Social Worker

As an identified group social worker I have often been asked by my talented medical social work colleagues to consult about group work in a medical setting. After many years of this rich collaboration I feel honored to represent the voices of these two sets of professionals with differing expertise.

It has been my experience that the role of the medical social worker varies depending on the culture of the particular medical setting. However, the literature indicates that certain aspects remain the same across environments. The general functions of the worker are to assess the psychosocial functioning of patients and families. Additionally, social workers provide support and intervention in order to maximize the patient's and family's ability to make use of the medical treatment or hospitalization. This includes overcoming obstacles or barriers such as family or other relational dynamics, psychological, cultural, financial, or concrete issues and that ultimately prevent the patient and family from making optimal use of health care. This is accomplished through connecting families with valuable resources or providing counseling or psychotherapy. Social workers are responsible for case management and complex resource coordination, crisis intervention, risk management, and ensuring a safe discharge and aftercare plan. An integral part of the role is to enhance the functioning of the health care team by helping to mediate team conflict, to recognize ethical and legal dilemmas, and to facilitate communication among team members. Medical social workers also provide psychosocial consultation to the medical team, along with recommendations to guide the patient and family through the hospitalization.

Ultimately, the work involves helping families strengthen their support systems. Medical social workers are creative and resourceful professionals. They are trained to advocate for patients and to understand how to navigate systems in order to empower families both during and after the treatment process. In addition to these aspects of their roles, they are important contributors in a team setting as program and policy developers, writers, researchers, and teachers.

Social work in a medical setting is by definition a collaborative practice. The medical team is a multidisciplinary team composed of doctors; nurses; nutritionists; physical, occupational, speech, and recreational therapists; and child life specialists. The social worker is frequently the only mental health professional. These multiple perspectives create a rich environment that facilitates a great deal of mutual learning.

Theoretical Framework

A Strengths-Based, Empowerment Perspective to Guide Practice

By design, the medical model focuses on the identification of a problem, illness or diagnosis, its origins, and treatment. Social workers are trained to contribute to the development of a treatment plan by giving attention to the whole person, in the context of his or her environment (Bronfenbrenner, 1979), rather than to just the illness. Strengths-based empowerment theory (Simon, 1994) provides the framework for all of social work.

Many of the clients for whom social workers advocate are coping with major life challenges in addition to their medical illnesses. Such challenges may include poverty or homelessness. They may have been victims of community and domestic violence or abuse. Or they may be coping with mental health needs, or they may have experienced marginalization or oppression due to race, ethnicity, age, or gender. Yet despite these challenges, many children grow up to be well adjusted adults, and I am continually inspired by their strength and courage. The literature shows that two indicators contribute to children's remarkable resilience in the face of adversity. First, the perception by some of adversity as a challenge and opportunity to grow and learn tends to result in better coping with stress than for those who view it as a roadblock. The other contributor to resilience is having strong social support (Christ, Sormanti,

& Francoeur, 2001). Strengths-based group work helps children and families build upon both factors. Where many professionals may see challenges or deficits, social workers are able to identify strengths and opportunities. They are trained to enhance support systems through the use of interpersonal and societal approaches. These may include individual therapy, family therapy, and group work, or organizational change and social action. In other words, social workers are trained specifically to recognize and build upon the very factors that contribute to resilience.

This chapter focuses on the role of the social worker as a group worker in a medical setting. The term *group worker* refers to the many different types of professionals and paraprofessionals who facilitate groups with children and families in medical settings. These workers may include psychologists, psychiatrists, nurses, physicians, child life specialists, recreational, occupational, and physical therapists, and research assistants.

Group Stage Theory

The following two group stage theories give a structure for group work practice with children and families coping with medical challenges. The Boston model was developed by James Garland, Hubert Jones, and Ralph Kolodny in 1965 at the Boston University School of Social Work. It is the leading group stage theory for work with children.

The five-stage theory proposes that members experience *preaffiliation* at the beginning of a group when they are weighing the cost and benefits of joining. This is a critical time for the worker to engage members. Clearly stating group purpose and using contracts can be invaluable during the beginning of a group. It can also be useful to have a group statement. For example:

> This is our group. Its success or failure is up to us. We come together in search of ourselves. What we have to share is honesty; what we hope to gain is trust. Through expressing our feelings, hopes, and dreams, we can become known to one another. Friendship and self-understanding are the rewards. We will respect the privacy of each member by keeping group business within the group. What we see here, what we say here, what we hear here, let it stay here. (Carrell, 2000, p. 39)

Once children decide to commit to the group, they quickly move into the *power and control* phase. Hierarchies are formed, alliances are made, and scapegoating may occur. This is when the highest amount of dropout happens. Workers should take an active role in helping members deal with conflicts through encouraging mutual aid and instilling hope. This may be accomplished by reminding them that what joins them is stronger than the sum of their differences (Steinberg, 2004). After weathering the storm and resolving conflicts, members move into the *intimacy stage,* in which there is a high level of self-disclosure, and they begin to take ownership of the group and rely less on facilitators. There emerges a mutual recognition that the group dynamic lends to growth and change. The language of members often shifts from "I" to "we." During the fourth stage, called *differentiation*, members see themselves as separate individuals and members of the group. Finally, during *separation*, members reminisce about shared experiences and revisit past loss. It is an indication that they are ready to terminate when they can integrate skills learned in the group into their lives. The worker takes a more active role during this phase in order to help members celebrate their growth while recognizing the difficulty endings can bring. (Garland, Jones, & Kolodney, 1965).

Thirty years later, Linda Schiller, also from Boston University School of Social Work, developed the first feminist group stage theory, called the *relational model*. The model emerged out of the recognition of feminist writing from the 1970s, 1980s, and 1990s, which proposed that women define power, relationships, and sense of self differently than men. Research and literature indicate that women's sense of self is closely related to the central role of connection and affiliation (Surry, 1991). This contrasts Sigmund Freud and Erik Erickson's emphasis on independence and autonomy as essential factors for healthy development into adulthood; whereas men tend to define power through status and hierarchy, women focus on developing connection, trust, and intimacy.

Though stages of *preaffiliation* and *separation* are consistent across both models, Schiller suggests that the three middle stages differ for women and for populations that have experienced oppression. In the second stage, called *establishing a relational base*, members spend time identifying similarities and seeking approval from each other and facilitators. Schiller believes that safety is essential for members to self-disclose and intimacy to develop. In the third stage, members move into what Schiller calls the *"sacred space of trust."* There is a respect for difference while preserving connection. Finally, during the fourth stage, *challenge and change*, members question their ways of coping or relating to the world. They may do this because of their insight or the feedback from their peers (Schiller, 1995).

Both of these models are useful when working with children and families coping with medical illness though it has been my experience that, this population tends to make the most progress when led through the relational model because of members' experiences of feeling isolated and marginalized and their need to feel safe and connected before growth and healing may occur.

Therapeutic Factors in Clinical Group Work

In the context of psychotherapy, Irving Yalom and colleagues (2005) created an important theoretical framework for clinical group work. He identified the following therapeutic factors, which patients valued in groups: altruism, group cohesiveness, universality, interpersonal learning, guidance, catharsis, identification, family reenactment, self-understanding, the instillation of hope, and existential factors. Many of these elements will be identified and put into context in the vignettes later in this chapter.

Different Types of Groups

There are four general categories of groups: educational, support, psycho-therapeutic, and task or social action (Garland, 1986). Additionally, I have found that healing groups play an integral role in helping children with medical illness and exist in a category of their own. They may include groups such as yoga, meditation, recreational therapy, expressive movement, dance, drama, and/or mindfulness. Having knowledge of these categories will assist workers in clearly stating the goal or purpose of the group. It will also provide guidelines for understanding the role of the worker as group facilitator.

Challenges and Roadblocks Associated with Group Work

Conducting group work in a medical setting presents many challenges. Space is often limited, and it is difficult for workers to devote the amount of time necessary to prepare for, facilitate, and process a group. There is seldom support available to the worker in the form of training, supervision, or consultation. Conflicting goals and expectations of the group often exist when working in an environment in which so many different professional perspectives are represented. Finally, there is often a lack of funding and resources to support the group. These are inherent in all group work. The good news is that there are creative ways to meet these challenges, with solutions clearly outweighing the reasons to abandon the endeavor.

Solutions to Addressing Challenges

The social worker must advocate for space, time, resources, and supervision. Providing education to colleagues and potential members will help with the recruitment process. Having a clearly stated group purpose and using contracts will help members engage and decrease the amount of attrition in the group. Meeting on a regular basis with co-facilitators to plan and process sessions will lead to the development of a strong, collaborative working relationship. Finally, it is essential that theory guide practice so members may have a common language when talking about group work.

I believe that the benefits of group work far outweigh challenges. Group work is a powerful mode of treatment alone or in conjunction with medical or psychosocial forms of treatment. It is a cost effective and efficient way of providing services to a large number of people in a short period of time. The group provides an opportunity for members to feel understood and validated by peers. In the context of working with parents, groups provide an opportunity to build a social network. Parents of children with chronic illness are often too busy caring for their children to foster social connections and therefore feel isolated while experiencing the stresses associated with their child's illness (Wharff, 1982). Members of a group can provide parents with strength and understanding during these difficult times. For children, the group offers a place for them to laugh, dance, express themselves, and play together as they learn to foster friendships and develop coping mechanisms. We should never underestimate the healing power of play for people of all ages. Additionally, members benefit from mutual aid and learn that they are capable of navigating challenging situations when they work together. Ultimately, these experiences lend to a sense of empowerment in the face of challenge. Members experience a sense of mastering of skills, and they feel connected and understood.

Case of Carl, Age 12

Carl is a kind, charismatic, 12-year-old, Caucasian boy who experienced acute kidney failure from a rare genetic disorder at the age of 3. This shift in his health happened overnight. He has subsequently had 40 surgeries, including an unsuccessful kidney transplant, has been on life support several times, and has undergone dialysis for the past nine years. He and his family refer to these medical challenges as "the medical mystery," and they are waiting for medical science to "catch up" so that Carl may get a kidney as a child. This has been his long-standing wish. As he so poignantly puts it, he feels his "childhood is slipping away," and it is difficult to cope with the uncertainty of the future. Carl lives with his wonderfully supportive mother, father, and younger brother. His parents have given written permission to write about their family's experience.

For the first year and a half of his illness, his parents were understandably operating on optimism, shock, and adrenaline. Several years later they recognized that they needed some psychological support to help Carl cope with his medical challenges. This was provided by several psychologists by means of creative, age-appropriate coping mechanisms taught bedside during his hospitalizations. Then, at age 7, when his family and treatment team realized that he was comfortable with adults but had no strong peer connections and therefore was suffering socially and emotionally, Carl was referred for an outpatient social-skills-building psychotherapy group.

Some children and families prefer to be around others who are coping with medical challenges. This can be normalizing, supportive, and healing during such an isolating process. Although there is much care and concern from loved ones, some find it uniquely satisfying to be with people who understand from personal experience, who speak a common language, and who are at different stages in the healing process. However, of equal importance, some children, such as Carl, choose to be in a group that does not focus on their medical challenges. This lovely young boy's spirit had been injured due to his illness, and it was time to expand his life and offer a perspective other than a medical one.

His goal was to develop a strong sense of self outside of his illness and to get his childhood back in a way other than through receiving a new kidney. Therefore, we placed him in social-skills-building groups in an outpatient setting. As his mother summarized, "Over the course of four years, he focused on kids more, shared, confronted, played, defended, forgave, and empathized. He has learned about give-and-take, listening, managing anger, and the complex myriad of details we all must navigate in order to be connected with one another." He now also perceives the hospital as a place where he may come for services other than for his intense renal treatment, a vital change in his personal narrative.

Carl's absence from normal school routine had interfered with his ability to form lasting friendships. It had also negatively affected his will to connect with peers, because he had missed so much academic work and felt left out socially. In fact, when we first met he had no interest in connecting with peers and avoided social situations. This is common among children who grow up spending most of their time in a medical setting, interacting with adults around the subject of their medical care. They may not even want to connect with children facing similar medical struggles in order to avoid identifying with their illness. It may feel easier and safer for them to interact with the professionals in their lives rather than take the risks associated with opening up to peers and navigating friendships.

When I first met Carl, I remember being impressed by how wise he was for a 7-year-old. He had experienced more hardship than many adults. Carl is the quintessential example of how to turn challenges and struggles into opportunities. He is a true inspiration and the epitome of resilience. Through his insight, honesty, and authenticity, he has taught me valuable lessons over the course of our four year relationship.

The following segments highlight Carl's journey through group therapy over the course of four years, beginning with the initial group meeting, then his weathering of several conflicts with peers, and ending with some of the most meaningful, emotionally intimate friendships imaginable. I refer to myself as the *worker* and to Carl as *Carl*. As other group members are introduced, I give a brief history about them. All of the sessions represented were co-facilitated by colleagues of different disciplines. Due to space constraints, the collective responses of facilitators are compressed representatively. Carl's identity is disguised by use of a psuedonym and his parents have given written permission to share the content of any of his treatment that would contribute to this chapter.

Vignette 1. Engagement and *Preaffiliation*

Following an initial phone call with Carl's parents, it was determined that he would benefit from the boys' relational group, and a prescreening meeting was arranged with Carl and his parents. A summary of the meeting is recounted in Table 9.1.

Table 9.1 First Impressions.

Content	Rationale/Analysis
Worker: "Welcome. It is so nice to meet you. We are going to spend some time together today talking about a wonderful group I cofacilitate. I will answer any questions you have about it and then you may decide whether you would like to join. "Let me begin with a description. It is a group for boys your age that meets for an hour each week for a total of 12 sessions. There will be six or seven boys in the group. We play games together, some of which I may introduce, and many of which the boys create. Sometimes we use acting and drama, dance, music, and art to express ourselves. We talk about challenges in our lives and provide support to each other. Boys really feel heard in group and they know this is their special time to care for themselves and for each other. The experience of giving and taking is a wonderful one. The group is a very private, safe, and	Giving a brief and detailed description of the group in the beginning helps to decrease children's and families' natural apprehensions about the nature of group. It gives them an opportunity to listen and take in the details rather than feeling as though they are being asked a lot of personal questions to see if they are the right fit for the group. This meeting often occurs after an initial phone conversation, at which time it is determined that a potential member would benefit from the group. *Preaffiliation* begins on the phone and in this initial meeting, as members are weighing the pros and cons of joining the group. It is important to remember that change is hard for everyone. Even if someone wants to change, it requires taking a great deal of risk and letting go of cherished ways of coping with challenges. It is a loss. Acknowledging this is one of the most important parts of engagement. It is always the facilitator's job to integrate the positive and

(continued)

Table 9.1 continued

Content	Rationale/Analysis
comfortable space. Boys often say, 'There is no place like it in the world.' While playing and talking, we also work on learning and practicing some important skills that help boys learn how to create and nurture friendships. Together, we learn about cooperation, negotiation, problem solving, and resolving conflicts. I assure you that it will be a great deal of fun and that there will be conflict. I know that conflict can feel scary, but we have a lot of creative ideas about ways to work through difficult times. The only commitment we need from you is that you will keep coming to group even when it is difficult. We will help you with the rest. Does this sound fair?" Carl: "Yes, it sounds fair."	negative aspects of experiences as a natural part of life. At the same time, the worker can assure children and their families that we have many creative solutions to working through conflict and that we have faith in the group's ability to stay connected.
Worker: "Now that I have described the group, would you be willing to join?" Carl: "No thanks. I don't really want to be around other kids and I don't have any favorite hobbies. I'm not allowed to do anything I want to do anyway! I can't eat or drink the things I want, can't swim, can't do a lot of things other kids can do." Worker: "I hear that you feel you haven't had the opportunity to do a lot of things you have wanted to do because of what you have been coping with for so long. This must be so hard for you." Carl: "Yes, it is hard!" Worker: "Well, may I ask you one thing?" Carl: "Yes." Worker: "I admire how many risks you take every day by doing things you don't want to do, especially related to medical treatment. If you take a risk, and pull from the same courage you use every day to cope with these challenges, I think you will be pleasantly surprised. It would also be great for you to share some of your courage with the other boys. They could learn so much from you. I believe you will learn a lot from them as well. Kids really look forward to coming to group every week. There may actually be a lot of things you can do that other children do. If you give it a chance, I think you will like it. Would you be willing to try?"	Carl's reluctance is normal. We are often asking people who are the most uncomfortable in social situations to participate in one. His thoughts about the group are negative at first; therefore, it is important to validate his feelings and their origins. He has experienced a lot of disappointment and is probably very scared. It is equally important to recognize and celebrate his strengths and resilience. This helps him and his family to see that you are aware of the challenges he faces and the inherent strength and courage he possesses. You are acknowledging the problem and pointing out that he already has many of the tools to fix it. This is the act of creating and instilling hope (Yalom & Leszcz, 2005), and it is essential throughout the life of the group.

Carl: "Okay. I'll *try* it . . . but no guarantees because I probably won't like it."

Worker: "Fair enough. Thank you so much for taking this risk. It says a lot about you that you are willing to do it even though you don't want to. Once boys agree to being in the group, they each identify one goal they would like to work on over the next 12 weeks. We only choose one because we want you to be able to focus on it completely. Each boy's goal is different. I will allow you to decide if you want to share it with the others."

As mentioned earlier in the contract, clearly stating the group purpose, expectations, and members' individual goal is essential in conducting effective group work. Taking the time to do this will greatly decrease the chances of having attrition. Choosing a small, attainable goal is important because it offers people an opportunity to focus on something specific and track their progress.

Worker: "Carl, what would you like your goal to be?"

Carl: "I don't really need to work on anything."

Worker: "It is important that every boy come to group with a goal. Is there anything you wish you could change in your social life?"

Carl: "Nope."

Worker: "May we see if your parents have any ideas?"

Carl: "Fine."

Parents: "Well, our favorite thing about you, Carl, is how determined you are about things. Your perseverance has helped you cope with a great deal of stress, and we have a lot of admiration for this quality. However, we wonder if this same determination may have a different result in social situations. Sometimes other kids may see it as inflexibility. Friendships, just like sibling relationships, require a lot of compromise, and this may be hard for you sometimes. We know there are so many things out of your control medically and so it makes sense that you may want to control as much as possible. We are just concerned because if things don't go your way you often give up on a relationship. There are so many great friendships out there for you if you would just give them a chance."

Carl: "That isn't true! I don't need to hear this. I'm leaving." [He walks to the door.]

Worker: "Carl, wait a second. It is understandable that you would want control. I would feel the same way if I were you. What if we just have you work on staying connected through the good and bad times? This is all you have to work on, and we will help you with the rest."

Collaborating about choosing a goal is one of the most important parts of group process and can also feel like the most difficult aspect. However, once the goal is identified by the member and it is made small and achievable, remarkable growth happens. All too often in life we are working on changing too many things at once or have very high expectations of ourselves. It is a luxury to be able to focus on a single, yet pertinent, goal and devote all energy to accomplishing it. Being more flexible probably felt like it was too daunting of a goal, but showing up and staying connected was one that Carl could agree to and which would ultimately help him with the larger goal when he was ready.

(continued)

Table 9.1 continued

Content	Rationale/Analysis
Carl: "I don't want to because it annoys me!" Worker: "It makes perfect sense that you leave when you are annoyed. The only problem is that there isn't an opportunity to work through those feelings. If you stay connected, there is a chance that you would feel less annoyed. Would you be willing to just give this a try?" Carl: "Fine (rolling his eyes), but I doubt it will work." Worker: "Thanks again for the taking the risk."	

Vignette 2. Jim and the Bumblebees: Moving from *Preaffiliation to Conflict to Intimacy*

One of Carl's first groups was composed of five boys, ages 7 to 10. Several had trouble controlling their impulses, some were struggling academically, one had very significant social anxiety, and another had witnessed a great deal of community and school violence and was experiencing subsequent anxiety. One of the boys emerged as the dominant member immediately. Jim had some of the most extreme symptoms of attention-deficit/hyperactivity disorder I have seen. I privately named the group "Jim and the bumblebees" because it somehow captured the incredible amount of energy buzzing in the group at any given moment. Our thought when composing this group was that big energy would equate to big potential for growth when used productively and constructively. All of the boys presented with different challenges, yet they all had one in common: difficulty making friends. We did not compose the group based on diagnoses, but rather chose boys who had very different communication and coping styles knowing that it would take some time for them to find ways to communicate meaningfully; yet the process of learning each other's styles would bring forth incredible learning opportunities. Table 9.2 recounts some of the group challenges.

Table 9.2 Weathering the Storm

Content	Rationale/Analysis
Within moments of our first session, our anxious members where hiding under tables. Jim was climbing all over the room and calling the other boys names. Carl was trying to keep everyone connected, but was clearly frustrated, as he kept attempting to leave the room. We gently invited Carl back to group and said to Jim, "Wow, you have a real gift!" He was curious, came over and wanted to hear more. "You have such a cool brain that you are aware of everything going on in this room and outside all at once. You have a very powerful mind, a superhero brain! It must also be overwhelming at times to have to pay attention to everything! You must get tired, or just want a	Instead of trying to control the members and change their behaviors right away, we created an alliance with their energy to demonstrate our willingness to accept and contain it without an immediate goal of changing it (Azima, 1989); instead, the focus was on self-understanding (Yalom & Leszcz, 2005). This stopped them in their tracks and piqued their curiosity. They wanted to know what we were all about.

break sometimes." He was nodding his head and said, "Yeah," in a soft voice, almost seeming amazed that someone understood his experience and even more astonished that his ability to multitask could be seen positively, since it often got him into trouble. The other bumblebees buzzed closer to us, and before we knew it we were back in a circle again, and we were the most interesting flowers in the room. Suddenly we were a group rather than a bunch of buzzing individuals.

We quickly grabbed their attention while they were intrigued and briefly had them brainstorm on the spot about the rules they wanted to create. The main rule they came up with in the moment was, "Nobody gets hurt, not their feelings or their bodies."

Having members create their own rules is empowering. The more they are invested in this process, the more committed they will be to following the guidelines. This is often the first time these children have been asked by an adult to make up their own rules; therefore, this experience will leave an impression. It will also lay the foundation for them to see the group as a unique and special place where they each have a powerful voice. Part of the engagement process with children and adolescents requires creating curiosity and interest in the midst of the anxiety and apprehension that exists around new experiences. It is useful to write their rules on a piece of poster board and bring them to group each week. The more permanence the rules have, the more they will be cherished. This process is an important component to creating clear expectations and is useful in groups with members of all ages.

We then talked about what to do when their first rule is broken, because it will be. They seemed relieved by this statement and decided that no one would be "kicked out of group or shamed." This indicated to us how many times this has happened to them in the past. Instead, we decided as a group that we would slow ourselves down by saying the word "freeze." As soon as the word was spoken, everyone would become still like a statue and we would explore why the freeze was called. The freeze would not be used to blame anyone, but simply to point out an event so we could all learn from each other and make sure it did not happen again in the same fashion. It was also decided that anyone could call a freeze.

The fact that rules will be broken is universal (Yalom & Leszcz, 2005), and normalizing it is critical. It gives people permission to make mistakes. Talking about how to handle it when they are broken is equally important, because it decreases children's anxieties about consequences. The "freeze" technique also helps children practice impulse control, and it is not a word that is negatively charged, such as "no" or "stop." In fact, the process becomes playful, because it resembles games that kids enjoy, such as freeze tag.

(continued)

Table 9.2 continued

Content	Rationale/Analysis
During the first session, in the midst of dialogue and play, we heard the following: Jim: "I'm going to kill you!" Carl: "Freeze!" Worker: "What happened?" Carl: "Jim just said he was going to kill me and it scared me; I'm out of here!" [Leaves the room.] Worker: [Meeting Carl outside the room.] "CB, please wait a moment and let the group respond to what you said." Carl: "I don't need to hear any response. I'm right and JV is wrong. What is the point of having rules if people are going to disrespect them?" [Crosses his arms.] Worker: "As we mentioned, the rules will be broken at first until we learn new skills." Carl: "I don't have time for this! If I go back in, he needs to apologize. Do you promise this will happen?" Worker: "Well, you can tell him how you feel and it will be up to him about how he responds. I am so proud of you for sticking with this. You are really working hard on your goal." [We start to reenter the room.] Carl: "Nope, forget it! I'm not going unless you can promise." Worker: "I think it will be more important for Jim to hear you tell him what you need than for me to say it. You are very good at telling people what you need. Let's go in as planned and I'll support you in expressing your feelings. Sound good?" Carl: "I guess, but this had better work or I'm out of here!" [Reluctantly reenters the room.] Worker: "Thank you for doing this even though it is hard." Jim: [To Carl as soon as he enters the room . . .] "I'm sorry. I was just kidding [smiling]." Carl: "But you are smiling and it isn't funny. It is serious! [Looking to me . . .] Do you see what I mean? He doesn't care." Worker: [To everyone . . .] "Do you guys ever smile at times other than when you are happy?" Other boys: "Yes."	During these interactions, members began to recognize that we believed in their ability to work through conflicts with a little guidance from us. Whenever possible, we invited all of the boys to participate in the resolution process so they could benefit as much as possible from mutual aid. We empathically reminded the boys that they are each in the group to work on something different and that it will take us some time to reach our goals. Doing this reminds members that the things linking them together are greater than the sum of their differences (Steinberg, 2004). While Jim could have been perceived as the bully and could have been scapegoated by the others, the members were able to take our lead and build an alliance with him and his behaviors without an immediate need to change him. They responded to him with forgiveness, understanding, and compassion. As a result, Jim was able to be accountable for his actions without fear of shame or punishment. His disclosure and accountability allowed him to emerge as a leader, and he earned respect from his peers. Interpersonal learning (Yalom & Leszcz, 2005) happened when Carl and the other boys in turn benefited from Jim's growth. Carl journeyed a great deal in this session as well. At first he was resistant to connect, then frustrated by the conflict and ready to give up, and finally confident in his ability to stay connected through hard times. Watching Jim openly talk about his goal and work on it seemed to inspire Carl to do the same. It was cathartic (Yalom & Leszcz, 2005) when he realized that he is in control of himself and the way he chooses to interact with others. Giving our group members choices provided an opportunity for them to see that they could create change in themselves and in the entire group culture.

Worker: "Like when?"

Another boy: "When I'm nervous."

All boys: "Yes, definitely."

Worker: "Do you think it would be helpful for Carl to stay in the room for a minute and let Jim respond to how he is feeling?"

Other boys: "Yes, please stay."

Carl: [Arms still crossed . . .] "Fine!"

Jim: "Sorry [genuinely]."

Carl: [Looking shocked yet pleased.] "It's okay."

The boys are now playing a game . . .

Jim: "I'll karate chop you!"

Carl: "Freeze"

Worker: "What happened?"

Carl: "After everything we went through, Jim just made another threat."

Jim: "No I didn't!"

Other boys: "Yes you did, but you aren't in trouble."

Carl: "There are other ways to play without saying mean things."

Jim: "Okay, I did say it. I don't even know I'm doing it."

Carl: "Well, we will help you. This why we come to group."

Jim: "Thanks."

Carl: "Sure."

Jim: "You're weird!"

Carl: "Freeze."

Jim: "I know, I know, I know . . . you don't need to say it. I was kiddin' around again and it hurt your feelings. Man, I really need to work on this. It's why I'm here. I feel out of control sometimes and do and say things I don't mean."

Worker: "Does this ever happen to any of you?"

All boys: "Yes."

Worker: "Jim, does it make you feel better to know that you are not alone?"

Jim: "Oh, yes! Sometimes I feel like the only one this happens to."

The other boys each give examples of times when it has happened to them.

(continued)

Table 9.2 continued

Content	Rationale/Analysis
Worker: "Thank you, Jim, for being so open and honest about the things you are working on. It took courage to do this. Would you boys agree?"	
Other boys: "Definitely!"	
Carl: "Thanks [proudly]."	
The boys are playing again . . .	
Jim: "You're too old to be in the first grade."	
Carl: "Freeze!"	
Jim: "It was me, *again*, sorry.	
Other boys: It's okay, we know, you are working on it. [All are laughing with him.]	

Vignette 3. Fight or Flight: The Wish for and Fear of Emotional Intimacy

Historic Background

Two years later, Carl was in session number 15 of a boys group that was about to terminate. There were five members, and three were present during this session. Carl was now nine years old and had been in several groups since the previous vignette. Up until a few sessions prior to this he had not disclosed his renal failure in the group. He made it a point to keep his "two worlds separate." He made his first disclosure several sessions prior to this vignette, at which time he informed his peers that he "had no kidneys and was hooked up to a dialysis machine to filter the waste" from his body. He proceeded to show them his catheter and many of his scars he received from past medical procedures. Last, he shared that there are many things he cannot eat or drink because of his medical situation and that he has to be particularly careful about his exposure to germs because he is immunosuppressed. His four peers had a difficult time processing the information. Their reactions ranged from fear for his safety to disgust about the details he shared. It was clear that Carl longed for them to respond more supportively and empathically, because he brought up the topic in each subsequent session.

The strengths Carl had displayed over the years in prior groups were his exceptional emotional intelligence, strong communication skills, empathic attunement, and motivation to form emotionally intimate friendships. It is clear that many of his original challenges had already been addressed by this time. His goals during this group were to be more flexible and to continue to stay connected during times of conflict, as shown in Table 9.3.

Table 9.3 Negotiation

Content	Rationale/Analysis
The group discussion revolved around voting on an activity for the day. A talking object was used to help members take turns listening to each other. Initially, the boys were able to come up with a list of possible games to play. However, they became stuck when they could not reach an	It is important to encourage group members to work together during times of conflict. In this case, all of the boys want to be friends, they are simply having a difficult time speaking the same language because they have such different communication styles and different

agreement. As members struggled to find resolution, the frustration level grew.

Carl: "I have some concerns about some of these games. I worry about playing dodgeball because of my dressing. If I were to be hit in the stomach, it could really hurt me. I remember when we used to play ball with Jim [from the earlier vignette, who had a difficult time controlling his impulses, much like James and Donald] that he used to accidentally hurt me sometimes."

James: "Gross. Stop talking. I'm going to throw up!" [In the past, James has shared that he wants topics of illness and death to be "off limits" in group.]

Carl: [Looks shocked and hurt by this statement and attempts to explain, with desperation.] "I need to share this information so that you will understand my experience. It is really important!"

James: [Gesturing by putting his fingers in his ears . . .] "I'm not listening to you! I told you I don't want to talk about these things!"

Donald: [Joining with James . . .] "Stop talking. We don't want to hear about your business; it's none of our business!!" [He screamed this across the room and appeared very frustrated and annoyed with Carl for bringing up the topic.]

Worker: "I just want to point out that we are all here for the same reason, which is to make friends. Sometimes friends experience difficult times. We have been struggling with this conflict for a few weeks now and it sounds like you boys have very different needs right now. How could we compromise so that everyone has their needs met?"

Carl: "Well, the reason we come to group is to talk about our feelings. That is what friendship is all about. We are supposed to talk about the things we need help with and to share our personal business. Group is personal and so is friendship."

Donald: "I come here to play games, that's it."

James: "Me too!"

definitions for, as well as expectations of, friendship. Carl had a wish for emotional intimacy and a need to express feeling vulnerable, whereas James and Donald had a wish for connection through play and physical activity and felt uncomfortable talking about emotions.

Interview with Carl

It was evident that Carl had transformed over the course of four years. He journeyed from not wanting friends to developing some of the most profound and intimate relationships with peers. He

(continued)

not only explored his feelings about his medical challenges but also about his coping style and relationships with family. This rich process inspired many other children as well as me. When interviewing Carl about his experience in group over the years, he stated that his most memorable moments consisted of "making some enemies and lots of friends, bubble contests, creative games, and confidence." His favorite aspect of group is that "no one gets left out." He further explained that in school someone is always an outsider. The privacy we create in group is also very important to him. "It is the only place where I can be myself and talk completely freely without being teased, because what's said in group stays in group. It was only after we created this rule that I felt comfortable opening up. It is different than seeing my psychiatrist or individual therapist because I know it is completely confidential and just my private space." I asked what lessons he has learned from the groups, and he stated, "to communicate better, make friends, and feel confident." In fact, during one of his final sessions of group to date, I asked him and his peers in a very casual fashion what they had learned from group, and their response was so profound that my cofacilitator grabbed the closest thing to write on and documented their responses on a paper plate. These were the boys' responses:

12/17/07
1. To respect each other.
2. Pay attention.
3. No hurting people.
4. Listening to others.
5. Having troubles and working them out.
6. Humor in bad situations is helpful.
7. Self-esteem.
8. Personal space.
9. No touching others.
10. Controlling anger.
11. How to get along.
12. Keeping group business in group.
13. Good sportsmanship.
14. Not judging.
15. *Go with the flow!!*

The co-facilitator and I were moved by the number of lessons listed so effortlessly by the boys as they were celebrating their experience and eating cupcakes during the ending ceremony.

Carl's family, treatment team, and I witnessed how much of a leader he has become over the years, especially on the dialysis unit. He has really nurtured and taught the younger patients about how to cope during medical procedures and has shown them an enormous amount of care and compassion.

In terms of his actual medical treatment, his mother states that "he can swallow eight pills at a time, give himself a daily injection, wheel into surgery stone sober, and hold the anesthesia mask over his own face as he chats with surgeons. He goes to hemodialysis three afternoons a week, where he holds perfectly still and verbally guides nurses as they insert juice-box-straw-sized needles into his thigh. Carl has done everything asked of him with aplomb. Superheroes have nothing on him. He is the bravest person I know."

Summary

Group work is an efficient and effective mode for treatment with children and families coping with illness. As evidenced in the case vignettes, members can make a great deal of progress in a short period of time due to the power of mutual aid and the experience of belonging. Additionally, feeling like a change agent in one's own life and in larger groups lends to the enhancement of self-esteem. It is common for children with chronic medical illness to want to be integrated into a group with children who are not struggling in this way. Groups are a microcosm of life and allow people to work through many of their past challenges in the present. This can be a powerful and corrective experience for everyone involved. It allows them to define themselves in ways other than their medical diagnosis. It is during intrapsychic and interpersonal conflict that many grow and learn the most, and this is certainly what lends to greater group intimacy. The more comfortable we all feel with conflict, the more we will see opportunities in life rather than roadblocks. Navigating these challenges together lends to a sense of greater group intimacy and social connection. These are the very factors that build on our clients' inherent resilience.

People of many disciplines may be group workers. In the context of this chapter, the role of the medical social worker has been reviewed and group work from a social work perspective discussed. The theoretical models that guide this practice are strength- and empowerment-based. They are grounded in group stage theory, with particular attention given to gender differences and populations who feel marginalized or oppressed. Historically, social workers are trained to recognize and build upon the intrinsic strength and resilience of clients coping with medical challenges. For these reasons, they are important members of treatment teams in medical settings. The vitality created through a multidisciplinary team representing varying perspectives, training backgrounds, and communication styles parallels the vitality we aim to create when composing groups of clients. Just as we model celebrating these differences as facilitators, it is equally important to do so with our colleagues.

As we are all aware but often don't fully appreciate in life, groups are ubiquitous. Everyone belongs to them and has experience as both a member and leader and social groups parallel therapeutic groups in many ways. Facilitators work to engage members, clearly state group purpose, and work to create a culture of safety and support in the beginning of the group. When members feel empowered, when conflict is welcomed, and when creativity and playfulness are encouraged, the group takes on a life of its own, and members move from being individuals to being individuals who contribute to a collective force. The experience of belonging, of having a powerful voice, and of feeling like a change agent in your life and in the world is invaluable. This is the magical space in which deep emotional and physical healing happens at times with great work and effort and sometimes with comfort and ease. As group healing continues, the lessons internalized by members will ripple through families, medical settings, and other vital arenas of our lives as the group continues.

References

Azima, F., & Richmond, L. (1989). *Adolescent group psychotherapy*. Madison, CT: International Universities Press, Inc.

Bronfenbrenner, U. (1979). *The ecology of human development: Experiments by nature and design*. Cambridge, MA: Harvard University Press.

Carrell, S. (2000). *Group exercises for adolescents* (2nd ed.). London, England: Sage Publications, Inc.

Christ, G., Sormanti, M., & Francoeur, R. (2001). Chronic physical illness and disability. In A. Gitterman (Ed.), *Handbook of social work practice with vulnerable and resilient populations* (2nd ed., pp. 124–162). New York: Columbia University Press.

Garland, J., (1986). The relationship between group work and group therapy. In M. Parnes (Ed.), *Innovations in social group work: Feedback from practice to theory*. New York: Hawthorn Press.

Garland, J., Jones, H., & Kolodny, R. (1965). A model for stages of development in social work group. In S. Bernstein (Ed.), *Explorations in group work* (pp. 17–71). Boston, MA: Milford House, Inc.

Gitterman, A. (Ed.). (2001). *Handbook of social work practice with vulnerable and resilient populations, second edition*. New York: Columbia University Press.

Gutierrez, L., Parsons, R., & Cox, I . (1998). *Empowerment in social work practice: A sourcebook*. Monterey, CA: Brooks/Cole Publishing Company.

Northern, H., & Kurland, R. (2001). *Social work with groups* (3rd ed.). New York: Columbia University Press.

Schiller, L. (1995). Stages of development in women's groups: A relational model. In R. Kurland & R. Salmon (Eds.), *Group work practice in troubled society*. New York: Haworth Press, Inc.

Schiller, L. (1997) Rethinking stages of development in women's groups: Implications for practice. *Social work with groups* (Vol. 20, no. 3, pp. 3–19). New York: Haworth Press, Inc.

Simon, B. (1994). *The empowerment tradition in American social work: A history*. New York: Columbia Press.

Steinberg, D. (2004). *The mutual-aid approach to working with groups, helping people help each other* (2nd ed.). New York: Haworth Press, Inc.

Surry, J. (1991). The self in relation: A theory of women's development. In J. Jordan, A. Kaplan, J. B. Miller, I. Stiver, & J. Surry (Eds.), *Women's growth in connection* (pp. 51–66). New York: Guilford Press.

Wharff, E. (1982). *Parents' group on a pediatric unit: A follow-up study*. Unpublished master's thesis, Smith College School of Social Work.

Yalom, I., & Leszcz, M. (2005). *The theory and practice of group psychotherapy* (5th ed.). New York: Basic Books.

Play and Expressive Therapies with Medically Challenged Children and Adolescents

Nancy Boyd Webb

Child therapists help children, adolescents, and their families deal with a variety of emotional problems related to interpersonal conflict, stress, unhappiness, and instability. School personnel, pediatricians, and others who notice that something is wrong may refer young people to mental health agencies or to private practitioners for specialized evaluation and treatment to resolve their relational or personal problems. Because chronic illness and disability affect approximately 15 percent of young people, any practitioner who treats children and youth will sooner or later encounter a child with some form of medical condition that coexists with the problem that prompted the referral. Occasionally, youth are brought for mental health assistance specifically to help them learn to cope with a chronic condition such as asthma, obesity, or diabetes. This chapter encompasses the use of play and expressive therapy for young people in *both* types of situations—those having difficulty adjusting and living with a chronic medical condition and those who have other family or personal problems in addition to serious health challenges.

Play and Expressive Therapies as Helping Interventions

Anyone, whether adult or child, who has a severe medical condition, worries about the impact of this illness or disability on his or her present and future life. The older the individuals, the more they will understand about the possible ill effects of their prognosis and its likely course. Many children and adolescents become very preoccupied about how their illness or disability will affect their capacity to participate in physical activities with their peers, and some become discouraged and even depressed when they realize that there will be necessary restrictions. Some worry about dying. Therapy gives these young people the opportunity to express and process their feelings of confusion, anger, fear, and sadness with someone who can understand and who can help them refocus on the positive aspects of their lives.

Play and Expressive Therapy

Treatment of children often employs various forms of play, using toys, puppets, dolls, drawings, and games to help them obtain mastery (in symbolic play) over their overwhelming anxieties. The rationale of play therapy rests on the assumption that the child uses play materials as projections of his or her inner world. The play therefore provides a sort of camouflage and the distance necessary for psychological safety (Bromfield, 2003). For example, in the minds of children at play, it is the toy dinosaur that is trying to win the race against the animal friends, not themselves.

As I have stated elsewhere, "clinicians who refer to themselves as 'play therapists' come from many different disciplines . . . and all have had specialized training and supervision on an advanced level" (Webb, 2003, pp. 149–150). Many play therapists employ art methods in their work with children (Goodman, 2007); others utilize stories (Mills, 2006); and still others use sandplay (Carey, 2006). The scope of the field of play therapy is defined more by its symbolic use of the child's play as a helping method than by the use of any specific play materials or techniques. Actually, "the possibilities of using play therapeutically are limited only by the imagination and creativity of the child and therapist" (Webb, 2007, p. 63).

Expressive and creative arts therapies incorporate and encompass many of the same principles and methods as play therapy. In fact, there is considerable overlap among these fields, and many training programs in expressive arts therapy include play therapy within the umbrella of the overall field. Conversely, play therapists routinely use art and music as ways to engage children in therapy. The goals of creative arts and expressive therapies are very similar to those of play therapy, namely, to help individuals express their feelings and obtain symptom relief through symbolic expression. One of the first graduate schools to offer courses in the emerging field of expressive therapies, 30 years ago (Lesley University, web site, 2008), states in its publicity that its program trains students to engage clients in healing through the therapeutic use of the arts. This is accomplished by integrating the modalities of dance, drama, music, poetry, literature, and visual arts with psychotherapy. Because of its wide range and intrinsic appeal to older youth (and even adults, throughout the life cycle), creative therapy approaches have been very useful in providing outlets for self-expression and personal growth. Readers who want to explore specific methods can refer to the following sources:

- Music therapy (Austin, 2006; Dileo, 1999; Loewy & Stewart, 2004)
- Drama therapy (Glass, 2006; Haen, 2008; Landy, 1994)
- Art therapy (Kramer, 1993; Malchodi, 2008; Rubin, 2005)

- Play therapy (Landreth, 2002; Schaefer, 2003; Webb, 2007)
- Sandplay (Carey, 1999; Dundas, 1994; Lowenfeld, 1993)

Frey (2006) suggests that some of the creative arts methods (e.g., art, poetry writing, or music) might be more appealing to adolescents than typical play therapy approaches, which teenagers might consider childish because they involve the use of puppets, dolls, blocks, or stuffed animals. Instead, adolescents may prefer the clinician's invitation to write in a journal or to view certain films and then discuss with the therapist their feelings about the main characters or about the circumstances depicted in the film. This method, called *video play therapy* (Frey, 2005), attempts to help the young person (or adult) identify certain themes or situations in a video or film that resonate with his or her own life. Sometimes the therapist suggests that the youth reenact segments of these stories with puppets or through sandplay. This enables further exploration of the motivation of the story characters, along with planning about what might happen to them in the future. All these creative arts methods are based on the principles of identification and displacement, and the story exploration is a metaphor for the young person's own life. When young people speculate about the future of a story character, they are often testing out a possible personal option. These creative methods therefore provide young clients a way to express feelings and to explore new avenues in a fantasy trial that may serve as a rehearsal for their own future.

Training in Play or Expressive Arts Therapy

It is essential that clinicians receive appropriate training and supervision in using creative arts for the benefit of their child clients. The appendix lists selected training locations in different parts of the country. Social workers, school counselors, nurses, and clinical pediatric psychologists are some of the many different professionals who provide therapy for children who are having emotional difficulties. All play or creative arts therapists must have master's-level knowledge of child development and psychology in addition to specialized training in the therapeutic use of expressive arts methods.

Using Creative Therapies with Medically Challenged Youth

Because the diagnosis of a serious medical illness can be very confusing and upsetting to children and adolescents and their families, creative art and play methods can help them express their feelings and obtain some relief. This may occur in the hospital setting, where *art or music therapists* are members of the staff who can offer helping interventions that provide comfort to the hospitalized child. (See examples in Loewy & Stewart,

2004; Martin, 2008; and Goodman, 2007.) Other times, a *child life specialist* may work with the child using either pretend or actual medical equipment in order to familiarize the young person regarding the hospital environment and a forthcoming medical procedure. (See Chapter 5 for more specifics and examples.) Because of the constraints of managed care, however, many children remain hospitalized for only short periods of time (Rae & Sullivan, 2005). Then the challenge of providing ongoing psychosocial therapy falls upon outpatient clinics and schools, where expressive therapists and other practitioners may deal with the youths' feelings about their past and current medical experiences.

During the early diagnostic phase of an illness, the young person may be hospitalized, at which point medical treatment is a primary concern. It takes time for the child and the family to comprehend the long-term implications of a serious medical condition. As indicated in Chapter 4, this initial hospitalization may actually qualify as a traumatic experience because of the child's (and parents') extreme anxiety about the unknown, and because of repeated experiences of painful medical procedures such as injections, spinal taps, and IV drips. Short-term crisis intervention can help by giving education about the illness and by providing helping methods to assist young people in dealing with their fears. Examples of some specific anxiety-reduction techniques are presented later in this chapter.

Once the child has been discharged and a medical protocol has been established, the child continues to benefit from counseling focused on processing his or her feelings related to the medical experiences as well as with various fears and anxieties about the long-term implications of the condition or disability. A consultation with a play therapist in an outpatient clinic or in private practice can provide a welcome opportunity for the child to deal with these issues in a nonthreatening atmosphere. In addition, because the child may require repeated hospitalizations over the course of many years, sequential contact with the same creative arts therapist in the medical setting often becomes a regular part of treatment for both the child and the parents (Goodman, 2007; Hom, in Chapter 1 of this book). This continuity in staff relationships offers the comfort of familiarity to a young person who is undergoing a series of painful medical procedures.

Medical Play Materials

A play therapist who anticipates working with children with acute or chronic health conditions should acquire an array of toys that will facilitate medical play. These include, for example, a toy medical kit with syringes, bandages, a toy or actual stethoscope, thermometer, and surgical masks. In addition, it is useful to have doctor and nurse puppets and dolls, pretend hospital beds, and hospital dollhouses, ambulances, and dolls that appear to have medical disabilities requiring crutches and/or wheelchairs. Some hospitals have separate playrooms that contain this equipment where the child and therapist meet alone or together with the parents. When the child is bedridden, the clinician sees the child in his or her room and brings an assortment of play and drawing material on a cart. Of course, this specialized play equipment makes it relatively easy for the child to engage in play that resonates with his or her own medical experience. However, some children may be too anxious or ill to attempt any such reenactments, and it is, of course, countertherapeutic to urge a child to engage in any play activity that causes excessive discomfort. Therefore, an array of nonthreatening, standard, and neutral play materials also should be available so that the child can pick and choose according to his or her inclinations and comfort level.

All play therapists subscribe to the belief in the importance of establishing a warm, supportive therapeutic relationship with the child as the foundation for engaging in play that may create anxiety. Involving the parent in the child's therapeutic play (either as an observer or a participant) may also help ease the child's anxiety. The goal of this play is to assist the child to develop a sense of understanding and mastery with regard to his or her experience. During medical procedures, the child has been helpless and disempowered. The play situation serves to reverse that temporarily by permitting the child to take on the role of the doctor, if he or she wishes, and to administer numerous shots and other treatments to the doll patient. In addition to medical play, other methods, such as art, music, or creative writing, encourage children and adolescents to express feelings symbolically and thereby gain a sense of mastery over the frightening experience.

Art Therapy

Some directive-structured techniques have been found to facilitate the expression and working through of an individual's complex responses to medical procedures. These techniques might include the drawing of a mandala, the drawing of how a family has changed due to medical circumstances, and the creation of a scary drawing (Sourkes, 1991). The art therapist responds to the child's drawings with questions intended to elicit the child's feelings about his or her medical experience and then makes some supportive comments regarding the content of the child's expression.

For example, the *mandala drawing exercise* (Sourkes, 1991) involves asking the young person to color in a circle with colors that correspond to the different feelings that surfaced when the child was first diagnosed with cancer. The youth is given a choice of eight colors to use in naming and coloring his or her different feelings about the experience. The exercise can also be used to identify feelings associated with other topics, such as anticipating the return to school or hearing about another patient's death. Children experience this technique as nonthreatening, and even enjoyable, because it requires little coordination or drawing ability, and the drawing and talking bring a sense of relief.

The *change-in-family drawing* (Sourkes, 1991) asks the child to first draw a picture of his or her family and then to either draw or say "what changed in your family after you got sick." The *scariest drawing* gives the child the opportunity to think about and then draw the scariest experience, thought, feeling, or dream since he or she became ill (Sourkes, 1991, p. 90). Obviously, all three of these drawing exercises will evoke complicated and powerful responses that encourage the child to express fears that might never be expressed through verbal means alone.

It has been said that a picture is worth a thousand words, and all child therapists know that the symbolic meaning of a child's drawing may convey a compelling message. This was true, for example, in the drawing by a five-year-old boy being treated for leukemia, as shown in Figure 10.1 (Goodman, 2007).

This child drew a "cactus family," with needles very prominently displayed on the "bodies" of the mother, father, and son cactus plants. The cactus son was in the middle and quite a bit larger than the other two; the boy said that it was because he was on prednisone (Goodman, 2007). The child made this drawing after several months of outpatient medical treatments, including chemotherapy, bone marrow aspirations, and spinal taps, during which time the art therapist had provided a variety of play and art activities to help the boy understand and express his feelings about these stressful experiences. She also had counseled the parents on a regular basis to help them deal better with the stresses of their child's illness and their divergent methods of handling this experience.

Figure 10.1

A Cactus Family

Another focus of the clinical work with this child involved helping him with his sense of self as a good, whole person despite his cancer. It is typical for young children to think that they acquired an illness because of something "bad" that they did. When the boy in this example began having temper tantrums, he sometimes screamed "I'm no good! I'm dumb and stupid! It's the chemo" (Goodman, 2007, p. 215). The therapist helped this child to deal with his frustration through a combination of art activities and positive reframing. She encouraged the boy to think of all the various ways that could help him get through the many difficult procedures he had to endure. The boy, his mother, and the therapist later made a list of 11 different coping strategies, such as deep breathing, thinking of nice things, and finding out what was going to happen and why (Goodman, 2007, p. 209). This cognitive strategy ("Tim's Tips") proved to be useful in calming the boy when he felt anxious about upcoming procedures.

Music Therapy

Music can be soothing, exciting, inspirational, or frightening depending on its rhythms, tones, instrumentation, and context. Because parents so often sing and rock their babies in their arms to comfort them, music seems to have the power to connect on a preverbal level.

The field of music therapy began in the 1950s, following World War II, to train practitioners about the "use of music to restore, improve, or maintain health and well-being" (Loewy & Stewart, 2004, p. 192). Since that time, it has developed into a field with more than 74 training programs in the United States, many of which prepare practitioners to work in the medical field. A medical music psychotherapy approach permits and encourages children and adults to improvise or write songs that deal with the significant issues in their lives, which often include their reactions to medical treatment.

In the hospital, music therapy sessions are held in a separate room (if available and if the child is physically able to leave his or her room). Another option is for the music therapist to wheel a cart with an assortment of different instruments near the hospitalized child's bed. The therapist then invites the child to select an instrument and play it. Typical instruments available include tambourines, drums, cymbals, gongs, and metallophones, to name just a few. After the child make a selection, the therapist then selects a different instrument and plays along with the child. The music therapist waits for the child to take the lead and then asks the child about his choice and whether he or she would like to make up his own special song to sing with his instrument. Or if he prefers, the therapist suggests that they select a familiar song, such as "Humpty Dumpty," "Ring Around the Rosy," or "The Wheels of the Bus" and create his *own* words to the melody. During the back-and-forth singing, the therapist encourages the child to change the words and sing whatever he or she wants. Much of the therapy session consists of elaborating and collaborating on the individual child's story song (Rubin-Bosco, 2002). Using this method, the therapist responds musically to the child's initial song selection and sings about new options and coping strategies within the context of the child's story theme. Obviously, this method requires great sensitivity and skill on the part of the music therapist, who must respond rapidly to the child's mood and content as part of the exploration of the musical play interaction.

An example of music therapy with a seven-year-old boy appears in Loewy and Stewart (2004) and is presented here with permission of the authors. Scotty, age 7, had a chronic illness that caused severe joint pain and that required hospitalization three or four times a year. During all these hospitalizations, Scotty was engaged in music therapy and also attended music therapy groups on an outpatient basis. The compelling issue for this child was his recurrent pain and separation fears.

The music therapy sessions with Scotty dealt with his ongoing fear of monsters, which contributed to the boy's sleep disturbance and separation difficulties. The hospital-based music therapist believed that these fears were related to the boy's underlying fear about being alone with his pain. In therapy sessions, many of the song stories in different scenarios dealt with how to confront or subdue the monsters (all in song and with the accompaniment of various musical instruments). Sometimes the monsters were subdued, and the story play concluded with the gentle singing of a lullaby, as Scotty peacefully rotated a rainstick and then quietly lay down to go to sleep. The lullaby may have provided soothing preverbal reminders of a time in infancy when he was being rocked and when he had no fears.

As is typical in many chronic medical problems, the goal for this child was not cure, since this was not a possibility given his particular condition. However, music therapy gave this boy considerable control over his fears and increased his ability to deal with the painful realities of his ongoing life.

Poetry and Writing as Therapy Aids

Whereas some children are drawn to art activities and others to music, the experience of putting words on paper appeals to individuals who want to capture their experiences through language. We have beautiful examples of the writing of terminally ill children who spontaneously wrote poems or stories about their lives (Grollman, 1988; Stepanek, 2001). For example, Shira Putter was diagnosed with a rare form of juvenile diabetes when she was five and a half, and she endured repeated hospitalizations and medical complications until her death three and a half years later. During her very short life, this child kept a journal and wrote poems about her feelings. The journals were a factual account of her times in different hospitals around the country, about her treatments, the medical personnel who cared for her, and the visits with her family in the hospital. In general, they convey an upbeat tone, in which this child genuinely seemed to enjoy the companionship of others. However, in her poems Shira expressed her anger and her frustration, including her acknowledgment that there was no cure for her condition, making her want to run away and hide until she was all better. Her final poem, at age 9, described how she was riding on a shooting star and going to a sunlit land where she would be free of all the tubes and doctors (Grollman, 1988, p. 70). She had made it clear to her family that she knew she was dying, and this young girl's acceptance of her certain death and her spirituality provided some comfort to them at this difficult time.

Like Shira, Mattie J. T. Stepanek wrote poems to convey his feelings about his illness. Mattie, who had muscular dystrophy, wrote poems and short stories from an early age. His book, *Journey through Heartsongs* (Stepanek, 2001), was written when he was 11 years old. Several of his siblings had died in their youth, and he described himself as a "leftover" child. His writings, filled with his strong spiritual beliefs, convey wisdom and insight about life, death, hope, and faith that have been an inspiration for many others with terminal illness.

Various workbooks have been created to assist young people who may not be self-directed to write about their feelings. Some of these include *Reactions: A Workbook to Help Young People Who Are Experiencing Trauma and Grief* (Salloum, 1998); *My Life Is Feelings: Starring Poly Polar Bear* (Josephson & Sourkes, no date); and *When Someone Has a Very Serious Illness* (Heegaard, 1992).

Each of these workbooks provides partially blank pages with instructions at the top about how the child can complete the page. Although the Salloum workbook was designed originally to be used with children who have gone through a traumatic grief experience (such as Hurricane Katrina), many exercises in it could benefit a young person with an acute or chronic medical condition. For example, the first page, titled "Supports," asks the child to write the names of people who care about him or her. Another page asks the child to "write or draw about what was the worst moment for you." And an additional exercise involves having the child rank nine separate feelings in terms of how intense they have been recently. There are some blank circles on the page in which the child may draw some of these feelings. Clearly, these exercises would be helpful to use with any child who has either an acute or a chronic medical condition. When used in therapy, they offer a window into the child's deep concerns and fears. Sometimes, the child's fears, as revealed in these exercises, may be excessive or inaccurate, and the therapist can correct these inaccuracies and/or exaggerations and thereby help the child feel less anxious.

The Poly bear book begins with a story about a little bear that has to have a finger stick or an IV. The story refers to how worried the bear is, and it mentions several possible procedures the bear may require. It goes on to list and describe some of the bear's feelings of anger and sadness because of the limitations put on his life by the illness. Following this story about Poly bear, the book has a half dozen blank pages on which the child is invited to draw or write what he or she would like to say to Poly.

All of these workbooks are designed to help children express their feelings about experiences (like medical procedures) that are beyond their control. Similar to the rationale in the art and music therapy approaches already described, all these methods have been developed to help young children express painful feelings, based on the belief that this type of expression will bring relief.

Lifebooks are still another way to help a child consider his or her life from infancy to the present. This tool was originally created to assist children in the child welfare system to keep track of their various moves and experiences with different families (Aust, 1981). I used this method with a 10-year-old girl who had HIV and who had experienced several traumatic moves after her mother's death when the child was 5 years old (Webb, 2003). I thought that it was important for this girl to retrieve and retain some memories of her mother, since her family was scattered and she had no photographs or other tangible belongings from her preschool years.

In creating the lifebook, therapists ask children to recall a very early memory and to draw it and then write or dictate a story about the drawing. My client actually chose to draw a picture of her mother in the casket with her three crying children surrounding it. This drawing offered a powerful visual portrait of the girl's grief and served as a way to help her express her feelings, about both her mother's death and her own medical condition. This case is discussed more fully in Chapter 15. It demonstrates how a serious medical illness such as HIV brings out strong grief reactions about the limitations that accompany it. This child mentioned to me, as we spoke about her illness, that she had decided never to have children of her own, but instead to become a nursery school teacher. Thus, the lifebook stimulated not only some very powerful memories of her past, but also led to some serious thinking about her future, and planning for it, related to the girl's perceptions about the limitations caused by her illness.

Selected Anxiety Management Techniques

Play therapists and others may employ various methods to teach young people to relax in order to reduce the physical tension that accompanies the severe stress associated with painful medical procedures. The following selected methods will be described in this section:

- Mindfulness
- Yoga
- Breathing exercises
- Self-control: Stop sign and change the channel
- Safe-place imagery

Mindfulness

This refers to the practice of "cultivating an appreciation for the fullness of each moment we are alive" (Kabat-Zinn, 1994, p. 3). It helps people focus on and appreciate all aspects of their lives at a particular moment, such as what is seen, heard, felt, smelled, and tasted. It involves appreciating the small blessings of each day rather than worrying about what *may* happen in the future (Cunningham, 2004). While we might expect that this approach would appeal more to adolescents and adults who have the cognitive ability to understand the futility of worry, younger children can also benefit from instruction about taking control of their own thoughts. Therapists may instruct the child to say, "I'm the boss of *me!*" Children with serious medical conditions may worry excessively about future procedures over which they have no control. Helping them learn to focus on "one good thing" (e.g., "Tim's Tips") can assist the child to substitute a positive thought as they deliberately push their worries away.

Yoga

There has been increased awareness about the advantages of developing mind-body awareness in children and teens through breathing strategies and movement exercises. A program called *YogaKids* (Wenig, 2003) describes various breathing poses that are useful for calming and energizing young people. Although some medically compromised children might not be able to achieve all of the physical postures of the yoga program, they certainly could benefit from the different breathing and meditation exercises. One exercise asks participants to sit with their eyes closed and then breathe in through their noses. As they breathe out, they are asked to either whisper or think the word *peace*. The instructor suggests that the participants feel peace around themselves. This is repeated several times. This exercise is very relaxing and soothing.

Breathing Exercises

One of the traditional ways of calming oneself has been to sit quietly and count one's breaths. This is very effective for adults, but may prove boring for children. It is much more interesting for young people to imagine blowing up a balloon until it gets bigger and bigger. The *YogaKids* training (Wenig, 2003) lists eight different breathing exercises that are intended to help calm and energize young people.

Self-Control: Stop Sign

All children are aware of traffic signs and that the stop sign brings cars to an inevitable standstill. I have found in my therapy with children who have attention-deficit/hyperactivity disorder (ADHD) that the stop sign can acquire special significance by encouraging the children to slow down and stop their incessant physical movements. I ask the child to draw a stop sign, cut it out, and to think of it when he or she becomes aware of becoming too hyper. Often, parents like the concept so much that they want to have the child hang up the sign at home as a visual reminder to periodically slow down.

This method can also be used following traumatic events in which the young person says, "I can't stop thinking about it." It also could be used helpfully when children are preoccupied with worries over past or future medical procedures. Once the child visualizes the stop sign to control his or her worries, the therapist then engages the young person to draw a "safe place."

Safe-Place Imagery

The therapist introduces this exercise by stating, "This will help you have something very pleasant and safe to think about when you become worried." I tell children that they can think of their heads as a TV in which hundreds and thousands of pictures go around and around. Some of the pictures are nice and interesting; others are not so nice and are scary. I tell the young people that they are in charge of their own TV in their heads and that if they don't like the pictures they are seeing, they should just think of a stop sign and then "change the channel." I then introduce the concept of their own special picture that they can substitute for the scary one.

It is important to involve children in imagining a detailed picture of their "safe place." I instruct them to close their eyes and think of a place, either real or imaginary, where they can go and feel totally safe, where nothing bad or scary can happen to them. I ask them to think about how it looks, smells, feels, and whether there are sounds there. After a few moments, I ask the children to open their eyes and draw their safe place. It is important for them to take time to draw all the details. Once the drawing is complete, I refer to it as "your own safe place where no one can harm or hurt you." Furthermore, I instruct them to use this when they start feeling worried or upset—after first thinking about the stop sign to push away their worries.

Cognitive Behavioral and Crisis Intervention Play Therapy

All the methods discussed here represent techniques that help the children and adolescents learn to control their thoughts. *Cognitive behavioral* therapy rests on the belief that thoughts control feelings and that feelings then control subsequent actions. Play therapists who choose to employ some cognitive strategies with young children may use toys such as puppets or dolls to act out a situation similar to that of the child's and then present a desirable outcome. As with all forms of play therapy this method emphasizes the importance of a positive therapeutic relationship and then builds on this using play as the means of communication with the child (Knell, 2003). The role of the cognitive behavioral therapist is quite directive, based on specific goals that have been set to help the child. In the case of Tim, the creation of his personal list of coping strategies helped him by giving him alternative thoughts that he could substitute for his intense fear responses. Although the boy could not stop the painful medical procedures, he could help himself by altering his thoughts during the process. This changed perception not only alleviated his feelings of distress, but also made him feel empowered. Thus, this approach utilizes education and modeling to change a child's perceptions and teach more adaptive coping skills.

Crisis intervention play therapy also attempts to repair a child's faulty perceptions, and it often offers information to clarify any incorrect attributions related to the cause of a crisis or traumatic event, such as acute or chronic illness. The crisis intervention therapist may provide specific toys suggestive of the child's traumatic experience in order to encourage the child to play out his or her feared experience. In the initial session, crisis intervention play therapists usually state directly to the child that they know about the terrible experience the child has endured, and they further state that their job is to help children by talking and by playing with them to reduce their worries about their frightening experience (Webb, 2007). This basically serves as a contract, or understanding, between the child and therapist, that makes it clear to the child that his or her problems will be understood either directly or indirectly through the means of play communication.

As I have outlined previously (Webb, 2006), crisis intervention play therapy helps relieve children and adolescents of their anxieties so they can move on with their lives. This particular form of play therapy achieves the following:

- Establishes a supportive therapeutic relationship with the child
- Teaches the child some relaxation methods to help keep anxiety in check
- Provides toys that will assist the child in re-creating the feared event
- Encourages a gradual reenactment of the feared event with the toys (after the child feels safe in the therapeutic relationship)
- Moves at the child's pace; does not attempt too much in one session
- Emphasizes the child's strength as a survivor
- Points out that the child is safe in the present

Working with children and adolescents who have acute and chronic medical conditions is difficult for both the child and the therapist. Clinicians who wish to use crisis intervention play therapy should be well-grounded in play therapy, in creative arts therapies, and in grief counseling. All should seek ways to obtain ongoing support and supervision for themselves in order to avoid what has been termed *vicarious traumatization*.

This refers to the personal reactions of therapists who become traumatized themselves in the course of their work with acutely anxious clients. This is discussed in Chapter 18.

We do know how to help children with acute and chronic medical conditions. It is most gratifying to observe children's reduced levels of anxiety and their enhanced ability to function and to consider their illness as only a part of their life. Encouraging a child's natural resiliency, while very challenging, is also very rewarding and well worth the struggle to overcome and cast out the demons of fear associated with medical experiences.

References

Aust, P. H. (1981). Using the life story book to treat children in placement. *Child Welfare, 60*, 535–560.

Austin, D. (2006). Songs of the self: Vocal psychotherapy for adults traumatized as children. In L. Carey (Ed.), *Expressive and creative arts methods for trauma survivors* (pp. 133–151). London and Philadelphia: Jessica Kingsley.

Bromfield, R. N. (2003). Psychoanalytic play therapy. In C. E. Schaefer (Ed.), *Foundations of play therapy* (pp. 1–13). Hoboken, NJ: Wiley.

Carey, L. (1999). *Sandplay therapy with children and families*. Northside, NJ: Aronson.

Carey, L. (2006). Sandplay therapy with a traumatized boy. In L. Carey (Ed.), *Expressive and creative arts methods for trauma survivors* (pp. 153–163). London and Philadelphia: Jessica Kingsley.

Cunningham, M. (2004). Avoiding vicarious traumatization: Support, spirituality, and self-care. In N. B. Webb (Ed.), *Mass trauma and violence: Helping children and families cope* (pp. 327–346). New York: Guilford Press.

Dileo, C. (1999). (Ed.). *Music therapy and medicine: Theoretical and clinical applications*. Silver Springs, MD: American Music Therapy Association.

Dundas, E. (1990). *Symbols come alive in the sand*. Boston: Coventure.

Encyclopedia of Mental Disorders. Retrieved July 20, 2008, from http://www.minddisorders.com/Br-Del/Creative-therapies.html.

Frey, D. (2006). Video play therapy. In L. Carey (Ed.), *Expressive and creative arts methods for trauma survivors* (pp. 193–205). London and Philadelphia: Jessica Kingsley.

Glass, J. (2006). Working toward aesthetic distance. Drama therapy for adult victims of violence. In L. Carey (Ed.), *Expressive and creative arts methods for trauma survivors* (pp. 57–71). London and Philadelphia: Jessica Kingsley.

Goodman, R. F. (2007). Living beyond the crisis of childhood cancer. In N. B. Webb (Ed.), *Play therapy with children in crisis: Individual, group, and family treatment* (pp. 197–227). New York: Guilford Press.

Grollman, S. (1988). *Shira: A legacy of courage*. New York: Doubleday.

Haen, C. (2008). Vanquishing monsters: Drama therapy for treating childhood trauma in the group setting. In K. A. Malchiodi (Ed.), *Creative interventions with traumatized children* (pp. 225–246). New York: Guilford Press.

Heegaard, M. (1992). *When someone has a very serious illness*. Minneapolis, MN: Fairview Press.

Kabat-Zinn, J. (1994). *Wherever you go, there you are: Mindfulness meditation in everyday life*. New York: Hyperion.

Kramer, E. (1993). *Art as therapy with children* (2nd ed.). Chicago: Magnolia Street.

Knell, S. M. (2003). Cognitive behavioral play therapy. In C. E. Schaefer (Ed.), *Foundations of play therapy* (pp. 175–191). Hoboken, NJ: Wiley.

Landreth, G. L. (2002). *Play therapy: The art of the relationship* (2nd ed.). Philadelphia: Brunner/Routledge.

Landy, R. J. (1994). *Drama therapy: Concepts, theories, and practices.* Springfield, IL: Charles C. Thomas.

Lesley University (2008). Retrieved February 15, 2008, from http://www.lesley.edu/gsass/56etp.html.

Loewy, J. V., & Stewart, K. (2004). Music therapy to help traumatized children and caregivers. In N. B. Webb (Ed.), *Mass trauma and violence: Helping families and children cope* (pp. 191–215). New York: Guilford Press.

Lowenfeld, M. (1993). *Understanding children's sandplay: Lowenfeld's world technique.* London: Bailey.

Malchiodi, K. A. (1998). *Understanding children's drawings.* New York: Guilford Press.

Malchiodi, K. A. (2008). (Ed.). *Creative interventions with traumatized children.* New York: Guilford Press.

Martin, E. S. (2008). Medical art and play therapy with accident survivors. In K. A. Malchiodi (Ed.), *Creative interventions with traumatized children* (pp. 112–131). New York; Guilford Press.

Mills, J. (2006). The bowl of light. A. story-craft for healing. In L. Carey (Ed.), *Expressive and creative arts methods for trauma survivors* (pp. 207–213). London and Philadelphia: Jessica Kingsley.

Rubin, J. A. (2005). *Child art therapy* (25th anniversary ed.). New York: Wiley.

Rubin-Bosco, J. (2002). Resolution versus reenactment. A story-song approach to working with trauma. In J. V. Loewy & A. Frich Hara (Eds.), *Caring for the caregiver: The use of music and music therapy in grief and trauma treatment* (pp. 118–127). Silver Springs, MD: American Music Therapy Association.

Salloum, A. (1998). *Reactions: A workbook to help young people who are experiencing trauma and grief.* Omaha, NE: Centering Corporation.

Schaefer, C. E. (2003). (Ed.). *Foundations of play therapy.* Hoboken, NJ: Wiley.

Sourkes, B. M. (1991). Truth to life: Art therapy with pediatric oncology patients and their siblings. *Journal of Psychosocial Oncology, 9*(2), 81–95.

Stepanek, M. J. T. (2001). *Journey through heartsongs.* New York: Hyperion.

Webb, N. B. (2003). *Social work practice with children.* New York: Guilford Press.

Webb, N. B. (2006). Crisis intervention play therapy to help traumatized children. In L. Carey (Ed.), *Expressive and creative arts methods for trauma survivors* (pp. 39–56). London and Philadelphia: Jessica Kingsley.

Webb, N.B. (2007). (Ed.). *Play therapy with children in crisis: Individual, group, and family treatment* (3rd ed.). New York: Guilford Press.

Wenig, M. (2003). *YogaKids: Educating the whole child through yoga.* Stewart, Tabori, & Chang.

Meeting the Spiritual Needs of Children with Chronic and Life-Threatening Illness

Paul Thayer

11
Chapter

This chapter begins by summarizing what is known about children's spirituality in general and explores five elements of children's spiritual lives: parental relationships, children's beliefs, rituals, the need to make meaning of life experiences, and the need to belong to a wider community. The particular needs of children coping with chronic illness are then examined, including the need for acceptance, the need to cope with issues of grief and loss, and needs of identity and self-esteem. This is followed by a discussion of five specific needs of children coping with life-threatening illness, including the need to leave a legacy, the need for hope, the necessity of having an ethical framework for medical decision making, the need for an understanding of death and afterlife, and the need for an understanding of suffering. Finally, the chapter concludes by presenting a model of spiritual care that is community-based, transdisciplinary, and holistic.

The Spiritual Lives of Children

Defining Terms

Any discussion of spirituality and religion should begin by defining how these terms are being used. The term *religion,* as used in this chapter, "is a set of creeds and covenants, of rituals and practices, that bring people together to worship a particular image of God" (Sommer, 1994, p. 8). Notice that this definition contains three important elements. First, a shared set of beliefs (creeds) defines a relationship to a higher power (covenant). Second, religion is not just about what one believes; it is about how one encounters the sacred (religious rituals) and how one acts in the world (ethics). Finally, religion is communal (community-based) with a shared purpose.

The term *religion* is sometimes used in this chapter to refer to a particular set of beliefs and practices that define one religion versus another in the sense of a particular religious denomination. Zinnbaueur et al. (1997, p. 561) defined religion by emphasizing the denominational elements—"organizational or institutional beliefs and practices such as church membership, church attendance, and commitment to the beliefs system of a church or organized religion."

The word *spirituality* is derived from the Latin term *spirare*, meaning "to breathe" (*Webster's Third New International Dictionary*). Michael Friesen (2000, p. 13) defines spirituality as "one's quest for vision, meaning, insight, and inspiration." Notice that, compared to religion, spirituality is often a more individualistic pursuit ("one's quest"). *Spirituality,* as used in this chapter, is defined not as a set of particular beliefs, but rather as a universal need to understand what lies beyond and beneath human experience, including vision, meaning, insight, and inspiration.

For many people, religion is their spirituality in the sense that their religion meets most, if not all, of their spiritual needs. Others may define themselves as "not religious" but as very spiritual. For most children and adults there is overlap between the two, making it important for the clinician or health care provider to listen carefully for how an individual might be using a particular term. For example, the term *faith* might be used to describe an absolute conviction in a particular religious belief ("faith that God will provide a miracle"), or it might be used more generally, as an expression of hope and spirituality ("faith that the treatment will work").

The Importance of Religion and Spirituality in Children's Lives

America is clearly a diverse but religious country, and religion seems to be important to American children and adolescents. According to a 2008 Gallup report (Gallup, 2008), 96 percent of 18- to 29-year-olds indicate that they believe in God or a universal spirit; 63 percent of teens ages 13 to 15 report that religion is very important to them; 69 percent of teens ages 13 to 15 report membership in a church or synagogue or faith community, with 69 percent reporting that they attend at least once a month.

It is not surprising, then, that religion is a major factor in how many individuals understand and cope with illness. Wallis (1996) reports that 80 percent of people believe in the power of God or prayer to improve the course of their illness. Keonig, Bearon, Hover, and Travis (1991) state that 43.8 percent of patients and 56.1 percent of families report that religion is important for coping. This contrasts to only 25.6 percent of nurses and 8.7 percent of physicians who state that religion is important for coping. These statistics suggest that many health care providers may overlook or under-estimate the important role that religion plays in coping with illness.

Robert Coles (1990) provides data to suggest that the religious needs of *children* coping with illness are even more likely to be overlooked. He makes an argument that adults often do not consider seriously enough the capacity of children to reflect on the meaning of their own experiences. Coles's (1990) interviews with children demonstrate that accidents, illness, bad luck, and moments of pain and danger prompt reflection in children as well as adults (p. 109) and that religious beliefs are often used by children to make sense out of unexpected life events.

The Spiritual Needs of Children Coping with Chronic Illness

How does one conduct a "spiritual care assessment" to learn about the role that religion and spirituality might play in a child who is coping with illness? The term *spiritual care assessment* refers to a careful consideration of an individual's religious and spiritual beliefs and the role that these beliefs play in coping with illness. While some hospitals or clinicians have very formal ways of assessing spirituality, no spiritual assessment tools have been tested systemically with children (*When Children Die,* IOM Report, 2003).

Any spiritual care assessment should be conducted with sufficient time to listen carefully. A rushed assessment will usually result in a minimum of information and may feel more like an interrogation than an interview. Coles (1990) states that learning about spirituality takes time and an "I wonder" attitude to see the connections between religious and spiritual life and other aspects of day-to-day life (p. 36). It is perhaps more useful to consider the spiritual assessment itself as a form of care. A spiritual care assessment that develops a relationship and cultivates a wonderment about the child's inner world becomes a way of both gathering information and providing care based on that information.

A spiritual care assessment usually begins with questions about religion. "Do you go to a church, mosque, or synagogue? What is that like for you? Do you talk (pray) to God? Does God talk back or communicate in any way? Have you met the hospital chaplain? Would you like to?" Carpenito's (1983) spiritual assessment for children was one of the first tools to focus on children's spiritual needs in addition to their religious needs. Her suggestions for starter questions about spirituality include:

What do you do for fun?

What bothers you about being sick?

Why do you think people get sick?

What makes you feel better when you are sad or lonely?

What can I do to help you feel better when you are sad or lonely?

Who do you like to talk to when you are scared?

Who do you think God is?

If you had three wishes, what would they be?

What would you do if you were in charge?

More recent spiritual care assessments recognize the importance of parental relationships, beliefs, rituals, meaning, and connection to a faith community. Each of these categories is considered here.

Parental Relationships

Robert Coles (1990, p. 119) writes that "God can be a friend or potential enemy, admirer or critic, ally or interference, source of encouragement or source of anxiety, fear, and panic." Whether children think of God as friend or enemy, admirer or critic frequently reflects their relationship with parents. Children whose parents are present, open, and honest are likely to conceive of God as caring and supportive. On the other hand, children whose parents are blaming, inconsistent, or abusive, are more likely to conceive of a God of wrath and punishment. Likewise, children whose parents are passive, closed, or rigid, are likely to have an image of God who is insulated from their suffering (Sommer 1994, p. 9). Therefore, a discussion about parents may help practitioners understand the child's fundamental model of God.

Beliefs

David Heller (1986, chap. 3) examines the wide range of ways that children might conceptualize their image of God: as a friendly ghost, an angry villain, a distant thing in the sky, a lover in heaven, an inconsistent God, a once and future king, or God the therapist. Heller's research demonstrates that religious denominations may emphasize different themes. Jewish children are more likely to rely on desert or water imagery. Catholic children are more likely to emphasize a God intimately involved in family life. Baptist children may emphasize a personal relationship with God. Muslim children may understand that suffering has a purpose and that God helps them with their suffering. Hindu children may emphasize the importance of community.

Belief systems change and evolve in response to life experiences. Children coping with serious illness often need to reconcile institutional religious teaching with their personal experience of living with illness. The experience of illness often raises questions about religious teachings. Therefore, when listening to the spiritual or religious concerns of children coping with illness, it is helpful to listen for not only what a child believes, but also areas that might lead to the questioning of belief.

Rituals

Religion is not just what one believes, but what one does. Religious rituals often provide safety and security for children. Friesen (2000) defines rituals as actions that stand apart from ordinary life. They are symbolic and point to that which is beyond words. Children's religious rituals may include bedtime prayers, grace at meals, worship, and, in many denominations, sacraments.

Religious rituals in the hospital setting may help a child to connect with that part of his or her life that is not defined by illness. The familiarity of a childhood prayer, for example, may provide comfort that words of consolation alone cannot provide. Rituals do not need to be specifically religious in order to be helpful. Care providers may want to develop rituals that set aside quiet times from the fast pace of an ordinary hospital day to encourage reflection and centering. Play can be an important part of any ritual, helping to encourage expression of emotions, laughter, and perhaps a brief respite from illness.

Meaning-Making

Meaning-making is the process of making sense of one's experiences. Meaning-making is often conveyed through personal narratives in which children tell stories about pain, lack of acceptance, helplessness, and personal struggles in light of their illness experience. Meaning-making may also involve cultural, religious, and family stories. For example, the biblical story of Job may be heard very differently by a child with serious illness than by healthy children.

Hearing the meaning in stories takes time and careful listening. Health care professionals are often under pressure to be efficient. Hospital assessment forms are often designed to gather patient information in the most efficient way for the professional. In contrast, meaning-making narratives often take longer and may take many unexpected turns. While brief assessments may be very appropriate for short hospital stays, one may need to take much longer to assess the spiritual needs of children with chronic and life-threatening illnesses.

Identity and Self-Worth

Children who live with chronic illness often struggle with issues of being different from other children and with issues of low self-esteem. Medical language about disabilities and illness often contributes to lowered self-esteem. For example, we usually say that a child has "failed chemo-therapy," when what we really mean is that chemotherapy has failed the child. We sometimes say that a child is anorexic, when it might be more helpful to say that the child has anorexia. Person-first language (child with a disability) recognizes that the child is not totally defined by his or her illness.

Religious beliefs that understand illness or disability as punishment from God may serve to further lower self-esteem. On the other hand, religious beliefs that help the child experience his or her self as a valued and loved creation of God can be a source of self-worth that is not tied to accomplishments or abilities.

Community Connections

Frequent hospitalizations, developmental delays, communication diffi-culties, and decreased ability to participate in sports and social activities may all increase the isolation experienced by children with chronic illness.

Participation in religious education, youth groups, rites of passage, and social activities are all potential ways to decrease the isolation of chronic illness, although these may need to be adapted to include children with special needs. Web sites for children with specific disabilities, such as cancer or diabetes, can be an important connection with other children coping with the same illness. Brainstorming how a faith community may better meet the needs of children with special health care needs can help religious organizations grow to become more inclusive.

The Spiritual Needs of Children Coping with Life-Threatening Illness

Legacy

It is a basic human need to want one's life to have made a difference and to know that one has made a difference to others. For many adults, their legacy is measured in accomplishments of the type that are listed in obituaries. Children with life-threatening illness usually do not have the time to accumulate a list of accomplishments. Their legacy is more likely to be measured by their relationships and impact on others. The need to give back to others is an important part of leaving a legacy that is often overlooked. Children will be remembered for their impact on those around them. Writing thank-you cards, giving gifts, and teaching others are all ways that children can give back to those who care for them.

A child whose life is coming to a close can benefit from life review. School-age children and older children are able to reflect on their contributions to others and talk about events that have had the most meaning for them. Life review may be conducted one-on-one or may be done in a group, such as a school group, sports team, or religious community. Journal writing can help children develop the ability to engage in a thoughtful reflection about the meaning of one's life and how one has made a difference.

Hope

Perhaps no issue is more important for children living with a life-threatening illness than the issue of hope. The uncertainty of the future brings the issue of hope to the forefront. Families become more aware of time and future through the process of waiting: "waiting for good news," "waiting for test results," "waiting for death."

Families and professionals all want to maintain optimism while waiting for a future that is uncertain at best. When the future is bleak, is it possible to have hope? When hope is defined only in terms of positive outcomes ("beating the disease," "being in remission," etc.), acknowledging "defeat" can result in loss of hope; on the other hand, denying the reality of the likely outcome can result in false hope.

The extremes of "no hope" and "false hope" both have their origins in an outcome-based understanding of hope. Lester's (1995) view of "functional hope" provides another alternative. Lester's view of hope is less about outcomes and more about the ability to understand the present in the context of a larger worldview that reaffirms a belief in the fundamental goodness of life. Fowler's (1981) view of faith is similar to Lester's view of hope. Fowler understands faith as the orientation of the whole person, giving purpose and goals to one's hopes, striving, and actions.

I define hope as "what one strives for." The striving provides hope and purpose without being measured only by successful outcomes. This definition of hope is broad enough to embrace those who choose to battle the disease and those who choose comfort measures only. In concrete terms, how one family strives for a cure and how another family strives to be able to go to the playroom may both be sources of hope.

Professionals often need to learn to actively wait with families, to listen for what families strive for, and to help them find what has meaning. Professionals need to resist the temptation to become cheerleaders in an attempt to "fix things" for families. In their active waiting, hopeful professionals provide honesty, availability, trust, presence, and the space for families to explore how their own spirituality might provide consolation and meaning.

Ethics

Adults often define end-of-life ethical issues as questions concerning "Do Not Resuscitate" orders, futility, and experimental treatments. Children, however, are much more likely to have ethical questions that are more immediate and concrete. They may be worried about the impact of having no hair for the prom or that other kids might make fun of their swollen face.

Children often raise ethical questions (e.g., "Why me?") that ask why suffering has entered their lives. In addition, children often complain about their medical treatments. Professionals might (correctly) hear whining and complaining as expressions of anxiety or fear and respond with comfort measures, distraction techniques, or reassurance. But what difference might it make if we also heard these expressions as ethical statements? It is developmentally appropriate that children and adolescents express ethical concerns as egocentric complaints. It may take some practice to listen less to the tone (whining) and more to the content (ethical questioning). Listening to their whining as expressions of ethical issues might lead to a very different conversation of the costs versus benefits of treatment, for example. This can open up space for deeper conversations about ethics and lay the foundation for later conversations about "bigger" end-of-life discussions about treatment options, advanced care preferences, and resuscitation orders.

Death and Afterlife

When listening to children's beliefs about an afterlife, it is helpful to know how children are likely to understand death at various developmental ages. Children under the age of two experience death as separation and are affected by disruptions in their routines but do not have a cognitive understanding of death. Toddlers and preschool-age children understand death as temporary and reversible. Younger school-age children understand death as a cessation of body function but may not yet understand that death is final and irreversible. School-age children gradually come to understand that death is final, irreversible, and universal. They also develop an understanding of causality and that disease processes that can lead to death. The formal operational thought processes of adolescents allow them to consider philosophies and theologies about death (Bluebond-Langer & DeCicco, 2006).

Beliefs about death and afterlife are not just influenced by cognitive development, however. For example, most religions have an understanding of an afterlife in which the person is alive again. A school-age child who understands death as reversible may be viewed as developmentally immature when viewed psychologically, but may be viewed as mature when viewed theologically.

Suffering

Suffering is a dimension of illness in which one experiences vulnerability or brokenness. Suffering can be caused by unrelenting pain, but suffering can also be emotional or spiritual. Religious beliefs may not be a source of comfort from suffering, especially if the child believes that he or she is being punished by God or that God does not care about his or her condition. For example, if the child believes that God is all-loving and all-powerful yet chooses to make the child suffer, then the child or parent may conclude that God is not all-loving, not all-powerful, or that there is no God. Religious beliefs about suffering may also teach that suffering has a greater purpose—that suffering is just an illusion, or that suffering is a part of the human condition. Reconciling religious beliefs with personal experience of suffering can lead to spiritual growth. Health care providers can often be helpful listeners, especially if the child's family or clergy do not allow questioning of religious belief.

A Model of Spiritual Care

Michael Friesen (2006, p. 16) defines seven principles of spiritual care that are essential elements of providing spiritual care. Friesen states that spiritual care must be intentional, integrated, inclusive, pluralistic, contextual, relational, and mutual. This section spells out a model of spiritual care for children with chronic and life-threatening illness by applying Friesen's seven-element model and adding four additional elements of care: care that is honest, community-based, transdisciplinary, and strengths-based.

1. *Care should be intentional*—Spiritual care must actively seek to understand and meet the spiritual needs of children. Intentional spiritual care recognizes the importance of spirituality in the child's illness experience and seeks to understand the unique spiritual needs of each child. Children will not usually bring up spiritual concerns unless they know that adults are truly interested. Intentional clinicians take the time to listen, learn, and appreciate the child's spiritual world. Intentional clinicians actively create reflective rituals that provide a form of expression for that which is beyond words.

2. *Care should be integrated*—Personhood includes physical, emotional, behavioral, and spiritual elements. A focus on spirituality and illness should always include questions about pain, emotions, and coping behaviors, in addition to questions that focus more exclusively on religion and spirituality.

3. *Care should be inclusive*—Inclusive care invites others into the caregiving circle. No one discipline has an exclusive claim on spiritual care. Nurses, child life specialists, social workers, physicians, volunteers, therapists, chaplains, and even dietary and housekeeping staff can play a role in meeting the spiritual needs of children. An obvious, but sometimes overlooked, need is to include the family fully in ethical decision making. Sometimes, health care teams make decisions and present them to the family in a way that fails to fully include the family.

4. *Care should be pluralistic*—Chronic illness and life-threatening illness affects Baptists, Muslims, Jews, Christians, Buddhists, Unitarians, Hindus, Hmong, and Native Americans, among others. Chronic and life-threatening illnesses affect fundamentalists, atheists, and agnostics. All have spiritual needs and a unique way of living out those needs. Spiritual care that is inclusive marvels at the many ways of expressing spirituality. Pluralistic care does not impose beliefs; it approaches spirituality with an attitude of "I wonder" rather than "I know."

5. *Care should be contextual*—The developmental level of the child, the family structure and functioning, the disease trajectory, and the unique health care experiences of the child all play a role in spirituality. Contextual care understands the need for some basic knowledge of child development, family systems theory, and the specific disease process that the child is going through. Contextual care understands that the family is the center of spirituality and often spiritual care of parents is the most important part of spiritual care for children. Contextual care recognizes that brief hospital stays are the norm and attempts to develop ways to provide spiritual care for families of children who are in the hospital only briefly.

6. *Care should be relational*—Relational care means that the clinician does not run away when the prognosis is poor or uncertain. Relational care understands that an assessment is a way to build relationships, not just a way to gather information. Relational care reaches out to others even when they are rejecting or angry. Relational care recognizes that healing is always relational.

7. *Care should be mutual*—Spiritual care allows for caregivers to be enriched as much as patients are enriched. Spirituality is meant to be shared, and often the sharing is between professionals and families. Parents may ask about the spiritual beliefs of the health care professionals who care for their family because they value views other than their own. Martin Luther (*Luther's Works* 54:7) stated, "It is by living, no rather by dying and being damned, that a theologian is made." What difference might it make if we understood pediatric patients who are coping with life-threatening illness as theologians who have something to teach us?

8. *Care should be honest*—Suffering and struggling should not be easily dismissed. Often, religion is misused by the use of easy platitudes that "all will be well." Spiritual care must recognize that health care providers do not have all the answers. "Theology, no matter how sweetly done, does not cure tribulation" (Forde, 1990, p. 29).

9. *Care should be community-based*—Health care clinicians who see patients only when they are hospitalized often undervalue the community foundation of spirituality. Clutter (2005) reminds us that, for most people, religion holds life value for the patient, and health care intervention is superimposed on the patient's life, not the other way around. I am reminded of my own experience at the funeral of a dear patient whom I had seen for psychosocial and spiritual support for many years. I had grown very fond of Nicholas, so much so that I thought of myself as the most important part of his life, with the exception of his family. The hundreds of school friends, scout troop, and church members at his funeral reminded me (with much humility) that he belonged to his local community much more than to the health care community.

   Community-based care often meets spiritual care needs in ways that health care cannot. Events such as weddings and religious rites of passage (e.g., bat and bar mitzvahs, confirmations) are important ways to participate in the life of the religious and cultural community. Often, teenagers, who know how to play and be with each other (hang out), are a welcome presence in a health care world that is so dominated by adult interactions. Small acts of kindness, including respite care, meals, transportation, babysitting, mowing the lawn, cleaning, phone calls, and cards, are sources of hope. As Lester (1995, p. 94) reminds us, "Hope is communal; we don't hope alone, we hope with," to which I would add that hope is also concrete, not abstract.

Community clergy are often-overlooked sources of hope and encouragement in the care of children with chronic and life-threatening illnesses. Community clergy often have lifelong relationships with families and can provide a historical perspective on family strengths and values. Families who are struggling with treatment options or ethical dilemmas may benefit from the presence of local clergy during team meetings. One word of caution, however; some clergy are not trained or comfortable with the care of children with serious or life-threatening illness. They may need some training from hospital staff about end-of-life care, including what is likely to be helpful to families at this critical time and how to cope with the stress of providing end-of-life care.

Hospital staff should be particularly attentive to the religious needs at the end of life. Often, priests, ministers, imams, and rabbis are requested by families to say prayers and perform end-of-life rituals. Too often, clergy are called too late or cannot be reached during this critical time, a problem easily avoided by remembering to obtain a clergy's cell phone number before it is needed. Hospital staff should also be attentive to the spiritual needs of families who are estranged from the religion of their family of origin or who are currently not part of a faith community. Families who were brought up in a particular religion but are no longer practicing may still find comfort in familiar childhood prayers, songs, or rituals. Finally, hospital staff should be attentive to the spiritual needs of families who are not religious. Rituals including music, poetry, and saying good-bye can be healing for all families. Many hospitals have memory boxes that allow families to make a hand- or footprint, collect a lock of hair, or take pictures. Some hospitals even have artists who sketch portraits of children without their tubes and medical equipment.

10. *Care should be transdisciplinary*—Transdisciplinary care is not the same as interdisciplinary care. Interdisciplinary care recognizes unique roles of the various health care professionals and emphasizes the importance of each profession and the need to coordinate the delivery of care by the many professions involved. For example, the hospital chaplain is usually responsible for the delivery of spiritual care in health care settings, but the chaplaincy services are coordinated with the physicians, nurses, social workers, and volunteers. Transdisciplinary care recognizes the uniqueness of each professional role, but additionally emphasizes the overlap between professions. When it comes to spiritual care, a transdisciplinary approach understands that no one profession is necessarily the best provider of spiritual care. While the chaplain coordinates spiritual care, nurses, physicians, and psychosocial staff are encouraged to attend to spiritual needs as well.

One model of transdisciplinary care is hospice care. The hospice team consists of a medical director, nurses, social workers, chaplains, and volunteers, among others. The team members meet regularly to discuss care and how to meet the medical, psychosocial, and spiritual needs of the family. While the hospice team cannot provide 24-hour care except in times of emergency, their ability to organize community support, teach families about giving care at home, and provide 24-hour backup and consultation allows many families to remain at home rather than returning to the hospital. The hospice model recognizes the importance of end-of-life spiritual care by mandating that a spiritual counselor be a part of the hospice transdisciplinary team.

11. *Care should be strengths-based*—Spirituality can be an important coping mechanism but should not be reduced to a coping mechanism alone. Spirituality and religion point to a value and purpose of existence that is not defined by illness. In doing so, they provide hope and sustenance in the face of suffering.

Professionals who care for children with chronic and life-threatening illnesses need to rely on a strengths-based core of personal commitment and professional skills. Health care is very results-oriented, and care that does not result in improvement, or that may even result in the death of a child, is very challenging and disturbing. End-of-life care often confronts health care providers with their own helplessness at not being able to achieve a cure. Helplessness is often diminished as we learn to focus on personal strengths rather than just professional skills. Ultimately, who we are becomes more important to children and families than what we do. We learn to focus on the importance of presence, or as Forde (1990, p. 29) states, "Don't just do something, sit there."

Professionals who care for children with chronic and life-threatening illnesses need to renew their strengths-based core of personal commitment and professional skills. To truly be present to those who suffer, we need to attend to our own spiritual life. Encountering suffering calls us to give away part of ourselves that needs to be refilled from a well of self-care. The best of care is not about being exhausted but about being drained and refilled. In the emptying of self we make room for change and growth that makes us more fully alive. Viewed this way, holistic care of children with chronic and life-threatening illnesses is not only about *including* spirituality, it is itself spiritual.

Family Resiliency Stories

The following stories are included to help the reader understand how the preceding principles of spiritual care can make a difference to children and families. The stories have been provided by family members who were asked to comment on the importance of spiritual care in their child's illness.

Inclusivity

"My daughter Stephanie was born with renal agenesia and renal dysplasia. Stephanie is medically fragile and is homebound due to risks from the possibility of contracting an illness from other children. As soon as I was able to bring Stephanie out of complete isolation, we began attending church. This year I wanted to enroll her in Sunday school so she could have the same religious experiences I had growing up, but the pediatrician said she needed to stay at home, at least for this year. Preparing to homeschool Stephanie, I brought her to visit the Sunday school just once. She was very excited about seeing the other children, and to this day whenever I ask her if she wants to go to church she asks, 'See kids?' I'm using things that Stephanie already had, like her rosary, cross, Bible, *Precious Moments* book, and even a stuffed Noah's ark! I'm hoping to bring Stephanie to church one day and that she will be able to attend Sunday school. For now, I'll follow the curriculum and set up our own lesson plans. Each year we will ask the doctors if Stephanie is strong enough to go to school and Sunday school. If so, she will participate in 'inclusive' religious education. If not, she will still participate in her own way."

Mutuality

"My son Nicholas is five years old and was diagnosed at birth with Prader-Willi syndrome. When he came home I felt helpless and guilty. So many endless days brought so many endless, hurtful, hard emotions. Slowly, I began to realize that these torturous feelings, these hardships, were important and even meaningful experiences. These awful extremes of emotion gave my life new meaning. I understood myself better.

"I understood others a lot better. These difficult experiences enabled us to see the many disguised angels traveling here on earth. Intelligent, kind, compassionate beings devoted simply to the healing of others. These guardians would now be a part of our lives forever. This horrifying new life of ours now seemed a little less scary."

Strengths-Based Perspective

"My son, now seven, continues to have issues from prematurity, including chronic lung disease, asthma, reflux, severe food allergies, and developmental delays. Though he weighed only two pounds at birth, Alexander was strong in spirit, a real fighter with fiery-bronze-colored hair. We named him *Baruch David*, 'Blessed Beloved,' and that he is.

"When Alexander was still in the NICU, the freshly hired rabbi from our congregation met us at the hospital. This spiritual leader told me that I would learn a lot from the baby. "Hmm, I thought, is this the kind of rabbinic wisdom we're to expect from the new guy? After all, wasn't the baby supposed to be learning from me?'

Well, in just the first year of Alexander's life, here is some of what he has taught me:

- Don't miss opportunities to laugh and smile or help others laugh and smile.
- Keep trying and be strong.
- Strive to give unconditional love.
- It's okay to make silly noises and faces.
- Live life as a musical by breaking out into song, if that's what your heart tells you to do

"Like the biblical Hannah, I cherish my children as gifts from God, guiding them in the spiritual ways of Judaism at home, bringing them to our congregation so they may better come to know Hashem, and helping them to be dedicated to our faith. I pray that they, like Hannah's son Samuel, may change the course of our history in some small way, perhaps finding paths to bring peace and healing to this Earth."

Legacy

The final story was not submitted by a family member; rather, it is from this author. I include this story in the hope that it will remind the reader of the importance of "listening" to nonverbal children. I had known Kaylie, now age 12, throughout the long course of her treatment for a brain tumor. Like many patients with advanced brain tumors, she had lost the ability to speak. I spent many visits talking to Kaylie's mother about the role that spirituality played in helping her cope with her daughter's life-threatening illness. One day her mother looked me in the eye and asked, "Why don't you ever ask Kaylie about *her* spirituality?" Her mother went on to explain that so many health care providers did not interact with Kaylie because she was nonverbal. I realized that while I had built a strong connection with her mother, I had not built a connection with Kaylie.

When I later spoke to Kaylie about her beliefs and fears, her mother was the child's verbal voice, but the eye contact, hand-holding, and gestures were all Kaylie's. I learned to appreciate the expression of spirituality in gesture, ritual, and personal connection that comes whenever one carefully listens to another. Kaylie's legacy to me was the lesson about how to "listen" more carefully when there are no words.

References

Bluebond-Langer, M., & DeCicco, A. (2006). Children's views of death. In A. Goldman, R. Hain., & S. Liben (Eds.), *Oxford textbook of palliative care for children*. Oxford: Oxford University Press.

Canda, E. R. (1988). Spirituality, religious diversity, and social work practice. Social Casework: *The Journal of Contemporary Social Work, 69*(4), 238–247.

Carpenito, L. J. (1983). *Nursing diagnosis: Application to clinical practice*. New York: J. B. Lippincott.

Clutter, L. (2005). Spiritual issues in children's health care settings. In J. Rollins, R. Bolig, & C. Mahan, *Meeting children's psychosocial needs across the health-care continuum*. Austin, TX: PRO-ED, Inc.

Coles, R. (1990). *The spiritual life of children*. Boston: Houghton Mifflin.

Feudtner, C., Haney, J., & Dimmers, M. A. (2003). Spiritual care needs of hospitalized children and their families: A national survey of pastoral care provider's perceptions. *Pediatrics, 111*(1), 192.

Field, M. J., & Behrman, R. E. (Eds.). (2003). *When children die: Improving palliative and end-of-life care for children and families*. Washington, DC: Institute of Medicine.

Friesen, M. (2000). *Spiritual care for children living in specialized settings*. Binghamton, NY: Haworth Pastoral Press.

Forde, G. (1990). *Theology is for proclamation*. Minneapolis: Fortress Press.

Fowler, J. (1981). *Stages of faith: The psychology of human development and the quest for meaning*. San Francisco: HarperCollins.

Gallup, G., Jr. (2008). *The Religiosity Cycle*. Retrieved June 22, 2008, from http://www.gallup.com/poll/6124/Religiosity-Cycle.aspx.

Heller, D. (1986). *The children's God*. Chicago: University of Chicago Press.

Koenig, H., Bearon, L., Hover, M., & Travis, J.,III (1991). Religious perspectives of doctors, nurses, patients, and families. *The Journal of Pastoral Care, 45*(3), 254–267.

Kohlberg, L. (1969). *Stages in the development of moral thought and action*. New York: Holt, Rinehart & Winston.

Lester, A. (1995). *Hope in pastoral care and counseling*. Louisville: Westminster John Knox Press.

Luther's Works 54:7. In D. Martin Luther's Werke: Kritische Gesamtaus-gabe, 5:163. In M. Solberge, Compelling Knowledge (57).

Sommer, D. (1994). Exploring the spirituality of children in the midst of illness and suffering. *The Association of the Care of Children's Health Advocate, 1*(2), 7–12.

Thurston, C., & Ryan, J. (1996). Faces of God: Illness, healing, and children's spirituality. *The Association for the Care of Children's Health Advocate. 2*(2), 13–15.

Wallis C. (1996, June 24). Faith and healing. *Time*, 58–63.

Webster's third new international dictionary. (1968). Springfield, MA: C. & G. Merriam Company.

Zinnbaueur, B. J., Pargament, K. I., Cole, B., Rye, M. S., Butter, E. M., Belavich, T. G., et al. (1997). Religion and spirituality: Unfuzzying the fuzzy. *Journal for the Scientific Study of Religion, 36*, 549–564.

Medical Conditions Present at Birth

Patrick Shannon

12

chapter

It was a difficult delivery that ended in a C-section after 24 hours of labor. I was waiting for my husband to tell me how beautiful she was, but I could tell by his expression that something was wrong. We refused all genetic testing during my pregnancy, so the fact that she had Down syndrome was a complete shock. In the ensuing days, weeks, and months I felt anger, joy, sadness, love, grief, hopefulness, anxiety, pride, embarrassment, hope, and despair. I was at times overly pessimistic and overly optimistic. What helped me to get through this period was my determination to know everything I could about Down syndrome. I wanted to know what the most effective programs were, who the best people were, and how to access them. The support of other families was invaluable, even though I felt my family made things worse.

—Claire, parent of a child
with Down syndrome
(quoted with permission from parent)

Discovering that a child has a disability can be a difficult experience for a parent. Some parents find out gradually as the child grows and develops. For example, the onset of autism symptoms begins in late infancy to two years of age, with fairly typical development prior to that point (Woodgate, Ateah, & Secco, 2008). Other parents find out the minute their child is born or even prior to birth as a result of genetic testing. For example, the physical features of spina bifida are evident at birth and can be diagnosed in utero (Vermaes et al., 2008). This chapter deals with medical conditions present at birth that result in a child having a disability and discusses some of the accompanying stresses and challenges for families.

The American Academy of Pediatrics (2001, 2006) has estimated that 12 to 16 percent of all children in America experience some type of disabling condition. This amounts to between 6.5 and 9 million children. Childhood disability, generally speaking, has been defined as "an ongoing chronic physical, developmental, behavioral, or emotional condition that requires health and related services beyond that required by peers" (Newacheck & Halfon, 1998, p. 610). This chapter, however, focuses on developmental disabilities because of the inclusiveness of the definition. The Administration on Developmental Disabilities (ADD) defines a *developmental disability* as a physical or mental impairment that begins before age 22 that alters or substantially inhibits a person's capacity to do at least three of the following (ADD Mission Statement, n.d.):

- Take care of themselves (dress, bathe, eat, and other daily tasks)
- Speak and understand clearly
- Learn
- Walk/move around
- Make decisions
- Live independently
- Earn and manage an income

Children with developmental disabilities face many challenges because their needs cross many developmental boundaries. Families often have to coordinate multiple services that can include special health care needs, learning challenges, physical limitations, and cognitive challenges. Developmental disabilities are caused by many factors, and sometimes the cause remains a mystery. However, exploring the etiology of developmental disabilities is an important first step to understanding how to respond to children and families.

Etiology

Many factors can cause disorders that result in disabling conditions. Disorders can result from environmental factors such as maternal substance use, poor nutrition, or exposure to toxic substances. They can result from genetic disorders such as muscular dystrophy, or they can result from a combination of genes and environmental factors (Batshaw, 2002). Understanding the causes of disabling conditions can lead to prevention, identification of complicating factors, and interventions to alleviate the developmental impact of the condition. Specifically, Percy (2007) believes that understanding causal factors can lead to (1) prevention of some genetic disorders, (2) better preparation for parents for inherited disorders such as fragile X syndrome, (3) prevention of disorders that have environmental causes, (4) interventions that will improve quality of life and maximize potential, and (5) the development of more effective interventions. This chapter profiles five conditions to present readers with a range of family experiences.

Medical Conditions

This sections offers a brief overview of the following medical conditions and syndromes that are leading causes of developmental disabilities: (1) cerebral palsy, (2) Down syndrome, (3) fragile X syndrome, (4) fetal alcohol syndrome (FAS), and (5) spina bifida. The impact of these conditions and syndromes on behavioral/emotional, cognitive, learning, and physical development varies considerably. After reviewing each of these, discussion focuses on common stresses and challenges for families.

Cerebral Palsy

Cerebral palsy (CP) occurs in approximately 2.5 per 1,000 live births (Stanley, Blair, & Alberman, 2000). According to Fehlings, Hunt, and Rosenbaum (2007), cerebral palsy refers to a "group of motor disorders with several common features, including (1) onset is before, during, or after birth; (2) motor difficulties that are secondary to brain impairment; (3) abnormal muscle tone and impaired control of movements, with poor motor coordination and balance or abnormal movements and postures; (4) the disorder is permanent but nonprogressive; and (5) it is often accompanied by disturbances of sensation, cognition, communication, perception, and behavior, and/or seizure disorder" (p. 279). There are several distinct types of CP, divided into two categories: spastic and extrapyramidal. Spasticity involves excessive stiffness in the muscles and can occur on one side of the body (hemiplegia), in both legs (diplegia), and stiffness in both arms and legs (quadriplegia). Extrapyramidal CP involves significant variability in an individual's muscle tone (e.g., low tone to excessive stiffness) and can sometimes include involuntary movements. Individuals can be affected by features of both spastic and extrapyramidal CP (Batshaw, 2002).

While CP may be present at birth, it is rarely diagnosed until the developing child begins missing developmental (motor) milestones (Dagenais et al., 2006). There are potentially multiple prenatal (e.g., premature birth, intrauterine infection), perinatal (e.g., neonatal encephalopathy), and postnatal (e.g., brain injuries or infections) causes of CP. The most recognizable feature of CP is difficulty controlling motor movements in the areas of the body that are affected. In addition, individuals with CP also frequently experience seizures, visual impairments, hearing loss, poor growth, swallowing difficulties, aspiration pneumonia, gastrointestinal reflux, and orthopedic complications (Fehlings, Hunt, & Rosenbaum, 2007). People with CP can have typical intelligence, but they are at much higher risk for experiencing cognitive delays and learning disabilities (Stanley, Blair, & Alberman, 2000).

Down Syndrome

Down syndrome occurs 0.92 times per 1,000 births, and there are currently more than 400,000 people with Down syndrome (Lovering & Percy, 2007). Infants with Down syndrome are easily identifiable at birth because of distinctive physical features, including three palm print patterns, Brushfield spots, which are colored speckles in the iris of the eye, neck skinfold, and widely spaced first toes (Blackman, 1990). Children with Down syndrome have an increased risk of abnormalities in nearly every organ and tend to grow less quickly than other children. Hearing and vision problems are very common in children with Down syndrome and should be addressed early. Additionally, individuals with Down syndrome are at higher risk for congenital heart disease; gastrointestinal conditions; ear, nose, and throat issues; oral health problems; skin conditions; eye problems; thyroid abnormalities; diabetes; hematological abnormalities; obesity; arthritis; and seizures (Lovering & Percy, 2007). Children with Down syndrome also tend to have more behavior and psychiatric problems than other children (Batshaw, 2002).

Fetal Alcohol Syndrome (FAS)

Fetal alcohol spectrum disorder (FASD) describes a collection of behavioral, cognitive, learning, and physical disabilities, which can have a developmental impact that lasts a lifetime, caused by prenatal exposure to alcohol. FASD refers to a set of mental and physical birth defects that are caused by alcohol abuse by women during pregnancy. FASD occurs approximately 9.1 to 10 per 1,000 live births in the United States, but rates vary by subpopulations (Nulman, Ickowicz, Koren, & Knittel-Keren, 2007). For example, rates are higher in poor inner-city communities than they are in suburban communities (Abel, 1995). Children with FASD experience a range of cognitive and physical challenges. Each child with FASD will experience challenges across a spectrum from mild to severe. The diagnostic categories for FASD include fetal alcohol syndrome (FAS), partial FAS, alcohol-related birth defects (ARBD), and alcohol-related neurological disorders (ARND).

FAS refers to the most severe form of FASD and is the leading cause of nongenetic intellectual and developmental disabilities (Nulman, Ickowicz, Koren, & Knittel-Keren, 2007). FAS prevalence estimates vary from 0.6 to 3 per 1,000 individuals. FAS involves brain damage, facial anomalies, and physical growth challenges. Individuals with FAS can experience hearing and vision problems, challenges with temperament and behavior, learning, attention, memory, and problem-solving abilities (Batshaw, 2002). Diagnosing FASD is challenging because of the extreme variation in level of intellectual function and physical anomalies. Children with FASD may present with behavioral and emotional challenges but have no obvious physical anomalies, thus making the linkage to FASD difficult. Finally, conditions such as phenylketonuria (PKU), fragile X syndrome, Turner syndrome, or Williams syndrome may present similar physical and neurodevelopmental features.

Children with FASD can experience secondary disabilities such as attention-deficit/hyperactivity disorder (ADHD), conduct disorder, depression, and psychotic episodes. Children with FASD often experience medical complications that are evident at birth. Interventions for FASD should target society in general as well as specific community and cultural groups to change patterns of alcohol-related behaviors that lead to alcohol abuse during pregnancy. Intervention should also target pediatricians and family practice physicians to improve knowledge of FASD related to prevention efforts, diagnosis, and multidisciplinary treatment. Early developmental screening and early intervention to prevent or alleviate the impact of secondary disabilities are essential to improving long-term developmental outcomes for children experiencing FASD (Nulman, Ickowicz, Koren, & Knittel-Keren, 2007).

Fragile X Syndrome

Fragile X syndrome is the leading inherited cause of mental retardation (Batshaw, 2002). Fragile X accounts for one-third of all X-linked causes of mental retardation and nearly 50 percent of X-linked causes of learning disabilities. Estimates suggest that 1 in 4,000 boys and 1 in 6,000 girls have a full mutation for fragile X. Individuals with fragile X account for just over 1 percent of children receiving special education services. Males with fragile X syndrome are affected much more negatively than females. The difference between men and women is due to the presence of a second, nonmutated X chromosome. Males with fragile X syndrome have characteristic physical features such as a long narrow face; prominent jaw and forehead; large, protruding ears; high, arched palate; flat feet; and mitral valve prolapse. Boys with fragile X often have low muscle tone and lack physical coordination. Males with fragile X experience mental retardation and have poor communication skills. Females with fragile X syndrome experience less severe cognitive limitations than males (e.g., mild mental retardation or learning disability). Women with the full mutation often look typical but may have a long narrow face and large ears (Mazzocco & Holden, 2007).

Spina Bifida

Spina bifida (SB) is a neural tube defect caused by malformation of the neural tube during embryonic development that results in relatively severe disabilities for individuals that experience the disorder (Lomax-Bream et al., 2007). In the United States, SB occurs approximately 3.2 times per 10,000 live births and is one of the leading causes of paralysis in children (Macias, Clifford, Saylor, & Kreh, 2001). Children with SB experience a variety of physical impairments related to ambulation (e.g., varying degrees of paraplegia), loss of sensation in the lower body, and loss of bowel and bladder control. Children with SB also experience congenital brain malformations involving the cerebellum, midbrain, and corpus callosum, and approximately 80 percent experience hydrocephalus that requires shunt diversion (Batshaw, 2002). Consequently, many children with SB experience challenges related to the development of cognitive, language, and adaptive behavior skills (Lomax-Bream, 2007).

Despite the affect of SB on the developing child's brain, children with SB rarely experience mental retardation. However, they do experience varying degrees of domain-specific strengths and challenges. For example, they may experience difficulties with focus and attention, visual perception, rule-based problem solving, and learning challenges related to reading comprehension and math (Macias, Clifford, Saylor, & Kreh, 2001). As children with SB reach school age, they often experience difficulties with the flexible use of language, especially related to their ability to engage in meaningful discourse with others (e.g., ability to understand and communicate the content of a conversation). As children with SB get older, they experience challenges with the acquisition of independent living skills due to having difficulties with setting goals and organizing behaviors to achieve goals.

Challenges Presented by Various Medical Conditions

We first started to really notice how challenging her needs were going to be our first night at home. She cried and cried—almost nonstop. Nothing consoled her. A lot of babies cry a lot in the first weeks at home, but we knew this was different but we couldn't put our finger on it. For the next few months our pediatrician told us to relax and she would eventually grow out of it. He assumed she was experiencing colic. It would be another two years before she was diagnosed with fragile X syndrome. In the meantime, we experienced intense fear, stress, and frustration.

—Amanda, parent of a child
with fragile X syndrome
(quoted with permission from parent)

Discovering that your child has a developmental disability can occur the moment your child is born (or prenatally) or it can occur over time as a child has difficulties or misses typical developmental milestones. Having a child with a disability has been thought to elicit a strong grief response from parents. Parental reactions to the birth of a child postulates that parents react with grief, shock, denial, and mourning (Roll-Pettersson, 2001). Macias, Clifford, Saylor, and Kreh (2001) described a process where parents must progress through stages of mourning but may react with defense mechanisms such as denial, isolation, reaction formation, projection, and regression if the progression is not completed. The result can be what Ohlshansky (1962) called "chronic sorrow," which can last a lifetime. However, the negative response to disability may be overstated. Some have suggested that this is due to society's prejudicial view of people with disabilities rather than to actual experiences.

A study by Sloper and Turner (1991) revealed that pediatricians tended to overestimate parental needs related to coping with a child with disability and overestimated the marital discord and overall negative effect on the family. Woodgate, Ateah, and Secco (2008) described parents experiencing mixed emotions such as fear/hope, anger/love, and grief/

pride with the birth of a child with a disability. Current thinking about the parental response focuses more on helping families to face the day-to-day challenges of parenting, systemic barriers they may face related to accessing services, and supporting families in dealing with their own personal psychological needs when and if they identify such a need.

Day-to-Day Parenting Challenges

The increased stress associated with raising a child with a developmental disability can create an immense amount of stress on a family system. Families are forced to engage in a considerable amount of time-consuming health and developmental care activities that can create both emotional and physical stress (Capper, 1996). Children with cerebral palsy and spina bifida, for example, have, depending on the severity of their condition, intensive health and physical care needs such as hygiene, toileting, physical transfer needs, medication management, and mobility needs (Dagenais, 2006; Lomax-Bream et al., 2007; Macias, Clifford, Saylor, & Kreh, 2001). Many families that have children with challenging health and physical care needs are often faced with frequent physician and therapy appointments, adding to the daily stress. Parents of children with other disorders, such as fragile X or autism, may face fewer health and physical care needs, but they are challenged by behavioral/emotional needs, learning challenges, and potential mental health issues (Roll-Petersson, 2001; Woodgate, Ateah, & Seccon, 2008). Nearly one-half of children with intellectual disabilities exhibit challenging behaviors that can greatly complicate parenting (Carr, Horner, & Turnbull, 1999).

Evidence suggests that families with a child with a developmental disability have fragile support systems (Shannon, 2004). When a child with a disability arrives in the home, many families report disruption in their social networks. Friends and family often sever ties, which serves to further isolate the family. The impact is compounded for families that have limited resources, especially for single mothers. Lack of money for basic life needs such as food, clothing, medical care, and housing can add a significant amount of psychological and emotional stress for families (Lloyd & Rosman, 2005). Child care for children with disabilities is difficult to find; high-quality child care is next to impossible (Taylor, 2005). Families, especially single mothers, face a difficult dilemma—they need to work to support their family but they cannot find suitable day care for their children with special needs.

Family stress can also increase the risk of maltreatment for children with disabilities (Shannon, 2006). Family stress may be associated with the presence of disabilities among children who have been maltreated. Pearson (1996) suggested that the added stress experienced by caregivers of children with disabilities may explain the increased risk of abuse for children with disabilities. Specifically, stress factors included parent disability, mental or emotional problem present in family member, family social isolation, involvement with the legal system, child alcohol or drug dependency, and gang activity or involvement (Sullivan & Knutson, 2000).

Child protection systems report having larger numbers of children with developmental disabilities placed in care (Govindshenoy & Spencer, 2006; Hughes & Rycus, 1998; Sullivan & Knutson, 2000). Nationally, it has been estimated that children with developmental disabilities are three to five times more likely to be maltreated than children who do not have developmental disabilities (Ammerman & Balderian, 1993; Sobsey & Varnhagen, 1988; Hibbard & Desch, 2007; Sullivan & Knutson, 2000). Sullivan and Knutson reported that the rate of maltreatment is 31 percent for children with disabilities compared to a 9 percent prevalence rate for children in general. Developmental disabilities have been treated as a secondary concern in CPS programs (Govindshenoy & Spencer; Hughes & Rycus). In addition to day-to-day challenges and psychological affects, families often experience systemic barriers related to services.

Systemic Challenges

Children with developmental disabilities and their families face many challenges that could qualify as oppressive. Families that include children with developmental disabilities often experience oppression and discrimination when trying to access services that most parents take for granted (e.g., child care, dental care; Levy, 1995). The presence of a child with a developmental disability can have a large impact on a family's financial stability, quality of life, available time and resources, relationships with extended family and friends, and family roles (Dewees, 2004). Disability can be stigmatizing for a child and his or her entire family. (Rounds, Weil, & Bishop, 1994).

Families experience barriers when trying to access most services. Levy (1995) reported that families struggle with finding physicians and dentists willing to provide care to their children with disabilities. While families of children ages 0 to 3 are entitled to a host of therapeutic services under Part C of IDEA, families often experience difficulty accessing services. In rural communities, for example, many services simply may not be available. Insurance companies often refuse to pay for recommended therapies or severely limit the number and frequency of visits (Parish & Cloud, 2006). Finally, when children reach school age, families often find themselves in an adversarial relationship with their school system. Schools are reluctant to take on the expense of intensive interventions and often deny families the services they need (Dewees, 2004).'

Raising a child with a disability costs more than raising a child who does not have a disability. Children with disabilities tend to experience multiple health and developmental issues that require treatment intervention, and support. Several studies have reported on the increased need for specialized therapies that require weekly appointments (Birenbaum, 2002; Dewees, 2004). Disability often requires families to purchase adaptive equipment and make expensive modifications to their homes (Parish & Cloud, 2006). The out-of-pocket expenses that families of children with disabilities incur have been estimated to be two to three times higher than for families that do not include a child with a disability (Newachek & McManus, 1988).

Psychological Well-Being

Capper (1996) described a range of emotions, including "anguish, guilt, anger, depression, anxiety, embarrassment, denial, grief, and hopelessness," she experienced as the extent of her daughter's disabilities became evident (p. 1). Vermaes et al. (2008) reported that having a child with spina bifida, for example, has a negative impact on the psychological functioning of parents that can create a permanent form of stress for them. Capper coped with her stress by becoming involved in her daughter's care as well as learning everything she could about her daughter's disability, needs, and the services available. Regardless, the added stress of parenting a child with a disability can have a negative effect on the family, and there is a significantly higher rate of divorce in families that include children with disabilities than in families that do not include children with disabilities (Capper, 1996). The dreams and hopes for the future that accompany new parenthood often vanish or at least are modified when a child is born with a disability.

Mothers raising children with developmental disabilities often experience high levels of emotional and physical stress (Lloyd & Rosman, 2005). Additionally, they are less likely to benefit from respite from their caregiving duties, which is essential for maintaining physical and mental health. As a consequence, mothers raising children with developmental disabilities experience higher rates of mental health concerns such as depression and anxiety, and they are more susceptible to high blood pressure, migraine headaches, and ulcers. Single parents report more psychological symptoms than dual-parent households, because dual-parent households report having more choices available to them and thus have lower reported levels of mental and physical ailments (Scorgie & Sobsey, 2000).

Professionals who ascribe too rigidly to a grief/mourning model or the denial/acceptance model may have difficulty understanding the complexity of the emotions that families experience and may underestimate their true needs and the strengths they possess. While most families do experience grief and sadness, most experiences of these emotions do not rise to the level of clinical pathology. Parents need help with understanding their feelings about their child and expressing their grief and sadness, but they also need help exploring their positive feelings about their child and taking advantage of their strengths. Professionals should not strive to work with families to reach acceptance of their child's disability, but rather they should assist them with exploring the possibilities for their child.

Interventions and Supports for Children and Families

The straw that broke our backs was when my mother said she could not babysit Justin anymore because he was too much for her to handle. What do you do when your own family won't help you with simple things like babysitting for two hours so you can go grocery shopping? We can't find paid babysitters who will sit for us for the same reason. Justin is a great kid, but his CP is pretty severe and he does need a lot of physical care with things like eating and the bathroom. I feel constant stress because I never get a break—my chest is tight, I don't sleep at night, and I have headaches all the time. Then I feel guilty because I am blaming my problems on him, when he is the one who has the real problems. I worry about what school is going to be like for him, I worry about his future, I feel sad because he has no friends, and I cry every time I try to imagine what it must feel like to be him. So, if you ask what I need help with, I say everything. Mostly, though, it is the little things, like someone to watch him, playdates, other parents to talk to who understand, and time for myself. There are big things, too, of course, like better insurance that will pay for therapy and all the additional medical expenses.

—Jennifer, mother of a four-year-old child
with cerebral palsy
(quoted with permission from parent)

When exploring how best to support children with developmental disabilities and their families, the community, social workers, medical providers, and other practitioners need to consider a range of possible interventions. Jennifer describes several areas where she needs help, including (1) access to physical therapy for Justin, (2) socialization (friends) for Justin, (3) educational planning to help him be ready for school, (4) networking and support from other parents, (5) respite care and babysitting, (6) possible personal care assistance for Justin, and (7) counseling support for herself to help her to cope with stress, grief, sadness, and depression. Most families that include children with disabilities experience these issues and more (Shannon, 2006). Therefore, intervention needs to focus on the child's needs related to their disabling condition (e.g., medical treatment, learning supports, daily living needs, and therapies such as occupational, physical, and speech/language) and the family (e.g., identifying formal and informal supports). Intervention, however, can begin before a child is even born, through genetic testing and counseling and newborn screening.

Genetic Testing and Newborn Screening

Many genetic conditions that cause developmental disabilities can be identified before a child is born. Having prior knowledge of a condition such as fragile X can help prepare parents for the needs that their child may face. Knowing the cause of a child's developmental problem will help parents to know what to expect and will help them with choosing the best available interventions. There are many types of tests that can be used to detect the presence of specific types of developmental disabilities, including ultrasound scans, maternal serum screening, amniocentesis, chorionic villus sampling, and percutaneous umbilical cord sampling (Percy, Lewkis, & Brown, 2007).

Ultrasounds and maternal serum screening can detect physical growth abnormalities such as those exhibited by children with spina bifida. In the case of spina bifida, corrective surgery can now be conducted in utero to repair the spinal cord, which can greatly decrease the risk for disabling conditions and their severity. Women over the age of 35 or who are believed to be at risk of having a child with a birth defect can choose to have amniocentesis, chorionic villus sampling, or umbilical blood sampling. These tests look for protein markers, extra or missing chromosomes, or structurally altered chromosomes that indicate specific types of disorders (Batshaw, 2002; Percy, Lewkis, & Brown, 2007). Finally, there has been a strong legislative push for universal newborn screening that will make many of these tests mandatory for all mothers. The hope is that all families will be given crucial information to help them make family planning decisions, to mentally prepare for the birth of their child and know what to expect, and to enable them to plan for interventions that will maximize their child's quality of life.

Specialized Medical and Related Health Interventions

An important concern for parents of newborns with developmental disabilities is to ensure that their child's primary medical needs are being met. Children with Down syndrome, for example, often experience life-threatening gastrointestinal blockages and cardiovascular problems that in the past were often fatal but now can be corrected by surgery soon after birth (Lovering & Percy, 2007). Other conditions also result in various chronic medical needs that require ongoing treatment.

Families require support (e.g., financial and informational) to meet all the specialized care that a child with a disability requires. While some support is available through the various federal and state disability-related programs described previously, such programs are not adequate in and of themselves. Professionals need to consider the trade-offs between the intensity of services and the ultimate outcome or benefit for a child and family. More services do not necessarily translate into services that have a greater impact on the child and family. Professionals need to work closely with families to strike a balance between the frequency or intensity of services, the cost of those services, and the ultimate impact on the child and family. Once a child's medical needs are being addressed, professionals should support families in accessing early intervention services.

Early Intervention

With comprehensive and effective intervention, developmental disabilities are often preventable, at the very least; there is much that can be done to limit the developmental consequences of many disabilities. Early intervention with children experiencing developmental delays has been shown to positively influence their health and development. The goal of early intervention services is to minimize or prevent the physical, cognitive, emotional, and resource limitations of children ages 0 to 3 who are at risk for or are experiencing developmental delays or disabilities (Blackman, 2002).

Part C of the Individuals with Disabilities Education Act (IDEA) mandated states to develop comprehensive, coordinated services for infants and toddlers experiencing developmental delays (Part C, 1997). Early intervention services for young children with developmental disabilities can substantially improve developmental outcomes for children who are experiencing delays in development (Guralnick, 1998). Children and their families are entitled to a host of services through the Individuals with Disabilities Education Act (IDEA). In 2001, nearly 250,000 children under the age of 36 months qualified for Part C early intervention services, although it is estimated that three times this number may be eligible for services (U.S. Department of Education, 2001). IDEA requires states to provide comprehensive programs for infants, toddlers, and school-age children and their families. The legislation promotes family-centered service delivery for all children with disabilities. Another important piece of federal legislation affecting children with disabilities is the Rehabilitation Act of 1973 (Public Law 93-112). The act focuses on providing training and placement of people with disabilities in full-time, part-time, or supportive employment in competitive jobs. Additionally, training provided under the act emphasizes skills needed to live independently in the communities in which individuals with disabilities live. Section 504 of the Rehabilitation Act protects rights of people with disabilities in schools and other educational programs that are federally funded by ensuring access to educational facilities and programs, including colleges and universities (Capper, 1996). A key component of early intervention is a focus on the family through family-centered planning.

Family-Centered Planning

Families of children with disabilities must serve many roles in order to meet the needs of their children who have disabilities. They must serve as the child's advocate to make sure they receive the services for which they are eligible, namely, primary caregiver (e.g., providing daily specialized health care needs or implementing behavioral plans) and case manager to coordinate the delivery of services that cross many service delivery boundaries (Chapman, Kincaid, Shannon, & Schall, 2002). Families need both formal and informal support in several areas, including respite care, counseling, parent support groups, parenting education, and someone to educate and advocate for parents regarding their child's disability and the programs available to them. Families need access to quality and affordable child care, and they need health insurance so that they have access to prenatal, preventative, and specialized health care. Families need access to safe and affordable housing.

According to Lizanne Capper (1996), "parents of a child with multiple disabilities, whatever the disability, are looking for the same thing—support" (p. vii). Advocacy and support begins with understanding the law, the rights of families, and the services available to meet the needs of children with disabilities and their families. Advocacy also requires assertiveness. Assertiveness is not a given for parents of children with disabilities, and many parents can struggle with asserting themselves with providers and policymakers to advocate for their children (Shannon, 2004).

Families that include a child with a developmental delay have experienced issues and concerns that could be considered oppressive. Levy (1995) argued that, despite recent changes in policies and practices that promote person- and family-centered practice, individuals with developmental disabilities have historically experienced oppression and discrimination in all aspects of their lives. The addition of a child with a developmental disability can have a large impact on a family's financial stability, quality of life, available time and resources, relationships with extended family and friends, and family priorities and roles (Dewees, 2004). In 1998, for example, 24 percent of all children under age 3 lived at or below the federal poverty line compared to 32 percent of families that included a child receiving early intervention services (Scarborough et al., 2004; Shannon, 2008). Disability can be stigmatizing for children and their families. This stigma is often compounded when the family is poor, racially or ethnically diverse, or headed by single parents (Rounds, Weil, & Bishop, 1994). Empowerment of families receiving early intervention services is a central feature of Part C and is considered to be an important goal for early intervention professionals (Dunst & Trivette, 1989). The concept of empowerment provided the conceptual foundation for the elements of Part C that promoted family-centered practice (Dunst, Trivette, & LaPointe, 1991). In fact, Dunst and Deal (1994) suggested that family empowerment was the most important feature of Part C and that it is crucial for professionals to understand the mechanisms of empowerment in early intervention.

Summary

Having a child with a developmental disability has been described by families as the best and worst experience a parent can have. Capper (1996) felt that her experience raising her daughter was challenging, yet taught her to be a better, stronger, more compassionate person. She felt that she did not come to terms with her daughter's disability, she came to understand that society has a lack respect for people with disabilities. Her initial feelings of sadness, grief, anger, and frustration have evolved into feelings of love, motivation to change society, and provide support for other families. Too often, professionals devalue people with disabilities by viewing them in purely clinical/pathological terms. This clinical focus can be negative and narrow. The complexity of the family experience and their strengths must be acknowledged as a starting point. Families need support; children with disabilities need support; and medical, school, and community professionals must work together to meet their diverse needs.

References

Abel, E. L. (1995). An update on the incidence of FAS: FAS is not an equal opportunity birth defect. *Neurotoxicology and Teratology, 17,* 437–443.

Ammerman, R. T., & Balderian, N. J. (1993). *Maltreatment of children with disabilities.* Chicago, IL: National Committee to Prevent Child Abuse.

Administration on Developmental Disabilities Mission Statement (n.d.). About ADD. Retrieved January 7, 2007, from http://www.acf.dhhs.gov/programs/add/addabout.html.

American Academy of Pediatrics, Committee on Children with Disabilities (2001). Developmental surveillance and screening of infants and young children. *Pediatrics, 108,* 192–195.

American Academy of Pediatrics, Committee on Children with Disabilities (2006). Identifying infants and young children with developmental disorders in the medical home: An algorithm for developmental surveillance and screening. *Pediatrics, 118,* 405–420.

Batshaw, M. L. (2002). *Children with disabilities* (5th ed.). Baltimore MD: Paul H. Brookes.

Birenbaum, A. (2002). Poverty, welfare reform, and disproportionate rates of disability among children. *Mental Retardation, 40,* 212–218.

Blackman, J. A. (1990). Down syndrome. In J. A. Blackman (Ed.), *Medical aspects of developmental disabilities in children birth to three* (pp. 107–112), Rockville, MD: Aspen Publishers.

Brown, I., & Percy, M. (2007). *A comprehensive guide to intellectual and developmental disabilities.* Baltimore, MD: Paul H. Brookes.

Capper, L. (1996). *That's my child: Strategies for parents of children with disabilities.* Washington, DC: Child and Family Press.

Carr, E. G., Horner, R. H., & Turnbull, A. P. (1999). *Positive behavior support for people with developmental disabilities: A research synthesis.* Washington, DC: American Association on Mental Retardation.

Chapman, C., Kincaid, D., Shannon, P., & Schall, C. (2002). It's about us: Families and positive behavior support. In J. M. Lucyshyn, G. Dunlap, & R. W. Albin (Eds.), *Families and positive behavior support: Addressing the challenge of problem behaviors in family contexts* (chap. 17). Baltimore, MD: Paul H. Brookes.

Dagenais, L., Hall, N., Majnemer, A., Birnbaum, R., Dumas, F., Gosselin, J., Koclas, L., & Shevell, M. I. (2006). Communicating a diagnosis of cerebral palsy: Caregiver satisfaction and stress. *Pediatric Neurology, 35,* 408–414.

Dewees, M. (2004). Disability in the family: A case for reworking our commitments. *Journal of Social Work in Disability & Rehabilitation, 3*(1), 3–20.

Fehlings, D., Hunt, C., & Rosenbaum, P. (2007). Cerebral palsy. In I. Brown and M. Percy (Eds.), *A comprehensive guide to intellectual and developmental disabilities* (pp. 279–286), Baltimore, MD: Paul H. Brookes.

Gibson, C. M., & Weisner, T. S. (2002). Rational and ecocultural circumstances of program take-up among low-income working parents. *Human Organization, 61,* 154–166.

Govindshenoy, M., & Spencer, N. (2006). Abuse of the disabled child: A systematic review of population-based studies. *Child Care, Health, and Development, 33,* 552–558.

Guralnick, M. (1998). Effectiveness of early intervention for vulnerable children: A developmental perspective. *American Journal on Mental Retardation, 102,* 319–345.

Hibbard, R. A., & Desch, L. W. (2007). Maltreatment of children with disabilities. *Pediatrics, 119.5,* 1018–1026.

Hughes, R. C., & Rycus, J. S. (1998). *Developmental disabilities and child welfare.* Washington, DC: Child Welfare League of America Press.

Leet, A. I., Dormans, J. P., & Tosi, L. L. (2002). Muscles, bones, and nerves. In M. L. Batshaw (Ed.), *Children with disabilities* (5th ed.). Baltimore, MD: Paul H. Brookes.

Levy, J. M. (1995). Social work. In B. A. Thyer & N. Kropf (Eds.), *Developmental disabilities: Handbook for interdisciplinary practice* (pp. 234–247). Cambridge, MA: Brookline Books.

Lloyd, C. M., & Rosman, E. (2005). Exploring mental health outcomes for low-income mothers of children with special needs: Implications for policy and practice. *Infants and Young Children, 18,* 186–199.

Lomax-Bream, L. E., Taylor, H. B., Landry, S. H., Barnes, M. A., Fletcher, J. M., & Swank, P. (2007). Role of early parenting and motor skills on development in children with spina bifida. *Journal of Applied Developmental Pyschology, 28,* 250–263.

Lovering, J. S., & Percy, M. (2007). Down syndrome. In I. Brown and M. Percy (Eds.), *A comprehensive guide to intellectual and developmental disabilities* (pp. 149–172), Baltimore, MD: Paul H. Brookes.

Macias, M. M., Clifford, S. C., Saylor, C. F., & Kreh, S. M. (2001). Predictors of parenting stress in families of children with spina bifida. *Children's Health Care, 30*(1), 57–65.

Mazzocco, M. M. M., & Holden, J. J. A. (2007). Fragile X syndrome. In I. Brown and M. Percy (Eds.), *A comprehensive guide to intellectual and developmental disabilities* (pp. 173–188), Baltimore, MD: Paul H. Brookes.

Meyer, G. A., & Batshaw, M. L. (2002). Fragile X syndrome. In M. L. Batshaw (Ed.), *Children with disabilities* (5th ed.). Baltimore, MD: Paul H. Brookes.

Newacheck, P. W., & McManus, M. A. (1988). Financing health care for disabled children. *Pediatrics, 81,* 385–394.

Nulman, I., Ickowicz, A., Koren, G., & Knittel-Keren (2007). Fetal alcohol spectrum disorder. In I. Brown and M. Percy (Eds.), *A comprehensive guide to intellectual and developmental disabilities* (pp. 173–188). Baltimore, MD: Paul H. Brookes.

Ohlshansky, S. (1962). Chronic sorrow: A responsive to having a mentally defective child. *Social Casework, 43,* 190–193.

Parish, S. L., & Cloud, J. M. (2006). Financial well-being of young children with disabilities and their families. *Social Work, 51,* 223–232.

Pearson, S. (1996). Child abuse among children with disabilities. *Teaching Exceptional Children,* Sept/Oct, 34–37.

Percy, M. (2007). Factors that cause or contribute to intellectual and developmental disabilities. In I. Brown and M. Percy (Eds.), *A comprehensive guide to intellectual and developmental disabilities* (pp. 125–148), Baltimore, MD: Paul H. Brookes.

Percy, M., Lewkis, S. Z., & Brown, I. (2007). Introduction to genetics and development. In I. Brown and M. Percy (Eds.), *A comprehensive guide to intellectual and developmental disabilities* (pp. 125–148), Baltimore, MD: Paul H. Brookes.

Roll-Pettersson, L. (2001). Parents talk about how it feels to have a child with a cognitive disability. *European Journal of Special Education, 16*(1), 1–16.

Rounds, K. A., Weil, M., & Bishop, K. K. (1994). Practice with culturally diverse families of young children with developmental disabilities. *Families in Society, 75*(1), 3–15.

Scorgie, K., & Sobsey, D. (2000). Transformation outcomes associated with parenting children who have disabilities. *Mental Retardation, 38*, 195–206.

Shannon, P. (2004). Barriers to family-centered care in early intervention. *Social Work, 49*, 301–308.

Shannon, P. (2006). Children with disabilities in child welfare: Empowering the disenfranchised. In N. Boyd-Webb (Ed.), *Working with traumatized youth in child welfare* (pp. 102–112). New York: Guilford Press.

Shannon, P. (2008). Childhood disability, poverty, and family life: A complex relationship. In C. A. Broussard, and A. L. Joseph (Eds.), *Family poverty in diverse contexts*. Binghamton, NY: Haworth Press.

Sloper, P., & Turner, S. (1991). Parental and professional views of the needs of families with a severe disability. *Counseling Psychology Quarterly, 4*, 323–341.

Sobsey, D., & Varnhagen, C. (1988). *Sexual abuse, assault, and exploitation of Canadians with disabilities*. Ottawa, Ontario, Canada: Health and Welfare Canada.

Stanley, F. J., Blair, E., & Alberman, E. (2000). *Cerebral palsies: Epidemiology and causal pathways*. London: McKeith Press.

Sullivan, P. M., & Knutson, J. F. (2000). Maltreatment and disabilities: A population-based epidemiological study. *Child Abuse and Neglect, 24*, 1257–1273.

Taylor, A. (2005). Hidden benefit. *Community Care, 1592*, 50–51.

U.S. Department of Education. (2001). *Twenty-third annual report to Congress on the implementation of the Individuals with Disabilities Education Act*. Washington, DC: Author.

Vermaes, I. P. R., Janssens, J. M. A. M., Mullart, R. A., Vinck, A., & Gerris, J. R. M. (2008). Parents' personality and parenting stress in families of children with spina bifida. *Child Care, Health, and Development, 34*, 665–674.

Wise, P. H., Wampler, N. S., Chavkin, W., & Romero, D. (2002). Chronic illness among poor children enrolled in the Temporary Assistance for Needy Families program. *American Journal of Public Health, 92*, 1458–1461.

Woodgate, R. L., Ateah, C., & Secco, L. (2008). Living in a world of our own: The experience of parents who have a child with autism. *Qualitative Health Research, 18*, 1075–1083.

Medical Conditions That Appear during Early Childhood

Roxia B. Bullock

13 Chapter

Introduction

When a woman is pregnant, she always hopes that she will deliver a physically and mentally healthy child. Regardless of the circumstance of the pregnancy—planned, unexpected, single parent, late life, or adolescent—the family hopes for a healthy baby, but what happens when this is not the case? When a new baby comes upon the scene, there is always an adjustment period in every family, but when the child is diagnosed with a medical condition, stress and anxiety increase significantly (Seligman, Benjamin, & Darling, 1997). After the diagnosis, parents experience the loss of the perfect child they had anticipated. The process of working toward acceptance includes grieving, developing coping skills, and finding support from family, friends, and the spiritual and therapeutic community (Webb, 2003).

According to statistics, about 10 million children under 18 years of age in the United States suffer some form of chronic illness (Goble, 2004). Medical technology has advanced and saves many infants who, 25 years ago, might have died. Today, many live, yet are afflicted with chronic medical conditions that may seriously compromise their development (Goble, 2004; Hiatt-Michael, 2004).

This chapter addresses the situation of children who are diagnosed with medical conditions early in childhood. The focus is not only on the numerous stresses placed on the family members and the chronically ill child, but on the challenges of schools to meet the educational needs of these children.

The School's Role

School systems, as well as parents, must deal with accommodating the needs of chronically ill children. Wood (2006) raised the question: Why educate children with chronic illness, especially those who will have shortened lives? Since 1948, every child has had the legal right to a "least restrictive education" (to be discussed later). Wood (2006) explains that education in a school setting is a normal part of every child's life. School provides a routine that gives chronically ill children a purpose in life, a distraction from the illness, a feeling of normalcy, a feeling of belonging to a peer group, a sense of accomplishment, the possibility of working to fulfill their potential, and a chance for parents to see their child participating in the normal development of childhood.

Educational Setting for Chronically Ill Students

Over the past 30 years, public schools have taken on many roles in addition to the legal requirements of teaching the academics of reading, writing, and arithmetic. As reviewed in Chapters 7 and 8, schools today have been delegated the responsibility of meeting the special needs of children. These needs include dealing with learning disabilities, chronic illness, and various developmental disorders. The Individuals with Disabilities Education Act (IDEA) and Section 504 accommodate these needs.

Section 504
What is a 504? The 504 is a section in the Rehabilitation Act of 1973. Other than IDEA (discussed in Chapters 7 and 8), this was the most comprehensive disability rights statute enacted prior to 1990 and was an amendment to a previous vocational rehabilitation law (Rothstein, 1995). The 504 policy and procedures states (Rothstein, 1995, p. 27):

> *No otherwise qualified handicapped individual in the United States . . . shall, solely by reason of his handicap, be excluded from the participation in, be denied the benefit of, or be subjected to discrimination under any program or activity receiving federal financial assistance.*

Public schools and educational programs must post the Department of Education's (DOE) "Notice of Non-Discrimination under 504" (www .schools.nyc.gov). Implementation of this policy begins with the principal of each school appointing a school-based 504 coordinator to oversee the administration of the 504 regulation at the specific school. It is the obligation of the coordinator to convene a 504 team to evaluate requests for accommodations, to oversee provisions of any accommodations, and to maintain data relevant to the school's regulations. Records identify which students have a current plan in place, the specific accommodations for each student, and any incident related to or resulting from a student's 504 plan.

Assessment and Evaluation   How does a concerned parent obtain an evaluation for his or her child? If a parent or teacher believes that a child has a disability that impairs a major life activity (neurological, respiratory, speech, hearing, vision, etc.), the 504 coordinator is notified in writing and an assessment to determine eligibility is arranged. Learning and medical needs are included in determining eligibility. However, if the student compensates in some way (medication, equipment, corrective devices) and is able to participate equally with his or her nondisabled peers, then the child is not considered eligible for 504 accommodations.

A parent can initiate a 504 request for his or her chronically ill child using the appropriate form supplied by the school. If school staff initiates the request, they contact the 504 coordinator, who then must notify the parent in writing and send appropriate forms to be completed by the parents and/or health care provider before assessment can begin. To determine whether a child is eligible for 504, the team must answer three questions: Does the student have a physical or mental impairment? Is a major life activity affected by the physical or mental impairment? Is a major life activity substantially impaired?

The following steps are initiated to determine eligibility:

- The team gathers information from all necessary sources.
- The team does an assessment.
- The team notifies the parents of the results of the assessment and informs the parents of their rights, including the right to appeal if they disagree.
- The modifications and/or accommodations are put in place.

Modifications and Accommodations   If the 504 team determines that the student has a physical or mental impairment that substantially impedes a major life activity, accommodations are put in place. The parent must be sent a minimum of two notifications to meet with the 504 team. If the parent chooses not to attend, the team can proceed with designing accommodations for the student. The 504 accommodation plan must be reviewed at the school level by the school-based 504 coordinator on an annual basis before the end of the school year. If there are no changes to the plan, the parent signs approval forms and the plan is disseminated and implemented for the next year. Specific step-by-step procedures can be obtained from www.schools.nyc.gov. If a student moves to a new school, a full team should convene to review a student's 504 plan.

Each case example in this chapter is a composite from this author's experience and the literature in this field. Family situations have been drawn from a variety of scenarios, and all names have been changed.

Case of Samantha, in first Grade

Samantha is a first-grader who is visually impaired. Sam, as her friends call her, is blind in her right eye and is progressively losing sight in her left eye due to a genetic condition. Her parents have decided, for now, to enroll Sam in her local public school, which, through Section 504, has arranged related services of special transportation, counseling, and a Braille-reading pullout program. At this time Sam is functioning academically on a par with her fellow students. Her condition will be reviewed periodically as a condition of Section 504.

Individual Disabilities Educational Act

In 1975, the Individual Handicapped Educational Act (IDEA) (Public Law 94-142) was created to provide consistency throughout all states in the area of special education. In 1990, the word "handicapped" was changed to "disabilities." IDEA is a federal funding statue. The federal government gives supportive funding to states that provide special education according to federal guidelines (Rothstein, 1995). IDEA provides education for school-age children of all ages who meet the eligibility requirements. This is especially significant for early intervention, as recent research has shown (Filipek, 1999). IDEA provides not only for education (learning disabilities), but also instruction in basic self-help skills such as feeding, toilet training, occupational training, and speech and language (Rothstein, 1995). Every eligible child is entitled to an annual review and a triennial reevaluation to monitor his or her progress.

Major Differences between IDEA and Section 504

The federal government provides funding for persons who meet IDEA eligibility. Although a school does not receive extra funds for Section 504, if that school is out of compliance it may lose federal funding. Some factors included in IDEA: evaluation of child by multidisciplinary team, written parental consent, reevaluation every three years and an annual review, IEP for an educational program, related services (speech and language), time frames, age limitations, child to reside in school district administering the evaluation, hearing officer appointed by impartial appointee, enforcement by U.S. Department of Education, Office of Special Education. Some factors included in Section 504 that vary from IDEA: assessment determined by a variety of sources, no written consent from parents (only notification), periodic reevaluation and before significant changes, covers the lifespan of the eligible person, provides related services, hearing officer appointed by school and enforced by U.S. Department of Education, Office of Civil Rights (de Bettencourt, 2002). Figure 13.1 offers an overview of support services.

School Personnel

The most important persons in the educational setting are the teachers. When dealing with a chronically ill child (or any child), the knowledge and training of the teachers are of the utmost importance (Berres & Knoblock, 1987). Administrative support through special training and workshops for teachers enhances the educational experience of the child. Twenty percent of school-age children have some form of chronic illness (Clay & Drotar, 2004). The IEP and 504 plans recommend modifications in the classroom for these children, such as sitting in the front of the classroom or using hearing devices, and teachers need to be trained in the appropriate use of these techniques. Teachers should develop a cooperative relationship with parents concerning absences, makeup work, tutoring, academic expectations, and social adjustment. The school psychologist and social worker are valuable resources for in-service

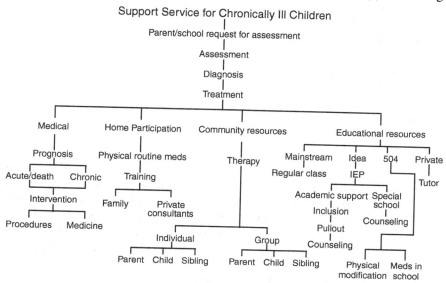

programs to help teachers become knowledgeable about treatment and its side effects (Clay & Drotar, 2004).

The school nurse is another important person to the chronically ill child. The nurse is not only trained to handle medical crises on school premises, but is involved with dispensing medication and can also share medical knowledge.

Resilience and Strengths

Living with a child with chronic illness is stressful and taxing. Parents develop coping skills as well as physical and emotional strengths to help and to teach the ill child regarding the extensive medical, emotional, and physical tasks they must master in the course of everyday life. Social workers and medical professionals are trained to acknowledge every individual's strength, respect his or her capacity to grow, and offer encouragement. These professionals can help support the parents and also work collaboratively with the family to find resources in the community according to the child's special needs (Saleebey, 1997).

Selected Medical Conditions

The sections that follow discuss the special challenges for families and schools in dealing with children diagnosed with the following medical conditions:

- Autism
- Seizure disorders

- Cystic fibrosis
- Multisensory deprivation
- Visual impairment
- Sickle cell disease

Autism

Definition

> The synonymous terms Autistic Spectrum Disorders and Pervasive Developmental Disorders refer to a wide continuum of associated cognitive and neurobehavioral disorders including, but not limited to, three core-defining features: impairments in socialization, impairments in verbal and nonverbal communication, and restricted and repetitive patterns of behaviors.
> —Filipek et al., 1999, p. 439

Recently, there has been concern about what appears to be an increase in the number of children diagnosed with autism. Previously, the rate of autism diagnosed in the general population had been less than the 1 in 160 of today (Filipek et al., 1999). However, as diagnosis and research have become better defined, the term *autistic spectrum disorder* has replaced the single word *autism* and now includes autism, Asperger's syndrome, Rett syndrome, childhood disintegrative disorder, and pervasive developmental disorder. Regardless of the etiologies of these disorders, early screening and diagnosis are essential (Brock et al., 2006; Filipek et al., 1999). Early screening allows for early interventions in education, speech and language training, socialization treatment, and family support (Filipek et al., 1999).

Treatment

Early Detection   Overt autistic symptoms generally do not appear until between ages 2 and 3. However, a parent will often say, "I knew there was something wrong from the very beginning." Some of the symptoms autistic infants might exhibit are not lifting their arms or changing posture in anticipation of being held, lack of cuddling, stiffening when held, lack of eye contact or smiling in social interactions, ignoring familiar persons, indiscriminate approach to strangers, and/or not responding to interactive play (Filipek, 1999). The attachment of the autistic child to the parent is exhibited differently from that of a typical child. An autistic child may become very upset with a change in routine and display tantrums. The child may seem aloof upon reunification, unlike a typical child, who might cling (Siegel, 2008). In addition, younger autistic children have difficulty with peer relationships and may not move beyond parallel play. Some autistic children want friends but do not understand the concept of reciprocity and sharing (Filipek, 1999). Stereotypic motor movements that are self-stimulating, such as hand clapping, arm flapping, spinning, and rocking, are characteristic of the autistic child. Language ranges from mute to fluency. Language delays are common, and some children develop language only to lose it later (Filipek, 1999).

Parents often are not taken seriously when, during their child's infancy, they express concern that "something is not right." However, when a knowledgeable pediatrician screens for autism or refers the child to a specialist for screening, the child and family may receive intervention as early as 12 months of age (Filipek, 1999; Greenspan, 2006; Openshaw, 2008; Schopler, 1993). Many times the parents must serve as their own advocates and search for adequate programs to help their child. Resources for parents include books on autism, state-run developmental evaluation clinics, school districts' early childhood assessment and evaluation intervention, the Autism Society of America, the *Journal of Autism and Developmental Disorders,* and support groups for parents.

Specific Programs   Most early intervention programs focus on speech and language, socialization, and behavioral training. Parents may avail themselves of public school programs or private early intervention agencies. Some models are Applied Behavioral Analysis (ABA), Treatment and Education of Autistic and Related Communication Handicapped Children (TEACCH), and Developmental, Individual-Difference, Relationship-Based (DIR) (Breakey, 2006; Greenspan, 2006).

Applied Behavioral Analysis   Applied Behavioral Analysis is grounded in B. F. Skinner's conditioned response approach (Breakey, 2006). This is a very intense and precise program of 30 to 40 hours per week in direct one-on-one teaching for two to three years. The implementation is by highly skilled professionals, parents, and family members. All persons involved work as a team (Breakey, 2006). For best results, early intervention is recommended.

Treatment and Education of Autistic and Related Communication Handicapped Children (TEACCH)   TEACCH offers a broad range of services to autistic people and their families, including diagnoses and assessment, individualized treatment programs, social skills training, vocational training, parent training, and counseling (Breakey, 2006). The goal of the program is to prepare autistic individuals to live and work up to their potential (Breakey, 2006). The principles of TEACCH are "improved adaptation, parent collaboration, assessment for individualized treatment, structured teaching, skill enhancement, cognitive and behavior therapy, and generalist training" (Breakey, 2006, pp. 46–51).

Developmental, Individual-Difference, Relationship-Based (DIR) Model ("Floortime")   The goal in working with the autistic spectrum disorder (ASD) child is to create a healthy foundation of development (Greenspan, 2006; Siegel,

2008). The goal for the child is to develop the ability to relate to others in a warm, pleasant, meaningful, and communicative way. The teacher follows the lead of the child and then brings the child into the shared world (Greenspan, 2006). As each family member finds his or her coping abilities, this in turn supports the care and education of the ASD child.

Considerations for the School

Parents must contact their school district and access available physical and educational services through a 504 referral and/or an educational evaluation with the school committee of special education. Depending on the severity of the autism, the DOE and the parents decide whether mainstreaming or a special school would constitute an appropriate setting. The New York City Department of Education is an example of a public school system that provides programs for autistic children at specific schools. This may not be true in all school systems. Often, parents have to change locations and schools for the autistic child and siblings to accommodate the academic and medical needs of the autistic child (Hines, 1994).

Case of Benjamin, Age 3

It was December in a public school in a large metropolitan city. The prekindergarten (three-year-olds) teacher came to me (school social worker) to discuss a very difficult child, Benjamin. He had not progressed since September, had exhibited extreme acting-out behavior, threw tantrums during any type of change, no matter how small, and had not developed language appropriate for a three-year-old. His parents had been called in four times to date and had argued that all children develop at different rates, and they insisted on giving their child at least one more year before considering an evaluation. After observing Benjamin in the classroom, I agreed with the teacher's assessment of him. He also showed signs of self-stimulating behaviors (hand flapping, spinning, and manipulating crayons for three or four minutes at a time). He showed little to no eye contact or interactive play with the teacher or with other children. I called his parents to set up an appointment.

I was anticipating resistance and anxiety from the parents, and I met with an exasperated Mr. and Mrs. Hines the next day. They did not want to hear any more complaints about Benjamin. I empathized with them and reassured them I was not going to complain but that I was here to help them help Ben. They admitted they were afraid that they sensed this conversation was bound to take place. Mrs. Hines took a deep breath and shared that Ben had been different since birth. He was their first child, but she certainly knew what typical behavior looked like. He did not babble or look at her or interact with her or her husband. He seemed detached and hard to cuddle. Benjamin required much of her attention. Mrs. Hines was becoming concerned, but admitted her fears prevented her from facing these strange behaviors. Her cousin had an autistic son, and she refused to think it could happen to her son, too. His physical exams ruled out any health issues. Her pediatrician told her not to worry, that he would outgrow these symptoms. With much empathy, I discussed an assessment to rule out or confirm their fears, after which I referred them to an autistic specialist. We are in a large metropolitan city where there are many resources. Self-education is important, so I gave them names of books to read.

After months of assessment with a new pediatrician specializing in autism, background reading, and evaluation by the Department of Education Committee on Special Education 0 to 5 (early intervention program), Mrs. Hines's fears were confirmed. Benjamin was diagnosed with autism. At first, Mrs. Hines was distraught, but soon used her internal strengths to begin finding resources for

Benjamin, both through the Department of Education and a professional from a private agency who came to the home four hours a day, five days a week to work with her son on socialization skills. This was not covered by the family's insurance, and Mrs. Hines had to reduce her work schedule to part-time so she could be home to continue the work that the professional taught not only Benjamin but her and her husband. Mrs. Hines continued to research autism, and after the diagnosis she joined a support group for parents with autistic children. I helped her contact the school social worker to set up a meeting with the administration of the special program Benjamin would attend. The social worker is key in coordinating the many services that the school can offer. The social worker can provide information regarding community resources that can supplement the school program (Openshaw, 2008).

Full inclusion in a mainstream classroom setting depends on the severity of a child's autism. There is controversy about inclusion versus pullout programs. But even some opponents recognize that some children need a pullout program for specific services such as speech and language, occupational therapy, and some academics (Simpson & Myles, 1998). As Benjamin advances in school, Mrs. Hines will work with the IEP team and decide what would be the best combination of academic and social programs to meet his needs. In addition to Mrs. Hines's in-school advocacy, she must reinforce the schoolwork with a home program. This is time-consuming, tedious work for the family but necessary for the child to function to his potential (Hiatt-Michael, 2004).

Seizure Disorders

Definition

A seizure is a change in sensation, awareness, or behavior caused by an electrical disturbance in the brain. The extent can range from a tingling to a grand mal, during which a person loses control and consciousness. The causes include birth defects, birth or head injury, brain tumor, or brain infection. Seizures are a symptom of epilepsy (Kutscher, 2006).

Epilepsy is usually diagnosed by a neurologist. The neurologist records a careful medical and developmental history of the child. The neurologist may then administer several possible tests, such as a blood test, electroencephalogram (EEG), a computerized axial tomography (CAT) scan, and/or a magnetic resonance imaging (MRI) scan (Kutscher, 2006).

Seizures are divided into two major categories: focal seizures and generalized seizures. Focal seizures, or partial seizures, occur in just one part of the brain. Generalized seizures occur on both sides of the brain simultaneously as a result of abnormal neuronal activity (Simpson & Myles, 1998; Kutscher, 2006).

Treatment

There is no known cure for epilepsy, but there are several medications that can prevent seizures. The physician may recommend several trials to find the most effective medication for a child. For persistent seizures that do not respond to medication, surgery is an option.

Considerations for the School

Parents need to inform the school staff that their child suffers from seizures, which type of seizures the child has, and how to handle the seizures. The child may want to educate his or her peers about seizures, thereby address-ing the "elephant in the room." Absences are often an issue. If there are other learning disabilities, the parents will need to request an educational evaluation and possibly a 504 referral to accommodate any medical needs, such as medication administration (Osborne, 1998).

Case of Sara, Age 5

Sara was a Hispanic kindergarten student in a public school in a large metropolitan area. It was midyear and the children in her class had known each other since prekindergarten. The teacher referred her to the social worker because she was being teased about being "spacey" and reacted by crying "too much." It was not anything new for her to be teased about being spacey and not paying attention. It happened when she was in prekindergarten as well. She began to cry in the class and no longer seemed able to defend herself when teased. I met with her parents and they confirmed the teacher's story of Sara being the class "ditz." As she became older, it bothered her more and more. I asked her parents to provide me with a developmental history. They seemed somewhat annoyed about this process. They just wanted me to talk to the other children and have them stop teasing Sara. I empathized with them, but there was something about this long-standing issue that left me unsettled. Sara was academically capable, articulate, and socially skilled. What could be causing this one problematic area? Developmentally, she was on target, but her parents commented that ever since early childhood she had this "staring thing" going on. I asked what her pediatrician thought about it. The parents confessed they had never mentioned it to the child's physician. I suggested that they begin with a hearing test and eye exam. In the meantime, I requested that the teacher allow me to form a small group of four kindergarten girls centered around the theme of teasing. After an eager beginning of activities and games, I observed Sara spacing out. There seemed to be no reason. She was engaged, active, involved, and then she spaced out, albeit momentarily. I asked her parents to have their doctor test Sara for epilepsy. I requested this as gently and tactfully as possible, suggesting it was something worth ruling out. The results came back: Sara was having petit mal seizures. This knowledge enabled appropriate treatment, and Sara became a much happier child.

Cystic Fibrosis

Definition

Cystic fibrosis (CF) is a genetically inherited fatal disease. In 1966, the life expectancy was 7.5 years. Presently, this has increased to 31.3 years (Berge & Patterson, 2004). If both parents carry the CF gene, each child they produce has a 25 percent chance of developing cystic fibrosis (Drotar, 2006). In the United States, 25,000 to 30,000 people have cystic fibrosis (Drotar, 2006). Cystic fibrosis is predominantly found in Caucasians, affecting 1 in 2,000 live births (Berge & Patterson, 2004). It is found in other ethnic groups at a rate of about 1 in 17,000 live births (Berge & Patterson, 2004).

Cystic fibrosis affects the respiratory, gastrointestinal, and reproduc-tive systems. The most common characteristic of the disease is thick mucus, which causes recurrent infections in the lungs. Thick secretions obstruct the pancreatic ducts and damage the pancreas, resulting in insufficient amounts of digestive enzymes assisting digestion, which leads to foul-smelling, bulky bowel movements, malnutrition, and slow growth and development (Drotar, 2006).

Treatment

Bluebond-Langner (1996, pp. 137–186), in her seminal work about siblings and parents living with a child with cystic fibrosis, lists six stages that describe a parent's response to diagnosis and treatment. The stages could apply to a parent living with any chronically ill child:

1. *Tasks of care and routine of CF treatment-related tasks*—Once a diagnosis has been determined, the parents and other family members must learn how to care for the ill child. This becomes a routine incorporated into the everyday life of the family. This includes the development of both stress and coping skills.

2. *Information about the disease and the child's condition and compartmentalization of information about CF and the child's condition*—With the diagnosis of CF comes the anxiety of death, along with the hope for a cure. Parents begin to gather information about the disease and recognize different symptoms in their child.

3. *Reminders of the disease and its consequences and avoidance of reminders of CF and its consequences*—Initially, parents seek out support groups of other parents with CF children. At some point, other children who are further along in the disease can serve as a reminder of its fatal future. Parents often begin to pull away from the support. The process can parallel other aspects of the family's life to avoid coming face-to-face with the reality of the disease (not keeping up with medical appointments).

4. *The child's difference from other children and the redefinition of normal*—In the first year, parents are aware of the difference between their child and a healthy child. Grief for the wished-for child is ever present. When the child is doing well, the parents want to avoid thoughts of the disease.

5. *Competing needs and priorities within the family and reassessment of priorities*—At the time of diagnosis, the focus of the family is on the sick child. As the sick child has periods of improvement, the family becomes more balanced. Siblings often feel left out, not as loved, and often mature beyond their years.

6. *The ill child's future and reconceptualization of the future*—CF comes with a death sentence. Parents begin to rethink the time and lifeline of their child.

Educating the parents in home treatments is one aspect of dealing with chronic illness. The administration of lifesaving medical interventions adds to the stress of an already overburdened family. Medical technology has developed new equipment to help parents and children with the necessary medical interventions of CF. Until recently, chest physiotherapy (CPT) required the caregiver to clap on the patient's chest to clear the mucus. Today the Fludder machine and vibrating chest vest aid in this process for children capable of taking responsibility for some of their own care. Even young children can take their necessary vitamins and nutritional drinks at each meal and learn to use an inhaler. As the ill child takes on more responsibility, he or she feels more empowered in dealing with the disease. This also frees other members of the family to deal with everyday life (Leaky, 1999).

Research has shown that positive psychosocial coping skills can benefit the health of the CF child in many ways, such as reduced family stress, increased parental involvement, parental participation in support groups, maintaining daily treatment routines, reduced maternal anxiety, and parents finding positive meaning in the situation (Berge & Patterson, 2004). For the CF child, pain, repeated medical procedures, fear of death, and being seen as different than their peers increases the risk for psychosocial problems (Berge & Patterson, 2004).

Considerations for the School
A major concern for the child with CF is absence from school due to hospitalizations, infections, and fatigue. To mitigate missed work, prompt tutoring needs to be set in place. Educators and parents need to be able to discern whether academic difficulties are due to missed work and time in the classroom and/or whether development delays are caused by learning disabilities or other neurological deficits.

When the CF child is healthy, he or she may participate in sports and/or extracurricular activities like a well child. Individual counseling or group counseling with peers (chronically ill or typical) may help to resolve anxieties regarding peer relationships and feeling embarrassed about being different (Drotar, 2004; Webb, 2002).

Multisensory Deprivation

Definition
A multisensory deprived (MSD) child is not like a deaf child without sight or a blind child without hearing. Blind-deaf children have lost more than just sight or hearing. They have lost perception of distance, ability to communicate, ability to anticipate the future, understand the consequences of their actions, and develop interpersonal relationships (McInnes & Treffry, 1993). Often, these children cannot compensate with alternate senses like children who are solely blind or deaf. Previously, most of these children were regarded as mentally retarded. This may not be the case. Their input systems may be damaged but not their processing systems (McInnes & Treffry, 1993).

Treatment
The cause of MSD is not always known, although many cases are a result of rubella or congenital afflictions (McInnes & Treffry, 1993). As with blindness or deafness, there is no cure. The treatment, other than possible

surgeries, is educational and sensory treatment by professionals and family members.

Considerations for the School

The basis of treatment for children with multisensory deprivation is rooted in the amazing work of Helen Keller and her teacher, Anne Sullivan (McInnes & Treffry, 1993). Through very early intervention and the absence of proven brain damage, one major goal is to develop adequate communication and an understanding of the environment. The MSD child is taught to use all of the residual potential in all sensory input modalities (McInnes & Treffry, 1993). Programs for these children, whether in local public schools or a residential setting, always include the parents and family members as part of the team. The degree of impairment will determine the type of academic program.

Hearing Impaired Solely

Hearing impairment can result from either "faulty transmission of sound across the conductive mechanisms of the middle ear, known as *conductive deafness*, or deafness which arises from damage to the nerves in the cochlea or auditory pathways, known as *sensori-neural deafness* "(Solity & Bickler, 1994, p. 153).

Treatment

The 2007 Joint Committee on Infant Hearing advocates early screening of all children to detect and intervene in order to access appropriate resources. Infants at high risk should have consistent follow-up assessment. Parents need to be educated about different professionals who will be involved with medical and educational options of their child: pediatrician, audiologists, otolaryngologists (physicians), speech/language pathologists, and educators. Parent support groups also provide education and resources. Intervention programs need to recognize and access the strengths, culture, and resources of each family in order to successfully engage the family in treatment.

The child's age at diagnosis influences the intervention and treatment. Treatment of hearing loss includes speech and language, receptive and expressive language, syntax, poor academics, and social and emotional adjustment (Cunninghan, 2003).

Considerations for the School

Each family must decide what educational setting is best for their child. The controversy is between oral perspective and manual perspective. Oral perspective makes use of residual hearing to develop speech. Manual perspective is language through signing.

Educational options are mainstreaming or a special school, whether residential or day school. Mainstreaming allows for the child's integration into the hearing environment. However, the hearing-impaired child in a mainstream setting may feel uncomfortable with the hearing population and remain close to special teachers and other hearing-impaired peers. The special school or residential setting provides academic and skills programs designed specifically for the hearing-impaired child. A special school may require families to move to another community to be near the school and hearing specialist (Solity & Bickler, 1994). Medical expenses, special schools, and relocating are a few of the adjustments families often incur.

The following case is an example of a mainstream setting for a hearing-impaired child. As a counselor and school social worker employed in an elementary school setting, I was approached by a first-grade teacher about one of her classroom children. Table 13.1 recounts the initial meetings.

Table 13.1 Mainstream Setting for Hearing Impaired Child.

Content	Analysis
Mrs. G: "Could I talk to you about Sally, a girl in my class? She has been a quiet, polite child so far this year. It is now November and she is beginning to act out. She is not paying attention, she is moody, she is failing her tests and not doing all of her homework, and, most unusual, she is yelling at and hitting her friends. Could you meet with her? Her mother is willing to have her seen by someone."	I had never met Sally before, so I was intrigued by this sudden appearance of acting out. Had something happened in her family recently? I would talk to her mother first. I called her mother and we set up an appointment for the next day.
SW: "Mrs. Phillips, thank you for coming in so soon. Mrs. G. tells me Sally is having a difficult time lately. How did Sally do in kindergarten?"	
Mrs. Phillips: "Thank you for helping Sally. Kindergarten was okay. I thought she would do better; she is smart, but she seemed to not get the reading as well as her cousin. They are in the same grade."	
SW: "I'm going to ask you some questions about her development to get to know her a little before I meet her. Have there been any changes in your family or any losses or deaths?"	I did a developmental history.
Mrs. Phillips: "No. She has a brother in the fifth grade. I am a single mother. Her father left when she was two. She was absent a lot from preschool because she had a lot of ear infections."	I was thinking hard, but came up with nothing except those ear infections and her absences. Was she missing her father?
SW: "I will meet Sally this afternoon." SW: "Hi, Sally, I am Dr. B. How are you today?"	I meet Sally, a cute, tall, African American child.
Sally: "I am fine. My mother came to see you today? Am I in trouble?" SW: "What makes you think that?"	Sally was an anxious child.

Sally: "I didn't do my homework last night. I didn't know how to do it, and I had a fight yesterday with James." SW: "Did you hit him?" Sally: "Yes."	There was something about her speech and language construction that caught my attention. No one had mentioned a hearing problem, but her speech sounded like someone with a hearing impairment.
SW: "Tell me what happened that made you so mad you hit James."	
Sally: "He said I was stupid because I failed the test. I got mad. Then he told the teacher he didn't say that, but I thought he did. I cried."	Sally began to cry; she was overwhelmed.
SW: "I'm going to teach you what you can do when you get so mad. Do you know what a thermometer is?"	I use the "thermometer angry scale," showing her the anger management technique using a thermometer scale to rate her anger.
Sally: "Yes." SW: "Sally, can you hear the teacher all the time?"	
Sally: "Well, better now. She put me up front because I talk too much. I have to ask my friend what the teacher said and she helps explain the work to me."	It is always best to rule out any physical problems first. I am going to call her mother and discuss a thorough hearing and speech evaluation.

Mrs. Phillips was annoyed to have to go to work late again, but she was concerned about Sally and did come in the following morning for an early appointment. I discussed my concern about Sally's speech and asked her to have a thorough hearing test done to rule out any hearing problems that could influence speech. I explained she could go to the Department of Education in the district and have a speech evaluation done. I asked her to bring me a copy of the results so we could discuss the evaluation, but in the meantime, while waiting for an appointment, I requested a hearing evaluation and gave her some names of agencies.

Mrs. Phillips had Sally undergo the auditological test. The results showed that Sally had serious hearing loss in her right ear and some minor loss in her left ear. She was fitted for hearing equipment to be used in the classroom. With a referral to the 504 team, accommodations were put in place and Sally began to improve in her schoolwork and peer relationships. She did go through some hard times with feeling different and occasional teasing from friends about the hearing equipment, but with individual counseling on how to handle these situations, Sally progressed to better academic performance and peer relationships.

This example shows how a child can progress to the first grade with severe hearing loss without being diagnosed. A variety of circumstances combined to delay awareness of Sally's condition: partial hearing, teachers unaware of speech and language issues, an overwhelmed single mom, and inadequate screening in schools and hospitals and lack of pediatric awareness. However, after Sally was diagnosed, her mother acted quickly and became involved in obtaining the necessary help. This really was a resilient child.

Visual Impairment Solely

Vision is the primary sense because it provides the most information to the brain. The visual system is made up of the optical system and the perceptual system (Bishop, 2004). According to Bishop (2004, p. 6):

Neither touch nor hearing have the same ability to perceive and understand multiple qualities simultaneously. Touch is sequential; you can only touch one thing or spot at a time. Hearing is largely sequential; you select one sound from a background or noise and focus on that sound; speech is a sequence of meaningful sound. Only vision is capable of perceiving a large number of bits of information, all at once.

The rudiments of vision are formed within three weeks of conception, thereby leaving vision vulnerable to deficits from the near beginning of conception (Bishop, 2004). Vision is completely developed at around two years of age (Bishop, 2004). Deficits are categorized in different areas: structural anomalies, extraocular muscle imbalances, refractive errors, diseases or defects, optic nerve defects, injuries, a premature visual system, and brain damage (Bishop, 2004).

Treatment

Although early intervention is best, testing for visual problems before the age of three or four years old is difficult. If formal testing is required, one or all of the following may be performed: a computerized axial tomography (CAT) scan, an electroretinogram (ERG), and/or a visual evoked potential (VEP) (Bishop, 2004).

Early interventions through departments of education, physician referrals, clinical referrals, and national organizations such as the American Foundation of the Blind (AFB) or National Association for Parents of the Visually Impaired, Inc. (NAPVI) begin the process of helping the visually impaired child move toward an independent life. Providing school readiness skills is a distinct benefit when the child enters a school setting. A team of professionals can guide parents to begin work at home, such as tutoring and movement under the guidance of a teacher of visually impaired (TVI).

Considerations for the School

The school setting needs to be carefully chosen so that the parents, TVI, and the school can work cooperatively (Bishop, 2004; Solity & Bickler, 1994). The parents can also request a 504 evaluation to modify the school setting for the appropriate education of their child. Corrective measures depend on the visual condition, age, setting, and needs of the child. Optical supports may be corrective lenses and contact lenses. Nonoptical supports include classroom seating, lighting, and special learning materials (large print or Braille).

Parents will have to decide whether a local public school with modifications or a special school setting for the visually impaired is best for their child. If there are additional learning disabilities, parents can request an evaluation from the school district's committee on special education to provide support in the academic environment.

Sickle Cell Disease

Definition

Sickle cell disease (SCD), or sickle cell anemia, is an inherited disease. It is most common in African Americans and those of Mediterranean ancestry. "Sickle-cell disease (SCD) is a spectrum of inherited disorders, each of which involves a mutation in the hemoglobin that causes normal red blood cells to take on a sickle shape, thus obstructing blood flow oxygen to tissues and organs" (Drotar, 2006, p. 179). Sickle-shaped blood cells do not pass through vessels as easily as normal red blood cells. These mutated cells can cause blockages that lead to damage to tissue and organs, including the lungs, spleen, kidneys, and liver (Drotar, 2006). Some of the symptoms of sickle cell experienced by young children are infections, strokes, pain and swelling of the hands, feet, and joints, fatigue, shortness of breath, eye problems, and delayed growth (Wethers, 2000). Sickle cell disease can be diagnosed at birth with a blood test. Early screening for high-risk infants is recommended.

Treatment

Although there is no cure for sickle cell disease, doctors have improved treatments for pain, infections, and strokes. Prophylactic penicillin, good nutrition, blood transfusions, and pain medicine are available (Wethers, 2000). Research has shown that positive patient coping is related to positive family functioning (Mitchell, 2007).

Considerations for the School

One of the major areas of difficulty in the school setting for a child with SCD is absence due to hospitalizations, pain, and infections (Wethers, 2000). The preschool experience can prepare the child for kindergarten and first grade, where important basic skills in reading and math are learned. Poor school performance and delayed early developmental skills may be an indication of central nervous system dysfunction in addition to SCD (Wethers, 2000). An evaluation for developmental delays may give guidance to support academic achievement. The parents and the school staff need to work together in communication, tutoring, and homework, especially when there are episodes of infection and pain that lead to absences or visits to the nurse.

Case of Zoey, Age 5

Zoey, an African American kindergarten child, was referred to the social worker for poor performance and acting-out behavior with other children. The teacher reported that Zoey did not do her work on a level comparable to typical students. She often complained of headaches, pain in her knees and hands, and was frequently irritable with children. She demanded much of the teacher's time for comforting and extra instruction. The teacher mentioned that Zoey has sickle cell disease but that her attendance had been adequate so far this year. The social worker called Zoey's parents to set up an appointment. Zoey's mother, Mrs. Collins, agreed to see her in two days.

Zoey's mother presented as tired and overwhelmed, yet eager to have some help with Zoey's behavior. Zoey's teacher was included in this meeting. Mrs. Collins discussed feeling guilty about Zoey's SCD. She did not know she or her husband were carriers of SCD. The developmental history informed the social worker of the sickle cell disease. She had been diagnosed at three months through a blood test. Prophylactic penicillin has been successful in reducing the number of infections Zoey has experienced. She did miss many days in prekindergarten, despite two hospitalizations and some days with severe join pain. This school year has been healthy except for some episodes of pain and headaches. Mrs. Collins had a new baby 10 months ago. There is no sign of SCD in the infant. Zoey feels angry and displaced by the new baby, and she is also angry that her new baby brother does not have SCD; Zoey exhibits "why me" and "it's not fair" frustration. The social worker asked Mrs. Collins to work with her on some behavior charts for Zoey. Mrs. Collins and the social worker discussed incorporating some pain management techniques into Zoey's daily routine. There would be a chart at home and one in the classroom. The social worker would teach some anger management techniques to Zoey and her mom for home and school. Initially, her mother would introduce pain management on the behavior modification chart. When Zoey was able to manage her pain consistently, the social worker would introduce controlling her anger. The social worker would initially engage Zoey in counseling to deal with feelings about her new brother and how she feels about her disease. She would combine some cognitive behavioral techniques with some psychodynamic interventions. Mrs. Collins gave written permission to the social worker to talk to Zoey's doctor to learn more about her SCD. Mrs. Collins agreed and, before she left, practiced some relaxation exercises to use with Zoey.

At first, Zoey was resistant to use the relaxation exercises. Her teacher realized that Zoey's pain served as a means of getting lots of attention from the teacher, so the teacher gave Zoey positive attention for passing out papers, raising her hand, and answering questions instead of for pain. Zoey learned that the relaxation exercises, along with medication, did help manage the pain. The extra attention for her positive endeavors, along with reduced pain, helped Zoey feel less irritable. Her peer relationships improved (Mitchell, 2007).

Her mother found ways for Zoey to help her with the new baby; this improved her attitude about her new brother. The social worker validated her anger about having this disease and its physical discomfort and was an empathic listener when she needed to vent. This also helped with peer relationships, because she learned how to vent to them in a more appropriate way and was able to engage their sympathy rather than incur their frustration.

Zoey improved in her behavior and somewhat in her academics. In terms of the academics, the teacher would take a wait-and-see approach until the January term to decide whether an academic evaluation was necessary.

Summary

In each of these chronic illnesses, the illness is forever or until some medical discovery improves the condition. There may be periods of improvement and even remission, but these young children will bring these conditions into latency, adolescence, and adulthood. Some conditions will worsen. The young child must develop lifelong coping mechanisms with medical procedures, apparatus, training, and emotional acceptance. Each child and family will find their own style of coping, and each will become resilient as they develop their own individual strengths.

References

Berge, J. M., & Patterson, J. M. (2004). Cystic fibrosis and the family: A review and critique of the literature. *Families, Systems, & Health, 22*(1), 74–100.

Berres, M. S., & Knoblock, P. (1987) *Program models for mainstreaming: Integrating students with moderate to severe disabilities.* Rockville, MD: Aspen Publication.

Bishop, V. E. (2004). *Teaching visually impaired children* (3rd ed.) Springfield, IL: Charles C. Thomas Publisher.

Bluebond-Langner, M. (1996). *In the shadow of illness.* Princeton, NJ: Princeton University Press.

Breakey, C. (2006). *The autism spectrum and further education: A guide to good practice.* London and Philadelphia: Jessica Kingsley Publishers.

Brock, S. E., Jimerson, S. R., & Hansen, R. L. (2006). *Identifying, assessing, and treating autism at school.* New York: Springer.

Clay, D. L., & Drotar, D. (2004). School teachers' experiences with childhood chronic illness. *Children's Health Care, 33*(3), 227–2239.

Cunningham, M. (2003). Hearing assessment in infants and children: Recommendations beyond neonatal screening. *Pediatrics, 111*(2) 436–440.

deBettencourt, L. U. (2002). Understanding the difference between IDEA and Section 504. *Teaching Exceptional Children. 34*(3), 16–23.

Department of Education, New York City. Retrieved March 26, 2008, from www.schools.nyc.gov.

Drotar, D., Witherspoon, D. O., Zebracki, K., & Peterson, C. C. (2006). *Psychological interventions in childhood chronic illness.* Washington, DC: American Psychological Association.

Filipek, P. A., et al. (1999). The screening and diagnosis of autistic spectrum disorders. *Journal of Autism and Developmental Disorders, 29*(6), 439–484.

Goble, L. A. (2004). The impact of child's chronic illness on fathers: Issues of comprehensive behavior. *Pediatric Nursing, 27,* 153–262.

Greenspan, S. (2006). *Engaging autism: Using the Floortime approach to help children relate, communicate, and think.* Cambridge, MA: Da Capo Press.

Harris, S. L. (1994). *Siblings of children with autism: A guide for families.* Bethesda, MD: Woodbine House.

Hiatt-Michael, D. B. (2004). *Promising practices connecting schools to families of children with special needs.* Charlotte, NC: Information Age Publishing.

Joint Committee on Infant Hearing. (2007). Year 2007 position statement: Principles and guidelines for early hearing detection and intervention programs. *Pediatrics, 120*(4), 898–921.

Kutscher, M. L. (2006). *Children with seizures: A guide for parents, teachers, and other professionals.* London: Jessica Kingsley Publishers.

Leaky, E. (1999). *One breath at a time: Living with cystic fibrosis.* Research Center University of Scranton film. Scranton, PA: University of Scranton.

McInnes, J. M., & Treffry, J. A. (1993). *Deaf-blind infants and children: A developmental guide.* Toronto: University of Toronto Press.

Mitchell, M. J. (2007). Parents' perspectives on pain management, coping, and family functioning in pediatric sickle cell disease. *Clinical Pediatrics, 46*(4), 311–319.

Openshaw, L. (2008). *Social work in schools: Principles and practice.* New York: Guilford Press.

Osborne, A. G. (1998). *Complete legal guide to special education services: A handbook for administrators, counselors, and supervisors.* New York: Parker Publishing Company.

Rothstein, L. F. (1995). *Special education law* (2nd ed.). New York: Longman Publishers.

Saleebey, D. (1997). *The strengths perspective in social work practice* (2nd ed.). New York: Longman.

Schople, E., Van Bourgondien, M. E., & Bristol, M. M. (1993). *Preschool issues in autism*. New York: Plenum Press.

Seligman, M., Benjamin, R., & Darling, R. B. (1997). *Ordinary families, special children: A systems approach to childhood disability* (2nd ed.). New York: Guilford Press.

Siegel, B. (2008). *Getting the best for your child with autism: An expert's guide to treatment*. New York: Guilford Press.

Simpson, R. L., & Myles, B. S. (1998). *Educating children and youth with autism: Strategies for effective practice*. Austin, TX: Pro-Ed.

Solity, J., & Bickler, G. (1994). *Support services: Issues for education, health and social service professionals*. London: Cassell.

Webb, N. B. (2003). *Social work practice with children* (2nd ed.). New York: Guilford Press.

Wethers, D. L. (2000). Sickle cell disease in childhood: Part I. Laboratory diagnosis, pathophysiology and health maintenance. *American Family Physician, 62,* 1013–1020.

Wood, I. (2006). School. In A. Goldman, R. Hain, & S. Liben (Eds.), *Oxford textbook of palliative care for children* (pp. 128–140). Oxford: Oxford University Press.

Other Conditions That May Occur in Childhood or Develop in Adolescence

M. Carlean Gilbert

14
Chapter

Introduction

As children grow up, they can acquire serious health conditions that impact them, their families, and their schools. This chapter reviews three disorders that can arise in childhood or adolescence and that challenge medical professionals to provide appropriate biopsychosocial services to these young people, their families, and their schools. The conditions discussed here are asthma, type 1 diabetes, and eating disorders. All present serious management challenges, affect large numbers of youth, and can be life-threatening. Following a brief discussion of the coping and family systems, theories related to chronically ill children, the etiology and epidemiology of each disorder, its typical prognosis, and treatment are summarized. Disease-specific physical and emotional effects on the developing youth and their families are reviewed and illustrated through fictitious case composites based on the author's interdisciplinary practice in hospital settings. Implications for service providers are discussed.

Theoretical Underpinnings
Coping with Chronic Health Conditions

Coping is an ambiguous term that is found in both everyday language and professional discourse. Practitioners can enhance their assessment and treatment of chronically ill children by categorizing their coping efforts, screening for overreliance on one type, matching coping attempts to the stressor, combining coping behaviors, and expanding the number of coping strategies. Members of various professions have made increasing efforts to clarify the concept of coping by describing the origins of coping behaviors in the "fight or flight" response (Miller, 1980), defining coping variables (Carver, Scheier, & Weintraub, 1989; Lazarus & Folkman, 1984; Pearlin & Schooler, 1978), and assessing the efficacy of coping responses in a multitude of situations. Folkman and Lazarus created a commonly used definition of *coping* as "constantly

225

changing cognitive and behavioral efforts to manage specific external and/ or internal demands that are appraised as taxing or exceeding the resources of the person" (p. 141). They identified two major types of coping: problem-focused and emotion-focused. The purpose of problem-focused coping is to manage the person or environmental situation that is the source of the stressful problem. Emotion-focused coping is intended to regulate the emotional impact of the stress. If a 10-year-old boy with asthma feels tightness in his chest, for example, he may cope in different ways with his frustrated desire to play soccer. A problem-focused coping response might consist of using his bronchodilator so that he can play soccer and avoid a full-blown asthma attack. An emotion-focused response might be confiding to his best friend or coach that he feels sad and left out when he is unable to play soccer so that he can gain their understanding and social support for missing practice.

Because early coping research was based on adult populations, pediatric researchers launched theory-driven efforts in the 1990s to further our understanding of children's coping. Gil, Williams, Thompson, and Kinney (1991) identified three major dimensions of children's coping in subjects with sickle cell disease. These pain-coping strategies include: (1) negative thinking, such as catastrophizing and making self-statements of fear and anger, (2) passive adherence, such as resting, and (3) cognitive and behavioral strategies such as diverting attention. Varni et al. (1996) distinguished the following five constructs that describe coping among children with musculoskeletal pain:

1. Cognitive self-instruction
2. Search for social support
3. Strivings to rest or be alone
4. Cognitive refocusing
5. Problem solving

In a qualitative study, Gilbert (1995) found that children with pediatric migraine who were classified as "copers" used a broader repertoire of strategies than "non-copers." Children in this study not only used affective, cognitive, and problem-focused coping, but also a variety of identified subtypes within these categories, such as spirituality, resignation, prevention, and expansion of their social support network. Coping efforts, of course, are mediated by children's developmental phase and environmental factors.

Folkman and Lazarus's (1984) previously described theory on stress, coping, and adaptation emphasizes the importance of the individual's primary and secondary cognitive appraisals and reappraisals in determining whether an event is perceived as a threat, challenge, or harm/loss. This concept is useful in understanding the parent-child dynamics in chronic illness. The term "vulnerable child" was coined by Green and Solnit (1964) to describe the maladaptive parent-child relationships that developed when parents had excessive anxiety about the health of their offspring following their child's recovery from a near-death experience. They suggested that this heightened parental perception of child vulnerability led to overprotective relationships that caused emotional and behavioral problems in the children. Later scholars observed similar interplay between parental perceptions of child vulnerability and mental health problems in pediatric patients with less serious health conditions. Children were found to mirror parents' perceptions of whether they were healthy or helpless victims of their illness (Gilbert, 1995), and vulnerable children had difficulty coping with their illness.

Family Considerations

A significant body of empirically based literature exists to guide practitioners in their work with families of children who suffer from chronic illness. Salvador Minuchin (1974) and colleagues (1975) applied the open systems model to their reconceptualization of families of sick children. Findings from their studies of children with diabetes, asthma, and anorexia nervosa and their families shifted the conceptualization of assessment and treatment from the individual to the child within a family system. Although the research of Minuchin and his colleagues has been criticized for methodological errors (Wood et al., 1991), this pioneering approach, which became known as *structural family therapy,* introduced many valuable concepts, such as enmeshment, disengagement, overprotection, triangulation, parent-child coalitions, and spousal, parental, and sibling subsystems. Unfortunately, misguided clinicians have applied the findings from this research with severely dysfunctional families to their practice with nonpathological ones. Advances in understanding the pathophysiology of these illnesses have assuaged the views that they are psychosomatic disorders resulting from dysfunctional parent-child interactions.

John Rolland (1984, 1987, 1994) developed the Family Systems-Illness model that provides a normative, preventative approach to the assessment and treatment of children and families. This social systems approach emphasizes the "goodness of fit" between the psychosocial demands of the illness or disability and the family system. Although this model focuses on the family system, it recognizes that the child and family are embedded in a larger ecosystem that may include the school, health care system, neighborhood, and community.

Rolland (1984, 1987, 1994) created a psychosocial typology of chronic illness that attends to both the commonalities and differences among chronic illnesses over the clinical course of the disease or disorder. He categorizes illnesses according to:

- Type of onset, which can be *acute* (e.g., a sudden clinical presentation such as traumatic brain injury) or *gradual* (e.g., juvenile rheumatoid arthritis)

- Type of course, which can be *progressive*, with continually symptomatic and worsening symptoms (e.g., type 1 diabetes), *constant*, with stabilized biological conditions (e.g., spinal cord injury), and *relapsing* or *episodic*, with periods of absent or minimal symptoms interspersed with disease flare-ups (e.g., asthma)
- Type of outcome, which can be *nonfatal, shortened life span,* or *possible sudden death* (e.g., type 1 diabetes), or *fatal*
- Type of incapacitation, which can be *none, mild, moderate,* or *severe*

To enhance his psychosocial schema regarding chronic health conditions, Rolland (1984, 1987, 1994) added another dimension, which is the developmental time phase of illnesses. The three time phases are *crisis, chronic,* and *terminal.* The *crisis* phase includes the prediagnostic time of symptom development, diagnosis, and initial treatment and requires patients and family members to assign meaning to the illness, to grieve the loss of pre-illness family identity, to balance awareness of possible future loss and hope, and to demonstrate individual and family system role flexibility. Understanding of the illness course and associated tasks is enhanced by the complex integration of individual, family, and illness developmental life cycle perspectives. The *chronic* phase spans the time between initial diagnosis and the terminal phase. This phase of taking "one day at a time" can be long or short and characterized by progressive, constant, or episodic symptomatology. In the *terminal* phase, the child and family shift from expectation of a cure to preparation for the inevitable death, and family members cope with issues of separation, anxiety, grief, and continuation of family life without the deceased member.

Family functioning is another focus of Rolland's (1984, 1987, 1994) framework, which is grounded in theories of individual and family developmental life cycles. He posits that clinicians cannot fully comprehend a family's responses to present illness without understanding its transgenerational history of adaptation to past illnesses and stressors. Rolland suggests that inquiring about coping with similar illness types (e.g., relapsing versus progressive) yields the most useful data. Families with ill children frequently experience organizational shifts in family structure and realignment of relationships (e.g., triangles and alliances). Family myths, taboos, beliefs, and expectations, some of which have cultural origins, also are transmitted among the generations (McGolderick, Giordano, & Garcia-Preto, 2006).

Selected Medical Conditions: Asthma, Type 1 Diabetes Mellitus, and Eating Disorders

Asthma

Asthma is one of the most common chronic diseases of childhood and affects approximately 6 million American youth (National Heart Lung and

Blood Institute [NHLBI], 2007). Asthma is an inflammatory disorder of the airways that is characterized by repeated episodes of symptoms that include coughing (especially at night), wheezing, breathing with difficulty, and tightening of the chest. The limited airflow is caused by complex interplay among three factors: (1) airway hyperresponsiveness, which is an exaggerated bronchoconstrictor response following exposure to stimuli such as allergens; (2) bronchoconstriction, which is the contraction of the bronchial smooth muscles after exposure to various stimuli that causes a narrowing of the airways; and (3) airway edema, which is characterized by fluid retention in tissue, increased mucus production, and the formation of mucus plugs that inhibit airflow.

Although a definitive cause of the inflamed airways that leads to childhood asthma remains elusive, research findings suggest that both individual and environmental conditions increase the risk of developing asthma (NHLBI, 2007). The two individual risk factors that contribute to asthma are genetics and an imbalance between Th1-type and Th2-type cytokines, which are hormonal messengers that affect the immune system. Major environmental risk factors that contribute to the development and perhaps severity of asthma are airborne allergens and respiratory infections. Common allergens include dust mites, pollen, molds, cockroaches and their droppings, and dried saliva or dander from the hair, fur, or feathers of animals and birds. Pollutants and irritants such as smoke from tobacco and wood-burning fireplaces, unvented stoves, polluted air, scented products, and volatile organic compounds found in materials like paint and new carpet also increase asthmatic symptoms. Asthma symptoms also may be exacerbated by exercise, cold air, or changes in air temperature.

The generally preferred long-term pharmaceutical treatment for children of all ages is inhaled corticosteroids (ICS), such as Alvesco or Flovent, which reduce swelling in the airways and decrease mucus production. Children also may be treated with a combination of ICS and a long-acting beta agonist such as Advair. These medications are considered preventers and must be used on a regular, daily basis to be effective. When asthma symptoms exacerbate, oral corticosteroids may be prescribed. The most common side effects of the ICSs are thrush, cough, or hoarseness. The initial concern that ICSs reduced growth velocity (Food and Drug Administration, 1998) has not been substantiated (Agertot & Pederson, 2000).

Children must also limit their exposure to the aforementioned pollutants and allergens, and the NHLBI (2007) provides comprehensive guidelines to control environmental factors. Allergy skin or in vitro tests can determine the presence of antibodies, but further testing of specific allergens is necessary to link them to asthma symptoms. Keeping a pet is often a high priority to children. Retention of this important family member is enhanced when high-efficiency particulate air (HEPA) cleaners are used and the pet is denied access to the child's bedroom and washed weekly.

Researchers have found that parents who perceive their children as vulnerable may be significantly more likely to keep them home from school, take them to their primary care physician, and use preventive medications regardless of the frequency or intensity of asthma symptoms (Spurrier et al., 2000). In contrast, emergency room visits and hospitalizations appear to be associated with severity of asthma symptoms rather than parental perceptions. These findings suggest that clinicians may focus interventions to increase school attendance, encourage participation in extracurricular activities, and prevent the overuse of medical resources on correcting parents' distorted images of their child's vulnerability. Another study found that there was a significant relationship between the mental health of children and family functioning, but not physical health and family functioning (Sawyer et al., 2001).

Emphasizing the therapeutic goal of minimizing asthma symptoms, experts recommend an interdisciplinary approach for comprehensive assessment and treatment of asthmatic symptoms (NHLBI, 2007). Four types of interventions are suggested:

1. Manage the frequency and functional limitations with corresponding adjustments of the treatment regime and monitor progression of disease severity.

2. Reduce the environmental and co-occurring conditions that increase asthma symptoms.

3. Educate children, parents, teachers, and significant others about asthma.

4. Use age-appropriate medications.

Even young children can understand the necessity of using an inhaler in school, as demonstrated in Figure 14.1, drawn by a preschooler who depicts a child using an inhaler (center bottom) in his detailed drawing of his classroom.

Figure 14.1

Child using inhaler in preschool.

Case Illustration of Child with Asthma: Jose Gonzalez, Age 5

Because 50 to 80 percent of children with asthma form symptoms before their fifth birthday (NHLBI, 2007), this case was selected to emphasize the importance of early health-related experiences to later development. Using coping and family systems theory, the practitioner applied an integrative therapeutic approach that included crisis intervention, case management, cognitive-behavioral treatment, advocacy, medical and psychosocial education, and family therapy within an inter-disciplinary context.

Presenting Problem

Jose Gonzalez was referred without delay to the clinical social worker, Ms. Meyer, by Dr. Goldsmith upon his admission to the emergency department (ED) of a large urban medical center. The physician wanted the family members to receive supportive treatment while she attended to Jose's medical crisis. Following six hours of worsening coughing and wheezing early that morning, Jose, age five, suddenly began to turn blue and to have extreme difficulty breathing. Terrified, his mother, Mrs. Sanchez, called 911 immediately for emergency services. Medical personnel rushed into the Sanchez home, completed an initial assessment of Jose, carefully placed him on a stretcher, loaded him into the emergency vehicle, and sped off with sirens and lights flashing. Mrs. Sanchez followed the emergency vehicle in her own car. En route to the hospital Jose required bag mask ventilation by emergency personnel, and within 30 minutes of his admission to the ED he was sedated and received endotracheal intubation because of his obvious respiratory failure. Jose was then transferred from the ED to the pediatric intensive care unit (PICU), where he was placed on a mechanical ventilator.

While Jose was being treated in the emergency department, Ms. Meyer introduced herself to the large family that was gathered in the waiting room and explained her role as the clinical social worker on the interdisciplinary pediatric pulmonary team. She offered to help them with immediate concerns, and she also informed them that at a future, less stressful, time she would like to complete a psychosocial history of Jose, which was part of the protocol for receiving care on the pulmonary service. Ms. Meyer observed the anxious parents and their spouses huddling near the treatment room door while four grandparents perched silently on a row of plastic, institutional chairs on the opposite side of the room. Shortly after Ms. Meyer introduced herself, Dr. Goldsmith entered the waiting room to explain that although Jose had a near-death experience, he had been intubated, stabilized, and transferred to the PICU. The news of this close encounter with death was so emotionally stressful that it precipitated a generalized seizure (his first) in Jose's biological father, Mr. Gonzalez.

The acute onset of Jose's illness time phase required crisis management skills to establish a therapeutic relationship with family members, process their emotional responses, provide emotional and instrumental support, identify major problems, search for problem solutions, and formulate an action plan that involved both hospital staff and family members. During the first day, team members attempted to restore equilibrium to Jose's family through various supportive services. Dr. Goldsmith immediately referred Mr. Gonzalez to the neurology service for evaluation and treatment of the father's possible seizure disorder. With the parents' agreement Ms. Meyer requested that the hospital chaplain, Father Smith, meet with this openly religious family, locate temporary lodging, and orient the family to hospital routines and protocols and ways to cope with them. At the end of the day Dr. Goldsmith, Father Smith, Ms. Meyer, and the PICU nurse had a brief case conference with all of Jose's family members to review the events of the day, to begin asthma education, and to discuss his treatment plan. Ms. Meyer noted that although the extreme closeness of the family during the crisis phase was adaptive, the family might have difficulty with the individual autonomy required during the chronic phase.

(continued)

Jose remained in the PICU for the next 72 hours. In order to prevent him from pulling out the breathing tube that was connected to the ventilator, Dr. Goldsmith administered a routinely used paralytic agent to render the boy immobile. Although he was conscious and able to understand the things that he heard, Jose was unable to withdraw from painful stimuli, talk, or even cry during this three-day ordeal.

Clenching little fists under his chin and sporting a New York Yankees baseball cap, Jose lay motionless in his hospital bed after being transferred to the pediatric ward. When Ms. Meyer went for her first post-PICU visit, Mrs. Sanchez confided her overwhelming fears that Jose might die or have permanent disabilities due to the surgery. She also believed that she could not leave him because she was the only one who understood Jose's omnipotent wishes, and he would not move or speak. His communication was limited to eye movements to fulfill needs such as water, whimpers when his mother attempted to leave the bed that they shared, and rapid breathing and other signs of extreme distress when she was gone. Indeed, this traumatized little boy had regressed to a level of function befitting a one-year-old child. Ms. Meyers arranged for both the surgeon and speech pathologist to examine Jose, and their evaluations confirmed her belief that his mutism did not have an organic cause.

Reassured that his motor abilities were intact, Ms. Meyers and the child psychologist, Dr. Davis, met with Jose's parents to share their provisional diagnosis of separation anxiety disorder, even though the onset was atypically acute and the duration was less than the required two weeks. They also believed that as Jose regained his age-appropriate autonomy and his sore throat improved, his speech would return spontaneously.

Assessment

Ms. Meyers's assessment of family functioning using Rolland's framework yielded essential information for the development of the treatment plan. Unable to handle the demands of parenthood, Mr. Gonzalez had abandoned his wife of 10 years when Jose was six weeks old. Jose became his depressed mother's only reason for living, and an intense mother-child bond developed. She married Mr. Sanchez when Jose was two. When Jose was three, he experienced a six-week separation from his mother, who was hospitalized with a high-risk pregnancy. The second son died within a week after birth. For various reasons, all family members developed an intense attachment to Jose. Jose's mother and stepfather learned that Mrs. Sanchez was unable to have more children, the maternal grandparents had been his primary caregivers, the guilt-ridden father and paternal grandparents wanted to make amends for the abandonment, and, ironically, Mr. Gonzalez's second wife was unable to conceive, and she also became invested in Jose. Based on the family history of many previous losses and the life-threatening presentation of Jose's asthma, family members' primary cognitive appraisal of his illness was harm/loss, even though, among children, deaths from asthma are rare. Ms. Meyers's treatment goals were to reduce separation anxiety, to restore Jose's age-appropriate behaviors, and to decrease the risk for his becoming a "vulnerable child." Early intervention was essential to decrease the opinion of all family members that Jose was extremely vulnerable. Failure to alter this perception would likely create a risk factor for the achievement of future developmental milestones such as separating for school in early childhood, forming peer relationships during latency, developing autonomy in adolescence, and attending kindergarten through twelfth grade.

Treatment

Mrs. Sanchez agreed that the focus of her work with Ms. Meyers was the enhancement of skills necessary to parent a chronically ill child. Ms. Meyers began the treatment of Jose by educating his mother about the normal reactions of early-school-age children to illness, such as temporary regression, incorrect ideas about causation of disease, fear of pain and bodily harm, distorted perceptions of death, impact on early moral development, misinterpretation of words and medical procedures, and the psychosocial crisis of initiative versus guilt. From the myriad of gifts that filled his room, Jose selected a special item, a plastic doll, which he constantly kept with him. This transitional object proved to be helpful in separating Mrs. Sanchez from Jose. Ms. Meyers used behavior-shaping techniques to move Mrs. Sanchez from lying in Jose's bed to sitting in bed to sitting on a chair next to the bed and then to progressively sitting farther away from the bed. Utilizing Jose's pride in his newly acquired skill of telling

time, Ms. Meyers next instructed the mother to leave Jose in the room alone for brief, time-limited periods and to return promptly at the agreed-upon time (e.g., "when the big hand gets to one") to restore his trust in her return. Despite some initial crying, which Mrs. Sanchez successfully ignored, Jose increased his alone time from one minute to ten minutes within a few days, and his speech, self-feeding skills, sense of humor, and playfulness rapidly returned. The doll also was used in medical play therapy to help Jose increase his understanding of his illness and treatment. When he returned home, Jose was able to regain his ability to sleep alone, communicate his needs, participate in age-appropriate activities with friends, and transition back to his school.

Type 1 Diabetes Mellitus

One in every 400 to 600 U.S. children and adolescents (0.22 percent) are diagnosed with type 1 diabetes (Centers for Disease Control and Prevention, 2005). Type 1 diabetes mellitus (T1DM) was previously called insulin-dependent diabetes mellitus and juvenile-onset diabetes. Type 1 diabetes develops from the autoimmune destruction of pancreatic beta cells, the only cells in the body that make the hormone insulin, which is needed to convert sugar, starches, and other food into energy. Without insulin, dysregulation of glucose, fat, and protein metabolism occurs. Although most children are not acutely ill when initially diagnosed with T1DM, approximately 30 percent present with diabetic ketoacidosis (DKA), a condition in which very high blood sugar levels and very low levels of insulin result in a dangerous accumulation of ketones (Silverstein et al., 2005). Children with DKA often are admitted to the intensive care unit because of the danger of coma or death.

Risk factors for T1DM may be autoimmune, genetic, or environmental (Centers for Disease Control and Prevention, 2005). The onset of T1DM is suspected to follow exposure to an "environmental trigger," such as an unidentified virus, that stimulates an immune attack against the beta cells of the pancreas in genetically vulnerable children. Children with T1DM are at risk of long-term complications such as heart disease, stroke, blindness, kidney failure, hypertension, and dental disease. Although data from death certificate reports is difficult to evaluate, the risk of mortality for persons with diabetes is about twice that of same-aged individuals without diabetes.

Children with T1DM and their families must follow a daily course of therapy that includes insulin replacement through, alternatively, two to five injections per day or an insulin pump (Silverstein et al., 2005; Wysocki et al., 2008), in addition to blood glucose monitoring using finger sticks. A complex treatment complex regimen balances an individualized nutrition plan, exercise levels that may vary according to seasonal activities and sports, and biological changes influenced by puberty. Silverstein and her colleagues present a comprehensive review article on the care of children and adolescents, and they provide detailed treatment guidelines based on the child's developmental status and current standards of care.

Like many other chronic illnesses, children with T1DM have varying abilities to manage their illness based upon physical, emotional, and cognitive development (Silverstein et al., 2005). Infants and toddlers are totally dependent upon their caregivers for metabolic control; children ages 3 to 7 can participate minimally by helping with blood glucose monitoring and documentation of food and exercise; and latency-age children can add supervised insulin injections and blood glucose testing with supervision. Early adolescence begins with the onset of puberty and is characterized by the acquisition of the fine motor skills necessary to manage the physical aspects of diabetic care. At a life stage when many believe that membership in the peer group is crucial, these diabetes-related tasks (e.g., checking blood glucose, injecting insulin, wearing pumps, and restricting food intake) can negatively affect body image and interfere with peer activities such as playing sports, having romantic relationships, or engaging in spontaneous behaviors. Adolescents may be embarrassed to wear necklaces or bracelets that identify them as individuals with diabetes. Peer groups in the community or online consisting of youth who have the same diagnosis can help adolescents feel less alone with their illness.

The intersection of the family life cycle, the developmental tasks of adolescence, and diabetes-specific issues places great demands on the family system. Most outcome studies of the association between family functioning and adolescent concerns have focused on metabolic control and psychosocial functioning. In contrast to families of healthy teenagers, Seiffge-Krenke (1998) found that family systems of diabetic adolescents were characterized by higher levels of control, structure, and organization. This comparatively rigid structure was associated with good to satisfactory metabolic control. Examining family climate rather than structure, others reported that children in families characterized by high cohesion, expressiveness, and lack of conflict also achieved good metabolic control (Hanson, De Guire, Schinkel, & Kolterman, 1995). Liss et al. (1998) reported that parents of children with DKA emphasized control more than empathy, were less well organized, and had less role and rule flexibility than non-DKA parents. These findings indicate that adolescents whose parents remain involved with diabetes management have improved metabolic control; their involvement, however, may impede adolescents' ability to separate from them.

Other researchers have examined the association between diabetes, mental disorders, and psychosocial functioning. Over the course of a 10-year longitudinal study, 47.6 percent of youth with T1DM were diagnosed with a psychiatric disorder; major depressive disorder was the most prevalent, at 27.5 percent, followed by conduct and generalized anxiety disorders (Kovac, Obrosky, Goldston, & Drash, 1997). Evaluating only children who were hospitalized with DKA, Liss et al. (1998) found that

88 percent of them met *DSM-III-R* criteria for a psychiatric disorder. The majority of study participants, mean age 13, experienced anxiety, mood, or disruptive behavior disorder, respectively; they also reported low self-esteem and social competence. Although the findings of these studies should be interpreted cautiously because of small sample sizes, they do suggest a neuroendocrine association between T1DM and psychopathology.

Case of Type 1 Diabetes Mellitus: Jim Wren, Age 15

This case illustrates how control of T1DM can become the focal point for an adolescent's struggle for identity, membership in the peer group, and autonomy from parents. The increased risk for a mental disorder is highlighted, and the growing influence of the larger environment (e.g., school) is emphasized.

Presenting Problem

Jim is a 15-year-old boy who is slightly below average in height for his age and sports a shock of red hair atop his slight, wiry frame. Jim was diagnosed with T1DM by his pediatrician when he was eight years old after several weeks of losing weight, drinking abnormally large amounts of fluid, and urinating excessive volumes of fluid. His diabetes had been managed satisfactorily on an outpatient basis until the past two months, when he was hospitalized three times for ketoacidosis. Jim had attended a small, rural middle school where his teachers and friends had supported him emotionally and in following his medical regime. As a result of school redistricting policies, Jim matriculated to a large, centralized high school approximately a month before his first hospitalization. Knowing few students at the new school, Jim was befriended by a group of students who described themselves as goths. Concurrently, his English teacher glimpsed the paraphernalia for his insulin injections, and she accused Jim of being a "druggie" in front of the class and sent him to the principal. Humiliated, Jim began to skip school and miss curfews to hang out with his new friends, and he refused to adhere to his medical plan because he wanted to be "normal." His single mother feared that he might die or suffer long-term effects such as kidney failure, and she and Jim had many heated arguments about her controlling parental style and his refusal to manage his illness.

Assessment

Entering the new school, Jim attempted to replace his lost social support with a lifestyle that threatened his health. Although separation from his overly involved mother was developmentally appropriate, he felt that he could achieve this only by keeping her out of his life, especially in regard to his diabetic care. Jim had a history of high academic achievement and admitted that he missed school. The evaluation also confirmed the mental health provider's suspicion that Jim was suffering from a major depressive disorder.

Treatment

The physicians on the interdisciplinary team stabilized Jim's medical condition and initiated psycho-pharmacological treatment for his depression. The teacher from the hospital school program collaborated with the high school teachers to help Jim get caught up with his assignments. Later, Jim, his mother, the diabetic nurse practitioner, and the mental health provider met with his school principal, nurse, counselor, and teachers to develop an individualized educational plan (IEP). Jim began individual psychotherapy for his depression and social concerns, and he and his mother used family sessions to work on age-appropriate autonomy. He also replaced his goth acquaintances with friends made in a school-sponsored support group for chronically ill students. Plante, Lobato, and Engel (2001) provide an excellent review of group interventions and summer camps for medically challenged pediatric populations.

Eating Disorders

The *DSM-IV-TR* (American Psychiatric Association, 2000) identifies three eating disorders: anorexia nervosa (AN), bulimia nervosa (BN), and binge eating disorder, which is the most common but has been less researched. Adolescents with AN fail to maintain or attain a body weight that is 85 percent of the expected weight for age and height due to restricting food intake or binge-eating and purging. The rule of thumb for ideal body weight of women is 100 pounds for five feet plus five pounds for each additional inch, with a 10 percent deviation. Teenagers with AN desperately fear gaining weight, have abnormal perceptions of their bodies, and, in the case of females, have missed three consecutive menstrual periods after the onset of menses. Adolescents with BN have a normal or slightly above normal body weight that can make the disorder difficult to detect unless clinicians notice dental erosion, abrasions on the dorsal surface of hands, and "chipmunk cheeks" from self-induced vomiting. In addition to vomiting, adolescents compensate for binge eating by using laxatives or diuretics, fasting, exercising excessively, or, with co-occurring diabetes, reducing their insulin. Ninety percent of patients with AN or BN are female. Several factors distinguish these disorders. The average age of onset for AN ranges between 14 and 18 years of age, with a mean of 17; the average age of onset for BN is 18. The prevalence rate of AN is 0.1 to 0.6 percent and of BN is 1 to 4 percent. Teenagers with AN have amenorrhea, deny the seriousness of low body weight, and have a distorted perception of body image in contrast to those with BN. Approximately 5 to 10 percent of persons with AN die from medical complications such as cardiac failure due to electrolyte imbalance or infections.

Eating disorders are both public and private issues. At a time when adolescents are experiencing sexual maturation and forming a self-identity, they are bombarded with print media, movies, television, Internet, and advertising that promote an unrealistically thin body. If these media messages are internalized, it is possible that the adolescent will strive to achieve this cultural ideal by developing an eating disorder. Frequently behind this celebrated public image of success, however, is private pain characterized by self-loathing, poor self-esteem, and shame. Although the causes of eating disorders have been attributed to genetic factors, psychological issues, family environment, and trauma, these explanations remain speculative (*Harvard Mental Health Letter*, 1997).

Case of Anorexia Nervosa: Sally Acorn, Age 15

Presenting Problem

When Sally was 15, she decided that she was a bit chubbier than other members of the high school gymnastics team and she began to diet. She began her diet by skipping breakfast, and two weeks later she began to eat only undressed leafy greens for lunch. Because she continued to work out for two hours after gymnastics practice ended at 6 p.m., her parents were unaware that she ate only a banana for dinner. Rapidly dropping from 130 to 100 pounds, Sally still was dissatisfied with how her stomach pouched out on her five-foot two-inch frame. She then began to use a combination of laxatives and diuretics after learning about them on a pro-ana (i.e., a movement that promotes anorexia as a "lifestyle choice") web site. Menses stopped, and Sally lost an additional 10 pounds, but still complained that she was too fat. Shortly thereafter, Sally was diagnosed with AN by her pediatrician after collapsing at the gym.

Assessment

Sally was 18 percent below her ideal body weight as a result of restricted caloric intake, purging, and exercise. Despite her amenorrhea, she denied having AN and maintained the belief that she was fat.

Treatment

Initially, Sally was hospitalized so that physicians, mental health providers, and dieticians could help her to reach her normal weight. Later, cognitive approaches were used to modify her false beliefs about perfectionism, control, food, and body image; in addition, behavioral approaches such as role plays and desensitization regarding phobic reactions to food were employed. Selected family interventions addressed adolescent issues.

Summary

It is critical for children with asthma, type 1 diabetes mellitus, and eating disorders to be routinely evaluated and subsequently treated to strengthen helpful coping strategies and to prevent or minimize maladaptive responses to chronic illnesses. A comprehensive assessment must be interdisciplinary. The preceding illnesses should ideally include a physical examination by a board-certified pediatrician or specialist (e.g., pediatric endocrinologist, pediatric pulmonologist, or child psychiatrist). Evaluations should also include a review of the youth's educational records, observation in multiple settings, reports from parents, teachers, coaches, guidance counselors, friends, clergy, and significant others, and specific psychological testing, as needed. Because perceptions of informants may be discordant and discrepancies between child and parent self-reports are common, a triangulation of data is needed to increase the likelihood of completing an accurate assessment and developing a comprehensive treatment plan.

Busy practitioners may find that screening instruments, some of which are illness-specific, can identify chronically ill children who may be at increased risk for poor adjustment and warrant in-depth biopsychosocial assessment and treatment. The Child Vulnerability Scale (CVS), for example, is an eight-item instrument that assesses parental perception of children's vulnerability to health problems using a four-point Likert scale (Forsyth, Horwitz, Leventhal, & Burger, 1996). Examples of self-report questions are "I often have to keep my child indoors because of health reasons" and "I often check on my child at night to make sure s/he is okay."

Forsyth found that the CVS had good construct validity; it identified children who were perceived as vulnerable, and these individuals had a significant increase in behavior problems and frequency of medical visits. Blount et al. (2007) extensively reviewed 12 instruments that measure children's stress and coping within a risk and resiliency framework. Because of the interplay between health and mental health issues, interdisciplinary and integrative interventions often are required.

In addition to providing individual and family assessment and treatment, clinicians must affect the larger environment to improve the health and mental health of ill children. Children have little control over their surroundings. To help these children succeed physically, academically, and socially, clinicians need to consult with school personnel and families to create an optimal educational environment. Seamless transitions between hospital and local schools help children maintain friendships and academic performance. Clay (2004) provides excellent guidelines for developing individualized educational plans and 504 plans, as well as useful assessment tools, intervention strategies, and checklists. Clinicians also need to advocate for social and environmental justice. Asthma, for example, disproportionately affects low-income and minority populations who live in impoverished neighborhoods (Brown et al., 2003). Asthma is affected by the home in which children live, the school that they attend, the transportation that they use, and the quality of air in their neighborhood.

In summary, children and adolescents with these disorders have unique risk factors that threaten their quality of life. With appropriate individual, family, and environmental protective factors, however, most adapt to their illnesses, gradually assume responsibility for medical management of their illness, and successfully meet developmental milestones.

Appendix

American Diabetes Association
   www.diabetes.org
American Lung Association
   http://www.lungusa.org
National Association of Anorexia Nervosa and Associated Disorders
   www.anad.org
National Diabetes Education Program. National Institutes of Health http://
   www.ndep.nih.gov/diabetes/youth/youth.htm

References

Agertot, L., & Pederson, S. (2000). Effect of long-term treatment with inhaled budesonide on adult height in children with asthma. *New England Journal of Medicine, 343,* 1054–1063.

American Psychiatric Association. (2000). *Diagnostic and statistical manual of mental disorders* (4th ed., revised). Washington, DC: American Psychiatric Association.

Bennett, D. S. (1994). Depression among children with chronic medical problems: A meta-analysis. *Journal of Pediatric Psychology, 19*(2), 149–169.

Blount, R. L., Simons, L. E., Devine, K. A., Jaaniste, T., Cohen, L. L., Chambers, C. T., & Hayutin, L. G. (2007). Evidence-based assessment of coping and stress in pediatric psychology. *Journal of Pediatric Psychology,* 1–25.

Brown, P., Mayer, B., Zavestoski, S., Luebke, T., Mandelbaum, J., & McCormick, S. (2003). The health politics of asthma: Environmental justice and collective illness experience in the United States. *Social Science & Medicine, 57,* 453–464.

Centers for Disease Control and Prevention. (2005). National diabetes fact sheet: General information and national estimates on diabetes in the United States. Atlanta, GA: Author.

Castro-Rodriguez, J. A., Holberg, C. J., Morgan, W. J., Wright, A. L., & Martinez, F. D. (2001). Increased incidence of asthmalike symptoms in girls who become overweight or obese during the school years. *American Journal of Respiratory and Critical Care Medicine, 163,* 1344–1349.

Clay, D. L. (2004). *Helping schoolchildren with chronic health conditions: A practical guide.* New York: Guilford Press.

Food and Drug Administration. U.S. Department of Health and Human Services Public Health Service. (1998, November 9). FDA Talk Paper.

Forsyth, B. W. C., Horwitz, S. M., Leventhal, J. M., & Burger, J. (1996). The Child Vulnerability Scale: An instrument to measure parental perceptions of child vulnerability. *Journal of Pediatric Psychology, 21*(1), 89–101.

Gilbert, M. C. (1995). Differences between "copers and "non-copers" with pediatric migraine. *Child and Adolescent Social Work Journal, 12*(4), 275–287.

Green, M., & Solnit, A. J. (1964). Reactions to the threatened loss of a child: A vulnerable child syndrome. *Pediatrics, 34,* 58–66.

Hanson, C. L., De Guire, M. J., Schinkel, A. M., & Kolterman, O. G. (1995). Empirical validation for a family-centered model of care. *Diabetes Care, 10,* 1347–1356.

Harvard Medical School. (1997). Eating disorders—Part I. *The Harvard Mental Health Letter, 14*(4), 1–4.

Kovacs, M., Obrosky, D. S., Goldston, D., & Drash, A. (1997). Major depressive disorder in youths with IDDM: A controlled prospective study of course and outcome. *Diabetes Care, 20*(1), 45–51.

Lazarus, R. S., & Folkman, S. (1984). *Stress, appraisal, and coping.* New York: Springer Publishing.

Liss, D. S., Waller, D. A., Kennard, B. D., McIntire, D., Capra, P., & Stephens, J. (1998). Psychiatric illness and family support in children and adolescents with diabetic ketoacidosis: A controlled study. *Journal of the American Academy of Child and Adolescent Psychiatry, 37*(5), 536–544.

McGolderick, M., Giordano, J., & Garcia-Preto, N. (2006). *Ethnicity and family therapy* (3rd ed.) New York: Guilford Press.

Minuchin, S. (1974). *Families & family therapy.* Cambridge, MA: Harvard University Press.

Minuchin, S., Baker, L., Rosman, B. L., Liebman, R., Milman, L., & Todd, T. C. (1975, August). A conceptual model of psychosomatic illness in children. *Archives of General Psychiatry, 32,* 1031–1038.

National Heart Lung and Blood Institute. National Institutes of Health. (2007). National Asthma Education and Prevention Program Expert Panel Report 3: Guidelines for the Diagnosis and Management of Asthma. (NIH Publication No. 08-5846). Retrieved on August 3, 2008, from http://www.nhlbi.nih.gov/guidelines/asthma/asthsumm.pdf.

Pearlin, L. I., & Schooler, C. (1978). The structure of coping. *Journal of Health and Social Behavior, 19,* 2–21.

Plante, W. A., Lobato, D., & Engel, R. (2001). Review of group interventions for pediatric chronic conditions. *Journal of Pediatric Psychology, 26*(7), 435–453.

Rolland, J. S., (1984). Toward a psychosocial typology of chronic and life-threatening illness. *Family Systems Medicine, 2,* 245–263.

Rolland, J. S., (1987). Chronic illness and the life cycle: A conceptual framework. *Family Process, 26,* 203–221.

Rolland, J. S., (1994). *Families, illness, & disability: An integrative treatment model.* New York: Basic Books.

Sawyer, M. G., Spurrier, N., Whaites, L., Kennedy, D., Martin, A. J., & Baghurst, P. (2001). The relationship between asthma severity, family functioning and the health-related quality of life of children with asthma. *Quality of Life Research, 9,* 1105–1115.

Seiffge-Krenke, I. (1998). The highly structured climate in families of adolescents with diabetes: Functional or dysfunctional for metabolic control? *Journal of Pediatric Psychology, 23*(5), 313–322.

Silverstein, J., Klingensmith, G., Copeland, K., Plotnick, L., Kaufman, F., Laffel, L., et al. (2005). Care of children and adolescents with type 1 diabetes. *Diabetes Care, 28*(1), 186–212.

Spurrier, N. J., Sawyer, M. G., Staugas, R., Martin, A. J., Kennedy, D., & Streiner, D. L. (2000). Association between parental perception of children's vulnerability to illness and management of children's asthma. *Pediatric Pulmonary, 29,* 88–93.

Wood, B., Watkins, J., Boyle, J., Nogueira, J., Zimand, E., & Carroll, L. (1989). The "psychosomatic family" model: An empirical and theoretical analysis. *Family Process, 28,* 399–417.

Acute Health Crises

Part

Outpatient Counseling for Children and Youth with Life-Threatening Conditions

Douglas Davies
Nancy Boyd Webb

15

Chapter

The fact that young children and adolescents can be diagnosed with serious health conditions which can cause their physical decline and eventual deaths seems cruel and unfair. Yet, statistics confirm that this is true of some types of cancer and of AIDS. Although both illnesses respond well to medications and the overall survival rates have greatly improved in recent years, some young people have cancers and HIV/AIDS that cannot be controlled, and fatalities still occur (Auslander & Freedenthal, 2006; Clay, 2004).

This chapter focuses on the particular stresses on the situations of these children and adolescents and their families who must live with the serious life-threatening illnesses of cancer or HIV/AIDS. The similarities and differences in the types of challenges presented by these different medical conditions are outlined, with implications regarding the counseling approaches that are appropriate and necessary for each. Douglas Davies is the author of the section on cancer, and Nancy Boyd Webb authored the section on HIV/AIDS.

Counseling Approaches for Childhood Cancer

Tremendous advances in treatment for childhood cancer in the past 30 years have increased the survival rate to approximately 80 percent (U.S. Cancer Statistics Working Group, 2004). But successful medical treatment may result in psychosocial and developmental side effects. The prolonged and invasive treatment common to cancer therapy protocols creates interferences to future development in some child cancer survivors (Rennick et al., 2002; Roddenberry & Renk, 2008).

The child in cancer treatment typically faces many stressors, including multiple hospitalizations, anxiety about dying, surgeries, distress from spinal taps, bone marrow aspirations and other procedures, malaise and weakness as side effects of chemotherapy, bodily changes such as hair loss, stress in the parent-child relationship, loss of familiar routines, school absence, and disruption of friendships. These stressors affect parents as well, who must contemplate the possible death of their child, as well as learn to manage a revised family life now dictated by cancer treatment. When a child is diagnosed with cancer, the medical crisis creates a family crisis.

Since cancer treatment encompasses many stressors over a long period, it is necessary to monitor children for psychological, relational, and social difficulties. The recent research literature on post-treatment adjustment suggests that the majority of child cancer survivors do not differ in degree of psychopathology from other children. However, a number of studies have shown that there is a subgroup of 25 to 30 percent who have social adjustment difficulties, ongoing posttraumatic stress symptoms, or problems with academic achievement, despite the fact that most do not have a diagnosable disorder (Patenaude & Kupst, 2005). Children may show age-expected development and adaptation yet also continue to struggle with distress and symptoms that may interfere with *optimal* development (Simms et al., 2002). Although recent studies find child cancer survivors resilient (Noll & Kupst, 2007), general resiliency research suggests that resilience developed in response to severe stress and risk conditions often has psychic costs (Luthar et al., 2000). For example, there is evidence that in the absence of intervention, post-traumatic symptoms of cancer survivors persist into young adulthood (Hobbie et al., 2000). In addition, some groups show poorer adjustment than other cancer survivors. These include children with brain tumors or bone tumors (some of which require amputation) and children who undergo bone marrow or stem cell transplants (Armstrong & Mulhern, 2000; Nargarajan et al., 2002; Simms et al., 2002; Phipps et al., 2000).

Intervention on behalf of children with cancer should be family-focused and collaborative among professionals. Work with parents and other caregivers combines crisis-oriented, psychoeducational, and supportive counseling. Individual therapy with children integrates play and cognitive approaches. The discussion begins with a presentation of frameworks that inform these therapy approaches.

Frameworks for Therapy of Children with Cancer

Attachment Perspective

The attachment relationship with parents is the major resource to help children cope with stress. Although school-age children have developed many autonomous coping strategies compared with younger children, even these older children are likely to show attachment-seeking behavior when confronted by the severe stressors of cancer diagnosis and intensive treatment. When a child is distressed or feels threatened—common reactions as treatment begins—parents in a functional attachment relationship offer emotional support and protection and help with regulation of emotions and explanation of the child's treatment.

An attachment perspective informs the goals of treatment when a family enters psychotherapy soon after a cancer diagnosis. The clinician helps parents to process their own distress and mobilize their internal and external resources so that they will be able to maintain a secure attachment as the child faces the necessary stressors of cancer treatment. The resilience found in child cancer survivors should be seen as the outcome of protection and support in the context of secure relationships rather than simply as an attribute of the child (Egeland, Carlson, & Sroufe, 1993). Since secure attachment is a crucial protective factor, the clinician must focus on supporting and augmenting established attachment processes during periods of crisis and increased risk.

Crisis Intervention Perspective

When psychotherapy begins soon after the child's diagnosis, assessment and initial treatment should be framed from a crisis intervention perspective that focuses first on the parents. A consistent finding in research is that the child's ability to cope with cancer stressors depends a great deal on the parents' ability to mobilize themselves to take an active role in supporting and advocating for the child. Good parent functioning buffers the child's stress (Vrijmoet-Wiersma et al., 2008). By contrast, if parents remain overwhelmed and distressed, they will be much less able to support the child, and research has consistently indicated that parents' persistent distress during treatment has long-term effects on children's posttreatment psychosocial functioning (Manne et al., 1996; Dolgin et al., 2007).

Consequently, the therapist should avoid a nondirective stance and instead take an active role in helping the parent respond to the cancer crisis: "Confronting rather than hiding or avoiding the pain, and summoning the courage to take action are important and necessary first steps" (Goodman, 2007, p. 220). Helping parents acknowledge the new reality and mobilize their resources is an early treatment goal. The initial work should take an informational and problem-solving approach (Sahler et al., 2005), but should also give parents a chance to express fears and doubts in response to their child's life-threatening illness.

Stress and Trauma Perspective

It is normative, rather than pathological, for children and parents to be distressed at diagnosis and during early treatment. Distress and symptoms of posttraumatic stress reflect reactions and initial adaptations to an overwhelming threat. Factors contributing to the development of trauma symptoms include the child's awareness that he or she could die, the intensity of medical treatment, lack of family support, and co-occurring PTSD or PTS symptoms in a parent (often stimulated by the parent's fears the child will not survive). (Saxe, Vanderbilt, & Zuckerman, 2003; Stuber, Shamesh, & Saxe, 2003).

Recent studies have found high rates of posttraumatic stress symptoms (68 percent of mothers and 57 percent of fathers) in parents of children in cancer treatment (Kazak et al., 2005; Brown et al., 2003). Parents' posttraumatic stress may be increased by their adult understanding: They know that treatment will take two to three years, that the outcome will be in doubt, that their child may suffer long-term effects, and that cancer can recur. Although normal, these emergency responses to a life-threatening illness have the potential to interfere with the parents' capacity for supporting the child. Posttraumatic stress symptoms are most likely to be present in the early phase of cancer treatment, but many parents report that they do not dissipate until the child is solidly in remission or after treatment is completed. Since parents' traumatic stress reactions may impair their ability to follow medical treatment recommendations and to support their child during the most intensive and anxiety-producing phase of treatment, it is important to assess for parents' trauma symptoms and offer focused trauma therapy and psychoeducation as part of the overall intervention (Kazak et al., 2005, 2006).

A traumatic stress model is a helpful lens for assessment and setting goals for the child's therapy as well, even though the child may not meet full criteria for PTSD. PTS symptoms, including intrusive imagery, fears, hyper-arousal, and affective numbing, are common in children with cancer, especially during early treatment when invasive procedures occur more frequently (Kazak et al., 2006). When children's subjective responses to medical treatment include fear, physiological arousal, and feelings of loss of control, PTS symptoms may emerge. It is helpful to offer the child individual therapy that focuses on symbolic and cognitive processing of the child's subjective experience of cancer treatment, with particular attention to normalization of affective responses, creation of a trauma story, correction of cognitive distortions, and enhancement of coping strategies.

Developmental Perspective
The child's level of cognitive development influences his or her subjective experience of cancer treatment. Older-school-age children have skills that allow them to understand the rationale for medical treatment, and they are more capable of compartmentalizing feelings about cancer and going on with a semblance of their normal lives. They are more able to utilize cognitive-behavioral interventions. By contrast, children under ages 6 or 7, because of cognitive immaturity, may be more at risk for egocentrically misunderstanding medical treatment and for becoming fearful and anxious or, alternatively, defending against anxiety by shutting down affectively (Chen et al., 2000; Davies, 2004). Prolonged medical treatment has the potential to interfere with developmental tasks, particularly those that are in process of becoming consolidated. For the preschool child, tasks such as the development of emotional regulation, autonomy, peer relationships, play and fantasy, regulation of bodily functions, and mobility may be temporarily derailed as the child's life is defined and restricted by the demands of cancer treatment. These developmental considerations for preschool children must be kept in mind, because the most common childhood cancers—leukemia and brain tumors—tend to strike in early childhood, with the peak incidence of diagnosis at about age 4.

Ecological Perspective
Given that the child's and parents' relationships with their familiar environments are altered by the cancer experience, the therapist must

be ready to help parent and child navigate a world that suddenly feels very different. Knowledge about cancer treatment and about medical systems is necessary.

When a therapist begins treatment with a child soon after the cancer diagnosis, it is essential that he or she learn about the child's medical treatment in detail. In cancers, like leukemia, that are treated primarily with chemotherapy, the early period involves high-dose chemotherapy that aims to bring the cancer into remission quickly. In consequence, the child is exposed during a concentrated period to many medical procedures and high doses of toxic medications. If the therapist is aware of what the child is experiencing, he or she can give words to the experience, providing clarification, empathy, and normalization of the child's anxiety and distress.

A broader perspective also implies collaboration. The therapist serves at times as a liaison or mediator between the parents and the medical system or the school system. A therapist can help parents frame questions to ask medical personnel, explore how they can participate during medical procedures to support the child, strategize how to communicate with teachers who may be unfamiliar with special needs of children with cancer, and in general help parents think about how to advocate with systems outside the family on their child's behalf. At times the therapist may consult with individuals in other systems directly, write reports to clarify the child's needs to school personnel, and advocate for special services for the child.

Long-Term Perspective

Cancer treatment is long. The child diagnosed with leukemia at age 5 typically undergoes three years of medical treatment and therefore will be 8 when treatment ends. It will be very helpful, frequently, for the child to have a chance to process the cancer experience with the new cognitive skills of an eight-year-old.

In some cases, taking a long-term perspective helps the clinician see the needs of children after cancer treatment concludes. For example, some children who defend against the stresses of treatment with a "repressive adaptation" (Phipps et al., 2001) may, when treatment is over, remain inhibited in ways that interfere with development. Intrusive imagery of cancer treatment and fears of dying may surface when suppression of affect no longer feels necessary for emotional survival. Katy, a five-year-old who had used suppression of affects during treatment for a brain tumor, seemed to become globally inhibited when she entered kindergarten, avoiding peers and academic challenges. Katy had been a stoic "good patient." However, in therapy with me after her cancer treatment was completed, she played out repeated scenarios presenting a subjective story of cancer treatment that had not been apparent to her parents and medical caregivers (Davies, 1992). Her play representations of medical treatment focused on intentional, sadistic hurting of child dolls by nurse and doctor dolls. Other play about angels registered her anxiety about dying. Her play presented a story of a young child who felt frightened, helpless, and angry, was confused by the pain of treatment that was supposed to help, and viewed herself as a victim of sadism. This affectively rich play representation was very different from her self-presentation while hospitalized, when she was subdued and compliant. Out of necessity, Katy had developed the ability to modulate and contain anxious reactions to all but the most painful or frightening procedures. Her precocious defenses and her ability to accept the support of her empathic and competent parents made it appear that she was coping well with her difficult medical treatment. However, as the content of her postcancer play suggested, it is important to distinguish between immediate coping and actual mastery. Play therapy enabled Katy to gain a significant degree of mastery over a series of extremely stressful experiences and to resume an adaptive developmental trajectory.

A long-term perspective also implies that therapists need to remain available, if possible, for future brief contacts as affects and stressful memories from the period of illness are triggered by normative developmental transitions. Finally, the therapist's ongoing availability is important because of the sad possibility of a recurrence of cancer. An existing relationship with a therapist serves an attachment function for parents and child during this demoralizing time. When renewed medical treatment is unsuccessful, the therapist should be familiar with grief work to help both child and parents when the child is dying.

Elements of Parent Work

Consistently, research has found that good parent support is a protective factor for the child undergoing cancer treatment and that parental distress increases children's distress (Robinson et al., 2007). For example, parents with high anxiety levels and persisting hyperarousal have trouble helping their children regulate their own anxiety during procedures: "Anxious parents may influence children's appraisals by behaving in ways that lead the child to perceive the medical procedure as unmanageable" (Dahlquist & Pendley, 2005, p. 627; McGrath, 2001).

An early task is to help parents understand their child's initial reactions to diagnosis and treatment. Many parents are shocked when their child becomes angry, has tantrums, becomes regressively needy, or withdraws emotionally. On one level, parents realize their child is under stress, but they may also feel he or she has become a different person. It is important to normalize the child's changed behavior as reactive to being sick and, at times (e.g., when the child is taking steroids), as a specific reaction to the treatment. Parents can provide support the child needs if they understand that these stress reactions are temporary coping devices.

The therapist can frame the stresses of treatment as *obstacles* to be overcome. For example, the first spinal tap generates a great deal of anxiety in parents and child, but preparation via explanation of the procedure and suggestions about how the parent and child can manage the procedure promote a sense of mastery—a sense that "we can get through this"—that helps make the next spinal tap seem manageable. To counter feelings of loss of control that emerge when life must revolve around the child's treatment regimen, the therapist can help parents and child develop adaptive strategies that allow some measure of control. For example, parents can be encouraged to learn as much as possible about the child's treatment and to ask medical professionals how they can participate in helping the child cope with distress during procedures. Many parents' levels of distress tend to decrease during the second six months of treatment, because they are coping better with treatment stress (Steele et al., 2004; Dolgin et al., 2007).

Families with a child with cancer face the adaptive task of achieving a "new normal" that integrates intensive medical treatment, illness-related changes in family routines and roles, increased focus on the ill child vis-à-vis siblings, monitoring the child's illness and its physical effects, and precautions against the child's exposure to contagious diseases into the regular functioning of the family. This is a significant task that some families will have trouble achieving. When parents are oriented soon after diagnosis to the changes the child's cancer will require of them, they are better able to create a "new normality" (Earle et al., 2006). When therapists encourage parents to actively confront problems associated with the child's illness and to seek professional and social support, their ability to cope increases.

A therapist can support recommendations that parents strive to make the child's life as normal as possible, while acknowledging, especially during the intensive treatment period, that life cannot be normal as it was prior to diagnosis. It is helpful for a therapist to collaborate with parents in thinking through the implications of the child's treatment for the parent-child relationship. Parents can be helped to understand that the "new normal" will likely involve parenting a child who is more frequently distressed and more dependent and reliant on them. From the perspective of attachment, the child will respond to medical procedures, bodily changes, and fears of dying by becoming more anxious and clingy. These behaviors should be normalized as responses to stress. At the same time, it is useful to predict that the child's (and parents') anxiety should lessen after the initial intensive treatment is completed. Alex, a six-year-old, looked at himself in the mirror after he had lost his hair for the first time. Because he was taking steroids, his face was very swollen. His mother reported that he cried and said he hated himself, and then he became furious with her. She told me that she could not bear to see him so upset and that she worried about permanent psychological damage. I suggested his strong reaction was understandable *and* temporary, and that she could help him by empathizing with his anger and then pointing out that his hair would grow back and that his face would look like himself again when he was no longer taking steroids. An attachment perspective can also help parents understand why younger children may direct anger and unreasonable demands toward them. For example, I suggested to Alex's mother, "You've always been able to help him with ordinary stress, and now it's as if he believes you can magically do something to make all this stop. And he's mad at you because you can't make it stop."

Many parents are temporarily disabled from knowing how to help their child cope because of their own transient trauma. The therapist can help them think about how to use their previous skills in helping the child regulate feelings in the new situation of cancer treatment. I said to Alex's mother: "I know you feel helpless because you can't cure his cancer or make this new reality go away. But you can help him with his upset. You haven't lost that ability." The goal is to help parents translate general feelings of parental competence into competence specific to helping their children cope with their illnesses. With the encouragement of their therapists, parents can learn about the medical treatment their children will undergo and prepare them verbally, helping their children know what to expect. At the clinic, parents can advocate for their children, based on their knowledge of their children as individuals. Parents' ability to help their children cope with treatment not only reduces their children's stress, but also counters the parents' feelings of helplessness. Parents' own sense of trauma will decrease as they reestablish themselves as "good enough" in this redefined caretaking role.

Parents become distressed in response to "regressive" behavior, and sometimes they receive mixed messages from medical staff about how to handle it. Parents are often relieved when therapists reframe regressive behavior in children undergoing cancer treatment as attachment-seeking behavior. Parents want to know how to respond to a child who is more needy, less competent in managing emotions, more angry, or more withdrawn. The treatment literature often suggests that parents should not "overindulge" or "reinforce" the child's needy behavior. Goodman, for example, states, "It is best to encourage social autonomy appropriate to the child's age, combined with reasonable limit-setting" (Goodman, 2007, p. 210; Rowland, 1989). While such recommendations are appropriate as the family's adaptation to cancer treatment stabilizes, a more nuanced perspective should inform the early period of treatment. To parents who recognize that their child is significantly distressed in response to medical treatment, such professional recommendations may feel unempathic and counterintuitive. The following recommendations are more useful:

- Expect the child to function autonomously for his or her age, with the caveat that the child often will not be able to because of illness-related stress.
- Tolerate temporary "regressive" behavior, recognizing that at times the child will not have the internal resources to function at an age-appropriate level.
- Continue to set limits, but be ready to "cut the child some slack" under some circumstances (e.g., when he or she is having a tantrum, is very clingy following a stressful procedure, or is affectively dysregulated because of the effects of steroids).

The parent of a child treated for leukemia said to the therapist during a session near termination of therapy: "I appreciated that you didn't push us to act as if everything was the same as before she was diagnosed. People at the hospital kept saying we should keep everything as normal as possible. I understood why they said that, but the truth was it *couldn't* be normal when we were in the hospital all the time at first, or when she was taking steroids and had those insane food cravings and intense anger. It helped a lot when you told us she needed to behave like a younger child then, and that the things we did to discipline her before she was diagnosed wouldn't work now." This parent also said it had been helpful to be told that research shows that children tend to resume their previous level of functioning following cancer treatment (Patenaude & Kupst, 2005).

As the family settles into cancer treatment, life becomes more predictable and therapy sessions may become less frequent. Nevertheless, the availability of the therapist remains important. It is common in cancer treatment for setbacks to occur. For example, the mother of a child with leukemia was very disturbed when her son's white cell counts remained low for almost a month and he was unable to attend school. This was a surprise, because the length of time his counts would be low following chemotherapy had been predictable for more than a year, and this departure from the norm prompted a recurrence of her earlier fears that he would not survive. More frequent parent sessions were helpful to her during this period. Parental stress in response to the long-term demands of cancer treatment may wax and wane, and it is important for parents to know that a therapist's support will be available throughout treatment, even if therapy is not ongoing.

Absence from school is a major issue for children undergoing cancer treatment (Vance & Eiser, 2002). Chemotherapy that kills cancer cells also radically reduces white blood cell counts. The child's immune system becomes so compromised that contracting a minor illness can be life-threatening. Consequently, when white counts are low, the child cannot attend school or go to other public places. In the early stages of leukemia treatment, for example, when high-dose chemotherapy is frequent, a child may miss two to three months of school. Later in treatment, when chemotherapy is administered monthly, the child may miss a few days to a week of school each month when white cell counts dip.

It is important for parents and health professionals to communicate with teachers and school nurses regarding the needs of children attending school while undergoing cancer treatment. These children must take precautions against infections by not handling materials touched by other children and by washing their hands frequently. Teachers can support children in these precautionary measures and monitor how they are feeling. Teachers need to know that at times they will have to change their expectations of children with cancer. For example, a child who has recently had chemotherapy may be fatigued and therefore less able to concentrate; a child who is taking steroids as part of a treatment regimen may be agitated and emotionally volatile. During periods when children are unable to attend school while recovering from surgery or because of infection risk, they can still feel connected to school through phone calls with classroom teachers, notes from peers, and visits from in-home teachers. Maintaining the connection smoothes the transition back to school as the period of intense treatment ends (Shiu, 2001).

In general, children do well academically and socially in school after treatment, although some studies have found that a significant number of children remain more isolative compared with peers (Vance & Eiser, 2002). Further, the school performance for children with brain tumors does not rebound as it does for children with other cancer diagnoses. In children with brain tumors, with those under age 7 being most at risk, cranial radiation therapy and methotrexate chemotherapy disrupt the growth of white matter that forms myelin sheaths insulating brain axons. The functioning of the circuits in the brain becomes less efficient, resulting in neurocognitive effects, including IQ decreases in the range of 15 to 25 points, slower rates of learning, and cognitive impairments in attention, memory, and processing speed (Moore, 2005; Palmer et al., 2007). Although pediatric cancer specialists are researching how to modify treatment to minimize neurocognitive effects, children treated for brain tumors and leukemia remain particularly at risk for lowered academic performance and learning disabilities posttreatment. Therapists can help parents understand these potential effects, explore their feelings about changed expectations for their child, and encourage them to advocate with school personnel for classroom accommodations and special education interventions (Upton & Eiser, 2006).

Therapy with Children Currently Undergoing Cancer Treatment

In individual therapy with children, treatment goals include promoting adaptation to medical treatment, reducing anxiety and posttraumatic symptoms, exploring idiosyncratic and developmentally based reactions with the aim of reducing cognitive distortions, and encouraging cognitive mastery.

If the therapist has the opportunity to work with the child shortly after medical treatment begins, a focus on helping the child (and parents) prepare for procedures should be considered as both an entry point for intervention and a means of establishing a therapeutic alliance. When there is no hospital-based medical social worker or child life specialist to do so, the therapist can help prepare the child for a procedure, such as bone marrow aspiration, and afterward review the child's experience and offer explicit recognition when a child has coped well with the procedure. Current medical practice for procedures such as bone marrow aspiration or port implantation surgery is to fully sedate the child within safe limits. When this is done during the first procedures after diagnosis, it tends to "prevent conditioned, maladaptive responses to subsequent procedures"

(Kazak et al., 2006, p. 349). Nevertheless, some children will be fearful of being hurt by procedures and consequently may experience mild pain or discomfort as affectively overwhelming. Children who have difficult experiences during an early procedure tend to exaggerate their distress as they remember it and will then anticipate later procedures with distress (Chen et al., 2000; Salmon, 2006). However, verbal processing of negative memories, followed by preparation using behavioral and cognitive rehearsal and discussion of specific coping strategies, can moderate children's expectations of distress and allow them to tolerate future procedures better (Blount, Piira, & Cohen, 2003; Vilas, chap. 5). Preparation for procedures is best practice, and therapists need to educate themselves about how to help children prepare.

Many cancer centers prepare children by offering a tour of the clinic, allowing children to inspect the medical equipment and demonstrating procedures using doll play. These preparatory approaches allow the child to develop a cognitive map of what to expect, making the procedure seem more predictable and manageable (Salmon, McGuigan, & Pereira, 2006). Several distraction techniques have been developed to reduce anxiety during the procedure by shifting the child's attention to activities like video games, stories told by the parent or clinician focusing on mastery of a difficult situation, and breathing exercises using guided imagery (Powers, 2002, chap. 5). Providing behavioral incentives and reinforcement is also helpful. However, distraction techniques, while helpful, should not be considered substitutes for detailed advance preparation and behavioral rehearsal (Salmon et al., 2006). Direct emotional support by parents during procedures also helps children cope.

Finally, when children are in therapy, it is useful for therapists to help them process the medical experience in words and play. Play therapy allows children to represent their subjective experience, allowing therapists to learn what the children found stressful, as well as to identify possible cognitive distortions about medical treatment (Davies, 1992; Gariépy & Howe, 2003). Cognitive processing helps children develop a sense of mastery over stressful procedures and enhances their ability to cope with the next procedure. Increasing children's procedure resilience is important, because they will have many procedures over the course of a long treatment. For example, with a five-year-old diagnosed with leukemia, it was valuable to underline his accomplishments. His parents and nurses prepared him well for bone marrow aspirations, and by the third time he had the procedure, he knew what to expect and was able to remain still without panicking. His mother reported this to me, and in our session I helped him elaborate the reasons he could cope with spinal aspirations: He said that he was "used to it," that he knew it wouldn't hurt now, that he knew how long it would take, that he knew he could lie still for that length of time, and that he could tell his mom or the nurse if he began to get worried or upset.

For young children, play is the best vehicle for uncovering the child's misunderstandings and negative reactions to treatment. My practice is to orient the child at the beginning of therapy by saying, "Our time together is a chance for kids to talk about and show their worries about cancer. I know how to help with those worries. One way kids show me is by playing." In response to such orienting comments, children intuitively feel they have permission to expose a range of reactions to medical treatment, and their play becomes a commentary on their medical experiences. It is helpful to have medical toys and supplies available, in addition to standard play therapy materials.

Play does not always take the form of a direct representation of cancer treatment, but therapists should observe for relevant themes and make interpretive links between play and the child's treatment. Since the therapy explicitly focuses on the child's responses to cancer treatment, the therapist actively looks for opportunities to make these links while staying within the child's play metaphors. I offer two examples from the play therapy of five-year-old Demetrius, who was being treated for leukemia. Demetrius frequently set up play scenarios in which he (or his character) was powerful and I (or my character) was vulnerable. In one session, he instructed me that my character was in danger and had to hide. Then a robot found him and Demetrius said, "He's sticking electrodes all over your head and body. And now you're getting shocks." I asked what I should feel, and Demetrius said. "You're scared!" I said, "What happened to my guy reminds me how kids feel sometimes when they're at the hospital. They might have electrodes stuck on them before a procedure and they wonder whether they'll get a shock, and they get scared. Really, kids don't get a shock. The only thing with the electrodes is that it might hurt a little when the nurse pulls them off. I like to play like this because it helps me understand some of the things that might scare you in the hospital."

In preschool children, developmentally normative concerns about body damage can be intensified by cancer treatment. Demetrius had lost his hair, at times felt weak and fatigued after receiving chemotherapy, and was jittery and emotionally labile when he was taking steroids. His play suggested that these physical changes in how he looked and felt, in combination with frequent invasive procedures, were creating fantasies about more severe body damage. For example, he pulled the limbs off a Spiderman figure, saying that a transformer figure with a circular saw on the end of his arm had cut them off. Then he reassembled Spiderman, putting the legs in the shoulder sockets and the arms in the hip sockets, and laughed. I asked how Spiderman was feeling now and Demetrius said, "He feels weird. He looks funny." Demetrius was amused when I spoke for Spiderman, saying, "I feel so weird, what's happened to my body, it doesn't work right!" As this scenario was repeated, I introduced a medical theme: "What's happening to Spiderman makes me think about what kids imagine when they go to the hospital. They wonder if their body will be hurt badly, even though it won't. It's no wonder they think that because weird things *do* happen to them, like getting all swollen and losing their hair." Demetrius's concerns about body damage were elaborated in a session soon after he had a port surgically implanted in his chest.

His play with action figures transparently focused on knife attacks, with a superhero figure stabbing another action figure in the chest. I suggested that his play reminded me of kids' worries when their skin is cut to put a port in, saying, "Even though kids are given medicine to keep the cutting from hurting, they're a little sore afterward, and they might have scary feelings about being cut. In their imagination, they might even worry that the doctors wanted to hurt them." I normalized these issues as what lots of kids feel, and then went on to reiterate medical information: "The port makes it easier for the doctors to give you medicine and draw blood. That's why they and your parents decided to put it in. It's going to be there for a long time, but it will be taken out when you don't need it any more when your cancer is gone."

The termination process in therapy offers the child a chance to gain perspective on medical treatment. Near the end of therapy, Lucia, an eight-year-old girl, provided the following concrete "advice," after her therapist asked her what she would tell a kid just diagnosed with leukemia. (This is an effective displacement device that encourages children to review their own thoughts and feelings in the guise of helping other children).

THERAPIST: *You know a lot about leukemia, and I'm wondering what advice you might give to a kid who's just been diagnosed and doesn't know much about it yet.*

LUCIA: *[Pauses, clearly thinking about the question.] You could tell her that leukemia isn't really a big thing. It doesn't bother you too much, except maybe in the first two or three months.*

THERAPIST: *Oh, yes, that's when a kid is having lots of procedures and lots of chemotherapy to get the cancer cells out of her blood.*

LUCIA: *Yes.*

THERAPIST: *But after the kid goes into remission . . . you know what remission means? . . . [Lucia nods] then she has to go to the clinic once a month.*

LUCIA: *And that's not so much.*

THERAPIST: *But at the beginning there are lots of procedures, and sometimes some hurting, and they might seem scary because the kid doesn't know what to expect. Would there be anything you would tell kids about the beginning?*

LUCIA: *They really don't hurt much at all because the nurse puts numbing cream on before they stick the needle in. I didn't look when they did it.*

THERAPIST: *It sounds like a good idea not to look. Was one of your parents there?*

LUCIA: *Yes. Most of the time it was my dad. He held my hand and he asked me some jokes, like knock-knock jokes.*

THERAPIST: *So it helps if a kid's parent is with them and talks to them while the procedure is happening. What could you tell other kids about spinal taps? Because I think they sound very scary when a kid first hears about them.*

LUCIA: *You feel some pressure; it doesn't really hurt. I didn't want them when I heard about it, but I got used to it.*

Such conversations with this child, who had been diagnosed at age 5 and now was 8, served to help her put her medical treatment in perspective, using the cognitive abilities of an eight-year-old. At age 8, she was able to think about her cancer experience more objectively. Characteristically for a school-age child, Lucia describes her experience matter-of-factly. Significantly, her statements seem free of misunderstanding or distortion, and the themes of mastery and understanding of the treatment come through strongly.

These examples illustrate the value of therapy during the period of cancer treatment. Therapy can help children understand their illness and treatment, clear up misconceptions, and help them compartmentalize, so that the illness, when the pace of treatment slows after the intense early period, can begin to take its place as part of their life, but not the dominant part. "Putting the illness in its place" frees children emotionally to resume many normal activities and, in a larger sense, normative developmental tasks.

Concluding Comments

The goal of intervention with children in cancer treatment and after treatment ends is to safeguard the children's future development by helping them cope with medical stresses and subjective meanings the illness holds for them. Central processes in intervention that contribute to this goal include:

- *Sustaining and strengthening the parent-child relationship* as the child's major resource for adaptation and coping. A focus on the illness and its treatment, and on their impact on the child-parent relationship, provides a clear direction and organization for intervention. Work on support, education, and active problem solving with parents is perhaps the most important safeguard for children.

- *Honoring the child's perspective.* Children's coping skills increase when adult partners, including parents and therapists, empathize with and respect the child's subjective experience of illness and treatment. This involves going beyond explaining reasons for treatment to acknowledging the whole range of the child's reactions. Recognizing the child's perspective also implies providing developmentally attuned and honest information about the child's illness and treatment.

- *Acknowledging play as an essential starting point* in work with children, especially those under age 8. Play therapy is usually excluded from reviews of evidence-based treatment, which focus primarily on cognitive-behavioral interventions. (The bias of outcome researchers against play approaches remains strong, in spite of recent meta-analytic findings that effect sizes of play therapy, at the .80 level, equal those of cognitive-behavioral treatment of children (Bratton et al., 2005). In fact, the orientations of cancer-focused play therapy and CBT are quite similar. Play interpretation is the entry point for cognitive interventions such as creating stress/trauma narratives, correcting cognitive distortions, cognitive processing of stressful medical experiences, and helping children gain an accurate understanding of past experiences based on their current level of cognitive development (Friedberg & McClure, 2002).

- *Advocating for family and professional collaboration as best practice.* This is an ideal that is often unrealized. Although children with cancer and their parents benefit tremendously when medical caregivers, therapists, and school personnel communicate regularly, more often the reality is that communication is sporadic and minimal, leaving parents with the additional responsibility of brokering between different people and systems. A therapist who maintains an ecological perspective can further support the parent by sharing the task of facilitating collaboration.

Counseling Approaches for Children and Youth with HIV/AIDS

Like young people with cancer, those with HIV/AIDS face the stresses of frequent hospital visits and painful medical procedures, absences from school due to the side effects of the illness or medications, fears about maintaining friendships with peers, and, underneath all, anxiety about the lurking fears of physical decline and eventual death. Often, children in families with HIV/AIDS have experienced the deaths of parents, siblings, or relatives, so they are acutely aware of the likelihood of a fatal outcome. Because of the nature of the disease transmission, many young children with HIV are infected at birth by mothers who were either substance abusers or involved with infected partners who passed on the disease through unprotected sex (Armstead, Kotchick, & Forehand, 2004). Many infected mothers die during their children's childhood, thereby resulting in the youth's premature loss of a parent, with all the associated reactions of traumatic bereavement. This is discussed later in a case example.

The occurrence of HIV in adolescence occurs primarily due to unprotected sex with an infected person (Mangione, Landau, & Pryor, 1998), although sharing contaminated needles in the process of injecting drugs can also result in infection (Auslander & Freedenthal, 2006). It is notable that many adolescents with HIV are unaware of their diagnoses and therefore do not follow safeguards to prevent the spread of the illness.

Definitions

HIV infection refers to a contagion caused by the human immunodeficiency virus. When this progresses to *HIV disease,* the body's immune system has become so compromised that it is vulnerable to infections with life-threatening clinical manifestations (Mangione, Landau, & Pryor, 1998; Auslander & Freedenthal, 2006). *AIDS* refers to the later stage of HIV disease in which the person's weakened and suppressed immune system makes him or her vulnerable to many diseases that ultimately cause death.

Transmission of HIV

HIV is transmitted in the following three ways: (1) to an infant from an infected mother in utero, in childbirth, or through breastfeeding, (2) unprotected sex with an infected person, and (3) exposure to infected blood or blood products, typically through intravenous transfusions, needle sticks, or injections. According to the Centers for Disease Control (CDC, 2005), approximately 91 percent of children with HIV have acquired their illness from their mothers through perinatal transmission (i.e., at birth). It is notable that at the latest available report, the rates of pediatric HIV (HIV in children under the age of 13) had been declining (due to improved medications for infected mothers), but the rates of *adolescent* HIV were increasing. The speculation is that some of the rise in adolescent rates is due to the increased longevity of children with perinatally acquired HIV disease as a result of the greatly improved effectiveness of specialized antiretroviral therapies since the mid-1990s (Steele, Nelson, & Cole, 2007).

Issues for Children and Youth with HIV/AIDS

HIV/AIDS is an illness with no known cure, requiring difficult and costly medical treatment and disturbing and painful side effects, such as susceptibility to ear, eye, and mouth infections, motor, speech, and language delays; and compromised intellectual functioning (Mangione, Landau, & Pryor, 1998). The requirements for adherence to a strict medical regimen causes great stress for both the victims and their families and caretakers. In addition to these numerous medical challenges, other factors seriously compromise the environment in which this incurable condition exists.

Sociological, Cultural, and Familial Factors
Children and youth with HIV/AIDS often live in poverty in multiproblem families characterized by substance abuse, domestic violence, parental abandonment, and imprisonment. These environments create many risks and few protective factors for the growing child. The child welfare system may become involved when overburdened parents develop addictions that contribute to child abuse or neglect. Studies have found that abuse was 14 times more common and neglect was 44 times more frequent in poor families (Sedlak & Broadhurst, 1996, as reported by Hendricks and Fong, 2006). Children with HIV/AIDS require home-based and medical attention that parents may not be able to provide because they may be overwhelmed or addicted or infected themselves. Sometimes children with special needs become more vulnerable to abuse (Shannon, 2006; Chapter 12 in this book).

African American and Hispanic youths are disproportionately affected by HIV/AIDS (U.S. Department of Health and Human Services, 2006), thereby adding the possibility of discrimination to the mix of poverty and health issues. When family members are unavailable to provide appropriate care for young people with medical needs, an out-of-home placement may be the only recourse. The case of Mario and Maria, which is discussed later, involves such a situation following a mother's death of AIDS and the lack of other family members to care for the children.

Multiple Losses of Children and Youth with HIV/AIDS

The stress of a chronic health condition may be only the tip of the iceberg for a young person growing up in a family and community struggling to survive due to economic conditions, discrimination, lack of resources, and various mental health and health problems. HIV/AIDS is a stigmatized illness due to its early association with gay men and drug addicts. Even churches may disapprove of the behavior that led to the illness, thereby causing relatives to feel unwelcome and unsupported. Despite the improved prognosis now due to new and stronger medications, people continue to fear this disease and to try to avoid contact with infected individuals and their relatives. Consequently, families with a member who has HIV/AIDS often attempt to hide it because they feel ashamed, and they erect a cloud of secrecy around the illness. When a family member dies, the true cause of death may not be disclosed because of fears of social ostracism. Their grief becomes enveloped with anxiety, and their true feelings of shame, rage, and despair are hidden. This situation qualifies as "disenfranchised grief" (Doka, 1989), constituting a loss that cannot be openly acknowledged or fully mourned, despite the great need for support from friends and the community. It is very confusing to children, who at a young age sense the shame and secretive behavior of their relatives.

Children and youth who have HIV/AIDS may not be told of their diagnosis, and when they later find out they may be cautioned against telling others about their illness. The American Academy of Pediatrics in 1999 recommended that children and adolescents with HIV be told of their diagnoses in an age-appropriate manner (APA, 1999). However, the issue of whether, when, and to whom to disclose the illness is very complicated. Parents may be uncomfortable about discussing their own HIV infection, and they may feel guilty because of associated questions about the child's paternity and about their own sexual behavior and substance abuse. Actually, studies show no clear evidence that children who have experienced full disclosure have better or worse psychological outcomes than those who do not (Wiener, Mellins, Marhefka, & Battles, 2007). However, young people with HIV/AIDS are at risk of developing a negative sense of their own identity, which, as they age and learn more about their future prognosis, may evolve into depression. These youth live with multiple losses on a daily basis, and they often do not have any way to cope with their confused feelings of anger and injustice. Family members may themselves be ill or bereaved, and they feel very isolated. Counseling and therapy can provide great relief and validation of their feelings.

Counseling and Therapy Options for Youth with HIV/AIDS

This section considers various treatment modalities (individual, family, group) and also key therapeutic issues in therapy with young people and their families who are affected by HIV/AIDS. Many of the perspectives and recommendations already presented with regard to counseling children and families with cancer also apply in helping youth and families with HIV/AIDS. Due to length considerations, these will not be repeated. Instead, the focus here is on two pivotal topics with special relevance to HIV/AIDS: (1) the disclosure of the illness to the young person, which often is very stressful for parents, caretakers, the child, and even the therapist, and (2) the necessity to provide bereavement counseling related to the child's many losses. A case example illustrates these selected issues with discussion regarding how best to address the needs of the child and the caretakers or family.

The Case of Mario, Age 12 and Maria, Age 10

Background Information

This case was referred to me (a child and family therapist) on a six-session consultation basis for the purpose of helping the child welfare caseworker respond to 10-year-old Maria's questions about why she had to take 14 pills every day. The girl had HIV, but had not been told about her diagnosis. Maria had a half brother, Mario, two years older. Maria's mother had died when the girl was six years old; the cause of the mother's death was not known but was presumed to be AIDS. Maria had stated that her mother died of a "weak heart." Maria's father was unknown, and there were no known relatives nearby. Mario's father was terminally ill with AIDS and lived out of state with Mario's older sister and her two young children.

Following their mother's death, Maria and Mario were initially cared for by the home health aide who had worked in their home during their mother's terminal illness. After a period of time, this woman decided that she could not continue to care for the children, and she virtually abandoned them. They were then placed in a Spanish-speaking foster home with foster parents and their three biological children. Maria shared a bedroom with a girl her same age, and she seemed to adjust fairly well. Mario, in contrast, was unable to adapt; he acted out aggressively and after a while was placed in a local residential treatment center. Mario was allowed to visit his sister in her foster home twice a month. At the time of my contact with this case, Maria had been living in this foster home for about a year and a half, and the family wanted to adopt her.

Planning the Sequence of Contacts

I realized that my clients in this case included the caseworker, the foster parents, and Maria and Mario. I decided to begin by meeting with the caseworker, since I knew that her involvement with the family would continue long after mine, and I also realized that she already had developed a relationship with the foster family and with Maria and Mario. The issue of disclosure of Maria's diagnosis had been the reason for the referral, and this needed to be addressed up front.

Next, I planned to meet with the foster parents, with the caseworker present; and finally, I wanted to meet with Maria to initiate some bereavement counseling. I knew that Mario was already receiving treatment at the residential center and that the caseworker was in contact with his counselor.

Session with the Caseworker to Discuss the Disclosure of Maria's Diagnosis:

The following designations are used: NBW = Nancy Boyd Webb (the consultant); CW = caseworker.

> **NBW:** *Please review for me your concerns and your questions about Maria.*
>
> **CW:** *She has been asking about why she has to take so many pills every day when her foster sister doesn't have to take any. She also asks me why she has to go for so many blood tests. I have managed to answer the last question by saying that I take a lot of foster kids to the hospital clinic for checkups, just to be sure they are healthy. She has kind of accepted this explanation, but I really don't know how to answer the question about the pills.*
>
> **NBW:** *Would you like to kind of rehearse it with me?*
>
> **CW:** *Yes, I really need help with this.*
>
> **NBW:** *First, let's consider when and where you could have this conversation.*
>
> **CW:** *She has an appointment at the clinic later this week, and we usually stop for a snack after the blood draw. So I thought I might bring it up then.*
>
> **NBW:** *That seems like a logical time. So, how can you introduce this topic?*
>
> **CW:** *I was thinking about telling her that I had not been completely honest with her about why she has to have the blood tests. I thought that I could say that maybe now she was old enough to understand the full reason.*
>
> **NBW:** *Great! You associate the disclosure with her being older. That is a good introduction.*
>
> **CW:** *Should I tell her the name of her diagnosis? Or just that she has a blood condition?*
>
> **NBW:** *Either way is the truth. How about asking her if she has ever heard of HIV/AIDS? I bet she has.*
>
> **CW:** *She must have, because her brother's father has AIDS and he is terminal. What if she asks me if she is going to die?*
>
> **NBW:** *I know that is a biggie, but with all the new meds, let's hope that they come up with new strong meds that will help her stay healthy. This is how you can talk about the pills. Say that the pills are to help make her strong cells stay healthy so they can fight the bad cells. And this is why it is so very important for her to take her meds every day without fail.*
>
> **CW:** *What about the ''Am I going to die?'' question? I'm afraid I will start to cry. I like her so much and I want to see her grow up and be healthy!*
>
> **NBW:** *Your affection for her is admirable. The truth is, no one knows who will die of this disease, but the medicines are getting more and more effective, so we really hope they will help her and keep her as healthy as possible. You can't promise a cure, but you can be hopeful, and it is important to be hopeful so she will feel positive about herself and her future.*
>
> **CW:** *Thank you so much. I feel much better about this, and I'll let you know how it goes.*

Several days later, the caseworker called and reported a very positive meeting. I invited her to be present at the forthcoming meeting with the foster parents.

Consultation Meeting with the Foster Parents

Although Maria had been living in their home for a year and a half, the foster parents had not met with anyone to discuss their questions following the placement. Because both parents were native Spanish speakers, they admitted to feeling reluctant to accompany Maria to the hospital to speak with her doctors there. This interview was facilitated by the caseworker's presence and her occasional translation from English to Spanish and vice versa.

As discussed earlier in the chapter with reference to children with cancer, collaboration with the parents should *always* be an integral part of helping children with acute and chronic illnesses. Maria was not their biological child, but these foster parents wanted to adopt her, so it seemed vital to meet with them to discuss any concerns.

This proved to be most fortunate, because the foster father did indeed have some serious concerns. He said that because Maria and his daughter shared the same bathroom, he was worried about possible

(continued)

transmission of the disease if the girls should happen to use one another's toothbrushes or if his daughter became exposed to Maria's menstrual blood later on when she began menstruating. I acknowledged the importance of these questions and urged the parents to accompany Maria and the caseworker to the hospital clinic at the time of her next visit so they could obtain the answers directly from the physician. I knew that there was no known transmission of HIV through casual contacts in home situations and in schools and day care settings (Mangione, Landau, & Pryor, 1998), but I felt that it was important for these parents to hear this from a medical doctor. I also wanted to set a precedent about seeking medical advice about future concerns.

I also told them about a support group based at the clinic for parents of children with HIV/AIDS. I suggested that they speak to the group leader when they visited the clinic and have her tell them about the group. I knew that these parents would need ongoing support as Maria entered adolescence, and I explained to them that all the people in the group would understand one another because they are all facing similar challenges.

Bereavement Counseling with Maria

When the caseworker brought Maria to me for the first time, I told her that I knew a lot about her background from the caseworker and that I had met with her foster parents. I explained my role as someone who helps kids and families with their worries and that I hoped to help their caseworkers understand more about how to help her in the future, because I would be meeting with her only a few times in the next weeks.

Maria related well and seemed very interested in the drawing materials I had laid out on the table. I invited her to draw a picture and she eagerly drew a picture of a woman in a long dress with a cigarette in her mouth. She said it was a picture of her mother on her wedding day. I was impressed that she spontaneously spoke of her mother, and I wanted to encourage her to recall more memories. I told her I knew that she was only six years old when her mother died, and I asked her to close her eyes and think back to a time when she was with her mother. As Maria began drawing, I realized that she was drawing her mother in a casket, with herself in front, crying, and her brother and her sister also crying as they stood at the rear of the casket. I was very moved and commented about how sad the picture was and that there was no adult there to take care of those children!

Maria then began talking about her "babysitter" (as she referred to her first foster mother) who "took us away and then brought us back." I commented that they must have been scared and worried about who would take care of them. Maria said some positive things about her current foster parents, and I then introduced the idea that we could make a book together about her life, because it was important for her to remember and record things about her life before and after her mother died. She seemed interested in this prospect, and then mentioned that she didn't even know where her mother was buried. I said that I would try to find out, and, if she wanted, we could go to the cemetery and visit her grave. Maria's whole face lit up and she said, "I really, really want to go!"

One month later the visit to the grave occurred. We had invited Mario to come also, and both children and the caseworker came to my office first so I could prepare them for the experience. I have a form letter that I showed them titled, "A Letter to the Person Who Died." It is lined paper and opens with the instructions to write a letter to the person who died. Both Mario and Maria wrote a letter and permitted me to make a copy in my office for their records. I said that they could do whatever they wanted with their letters at the cemetery: Some people like to read them out loud at the grave, and other people read them silently to themselves. The caseworker had brought flowers for the children to place on the graves.

When we later made the trip by car and found the grave, Maria immediately dropped to her knees and began digging in the dirt. She buried her letter in her mother's grave and then proceeded to gently smooth out the dirt and groom the grave. This continued for about 15 minutes while Mario walked around looking at the other tombstones. This was one of the most moving experiences I have had in my more than 30 years as a child therapist! I knew that Maria would always remember the visit to her mother's grave and that the letter had provided her a way to communicate with her mother and ask some meaningful questions.

When I later examined the copy of the letter in my office I saw that two of Maria's questions to her mother were: "How did you die?" and "Who is my father?" Maria had lost not only her mother but the key to her own life history. I filed these questions in my mind for exploration in Maria's future therapy.

We had one more concluding session with the caseworker and Maria in which we reviewed the Life Book filled with Maria's drawings, stories, and photos of the grave, of the caseworker, and of me. We had some special snacks, and I was able to say good-bye knowing that this caseworker would continue to support and sustain this child. I had made a recommendation for individual play therapy and for group therapy with kids Maria's age who also have HIV. She would continue to have ongoing therapy and the opportunity to continue to explore her bereavement and identity issues.

Concluding Comments

Children with HIV and their families suffer many losses, and face an uncertain future. No cure is yet on the horizon, but we do know how to support and comfort these individuals through a variety of individual, group, and family treatments. Although not addressed in this abbreviated case example, the foster children (or siblings) in the family also require the opportunity to ask questions and to receive some recognition. When the attention is focused on the child with the diagnosis, the other children in the family may feel invisible. Fortunately there are web sites addressed specifically to siblings (see supersibs.org).

Space does not permit discussion here of the impact on the counselors and therapists who deal with children who are chronically ill and dying. See Chapter 18 in this book for further discussion of the vital need to help the helpers. Many children continue to have fun and participate in the activities of childhood despite limitations such as reduced energy following chemo treatments. Their resilience is remarkable and serves as a model for helping professionals. If we can assist chronically and terminally ill children and youth to enjoy their lives more, our work takes on great meaning, not only for the young people and their families, but also for those of us who provide services to them.

References

American Academy of Pediatrics (APA). (1999). Committee on pediatric AIDS. Disclosure of illness status to children and adolescents with HIV infection. *Pediatrics, 103,* 164–166.

Armstead, L., Kotchick, B. A., & Forehand, R. (2004). Teenage pregnancy, sexually transmitted diseases, and HIV/AIDS. In L. A. Rapp-Paglicci, C. N. Dulmus, & J. S. Wodarski (Eds.), *Handbook of preventive interventions for children and adolescents* (pp. 237–254). Hoboken, NJ: Wiley.

Armstrong, F. D., & Mulhern, R. K. (2000). Acute lymphoblastic leukemia and brain tumors. In R. T. Brown (Ed.), *Cognitive aspects of chronic illness* (pp. 47–77). New York: Guilford.

Auslander, W., & Freedenthal, S. (2006). Social work and chronic disease: Diabetes, heart disease, and HIV/AIDS. In S. Gehlert & T. A. Browne (Eds.), *Handbook of health social work* (pp. 532–567). Hoboken, NJ: Wiley.

Blount, R. L., Piira, T., & Cohen, L. L. (2003). Management of pediatric pain and distress due to medical procedures. In M. Roberts (Ed.), *Handbook of pediatric psychology* (3rd ed., pp. 216–233). New York: Guilford.

Bratton, S. C., Ray, D., Rhine, T., & Jones, L. (2005). The efficacy of play therapy with children: A meta-analytic review of treatment outcomes. *Professional Psychology: Research and Practice, 36*, 376–390.

Brown, R. T., Madan-Swain, A., & Lambert, R. (2003). Posttraumatic stress symptoms in adolescent survivors of cancer and their mothers. *Journal of Traumatic Stress, 16*, 309–318.

Butler, R. W., & Mulhern, R. K. (2005). Neurocognitive interventions for children and adolescents surviving cancer. *Journal of Pediatric Psychology, 30*, 65–78.

Centers for Disease Control and Prevention (CDC) (2003). HIV/AIDS Surveillance Report (Vol. 15). Retrieved from http://www.did.gov/hiv/stats/2003SurveillanceReport/cover.htm.

Chen, E., Zeltzer, L. K., Craske, M. G., & Katz, E. R. (2000). Children's memories for painful cancer treatment procedures: Implications for distress. *Child Development, 71*, 933–947.

Clay, D. L. (2004). *Helping schoolchildren with chronic health conditions. A. practical guide.* New York: Guilford Press.

Dahlquist, L. M., & Pendley, J. S. (2005). When distraction fails: Parental anxiety and children's responses to distraction during cancer procedures. *Journal of Pediatric Psychology, 30*, 623–628.

Davies, D. (1992). Psychotherapy of a preschool cancer survivor: Promoting mastery and understanding. *Child and Adolescent Social Work, 9*, 289–305.

Davies, D. (2004). *Child development: A practitioner's guide* (2nd ed.). New York: Guilford.

Doka, K. J. (1989). (Ed.). *Disenfranchised grief: Recognizing hidden sorrow.* Lexington, MA: Lexington Books.

Dolgin, M. J., Phipps, S., Fairclough, D. L., Sahler, O. J. Z., Askins, M., Noll, R. B., Butler, R. W., Varni, J. W., & Katz, E. R. (2007). Trajectories of adjustment in mothers of children with newly diagnosed cancer: A natural history investigation. *Journal of Pediatric Psychology, 32*, 771–782.

Earle, E. A., Clarke, S. A., Eiser, C., & Sheppard, L. (2006) Building a new normality: Mothers' experiences of caring for a child with acute lymphoblastic leukaemia. *Child: Care, Health, and Development, 33*, 155–160.

Egeland, B., Carlson, E., & Sroufe, L. A. (1993). Resilience as process. *Development and Psychopathology. 5*, 517–528.

Friedberg, R. D., & McClure, J. M. (2002). *Clinical practice of cognitive therapy with children and adolescents: The nuts and bolts.* New York: Guilford Press.

Gariépy, N., & Howe, N. (2003). The therapeutic power of play: Examining the play of young children with leukaemia. *Child: Care, Health, and Development, 29*, 523–537.

Goodman, R. F. (2007). Living beyond the crisis of childhood cancer. In N. B. Webb (Ed.), *Play therapy with children in crisis: Individual, group and family treatment* (3rd ed., pp. 197–227). New York: Guilford Press.

Hendricks, C. O., & Fong, R. (2006). Ethnically sensitive practice with children and families. In N. B. Webb (Ed.), *Working with traumatized youth in child welfare* (pp. 135–154). New York: Guilford Press.

Hobbie, W. L., Stuber, M. L., Meeske, K., Wissler, K., Rourke, M., Ruccione, K., et al. (2000). Symptoms of posttraumatic stress in young adult survivors of childhood cancer. *Journal of Clinical Oncology, 18,* 4060–4066.

Kazak, A. (1998). Posttraumatic distress in childhood cancer survivors and their parents. *Medical and Pediatric Oncology* (Suppl. 1), 60–68.

Kazak, A. E. (2005). Evidence-based interventions for survivors of childhood cancer and their families. *Journal of Pediatric Psychology, 30,* 29–39.

Kazak, A. E., Bouving, C. A., Alderfer, M. A., Hwang, W-T., & Reilly, A. (2005). Posttraumatic stress symptoms during treatment in parents of children with cancer. *Journal of Clinical Oncology, 23,* 7405–7410.

Kazak, A. E., Kassam-Adams, N., Schneider, S., Zelikovsky, N., Alderfer, M. A., & Rourke, M. (2006). An integrative model of pediatric medical traumatic stress. *Journal of Pediatric Psychology, 31,* 343–355.

Luthar, S. S., Cicchetti, D., & Becker, B. (2000). The construct of resilience: A critical evaluation and guidelines for future work. *Child Development, 71,* 543–562.

Mangione, C., Landau, S., & Pryor, J. B. (1998). HIV and AIDS (pediatric and adolescent). In L. A. Phelps (Ed.), *Health-related disorders in children and adolescents: A guidebook for understanding and educating* (pp. 328–336). Washington, DC: American Psychological Association.

Manne, S., Miller, D., Meyers, P., Wollner, N., & Steinherz, P. (1996). Depressive symptoms among parents of newly diagnosed children with cancer: A 6-month follow-up study. *Children's Health Care, 25,* 191–209.

McGrath, P. (2001). Findings on the impact of treatment of acute lymphoblastic leukaemia on family relationships. *Child and Family Social Work, 6,* 229–237.

Moore, B. D. (2005). Neurocognitive outcomes in survivors of childhood cancer. *Journal of Pediatric Psychology, 30,* 51–63.

Nargarajan, R., Neglia, J. P., Clohisy, D. R., & Robison, L. L. (2002). Limb salvage and amputation in survivors of pediatric lower-extremity bone tumors: What are the long-term implications? *Journal of Clinical Oncology, 20,* 4493–4501.

Noll, R. B., & Kupst, M. J. (2007). Commentary: The psychological impact of pediatric cancer. Hardiness, the exception or the rule. *Journal of Pediatric Psychology, 32,* 1089–1098.

Palmer, S. L., Reddick, W. E., & Gajjar, A. (2007). Understanding the cognitive impact on children who are treated for medulloblastoma. *Journal of Pediatric Psychology, 32,* 1040–1049.

Patenaude, A. F., & Kupst, M. J. (2005). Psychosocial functioning in pediatric cancer. *Journal of Pediatric Psychology, 30,* 9–27.

Phipps, S., Dunavant, M., Srivastava, D. K., Bowman, L., & Mulhern, R. K. (2000). Cognitive and academic functioning in survivors of pediatric bone marrow transplantation. *Journal of Clinical Oncology, 18,* 1004–1011.

Phipps, S., Steele, R. G., Hall, K., & Leigh, L. (2001). Repressive adaptation in children with cancer: A replication and an extension. *Health Psychology, 20,* 445–451.

Powers, S. W. (1999). Empirically supported treatments in pediatric psychology: Procedure-related pain. *Journal of Pediatric Psychology, 24,* 131–145.

Roddenberry, A., & Renk, K. (2008). Quality of life in pediatric cancer: The relationships among parent's characteristics, children's characteristics, and informant concordance. *Journal of Child and Family Studies, 17,* 402–426.

Rennick, J. E., Johnston, C. C., Dougherty, G., Platt, R., & Ritchie, J. A. (2002). Children's psychological responses after critical illness and exposure to invasive technology. *Developmental and Behavioral Pediatrics, 23,* 133–144.

Robinson, K. E., Gerhardt, C. A., Vannatta, K., & Noll, R. B. (2007). Parent and family factors associated with child adjustment to pediatric cancer. *Journal of Pediatric Psychology, 32*, 400–410.

Rowland, J. H. (1989). Developmental stage and adaptation: Child and adolescent model. In J. C. Holland & J. H. Rowland (Eds.), *Handbook of Psychooncology* (pp. 519–543). New York: Oxford University Press.

Sahler, O. J. Z., Fairclough, D. L., Phipps, S., Mulhern, R. K., Dolgin, M. J., Noll, R. B., Katz, E. R., Varni, J. W., Copeland, D. R., & Butler, R. W. (2005). Using problem solving skills training to reduce negative affectivity in mothers of children with newly diagnosed cancer: Report of a multi-site randomized trial. *Journal of Consulting and Clinical Psychology, 73*, 272–283.

Salmon, K. (2006). Commentary: Preparing young children for medical procedures: Taking account of memory. *Journal of Pediatric Psychology, 31*, 859–861.

Salmon, K., McGuigan, F., & Pereira, J. K. (2006). Brief report: Optimizing children's memory and management of an invasive medical procedure: The influence of procedural narration and distraction. *Journal of Pediatric Psychology, 31*, 522–527.

Saxe, G. N., Vanderbilt, D., & Zuckerman, B. (2003). Traumatic stress in injured and ill children. *PTSD Research Quarterly, 14*, 1–7.

Sedlak, A. J., & Broadhust, D. D. (1996). *Third national incidence study of child abuse and neglect. Final report.* Washington, DC: Department of Health and Human Services. Administration on Children, Youth and Families. National Center on Child Abuse and Neglect.

Shannon, P. (2006). Children with disabilities in child welfare. Empowering the disenfranchised. In N. B. Webb (Ed.), *Working with traumatized youth in child welfare* (pp. 155–170). New York: Guilford Press.

Shiu, S. (2001). Issues in the education of students with chronic illness. *International Journal of Disability, Development, and Education, 48*, 269–281.

Simms, S., Kazak, A. E., Golomb, V., Goldwein, J., & Bunin, N. (2002). Cognitive, behavioral, and social outcome in survivors of childhood stem cell transplantation. *Journal of Pediatric Hematology/Oncology, 24*, 115–119.

Steele, R. G., Dreyer, M. L., & Phipps, S. (2004). Patterns of maternal distress among children with cancer and their association with child emotional and somatic distress. *Journal of Pediatric Psychology, 29*, 507–517.

Steele, R. G., Nelson, T. D., & Cole, B. P. (2007). Psychosocial functioning of children with AIDS and HIV infection. Review of the literature from a socioecological framework. *Journal of Developmental and Behavioral Pediatrics, 28*(1), 58–69.

Stuber, M. L., Shemesh, E., & Saxe, G. N. (2003). Posttraumatic stress responses in children with life-threatening illnesses. *Child and Adolescent Psychiatric Clinics of North America, 12*, 195–209.

Upton, P., & Eiser, C. (2006). School experiences after treatment for a brain tumour. *Child: Care, Health, and Development, 32*, 9–17.

U.S. Cancer Statistics Working Group. (2004). *United States cancer statistics: 2001 incidence and mortality.* Atlanta, GA: Department of Health and Human Services, Centers for Disease Control and Prevention and National Cancer Institute.

U.S. Health and Human Services. (2006). Youth and HIV/AIDS in the United States. Rockville, MD: Human Resources and Services Administration HIV/AIDS Bureau. www.hab.hrsa.gov.

Vance, Y. H., & Eiser, C. (2002). The school experience of the child with cancer. *Child: Care, Health, and Development, 28*, 5–19.

Vrijmoet-Wiersma, C. M., van Klink, J. M. M., Kolk, A. M., Koopman, H. M., Ball, L. M., & Egeler, R. M. (2008). Assessment of parental psychological stress in pediatric cancer: A review. *Journal of Pediatric Psychology, 33,* 694–706.

Webb, N. B. (1996). *Social work practice with children.* New York: Guilford Press.

Webb, N. B. (2004). *Social work practice with children* (2nd ed.). New York: Guilford Press.

Wiener, L., Mellins, C. A., Marhefka, S., & Battles, H. B. (2007). Disclosure of an HIV diagnosis to children. History, current research, and future directions. *Journal of Developmental & Behavioral Pediatrics, 28*(2), 155–166.

Hospital Treatment of Children and Youth with Life-Threatening Conditions

Elaine C. Meyer

16
Chapter

Life-threatening illnesses can have significant, far-reaching effects on children and their families and generate major disruptions in daily home, school, and work lives (Holmes, 2004; Haines 2005). Children with life-threatening conditions vary widely in age (newborn to young adult), reasons for admission, previous health care experiences, familiarity with the hospital culture, expectations, and relationships with health care providers. Children who are previously healthy can be diagnosed with overwhelming infection, be victims of traumatic injury, or present with a range of life-threatening acute medical illnesses that require hospitalization. Children who have chronic medical conditions can develop acute illnesses, experience worsening of their underlying condition, or suffer complications from necessary medical and surgical interventions. The parents of chronically ill and technology dependent children bring valuable experience and hard-earned expertise that can be tapped to optimize diagnostic and treatment planning (Pate, 2008). This chapter discusses the nature of critical illness and the demands of the pediatric intensive care unit (PICU) and reviews interdisciplinary interventions to support children and their families.

Introduction

The critical care environment can be an intimidating, noisy, emotionally overwhelming place that is dominated by advanced technological monitoring and life-support equipment (Meyer, DeMaso, & Koocher, 1996). Stress is ubiquitous and often palpable. There are many busy interdisciplinary staff members working as a team to deliver care, including physicians, nurses, respiratory therapists, social workers, child life specialists, chaplains, nutritionists, pharmacists, and hospital volunteers. It is not unusual for a huddle of 10 to 15 practitioners to participate in daily rounds when the child's diagnostic tests and treatment plans are discussed. The presence of parents, siblings, extended family members, friends, and community members at the child's bedside also characterize and enliven the PICU. Unlike adult hospitals, pediatric settings naturally host greater numbers of family members who remain present and vigilant to provide their youngsters with care, supervision, and nurturance. Children's toys, games, stuffed animals, photographs, school memorabilia, and artwork help to humanize the PICU, yet make a startling contrast against the backdrop of technology. Such personal items can be potent reminders of the children's typical daily lives and their place in the world and can serve as a source of comfort and conversation (Macnab et al., 1997).

The Child's Experience

Acute medical distress can be experienced by children and adolescents requiring general pediatric hospital admission (Shaw & DeMaso, 2006), and those in need of intensive care may be especially vulnerable (Rennick et al., 2002; Colville, 2008). The unfamiliar environment, dependence on health care providers, and disruptions in daily routines can erode a child's sense of predictability and security. Youngsters in the PICU must often endure an onslaught of aversive stimuli (e.g., beeping monitors, bright lights) and procedures such as vital signs, clinical examinations, diagnostic tests, intravenous line placements, suctioning, and dressing changes that can exact a heavy physical and emotional toll (Playfor et al., 2000). Preparation prior to procedures and adequate sedation and pain management can help to combat anxiety and distress. The amnesic effects of medication administered for sedation and analgesia can serve a protective function from the development of emotional sequelae, since some children's memories of the procedures and hospitalization may be neutral or forgotten (Board, 2005). However, others have reported that children can harbor frightening memories of invasive procedures in the form of nightmares and hallucinations and experiences of pain, all of which highlight the need for comprehensive assessment and emotional support (Colville, Kerry, & Pierce, 2008, chap. 4).

Individual factors such as coping style, cognitive capacity and developmental level, temperament, and previous health care experiences will influence the child's response to hospitalization and the likelihood of acute medical distress, fearfulness, isolation, sadness, or anger (Sourkes, 1995; Shaw & DeMaso, 2006). Although hospitalization represents a significant stressor, many children and families can and do cope well with adequate support services, and adjustment difficulties are not inevitable. Jones and colleagues (1992) reported that compared to other general pediatric patients, PICU patients exhibited higher levels of distress in the days immediately following extubation (i.e., withdrawal of the respirator). Children with prolonged or repeated hospitalizations, as well as those with preexisting mood and anxiety disorders, were also at greater risk during hospitalization.

Acute stress disorder (ASD) and posttraumatic stress disorder (PTSD) have been reported in children across multiple medical and surgical diagnoses and experiences, including cancer (Stuber & Shemesh, 2006), solid organ transplantation (Mintzer et al., 2005), motor vehicle accidents (DeVries et al., 1999), and cardiac surgery (Connolly et al., 2004). Such symptomatology may be related to the injury or illness itself in addition to treatment-related variables, and it has also been speculated that the PICU environment may be a further source of trauma, including exposure to distressing experiences or deaths of other patients. Risk factors that have been associated with the development of trauma symptoms include uncontrolled pain, high emotional distress or levels of trait anxiety (i.e., high baseline level of anxiety), and subjective appraisal of life threat (Stuber & Shemesh, 2006).

The Family's Experience and Perspectives

Miles and Carter (1982) were among the first to describe the parental experience and stressors inherent in the PICU, including unfamiliar and daunting sights and sounds, the altered appearance and behavior of the child, procedures, challenges, and alterations in parental role, and staff communication and behavior. Mothers whose children required PICU level of care experienced greater states of anxiety, depression, confusion, and anger than mothers of healthy nonhospitalized children and those whose children needed hospitalization on general pediatric units (Board & Ryan-Wenger, 2003). Similar findings are seen in fathers of PICU patients, who reported higher levels of perceived stress and stress symptomatology compared to fathers of pediatric patients on general hospital units (Board, 2004). Studies investigating the short-term psychological impact of critical care hospitalization on family members have documented significant heightened anxiety, depressive symptoms, and acute and posttraumatic stress symptoms that warrant early case identification and intervention (Paparrigopoulos et al., 2006).

A survey of more than 50,000 parents identified several priorities and "solution starters" to improve pediatric care (Miceli & Clark, 2005). Specifically, parents rated, and offered their overall assessment of, the admission process, the child's room, meals, nursing care, tests and treatments, child's physician, family, and visitors, discharge, personal issues. They identified the following areas that needed improvement: (1) staff sensitivity to the inconvenience that hospitalization entails; (2) the degree to which staff address emotional and spiritual needs; (3) staff response to concerns and complaints; (4) staff efforts to include parents in the treatment decision-making process; (5) accommodations and comfort for visitors; (6) information provided about facilities for sleeping, eating, showering, and talking; and (7) efforts to ensure the child's rest and recovery. It is vital for practitioners to solicit and pay attention to patient and family perspectives when designing services and to regularly inquire about satisfaction with the care provided. Such efforts can enhance family-provider relationships and improve the quality of care.

Brothers and sisters of children requiring critical care hospitalization have unique needs and can benefit from psychosocial assessment and emotional support. Often, parents may seek help with how to "talk to" and support their other children at home, and they may particularly seek advice about visitation and ways to balance the demands of child care and family life when one child requires hospitalization (DeMaso, Meyer, & Beasley, 1997). Siblings can experience a range of emotional responses to their sibling's hospitalization and the accompanying unavoidable disruption in child care arrangements and family life, including increased stress, fearfulness, worries, sadness, or anger (Spinnetta, 1981). Brothers and sisters can be particularly susceptible to complicated feelings of isolation, displacement, jealousy, and guilt when their sibling has a critical illness.

Conceptual Models and Treatment Approaches

The Nursing Mutual Participation Model of Care (NMPMC) is a parent educational and supportive nursing intervention that has demonstrated clinical effectiveness in the PICU (Curley, 1988; Curley & Wallace, 1992). The model is based on the premise that there are many stressful aspects surrounding parenting in the PICU and that individual variation in coping, adjustment, and perceptions of stress need to be considered when customizing educational and supportive interventions. Upon admission, nurses extend care to include parents and acknowledge their importance and centrality to the child's health and well-being. Daily bedside encounters with nurses incorporate strategies to equip parents with health care system savvy by providing information and instrumental resources and offering anticipatory guidance. Nurses ask parents open-ended questions aimed at building rapport such as "How are you doing today?" "How does [child's name] look to you today?" "What troubles you most?" and "How can I help you today?" Parents' suggestions and preferences pertaining to the child's care, as well as their own participation in that care, are invited. The NMPMC has been demonstrated to diminish levels of perceived parent stress both during hospitalization and following discharge.

The medical crisis counseling (MCC) model proposed by Pollin (1994, 1995) is a crisis-oriented, pragmatic approach that has been adapted to working with medically traumatized children (Bronfman, Campis, & Koocher, 1998). The model is predicated on the belief that traditional models of psychotherapy cannot fully address the emotional and social needs of individuals and their families who are in turmoil due to a medical crisis. The model emphasizes the disruption of normal life tasks that are challenged by medical crisis and considers the accompanying emotional distress as a normal and somewhat predictable response rather than a pathological process. Eight common fears are described: loss of control, loss of self-image, dependency, stigma, abandonment, expressing

anger, isolation, and death. Practitioners implementing the model function as good communicators, listeners, educators, and counselors (Williams & Koocher, 1999). Treatments focus on the medical condition and
integrate psychosocial interventions with medical care delivery, normalize
the experienced distress, and work with the client to collaboratively
identify concrete actions toward adaptive coping, all within a limited
time frame and with a focus on both symptom relief and prevention.

Treatment and Interventions

By its nature, the PICU care focuses on lifesaving treatments that must take
priority. Ideally, psychosocial care delivery can be comprehensive and well
integrated into the overall plan of care and not impinge on or compete with
the child's critical health care needs (Small & Melnyk, 2006). Although the
PICU has more than its share of stress and sorrow, that should not necessarily hamstring or limit the possibilities for creative interventions. First,
consult with the child's nurse and parents to determine the priorities for
care, what kind of a day the child is having, whether the child is in pain or
discomfort, whether the child is sleeping or on special isolation precautions,
and whether any tests or treatments are scheduled. Being flexible and
creative about where, when, and how long to meet with children and
parents is important. One must always balance the child's need for rest
and essential interventions, family members' wishes to remain at the
bedside, and the demands of critical care (Miceli & Clark, 2005).

   It is advisable to address the immediate issues at hand, offer practical
and doable suggestions, model good communication and family–staff
relationships, and foster a climate of psychological safety and well-being
(DeMaso & Meyer, 1996). Being responsive and positive and offering a
different and optimistic perspective can do worlds of good for children,
their families, and staff members. When medically feasible, physical
activity (e.g., getting out of bed or walking around the unit) or a change
of environment (e.g., a trip to the garden or hospital gift shop) can help to
promote mental health, autonomy, and independence. Effective interventions need to take into consideration any physical limitations or
restrictions imposed by the child's illness and/or its treatment (Hansen
et al., 1986). Special snacks and physical activities need to be approved by
nursing and medical staff, since children can be on restricted diets or have
limitations on physical activity. Behavioral contingency plans should be
customized to include desirable behaviors and rewards that are permissi-
ble within the PICU environment (Cataldo et al., 1979). When children
cannot be taken out of doors safely due to physiological instability, it may
be possible to bring the outdoors to them (e.g., the child life specialist could
bring in a fresh bin of snow or a basketful of leaves). Document and
describe psychosocial interventions and activities, and the child's level of
interest and response, to promote a greater variety of activities and
consistency of care. Staff members appreciate hearing from others what

works, and attention to these details and little kindnesses can matter a great deal to families (Meyer et al., 2002).

Treatment approaches for hospitalized children are optimally guided by knowledge about the child's cognitive and developmental level, illness condition, and normative behaviors that characterize different stages of development. Children should be provided with truthful developmentally appropriate information whenever possible, as well as some degree of control and choice regarding their care (Meyer, DeMaso, & Koocher, 1996). This is particularly important since children's cognitive understanding of the disease and its treatment can facilitate coping with the trauma of illness (Sourkes, 1995). Jansen et al. (1989) describe pragmatic and developmentally motivated interventions, including consistency within the health care team to foster children's growing sense of trust and stability, implementation of a predictable and comprehensive daily schedule to increase consistency in day-to-day routines, and regular opportunities to engage in normal childhood play activities with the benefit of good child life programming.

Celeste, Age 6

Celeste is a bright and engaging six-year-old girl who was born with a rare form of dwarfism and severe scoliosis (curvature of the spine) that render her unable to sit or walk. She was electively admitted for a spinal fusion to help stabilize her spine, improve her posture, and optimize her respiratory function. She requires routine urinary catheterization. At home, she successfully uses adaptive equipment and is fully participatory in first grade at her local public school with the assistance of an aide. Celeste lost considerable blood during the surgery and was weaned slowly from the ventilator. She is eager to return home and to school and says, "Once I get rid of this (intravenous line in her arm), I'll be free as a bird."

- Elicit and try to understand the child's perspective of the illness. Here, Celeste lets us know that despite her many health issues and challenges, the intravenous line is currently her biggest concern. Does she understand the importance and role of the intravenous line to provide her medications? Ask the medical team to estimate how much longer the IV is expected to remain in place, and make a calendar to count down the days together (preparing her for the possibility that sometimes there are unexpected complications).

- Be mindful of the assumptions that we bring to the child's situation. Ask the child and family how they view the current situation, what is important to them, and what would be helpful. Celeste described missing her schoolmates and teacher and feeling disappointed that she had not been outdoors in a long time. Listen to her concerns and ask for her ideas. A special visit from Celeste's teacher and aide to deliver cards and artwork from classmates could be planned. If prolonged hospitalization is expected, in-hospital tutoring can help Celeste keep up with her schoolwork. Similarly, a trip to the garden or, if that is not possible, to a sunny window and a chance to talk and work on some nature crafts may be uplifting. Ensure excellent child life programming and generate ideas together about creative activities.

- Take the time to fully assess and document Celeste's estimation of pain and discomfort. Let her know that her comfort is a big priority, and encourage her to tell staff and her parents if she is uncomfortable.

- Celeste illustrates resilience and forward thinking in a young child. Let her know what she might be able to do to enhance her own healing and recovery. Does she have any physical therapy exercises to practice? Is her adaptive equipment available to her in the hospital? Is she eating well and getting good nutrition to promote her health? Letting children and families know how they can actively contribute to care and recovery can be empowering and rewarding. Crafting a daily routine that balances treatment requirements, pleasurable activities, visits, and adequate rest can be helpful to children, families, and staff members alike.

Francesco, Age 11

Francesco is an 11-year-old Italian American boy who has cerebral palsy, mental retardation, and severe developmental delays. He has a tracheostomy and requires ventilation during sleeping hours, and he receives his nutrition through a gastrostomy tube. He was emergently admitted to the PICU following a traumatic tracheostomy change at home during which he bled profusely. He required surgery to stop the bleeding and subsequently developed respiratory distress and pneumonia. He is now on a ventilator receiving sedation and antibiotic therapy. Prior to admission, Francesco communicated primarily through nonverbal means by smiling and visual gaze. He lives at home with his mother, father, and two sisters and has home-based school programming. His family is anxious about the upcoming tracheostomy change after surgery and his respiratory recovery, and they are concerned about their ability to safely care for him at home. As Francesco began to be weaned from sedation, the mother was asked about her son's likes and dislikes. She exclaimed, "Oh, Francesco loves the Three Tenors. He loves his music!"

- Francesco and his mother remind us that all children have their likes and dislikes regardless of their illness or developmental delays. An unrushed conversation and simple open-ended questions such as, "Tell me about your child" or "How can I be helpful?" can yield valuable insights and suggestions. Learning about Francesco's love of music offered a wonderful avenue to incorporate music to improve and humanize the environment.

- Parents of children with complex health care needs often bring a wealth of experience and valuable suggestions. Parents can serve as historians of the child's illness, reminding the team of strategies and approaches that have worked best (or failed) in the past. Build and draw on strong partnerships with parents and community health providers such as pediatricians and home health nurses.

- A consultation with a speech-language pathologist may be very useful. Is Francesco able to communicate and signal his wish to hear music, either through pointing, vocalizing, or pressing a switch? Sometimes the hospitalization can serve as an opportune time to reassess abilities and fine-tune communicative strategies.

- The circumstances of Francesco's admission to the PICU were traumatic and occurred in the home setting. Assessment and supportive intervention may be helpful for the family. The opportunity to revisit and tell one's story to an attentive listener can help family members who witnessed the emergency event to better understand the circumstances and generate preventive strategies.

- Careful coordination can improve care and mitigate future parental anxiety. Are emergency providers readily available at home? Could the parents benefit from additional teaching? Are the home health nurses and community pediatrician available for a joint discharge planning meeting? Provide parents with graduated responsibility for Francesco's care within the security of the hospital environment prior to discharge to help them feel more ready and confident.

Interdisciplinary Collaborative Practice

Meeting the psychosocial needs of children and families in the PICU demands first-rate interdisciplinary collaborative practice across medical, nursing, child life, pastoral care, and psychosocial professionals. Services provided by medical interpreters, lactation consultants, massage therapists, and parent educators and advocates, among others, can immeasurably enhance the quality of the child's hospitalization. Regularly scheduled psychosocial rounds can increase the visibility and stature of psychological care, expedite referrals, and promote better care coordination. Interdisciplinary collaboration and ethics consultation can also be helpful in the context of the highly complex ethical issues and decision making that is often characteristic of the PICU (Colville, 2001). Consultation with a speech-language pathologist around augmentative and alternative communication strategies can be of enormous benefit in restoring a child's sense of autonomy and control (Costello, 2000). Children who do not have an effective means to convey their needs, wishes, questions, and worries due to intubation, surgery, or immobilization can be at increased risk for emotional distress, frustration, and feelings of isolation. Community-based practitioners are also vitally important to bridge the transition between hospital and home, including community pediatricians, home-based nurses, school staff, and religious personnel (Meyer et al., 2002).

Family-Based Practices

Family-based practices, such as family conferences and parent participation on rounds, can positively influence the child's hospital experience, increase the family's satisfaction with care, and decrease family–staff conflict (Kleiber et al., 2006). Parents identify the need for honest and complete information, the ability to stay close and contribute to their child's care, and ready access to the health care team as vital to their coping during critical care hospitalization (Meyer et al., 2006). Policies about visitation hours, family conferences, parent presence during invasive procedures, and bedside rounds reflect the place of parents, the integration of family-centered care principles, and the degree of parent–professional partnership.

Good Bedside Manners

"Etiquette-based" medicine emphasizes the importance of good bedside manners, attentiveness, and respectful patient–provider interactions (Kahn, 2008). Simple bedside manners such as asking permission to enter a patient's room, greeting and shaking hands, introductions, and attentive listening can go a long way to demonstrate professionalism and establish trust. When professionals sit down and lend their full attention, this conveys they have the time and interest to listen. Rituals and social scaffolding of the family–staff interaction can aid the child, family, and practitioner alike by engendering a calm, nonanxious therapeutic environment. Practitioners who are polite and have gentle manners lend predictability and consistency to their visits, which can be especially helpful for wary, anxious, or fearful children.

Good Communication Practices and Family–Provider Relationships

Patients and family members highly value good communication and empathic relationships with their health care providers and often base their perceptions of the quality of care on these factors (Mack et al., 2005). Good communication can provide important information, promote better understanding, improve treatment adherence, and promote good decision making (Levetown, 2008). For children and their families to feel understood and well cared for, practitioners are encouraged to be attentive, show genuine curiosity and emotion, listen well, and hold health care conversations on a deeper, more relational level. Conveying troubling news and engaging in difficult conversations are vitally important yet anxiety-provoking components of practice in the PICU. Rather than launching into a predetermined agenda, begin conversations with children and families by asking them about their understanding and what matters most to them. Encourage families to jot down any questions that come to mind, and take the time to answer them.

Family Visitation

In some settings, visitation is highly regulated, and families are not permitted during nursing changes of shift, medical rounds, when patients are being admitted, or while procedures are being performed. That parents are considered "visitors" reflects underlying dynamics of family–staff control, power differential, and ownership (Smith, Hefley, & Anand, 2007). Visitation can also be restricted due to concern or fear that family members may compromise the therapeutic environment, distract practitioners, or disrupt the workflow. Conversely, other units embrace 24-hour family visitation, welcome parents to participate in the child's care and treatment decision making, and provide convenient in-room sleeping and showering accommodations. In these settings, parents are viewed not as visitors or intruders, but rather as well-regarded partners who have a rightful and vital place in the care and healing of their children.

Family Presence during Invasive Procedures and Resuscitation

Parent presence during invasive procedures and resuscitation is a growing yet controversial practice. Clinicians can harbor deep concerns about the value, safety, and logistics of parent presence. Concerns focus on the potentially traumatic nature of the procedures, performance anxiety, interruption in the clinical workflow, maintenance of a safe therapeutic environment, ability to meet parents' needs, compromise in procedural teaching opportunities, and potential risk for malpractice claims (Dingeman et al., 2007). In general, the concerns of practitioners have been largely unfounded in settings that have embraced comprehensive staff education, instituted policy and procedure guidelines, and formalized a facilitator role.

Most family members prefer and appreciate having a choice regarding whether to remain present or not during their child's invasive procedures and resuscitation (Boie et al., 1999; Mangurten et al., 2005). Some parents prefer to step aside, whereas others strongly believe their presence is essential. For some, remaining present during procedures is considered a parental duty that must be fulfilled. Since parents and family members may be reluctant to ask, or may not realize that they may remain present during such times, it is recommended that practitioners educate parents and extend the opportunity whenever possible. Although findings are not conclusive, family members may experience less anxiety and depression, and better bereavement adjustment, if present during resuscitation efforts (Boudreaux et al., 2002). Eichhorn and colleagues (1996) recommend that family-witnessed resuscitation include the following elements of preparation: Discuss the plan in advance with the resuscitation team; assign one team member to remain with the family to answer questions, clarify information, and offer emotional comfort; provide sufficient space to accommodate family members; and team members should remain mindful of family presence when communicating.

Open Bedside Rounds

Open bedside rounds is a variable practice in pediatric critical care settings. Clinicians are concerned that parents on rounds may breach confidentiality, inordinately increase the time of rounds, degrade the teaching environment, and undermine respect for junior practitioners (Kleiber et al., 2006). Newly constructed units that provide parent accommodations will need to grapple with ways to build partnerships with families and share information while still accomplishing the work of the unit.

Sibling Support

Brothers and sisters need to have truthful, accurate, developmentally appropriate information about their sibling's illness (Spinnetta, 1981). Children need to feel welcome in the hospital and be regarded as important and vital members of the family. Having explanations about the hospitalization, consistent security-enhancing child care arrangements, and, if appropriate, a school-based liaison are recommended. Depending on the child's age and circumstances of admission, some siblings relish the chance to make artwork to decorate the room, bring toys and music from home, and spend special time with the ill child. Some units provide structured sibling groups and opportunities for brothers and sisters to learn about the hospitalization, share in play and expressive arts activities, and meet with other siblings. Opportunities to make active contributions to their sibling's care (e.g., learning about medicine, helping with physical therapy) can make a world of difference. When trauma has struck or death appears likely, parents appreciate the services of the mental health provider to offer emotional support, anticipatory guidance, and a road map for how to navigate (DeMaso, Meyer, & Beasley, 1997). For many parents, being able to provide well for their other children bolsters parental self-esteem and offsets the helplessness and vulnerability that so often accompanies pediatric critical care illness.

Miranda, Age 14

Miranda is a 14-year-old athletic adolescent female who had experienced two days of intermittent dizziness and headaches prior to collapsing during basketball practice. Diagnostic tests revealed a significant congenital arteriovenous malformation and bleeding on the left side of her brain (stroke) that is expected to affect the right side of her body and her speech. Miranda has periods of wakefulness, but she is quite agitated, unable to communicate clearly, and is not consistently oriented to person, place, or time. Parents are uncertain how best to comfort her and feel discouraged that they cannot seem to help her more. The extent of Miranda's neurological sequelae is uncertain and is a cause of great concern and worry for her parents. Miranda is the adopted daughter of her parents and has one older brother who is enrolled in his second semester of college. She is an average student who prides herself in her athletic ability and prowess. Several of Miranda's friends have sent e-mail get-well messages and want to visit her in the PICU. Her parents are unsure how to handle her friends' requests to visit and feel that they would need to tend to the friends' emotional needs.

- Parents have many questions about Miranda's current and future neurological status and could benefit from a family meeting with the nursing staff, intensive care physicians, and consulting neurologist. It would be helpful for parents to be educated about Miranda's head injury and the expected trajectory of recovery. It may relieve their anxiety to know that it is not unusual for patients to be agitated and disoriented following brain injury. Based on the parents' learning style and wishes, they may be interested in participating in daily rounds.

- Adolescent patients often have many friends who wish to visit. The circumstances of Miranda's admission (students witnessing her fall during basketball practice) suggest that the school psychologist and basketball coach would be likely resources to help coordinate education and supportive intervention for the students. Fellow student visitors to the PICU are best limited, especially since Miranda is not able to express her views and wishes about who visits. If parents are feeling overwhelmed with the needs of Miranda's friends, heed those concerns and offer to have hospital psychosocial staff assist.

- Miranda needs careful assessment about her comfort level, her ability to tolerate stimulation and interventions, and strategies that reduce her agitation. Use Miranda's name and offer preparation and anticipatory guidance throughout the day so that she knows what to expect (e.g., "Now it is time to sit up in the chair and eat some lunch"). Environmental interventions to aid her orientation, such as a clock and calendar within view and a predictable daily schedule, can be very helpful. Since the days and nights can be blurred in the PICU, be sure to turn off lights and

(continued)

minimize noises and interruptions at night to foster a healthy diurnal pattern. Incorporate familiar routines such as grooming (washing face, combing hair) and reading time into her day and night.

- Referral to a speech-language pathologist may be helpful to optimize Miranda's ability to communicate her needs and wishes. The use of conventional gestures (e.g., nodding, pointing, smiling, clapping, thumbs-up) and picture symbols can be very useful to the patient and staff members to shore up communication and reduce frustration.

Anticipatory Bereavement and End of Life

Without question, clinicians based in the PICU will come face-to-face with dying children and their families, yet often feel unprepared and uncertain about how to help and intervene. It is advisable to observe and apprentice oneself to experienced staff members and to become familiar with the culture of death in the PICU before assuming direct clinical care responsibility. Most often, but not always, the dying child will be intubated and sedated in the PICU, necessarily limiting the direct interventions that are possible. If the child is awake and alert, however, the most important aspects of psychological care include ensuring adequate pain management and comfort; facilitating a means for the child to effectively communicate his or her needs, wishes, and fears; fostering opportunities for tender, uninterrupted intimate time with loved ones; and offering anticipatory guidance, emotional support, and reassurance (Sourkes, 1995; IOM, 2003).

When faced with end-of-life decision making, parents identify the child's quality of life, the likelihood of getting better, expected neurological outcome, the perception of the child's pain and suffering, and the child's perceived wishes and will to live as most important (Meert et al., 2000). Parents can differ widely in their capacity, approach, and preferences when faced with news that the child has not responded to treatment and that death is likely. Parental priorities for end-of-life care include honest and complete information, ready access to staff, communication and care coordination, emotional expression and support by staff, preservation of the integrity of the parent-child relationship, and faith-based services, if desired (Meyer et al., 2006).

Tiara

Tiara is a 21-month-old previously healthy Hispanic toddler who sustained a massive traumatic head injury when she fell from the family's new third-floor apartment porch. She is unresponsive and maintained on life support treatment. The neurologist and team have spoken with the family about performing diagnostic tests and clinical examination to determine brain death. Parents and paternal grandfather have requested to be present during the exam for brain death. The father simply states, "If I don't see it with my own eyes that she is unable to breathe on her own and wake up, I'll never believe it." The parents have taken to pinning photographs of Tiara over their hearts. The family and local church community have been praying for a miracle, but her mother tearfully whispers, "I am not sure that God is listening."

- Given the crisis nature of the situation, it is important to begin by establishing a trusting relationship with the family and quickly assessing their psychosocial needs and wishes. Psycho-education and anticipatory guidance about the upcoming tests and deteriorating clinical course (i.e., brain death likely) are vital. Parents have requested to be present during the neurological brain death examination, and this request should be brought forth to the neurologists and supported. Parent presence during such procedures can be of enormous psychological importance to parents, and, whenever possible, offering parents a choice and adequate support is recommended. A family meeting will be important to discuss the findings of the clinical examination and, if withdrawal of life support is to be considered, to provide families with ample time, information, discussion of values, and emotional support.

- Acknowledge the family's photographs of Tiara and invite conversation about their little girl and their relationship with her. Offer simple commemorative activities, such as making hand- and footprints with colored tempura paint. If the family is interested, perhaps the photographs of Tiara may be made into sturdy pins that can be worn and distributed to family members.

- Welcome and support the family's spiritual and religious perspectives. Community religious providers are welcome at the hospital at the family's invitation, and hospital-based chaplains are also generally available around the clock. The mother's comment that she is "not sure God is listening" is suggestive of spiritual distress, and a consultation with the hospital chaplain is in order.

- Given Tiara's accidental fall, parents may well experience strong emotional responses such as sadness, guilt, and anger. Provide the family with privacy and supportive psychological intervention, including attentive listening, empathy, and opportunities to express their emotions freely. Parents may direct anger at the landlord; this is natural and has its place. Sometimes parents need to have their anger and frustrations validated; remind them that there will be a future time to address issues of anger and responsibility, but now the focus needs to remain on Tiara and her medical situation.

- Referral to a consistent medical interpreter may be very helpful and supportive for the grandfather. The interpreter may serve as a language resource and cultural broker dedicated to the grandfather during this difficult time.

Summary

Pediatric critical care hospitalization has significant and far-reaching psychological effects on the child and family. The PICU is a busy and technologically sophisticated setting that is devoted to lifesaving interventions. Amid its traumatic ecology, health care's highest highs and lowest lows unfold, and this is at once a place of promise, triumph, heartbreak, and devastating loss. Underneath the whirl of activity and technological brinksmanship lie vitally important and real relationships between children, their families, and interdisciplinary staff members. In the context of these relationships, creative and meaningful psychosocial interventions can flourish to support the emotional well-being and resilience of our young patients and their families.

References

Board, R. (2004). Father stress during a child's critical care hospitalization. *Journal of Pediatric Health Care, 18*, 244–249.

Board, R. (2005). School-age children's perceptions of their PICU hospitalization. *Pediatric Nursing, 31*(3), 166–175.

Board, R., & Ryan-Wenger, N. (2003). Stressors and stress symptoms of mothers with children in the PICU. *Journal of Pediatric Nursing, 18*(3), 195–201.

Boie, E. T., Moore, G. P., Brummet, et al. (1999). Do parents want to be present during invasive procedures performed on their children in the emergency department? *Annals of Emergency Medicine, 34*(1), 70–74.

Boudreaux, E. D., Francis, J. L., & Loyacano T. (2002). Family presence during invasive procedures and resuscitations in the emergency department: A critical review and suggestions for future research. *Annals of Emergency Medicine, 40*(2), 193–205.

Bronfman, E. T., Campis, L. B., & Koocher, G. P. (1998). Helping children to cope: Clinical issues for acutely injured and medically traumatized children. *Professional Psychology: Research and Practice, 29*(6), 574–581.

Cataldo, M. F., Bessman, C. A., Parker, L. H., Reid Pearson, J. E., & Rogers, M. C. (1979). Behavioral assessment for pediatric intensive care units. *Journal of Applied Behavioral Analysis, 12*, 83–97.

Colville, G. (2001). The role of a psychologist on the paediatric intensive care unit. *Child Psychology and Psychiatry Review, 6*(3), 102–109.

Colville, G. (2008). The psychologic impact on children of admission to intensive care. *Pediatric Clinics of North America, 55*, 605–616.

Colville, G., Kerry, S., & Pierce, C. (2008). Children's factual and delusional memories of intensive care. *American Journal of Respiratory and Critical Care Medicine, 177*(9), 976–982.

Connolly, D., McClowry, S., Hayman, L., Mahony, L., & Artman, M. (2004). Posttraumatic stress disorder in children after cardiac surgery. *Journal of Pediatrics, 144*(4), 480–484.

Costello, J. M. (2000). AAC Intervention in the intensive care unit: The Children's Hospital Boston Model. *Augmentative and Alternative Communication, 16*, 137–153.

Curley, M. A. Q. (1988). Effects of the nursing mutual participation model of care and parental stress in the pediatric intensive care unit. *Heart and Lung, 17*, 682–688.

Curley, M. A. Q., & Wallace, J. (1992). Effects of the nursing mutual participation model of care on parental stress in the pediatric intensive care unit: A replication. *Journal of Pediatric Nursing, 7*, 377–385.

DeMaso, D. R., & Meyer, E. C. (1996). A psychiatric consultant's survival guide to the pediatric intensive care unit. *Journal of the American Academy of Child and Adolescent Psychiatry, 34*(10), 1411–1413.

DeMaso, D. R., Meyer, E. C., & Beasley, P. J. (1997). What do I say to my surviving children? *Journal of the American Academy of Children & Adolescent Psychiatry, 36*(9), 1299–1302.

DeVries, A. P. J., Kassam-Adams, N., Cnaan, A., Sherman-Slate, E., Gallagher, P. R., & Winston, F. K. (1999). Looking beyond the physical injury: Posttraumatic stress disorder in children and parents after pediatric traffic injury. *Pediatrics, 104*(6), 1293–1299.

Dingeman, R. S., Mitchell, E. A., Meyer, E. C., & Curley, M. A. Q. (2007). Parent presence during complex invasive procedures and cardiopulmonary resuscitation: A systematic review of the literature. *Pediatrics, 120*(4), 842–854.

Eichhorn, D. J., Meyers, T. A., Mitchell, T. G., & Guzzetta, C. E. (1996). Opening the doors: Family presence during resuscitation. *Journal of Cardiovascular Nursing, 10*(4), 59–70.

Field, M. J., & Behrman, R. E. (Eds.). (2003). For the Institute of Medicine Committee of Palliative and End-of-Life Care for Children and Their Families. When children die: Improving palliative and end-of-life care for children and their families. Washington, DC: National Academies Press.

Haines C. (2005). Parents' experiences of living through their child's suffering from and surviving severe meningococcal disease. *British Association of Critical Care Nurses, Nursing in Critical Care, 10*(2), 78–89.

Hansen, M., Young, D. A., & Carden, F. E. (1986). Psychological evaluation and support in the pediatric intensive care unit. *Pediatric Annals, 15*(1), 60–69.

Holmes A. (2004). An emotional roller coaster: A parent's perspective of ICU. *Pediatric Nursing, 16*, 40–43.

Jansen, M. T., DeWitt, P. K., Meshul, R. J., Krasnoff, J. B., Lau, A. M., & Keens, T. G. (1989). Meeting psychosocial and developmental needs of children during prolonged intensive care unit hospitalization. *Care of Children's Health, 18*(2), 91–95.

Jones, S. M., Fiser, D. H., & Livingston, R. L. (1992). Behavioral changes in pediatric intensive care units. *American Journal of Diseases of Children, 146*(3), 375–379.

Kahn, M. W. (2008). Etiquette-based medicine. *New England Journal of Medicine, 358*(19), 1988–1989.

Kleiber, C., Davenport, T., & Freyenberger, B. (2006). Open bedside rounds for families with children in the pediatric intensive care units. *American Journal of Critical Care, 15*(5), 492–496.

Levetown, M., and Committee on Bioethics. (2008). Communicating with children and families: From everyday interactions to skill in conveying distressing information. *Pediatrics, 121*, e1446–1460.

Mack, J. W., Hilden, J. M., Watterson, J., et al. (2005). Parent and physician perspectives on quality of care at the end of life in children with cancer. *Journal of Clinical Oncology, 23*, 9155–9161.

Macnab, A. J., Emerton-Downey, J., Phillips, N., & Susak, L. E. (1997). Purpose of family photographs displayed in the pediatric intensive care unit. *Heart and Lung, 26*(1), 68–75.

Mangurten, J. A., Scott, S. H., Guzzetta, C. E., Sperry, J. S., Vinson, L. A., Hicks, B. A., Watts, D. G., & Scott, S. M. (2005). Family presence: Making room. *American Journal of Nursing, 105*(5), 40–48.

Meert, K. L., Thurston, C. S., & Sarnaik, A. P. (2000). End-of-life decision-making and satisfaction with care: Parental perspectives. *Pediatric Critical Care Medicine, 1*(2), 179–185.

Meyer, E. C., Burns, J. P., Griffith, J. L., & Truog, R. D. (2002). Parental perspectives on end-of-life care in the pediatric intensive care unit. *Critical Care Medicine, 30*, 226–231.

Meyer, E. C., DeMaso, D. R., & Koocher, G. P. (1996). Mental health consultation in the pediatric intensive care unit. *Professional Psychology: Research and Practice, 27*(2), 130–136.

Meyer, E. C., Ritholz, M. D., Burns, J. P., & Truog, R. D. (2006). Improving the quality of end-of-life care in the pediatric intensive care unit: Parents' priorities and recommendations. *Pediatrics, 117*(3), 649–57.

Miceli P. J., & Clark P. A. (2005). Your patient—my child. Seven priorities for improving pediatric care from the parent's perspective. *Journal of Nursing Care Quality, 20*(1), 43–53.

Miles, M. S., & Carter, M. C. (1982). Sources of parental stress in pediatric intensive care units. *Child Health Care, 11*, 65–69.

Mintzer, L. L., Stuber, M. L., Seacord, D., Castaneda, M., Mesrkhani, V., & Glover, D. (2005). Traumatic stress symptoms in adolescent organ transplant recipients. *Pediatrics, 115*(6), 1640–1644.

Paparrigopoulos, T., Melissaki, A., Efthymiou, A., Tsekou, H., Vadala, C., Kribeni, G., Pavlou, E., & Soldatos, C. (2006). Short-term psychological impact on family members of intensive care unit patients. *Journal of Psychosomatic Research, 61*(5), 719–722.

Pate, M. F. D. (2008). Supporting families of technology-dependent patients hospitalized in a pediatric intensive care unit. *AACH Advanced Critical Care, 19*(2), 125–129.

Playfor, S., Thomas, D., & Choonara, I. (2000). Recollections of children following intensive care. *Archives of Disease in Childhood, 83*(5), 445–448.

Pollin, I., with Golant, S. K. (1994). *Taking charge: Overcoming the challenges of long-term illness.* New York: Times Books.

Pollin, I., with Kanaan, S. (1995). *Medical crisis counseling: Short-term therapy for long-term illness.* New York: W.W. Norton & Company.

Rennick, J. E., Johnston, C. C., Dougherty, G., Platt, R., & Richie, J. A. (2002). Children's psychological responses after critical illness and exposure to invasive technology. *Developmental and Behavioral Pediatrics, 23*(3), 133–144.

Shaw, R. J., & DeMaso, D. R. (2006). *Clinical manual of pediatric psychosomatic medicine: Mental health consultation with physically ill children and adolescents.* Washington, DC: American Psychiatric Publishing, Inc.

Small, L., & Melnyk, B. M. (2006). Early predictors of post-hospital adjustment problems in critically ill young children. *Research in Nursing and Health, 29*(6), 622–635.

Smith, A. B., Hefley, G. C., & Anand, K. J. S. (2007). Parent bed spaces in the PICU: Effect on parental stress. *Pediatric Nursing, 33*(3), 215–221.

Sourkes, B. M. (1995). *Armfuls of time: The psychological experience of the child with a life-threatening illness.* Pittsburgh, PA: University of Pittsburgh Press.

Spinnetta, J. (1981). The siblings of the child with cancer. In J. Spinnetta & P. Spinnetta (Eds.), *Living with childhood cancer* (pp. 181–236.). St. Louis, MO: C. V. Mosby Company.

Stuber, M. L., & Shemesh, E. (2006). Post-traumatic stress response to life-threatening illness in children and their parents. *Child and Adolescent Psychiatric Clinics of North America, 15*(3), 597–609.

Williams, J., & Koocher, G. P. (1999). Medical crisis counseling on a pediatric intensive care unit: Case examples and clinical utility. *Journal of Clinical Psychology in Medical Settings, 6*(3), 249–258.

Helping in the Emergency Room after Accidents and Traumatic Injury

Leslie H. Wind

17

Chapter

Childhood injuries constitute a major health challenge worldwide. According to the Centers for Disease Control (2004), in 2002, in the United States alone, more than 6.5 million children under 14 years of age were admitted to hospital emergency rooms. Of the 12,200 who died of injuries, 2,300 children were ages 4 to 11. Almost 4.7 million adolescents were nonfatally injured in 2003. In the same year, more than 1.8 million children under four years of age were injured, with the majority of injuries due to falls. While motor vehicle accidents have been the leading cause of death among children and adolescents in the United States (CDC, 2006), more than 30,000 hospital admissions are due to pediatric burns (Passaretti & Billmire, 2003). Of the burn admissions, 80 percent are accidents due to child or adolescent behavior. Among intentional injuries, child maltreatment by blunt head trauma or violent shaking is the leading cause of head injury among infants and young children. In 2005, more than 721,000 youth ages 10 to 24 were treated in emergency departments for injuries due to violence (CDC, 2007). While not all childhood injuries requiring emergency room treatment are traumatizing, research indicates that pediatric injury can result in traumatic stress symptoms, acutely and chronically, in both injured children and their parents (Stuber, Schneider, Kassam-Adams, Kazak, & Saxe, 2006).

Impact of Traumatic Injuries

There is considerable empirical evidence indicating that, following traumatic injury, children and their families can experience acute and long-term psychological difficulties, such as acute stress disorder, posttraumatic stress disorder (PTSD) (Caffo & Belaise, 2003; Stallard, Salter, & Velleman, 2004), depression, and anxiety (Bryant, Mayou, Wigs, Ehlers, & Stores, 2004), which can interfere with children's social and educational development as well as physical health (Seng, Graham-Bermann, Clark, McCarthy, & Ronis, 2005). For example, studies have reported 10 to 36 percent of children injured in traffic accidents as experiencing clinically significant distress, meeting criteria for acute stress disorder (Holbrook, Hoyt, Coimbra, Potenza, Sise, & Anderson, 2005; Meiser-Stedman, Yule, Smith, Glucksman, & Dalgleish, 2005; Winston, Kassam-Adams, Vivarello-O'Neill, Ford, Newman, & Baxt, 2002). Among injured pediatric emergency patients, 10 to 35 percent have been found to develop PTSD (DeVries, Kassam-Adams, Cnaan, Sherman Slate, Gallagher, & Winston, 1999; DiGallo, Barton, & Parry-Jones, 1997; Keppel-Benson, Ollendick & Benson, 2002; Stallard, Velleman, & Baldwin, 1999). Understanding the factors that influence the injured child's and family's experience in the emergency room is essential to effective intervention aimed at reducing the likelihood of longer-term negative outcomes.

Organizing Theoretical Framework: Model of Pediatric Medical Traumatic Stress (PMTS)

In this chapter, the *pediatric medical traumatic stress* (PMTS) model is used as an organizing theoretical framework for understanding the impact of pediatric traumatic injury and guiding intervention. Kazak and colleagues (2006) identify a developmentally based "set of psychological and physiological responses of children and their families to pain, injury, serious illness, medical procedures, and invasive or frightening treatment experiences" (National Child Traumatic Stress Network, 2008). PMTS is conceptualized as a continuum of posttraumatic stress symptoms that may be present without meeting criteria for acute stress disorder or posttraumatic stress disorder.

PMTS identifies three general phases, each indicative of a child and family's experience of a potentially traumatic event (PTE) that corresponds to time in relation to the precipitating event. Phase I, the peritrauma phase, includes the actual occurrence of the PTE and its immediate aftermath. Phase II includes acute, ongoing, and evolving traumatic stress responses resulting from physical sequelae of the precipitating event and treatment. Phase III refers to the longer-term traumatic responses that occur when the immediate physical sequelae, treatment, and threat have been resolved. While PMTS describes a process in which traumatic stress symptoms may emerge at various points during the course of treatment, this chapter focuses on phase I within this model.

Based on growing evidence (Balluffi, Kassam-Adams, Kazak, Tucker, Dominguez, & Helfaer, 2004; Stuber, Kazak, Meeske, Barakat, Guthrie, Garnier, et al., 1997), Kazak and colleagues (2006) emphasize the individualized response to injury and the importance of understanding the patient's and family's subjective experience of the injury as determining whether or not it is traumatic. Their subjective experiences are likely filtered through preexisting factors such as psychological functioning and coping capacity, factors that are also predictive of later posttraumatic stress symptoms (Stallard & Smith, 2007). For example, it is thought that children with preinjury emotional or behavioral problems, particularly anxiety disorders, may appraise their injury as more life-threatening and have lower threat thresholds (Muris, Rapee, Meesters, Schouten, & Geers, 2003), thereby increasing risk for posttraumatic stress symptoms.

Parental posttraumatic stress symptoms have also been found to moderate children's acute biological response and later posttraumatic stress symptoms (Nugent, Ostrowski, Christopher, & Delahanty, 2007). A prospective study of 272 families of children admitted to an intensive care unit found one-third of the parents met criteria for ASD days after their child's hospitalization, and one-fifth qualified for a diagnosis of PTSD four months later. During admission, the presence and severity of acute stress symptoms in parents and parents' subjective appraisal of life threat to their child predicted later PTSD (Balluffi, Kassam-Adams, Kazak, Tucker, Dominguez, & Helfaer, 2004).

The event context has also been found to impact both acute stress and chronic stress symptoms. Research indicates that among children with burn injuries, the relationship between the size of the burn and ASD was mediated by child's heart rate, body image, and parent's stress symptoms (Saxe, Stoddard, Hall, Chawla, Lopez, Sheridan, King, King, & Yehuda, 2005) and the relationship between the child's pain and traumatic stress symptoms was mediated by parents' acute stress symptoms (Stoddard, Saxe, Ronfeld, Drake, Burns, Edgren, & Sheridan, 2006). Extreme rates of posttraumatic stress symptoms (up to 98 percent) have been found in children with disfiguring injuries (Rusch, Grunert, Sanger, Dzwierzynski, & Matloub, 2000), particularly those within the facial triangle (Kish & Lansdown, 2000). Studies suggest that a child's intensity of fear, perception of life threat, and loss of control during and immediately after an unintentional injury increases the risk of posttraumatic stress symptomatology (Langeland & Olff, 2007). In the case of gunshot wounds to the abdomen (Gill, 2002), severe head injuries (Gerring, Slomine, Vasa, Grados, Chen, Rising, et al., 2002), and burns (Saxe et al., 2005), the mechanism and severity of injury (Kassam-Adams & Winston, 2004) can influence development of acute posttraumatic stress symptomatology and, later, persistent PTSD.

Spirituality and corresponding religious traditions provide a framework for child and family views of their world, including how they perceive the meaning of what happens to them and how they cope (both positively and negatively) with medical crises (Sexson, 2004). Spirituality also facilitates coping through social support, a shared value base, and family cohesion (Moncher & Josephson, 2004). One study found that among families of children with long-term illness, 60 to 80 percent were fearful and anxious, had difficulty coping with their child's pain, questioned why they were going through their situation, and wondered about the purpose of suffering and felt guilty (Feudtner, Haney, & Dimmers, 2003). These same responses are also likely to some degree within the emergency room context.

Guided by research, five assumptions are fundamentally related to the understanding of child and family adjustment to pediatric traumatic injury, and these guide planned interventions aimed at preventing or reducing PMTS. First, regardless of the type of injury, parents and older children and adolescents perceive the presence of a *life threat*. It is the perception of a life threat that makes the experience of the injury generate a traumatic response. This may occur at the time of the event, such as parents watching in horror as a car barrels into their driving lane and hits their car or in the emergency room where their child experiences pain and everyone struggles to comprehend the uncertainty of the outcome of the injury. Second, nearly all children and family members experience some acute stress reactions, many of which are considered normative. These stress responses may serve an adaptive function in the early stage. For example, frequent thoughts of the event may help accommodate the injury exposure and assist fitting of the traumatic event into the child or parent's identity and worldview. Third, patients and families have a range of preexisting psychological functioning. This assumption guides assessment and intervention that builds on competence while recognizing there are some families who struggle with greater distress or psychological challenges. Fourth, a developmental lens on the aftermath of trauma that includes a focus on growth and development is essential. For example, following traffic accidents, younger-school-age children have been more likely to report acute stress symptoms than adolescents (Kassam-Adams & Winston, 2004). Finally, a social ecological or contextual approach, viewing the child across multiple contexts, considers the multilevel systems that impact the well-being of children and is considered optimal for intervention (Kazak, Rourke, & Crump, 2003). The parent's response to trauma may be influenced by multiple factors, such as child age, severity of the injury, witnessing the accident, being the driver in a vehicular accident, and ongoing family strains (DeVries et al., 1999; Winston et al., 2002, 2005). Parent-child interactions and interactions between child, family, and the treatment team impact numerous aspects of the health care experience (Power, DuPaul, Shapiro, & Kazak, 2003). These five assumptions then support emergency-based assessment and intervention.

Collaborative Intervention

According to the PMTS framework, the goal of intervention is to change the subjective experience of the potentially traumatic event (Kazak, Kassam-Adams, Schneider, Zelikovsky, Alderfer, & Rourke, 2006), thereby reducing the likelihood of persistent posttraumatic stress symptoms and promoting resilience. To do so requires both child and family assessment and, based on that assessment, planned intervention. Winston, Kassam-Adams, and Marks (2008) recommend the D-E-F protocol (developed by the Medical Traumatic Stress Working Group of the National Child Traumatic Stress Network) as a useful framework for emergency care providers to identify, prevent, and address traumatic stress responses during the acute time frame. The protocol emphasizes a multi-disciplinary, collaborative approach aimed at reducing **D**istress, promoting **E**motional support, and including the **F**amily. These components, grounded in the five assumptions defined previously, are discussed next within the context of assessment and intervention in the aftermath of serious pediatric injury during treatment in the emergency room.

Assessment

Trauma situations require interdisciplinary assessment and intervention along with clearly defined functions for each discipline (Heggar, 1993). Assessment of distress includes evaluation of both the injured child or adolescent and his or her family. Assessment can contribute to hope and promote the therapeutic relationship. After addressing the child's basic physical health, physicians and nursing staff attend to the child's pain. For children and adolescents who are conscious in the emergency room, the Faces Pain Scale—Revised utilizes a scale of six faces scored 0 to 10 and can be used with children ages 4 to 16 (Hicks, von Baeyer, Spafford, van Korlaar, & Goodenough, 2001). The D-E-F protocol recommends concretely asking children and adolescents, "How is your pain right now?" (Winston, Kassam-Adams, & Marks, 2008). In the event of significant pain, pharmacological pain management can diminish the impact of a traumatic event by reducing confusion, anxiety, fear, and overall suffering (Stoddard and Saxe, 2001).

Additional triage is initiated to determine the need for psychosocial services assistance. For example, an emergency room protocol leading to initiation of psychosocial services may be based on concrete criteria such as sudden death, road accidents resulting in loss of limb or severe injuries, sexual or physical assaults, and the presence of family members present in relation to any of these situations (Heggar, 1993).

To assess children's fears and anxiety, the D-E-F protocol (Winston, Kassam-Adams, & Marks, 2008) recommends the following statements and questions:

> Sometimes children are scared or upset when something like this happens. Is there anything that has been scary or upsetting for you? What worries you the most?

To assess grief or loss, the D-E-F protocol recommends asking:

> Was anyone else hurt?
> Have you had other recent losses?

To assess emotional support, the D-E-F protocol recommends assessment of what the child needs to help him or her cope in the emergency room, what resources are available to help the child, and how existing supports can be mobilized. For example, to determine what the injured child or adolescent needs, asking parents, "What helps your child cope with upsetting or scary things?" and asking the child or adolescent, "What has been the best thing that helps you feel better?" To identify those who are available to help the injured youth, asking, "Do you [the parents] understand the injury and intervention?" "Are you able to help calm your child?" "Are you able to be with your child during this procedure?"

The D-E-F protocol also emphasizes the importance of assessing the distress of parents, siblings, or others and gauging family stressors and resources (NCTSN, 2008). Recommended questions during assessment include, "Who is having an especially difficult time?" "Are there other stresses in your family right now?" "Are there other worries that make it particularly difficult to deal with this situation?"

Time constraints in the emergency room will preclude in-depth assessment of all injured children. Practical and effective ways to screen for children and families at risk of ASD or PTSD are critical to good practice. Use of early screening tools, such as the Child Trauma Screening Questionnaire (Kenardy, Spence, & MacLeod, 2006) and the Screening Tool of Early Predictors of PTSD (STEPP) (Winston et al., 2003), are recommended to identify those children who may be more at risk for persistent posttraumatic stress. The STEPP is a 29-item instrument that effectively screens for predictors of PTSD outcomes, including prior PTSD, behavioral and emotional concerns, family stress, acute pain, traumatic exposure, and available social support (Center for Injury Research and Prevention, 2008). The Immediate Stress Response Checklist (ISRC) can be used to evaluate acute stress symptoms in violently injured youth eight years and older.

Heggar (1993) emphasizes beginning with assessment of the trauma survivor. In addition to talking with the patient, Heggar recommends (1) interviewing individuals who can provide detailed information about the event leading to the emergency room visit (e.g., survivors, police, physicians, nurses, anyone at the scene) in order to understand the context of the injury; (2) talking with or observing survivors of the event to assess mental status and emotional states; (3) determining which family members need to be notified and how; (4) assessing family relationships and social supports available and needed; (5) assessing group status in the event of a group trauma, such as a school bus accident (e.g., finding out who is connected to whom, who leads the group, how cohesive the group is); and (6) determining whether multiple social workers are needed to address immediate psychosocial needs of everyone impacted by the traumatic injury.

Understanding what the trauma means to the child and his or her family is an important aspect of assessment. Thoughts, beliefs, and explanations that define the meaning of the event and its outcome will determine affective and behavioral responses (Collins & Collins, 2005). Recognizing the influence of spirituality and religious traditions on child and family coping, Barnes, Plotnikoff, Fox, and Pendleton (2000) recommend a series of questions to assess the family belief system. Considering the context of child injury, here are some examples of questions: How does the family explain illness and suffering? How is the specific injury of the child explained? For example, children may perceive their injury as punishment by God (Koepfer, 2000; Sexson, 2004). A five-year-old boy seen for a broken leg due to exposure during Hurricane Katrina comments that "God was mad at me for being bad." A parent asks, "Is my child's injury punishment for our family's sins?" A mother whose child is attacked by a neighborhood dog when she leaves the front door open feels guilty for not effectively protecting her child and struggles with worries about being forgiven. Other questions recommended by Barnes and colleagues are: What treatments are necessary for the child? Who is the qualified person to address treatments for various aspects of the child's healing? Moncher and Josephson (2004) also recommend asking about spiritual rituals and practices that are meaningful and that may support coping processes. Because parents' perception of their children's symptoms may be biased by their own mental health, additional recommendations include assessing children and parents separately (Kassam-Adams et al., 2006).

Assessment also includes an ecological evaluation focusing on the interaction between the patient and family and the environmental context of the emergency room as well as the community and society in which the client(s) is embedded. At a minimum, Collins and Collins (2005) suggest identifying the family's culture (e.g., values, traditions, and dominant belief systems), availability and quality of social supports (e.g., family, friends, and others), and community resources. It is the combined knowledge from all aspects of screening and assessment that provide the basis for intervention.

Intervention

Because not all injured youth and their families require the same level of intervention after serious injury, models of preventive care such as the D-E-F protocol emphasize considering matching the type and degree of intervention to the level of individual and family risk (NCTSN, 2008). According to this approach, during emergency care, universal interventions that are considered helpful, regardless of risk level, would be provided to assist all children and their families. These include providing the child and family with information about what is happening, providing reassurance and realistic hope and encouraging parents and empowering them to comfort and help their child or adolescent, and providing the child and family with information about common post-traumatic reactions and suggestions for successful coping. Targeted interventions would be provided for those youth and families whose screening identified risk indicators known to be related to acute and persistent traumatic stress identified during the assessment. Targeted interventions include additional support and anticipatory guidance as well as provision of relevant referrals.

Applied Assessment and Intervention

Case of Shelia, Age 14

Sheila is a 14-year-old girl who arrives in the emergency room after being hit by a stray bullet in her neighborhood. While outside on her porch talking with a friend, gang members in two cars began shooting at one another as they drove past her home. According to Sheila's parents, her friend began screaming, and Sheila's parents came running out. While her dad carried her inside their home, her mother ran to call 911. Sheila sustained injuries to her abdomen and upper arm. She was brought to the emergency room by ambulance. Sheila's parents watch in horror as bloodstained clothing is cut away during their child's medical examination. Her mother cries uncontrollably. Her father yells at the doctors and nurses, trying to understand what is happening to their child. Her distraught parents are asked by the ER social worker to accompany her to a nearby consultation room. As they move down the hall, they hear their daughter screaming in pain, yelling for her parents. In the room just down the hall from the ER, Sheila's father paces back and forth, stopping now and then to try to comfort his wife who is crying hysterically. They cling to one another, fearing their daughter is going to die, feeling utterly helpless.

In this situation, the doctors and nurses try to minimize the potentially traumatic aspects of the medical procedures by explaining to Sheila what has happened and what they are doing as they dress her wounds. They use age-appropriate explanations and try to respond to any questions reassuringly yet honestly. They follow the adolescent's lead in order to understand what she is able to hear and cope with. Once Sheila's wounds are dressed, they assess her level of pain. Recognizing Sheila's difficulty focusing, they ask her, "How is your level of pain right now?" Based on that assessment and their knowledge of pain related to abdominal wounds, they provide medication for pain management. While physicians and nurses are implementing lifesaving medical procedures, the social worker assists the family. They move the family to a quiet room nearby, where assessment and family intervention can occur privately. There, the family is intermittently informed by members of the medical team about their child's condition. The social worker ensures that family and relatives are informed about the child's situation in clear, nonclinical language and assists Sheila's parents in obtaining needed information or in formulating questions and concerns to be addressed by medical and nursing staff to decrease anxiety. The social worker gathers detailed information about the shooting from the family, police, medical staff, and any others who were at the scene of the accident in order to understand the context of this injury. When it's possible to do so, the social worker will talk with the survivor of the shooting to assess her mental and emotional states. She will talk with the family about who they might call to support them. Because Sheila's injury is serious, she decides to call another social worker to assist. While one social worker stays with the family to offer support, the other makes outside contacts, as needed.

The social worker with the family allows them to vent emotions and fears, making sure they are not left alone. Knowing that parent-child separation at this time can increase the potential for traumatic stress in both youth and their parents, Sheila's parents are accompanied to join their daughter as soon as her wounds are dressed. Once Sheila is stable and resting, the social worker provides anticipatory guidance to the parents. Keeping in mind the developmental needs of the adolescent, she discusses helping their daughter manage psychological symptoms and pain, identifying the child's coping strengths and challenges. Recognizing that the parents as well as other family members may also be impacted and in need of assistance, the social worker assesses parent distress as well as previous functioning and counsels the parents about effective coping strategies they might use to manage their own stress reactions. The social worker also discusses potential signs of future distress in their daughter and themselves and other family members that might indicate a need for additional assessment and intervention.

Unlike Sheila's situation, some traumatic injuries result in the death of the child or adolescent. For example, consider the following case.

Case of James, Age 16

James is a 16-year-old boy who was riding his motorcycle home after visiting his girlfriend when a drunk driver ran a stop sign and hit him, knocking him 76 feet across an intersection. The drunk driver's car continued up an embankment, stopping when it hit a tree. Both James and the drunk driver are rushed to the emergency room. James is unconscious when he arrives at the emergency room. Medical examination reveals a ruptured spleen, a swelling brain, a crushed forearm, and a broken leg. When his parents arrive at the emergency room, they are notified about his serious medical status as well as his poor prognosis. As they anxiously await more information about their son's condition, they hear hospital personnel say the driver who hit their son is in the ER as well. They also hear that the driver was drunk, had drugs in the car, and was relatively uninjured, with only minor cuts and scrapes. While James is in surgery, his parents struggle with their fears that James will die. They also experience a desire to confront the drunk driver that hurt him. Three hours after admission, James's parents are informed that he has died.

Emergency rooms have established protocols for sudden bereavement (see Heggar, 1993). In the event of a child's or an adolescent's death, treatment team representatives inform the family of their child's death, using direct and clear language such as, "I'm sorry. We tried everything we could, but James died." Clear and direct communication provided compassionately reduces misunderstandings and family denial as well as increases acceptance (Wells, 1993). In the event family members exhibit denial, it may be necessary to repeat the facts regarding injury and death. For example, when the parent who responds to pronouncement of his or her child's death by saying, "You must be mistaken. My son is going to be fine after the surgery," the emergency room personnel working with the family may need to repeatedly state facts about the child's death, providing enough information to penetrate the denial of loss while being cautious to not further traumatize the family. They might say, for example, "During the surgery James's heart stopped beating. We attempted to restart his heart several times, but we were unsuccessful. I'm sorry, James died." Compassionate repetition of the facts is provided until families can verbalize factual events, a step toward internal acceptance of their loss (Wells, 1993). Sensitive notification includes providing parents with sufficient time to ask questions and information about who to contact with subsequent questions. Parents often wish to stay with their child after notification, even when there was significant visible injury. The viewing of their child's body facilitates the grief reaction. To dissuade parents from viewing their child's body can lead to ongoing anger and regret and prolonged grief (Dubin & Sarnoff, 1986). If parents are unsure whether or not to view their child's body, it is recommended that emergency personnel take a neutral stance and discuss the merits of doing so without making family members feel it is wrong not to do so. When families choose to spend time with their deceased child, the social worker or other emergency staff should remain nearby outside of the room for needed support (Dubin & Sarnoff).

In the event of a child or sibling death, family members may exhibit guilt and self-blame. For example, a mother states, "If only I had fed him more, he wouldn't have been so thin. Then he might have been stronger; he might have been okay." Wishful thinking is a frequently exhibited coping strategy requiring additional support and comfort by those working with the family.

Because there is often a religious perspective about death that influences the family's response, offering the assistance of the hospital chaplain or helping the family contact their family clergy may be comforting. Generally, a treatment team member, such as the social worker, will guide the family through postdeath details, such as completing required paperwork, to ensure that family members do not have to make return visits. A treatment team member will also inform family members of the options regarding organ donation and information about any requirements for autopsy (Wells, 1993). The social worker will typically offer assistance to notify additional family members, to notify the primary care physician, to arrange for needed transportation for the family, and to arrange for consultation with community resources. Throughout this process, the family needs a consistent, comforting treatment team member who can facilitate discussion, education, assistance, and support.

The intense interaction between highly stressed family members and hospital staff in life-threatening situations can create significant conflict (Studdert, Burns, Mello, Puopolo, Troug, & Brennan, 2003). One survey of pediatric emergency room directors found that 77 percent reported one or more physical attacks on staff annually (Carroll, 1993). However, potential targets of violence in the ER include patients, visitors, and ER personnel (Walsh-Kelly & Strait, 1998). Consider the preceding case of James. After notification of their child's passing, his parents must struggle to accommodate the shock of losing their son. The presence in the ER of the person who caused his death may trigger a violent response. Imagine James's father storming through the ER looking for the drunk driver. He pushes patients, visitors, and staff out of the way yelling, *"Where is he? I'm gonna kill him!"* Or a hysterical mother pounds her fists on the doctor who informs her of the death of her child. Individuals displaying aggression need to be contained in a quiet and secure location with security personnel. Crisis intervention methods of communication (e.g., a calm demeanor, gentle eye contact, a quiet voice) may help diffuse confrontations. If crisis intervention is unsuccessful, assistance from law enforcement, chemical and/or physical restraint, or even ER evacuation may be required. All emergency rooms need written policies defining protocol for response to, and containment of, violent situations (see Walsh-Kelly & Strait, 1998, for examples of protocols for both victims of violence and management of perpetrators of violence).

Summary

Children and families faced with serious and traumatic injury demonstrate a broad array of emotional and behavioral responses requiring effective, collaborative intervention by trained interdisciplinary emergency room professionals. While most emergency medical personnel recognize that traumatic injury is extremely stressful for children and their families, they generally receive little training in the acute and long-term impact and developmental emotional and behavioral responses of children and adolescents. Time constraints in the emergency room preclude in-depth assessment of all injured children. However, recent studies indicate that brief screening of acute stress symptoms and other risk factors can be helpful (Winston, Kassam-Adams, Garcia-España, Ittenbach, & Cnaan, 2003). While a primary focus within this context is child survival, greater knowledge of trauma and incorporation of trauma-sensitive intervention can support prevention of some traumatic exposure and related post-traumatic stress postinjury (Stuber, Schneider, Kassam-Adams, Kazak, &

Saxe, 2006). In addition, the multidisciplinary collaboration required for effective intervention with traumatically injured children and families in the emergency room is often hindered by lack of a clear understanding and valuing of differing roles and related protocols.

Effective intervention with traumatically injured youth seen in the emergency room seeks to alter the subjective experience of the traumatic event in ways that reduce the likelihood or severity of posttraumatic stress responses in patients and their families. Clearly delineated and trauma-theory-informed protocols grounded in empirical evidence, such as PMTS, are easily integrated into current models of care (Kazak, Kassam-Adams, Schneider, Zelikovsky, Alderfer, & Rourke, 2006) and provide a structure and opportunities for achieving this goal.

The pyramid framework for preventing and treating traumatic stress reactions uses a family-centered approach that is consistent with pediatric health care settings. Training materials and convenient tools supporting trauma-informed practice have been developed by the Medical Traumatic Stress Working Group of the National Child Traumatic Stress Network and are available online at www.nctsn.org.

Traumatically injured children and their families enter the emergency health care setting with both physical and emotional challenges. In addition to discipline-specific medical training, all emergency room health care providers need to have an understanding of traumatic stress upon which they can base their interactions with patients and their families. Utilizing the traumatic stress lens and providing screening to identify children and families at risk or in distress, preventive measures and anticipatory guidance can minimize the potential for trauma during medical care and reduce the likelihood of posttraumatic symptoms later. In addition, emergency room health care workers need to be able to work assertively and cooperatively with the multiple disciplines present on the health care team (registration staff, nurses, physicians, community service personnel such as police officers, paramedics, etc.). In order to implement effective assessment, it is recommended that all physicians, nurses, and social workers possess psychiatric diagnostic skills. They will need to maintain a current working knowledge of community resources and be able to manage multiple crisis situations simultaneously that include constant time pressure. For social workers in particular, skills in crisis intervention, education, and advocacy are essential. Social work departments in large hospital systems such as teaching hospitals offer multi-session courses combined with a supervised practicum to prepare social workers for the demanding work in the emergency room. For example, topics applicable to work in the ER include the roles of the emergency room social worker, regional resources, psychiatric assessment and diagnosis, suicide evaluation, grief reactions, sexual assaults, domestic violence, and practice ethics (Clement & Klingbeil, 1981). Additionally, useful skills include the capacity to educate medical staff in evaluation and consideration of psychosocial difficulties that may impact a patient's or family's response to medical care, the ability to effectively engage in evaluation of the quality of care provided, and capability to work with the community and the hospital in developing needed resources (Bergman, 1976).

Working with traumatic injury of children and adolescents in a hospital emergency room, and especially those that include deaths of pediatric and adolescent patients, can be extremely stressful. Repeated exposure to others' trauma stories can lead to alterations in practitioners' sense of self and worldview, their capacity to manage distress, and their ability to engage others, resulting in depression, cynicism, alienation, impairment of professional judgment, physical difficulties, and premature departure from employment (Pearlman & Saakvitne, 1995). In a sample of 53 emergency room professionals, Laposa and Alden (2003) found that 12 percent met full criteria for a diagnosis of PTSD, 44 percent demonstrated clinically significant peritraumatic dissociation, and 27 percent reported their symptoms interfered with their work. A traumatic stress framework can assist staff with the needed support when confronted with the impact of traumatic events (either exposure to traumatized patients or aggression toward others or themselves) and can also foster greater understanding and compassion for the traumatic experience of patients, families, and colleagues. The collaboration of two or more social workers assisting families in the ER can also provide the opportunity for mutual emotional support both during and after traumatic events. Crisis response for ER staff may include immediate debriefing after an incident and subsequent psychological support (Walsh-Kelly & Strait, 1998). Pearlman and Saakvitne (1995) emphasize use of a range of strategies to combat the impact of vicarious trauma. In addition to maintaining a positive and fulfilling personal life, they encourage use of personal psychotherapy, regular use of supervision and consultation, attending workshops and seminars on the topic of vicarious trauma that can promote positive professional connection, and engaging in a variety of healing activities such as art, music, time with family and friends, journaling, exercising, massage, and activism, to name a few.

Working with traumatically injured youth and their families can also be extremely rewarding. Family-centered intervention within the emergency room context is based on collaborative partnerships between the multidisciplinary professionals providing emergency services and between services providers and patients and their families. Effective assessment can support positive adaptation to traumatic injury, providing hope to children and adolescents and their families. Positive early engagement during this crisis phase can also set the stage for the positive therapeutic relationship that can be critical as children address physiologic changes and emotional adjustment (Caffo & Belaise, 2003). Using the PMTS model and following evidence-based assessment and intervention such as the D-E-F protocol in the emergency room promotes a sense of care and safety, which thereby decreases the patient's and family's vulnerability and promotes resilience as well as a sense of compassion and satisfaction for emergency personnel.

The number of children and families impacted by accidents and traumatic injury is staggering. Effective intervention with children and families in the emergency room who are confronted by accidents and traumatic injury is complex, challenging, rewarding, and critical to the well-being of children and adolescents. This chapter is intended to assist students preparing to be part of an emergency medical team and emergency medical personnel in learning and utilizing a trauma-sensitive, family-centered approach with this vulnerable population.

References

Balluffi, A., Kassam-Adams, N., Kazak, A., Tucker, M., Dominguez, T., & Helfaer, M. (2004). Traumatic stress in parents of children admitted to the pediatric intensive care unit. *Pediatric Critical Care Medicine, 5*(6), 547–553.

Barnes, L. L., Plotnikoff, G. A., Fox, K., & Pendleton, S. (2000). Spirituality, religion, and pediatrics: Intersecting worlds of healing. *Pediatrics, 106*(4), 899–908.

Bergman, A. S. (1976). Emergency room: A role for social workers. *Health and Social Work, 1*(1), 32–44.

Bryant, B., Mayou, R., Wiggs, L., Ehlers, A., & Stores, G. (2004). Psychological consequences of road traffic accidents for children and their mothers. *Psychological Medicine, 34,* 335–346.

Caffo, E., & Belaise, C. (2003). Psychological aspects of traumatic injury in children and adolescents. *Child and Adolescent Psychiatric Clinics of North America, 12,* 493–535.

Carroll, V. (1993). Assessing and addressing violence in the acute care setting. *The Kansas Nurse, 68,* 3–4.

Centers for Disease Control (2004). Web-based Injury Statistics Query and Reporting Systems. National Center for Injury Control and Prevention. Retrieved May 15, 2008, from www.cdc.gov/ncipc/wisqars.

Centers for Disease Control (2006). Web-based Injury Statistics Query and Reporting System. National Center for Injury Control and Prevention. Retrieved May 15, 2008, from www.cdc.gov/ncipc/wisqars.

Centers for Disease Control (2007). Web-based Injury Statistics Query and Reporting System. National Center for Injury Control and Prevention. Retrieved May 15, 2008, from www.cdc.gov/ncipc/wisqars.

Clement, J., & Klingbeil, K. S. (1981). The emergency room. *Health and Social Work, 6*(4), 83–90.

Collins, B. G., & Collins, T. M. (2005). *Crisis and trauma: Developmental-ecological intervention.* Boston, MA: Houghton Mifflin Company.

DeVries, A. P. J., Kassam-Adams, N., Cnaan, A., Sherman Slate, E., Gallagher, P. R., & Winston, F. K. (1999). Looking beyond the physical injury: Post-traumatic stress disorder in children and parents after pediatric traffic injury. *Pediatrics, 104,* 1293–1299.

DiGallo, A., Barton, J., & Parry-Jones, W. L. (1997). Road traffic accidents: Early psychological consequences in children and adolescents. *British Journal of Psychiatry, 172,* 443–447.

Dubin, W. R., & Sarnoff, J. R. (1986). Sudden unexpected death: Intervention with the survivors. *Annals of Emergency Medicine, 15*(2), 54–57.

Feudtner, C., Haney, J., & Dimmers, M. A. (2003). Spiritual care needs of hospitalized children and their families: A national survey of pastoral care providers' perceptions. *Pediatrics, 111*(1), e67–72; *Annals of Emergency Medicine, 15*(2), 54–57.

Finlay, I., & Dallimore, D. (1991). Your child is dead. *British Journal of Medicine, 302,* 1524–1525.

Gerring, J. P., Slomine, B., Vasa, R. A., Grados, M., Chen, A., Rising, W.,et al. (2002). Clinical predictors of posttraumatic stress disorder after closed head injury in children. *Journal of the American Academy of Child and Adolescent Psychiatry, 41,* 157–165.

Gill, A. C. (2002). Risk factors for pediatric posttraumatic stress disorder after traumatic injury. *Archives of Psychiatric Nursing, 16*(4), 168–175.

Heggar, A. (1993). Emergency room: Individuals, families and groups in trauma. *Social Work in Health Care, 18*(3/4), 161–168.

Hicks, C. L., von Baeyer, C. L., Spafford, P., van Korlaar, I., & Goodenough, B. (2001). The Faces Pain Scale—Revised: Toward a common metric in pediatric pain measurement. *Pain, 93,* 173–183.

Holbrook, T. L., Hoyt, D. B., Coimbra, R., Potena, B., Sise, M., & Anderson, J. P. (2005). Long- term posttraumatic stress disorder persists after major trauma in adolescents: New data on risk factors and functional outcome. *Journal of Trauma, 58,* 764–771.

Kassam-Adams, N., Garcia-España, J. F., Miller, V. A., & Winston, F. (2006). Parent-child agreement regarding children's acute stress: The role of parent acute stress reactions. *Journal of the American Academy of Child and Adolescent Psychiatry, 45*(12), 1485–1493.

Kassam-Adams, N., & Winston, F. K. (2004). Predicting child PTSD: The relationship between acute stress disorder and PTSD in injured children. *Journal of the American Academy of Child and Adolescent Psychiatry, 43*(4), 403–411.

Kazak, A. E., Kassam-Adams, N., Schneider, S., Zelikovsky, N., Alderfer, M. A., & Rourke, M. (2006). An integrative model of pediatric medical traumatic stress. *Journal of Pediatric Psychology, 31*(4), 343–355.

Kazak, A. E., Rourke, M., & Crump, T. (2003). Families and other systems in pediatric psychology. In M. Roberts (Ed.), *Handbook of pediatric psychology* (3rd ed., pp. 159–175). New York: Guilford.

Kenardy, J. A., Spence, S. H., MacLeod, A. C. (2006). Screening for posttraumatic stress disorder in children after accidental injury. *Pediatrics, 118,* 1002–1009.

Keppel-Benson, J. M., Ollendick, T. H., & Benson, M. J. (2002). Posttraumatic stress in children following motor vehicle accidents. *Journal of Child Psychology and Psychiatry and Allied Disciplines, 43,* 203–212.

Kish, V., & Lansdown, R. (2000). Meeting the psychosocial impact of facial disfigurement: Developing a clinical service for children and families. *Clinical Child Psychology and Psychiatry, 5*(4), 497–512.

Koepfer, S. R. (2000). Drawing on the spirit: Embracing spirituality in pediatrics and pediatric art therapy. *Art Therapy: Journal of the American Art Therapy Association, 17*(3), 188–194.

Langeland, W., & Olff, M. (2007). Psychobiology of posttraumatic stress disorder in pediatric injury patients: A review of the literature. *Neuroscience and Biobehavioral Reviews, 32,* 161–174.

Laposa, J. M., & Alden, L. E. (2003). Posttraumatic stress disorder in the emergency room: Exploration of a cognitive model. *Behavior Research and Therapy, 41,* 49–65.

Meiser-Stedman, R., Yule, W., Smith, P., Glucksman, E., & Dalgleish, T. (2005). Acute stress disorder and posttraumatic stress disorder in children and adolescents involved in assaults or motor vehicle accidents. *American Journal of psychiatry, 162,* 1381–1383.

Moncher, F. J., & Josephson, A. M. (2004). Religious and spiritual aspects of family assessment. *Child and Adolescent Psychiatric Clinics of North America, 13*(1), 49–70.

Muris, P., Rapee, R., Meesters, C., Schouten, E., & Geers, M. (2003). Threat perception abnormalities in children: The role of anxiety disorders symptoms, chronic anxiety, and state anxiety. *Anxiety Disease, 17,* 271–287.

National Child Traumatic Stress Network (2008). Pediatric medical traumatic stress: A comprehensive guide. Retrieved May 19, 2008, from http://www.nctsnet.org/nccts/nav.do?pid=typ_mt_ptlkt.

Nugent, N. R., Ostrowski, S., Christopher, N. C., & Delahanty, D. L. (2007). Parental posttraumatic stress symptoms as a moderator of child's acute biological response and subsequent posttraumatic stress symptoms in pediatric injury patients. *Journal of Pediatric Psychology, 32*(3), 309–318.

Passaretti, D., & Billmire, D. (2003). Clinical experience: Management of pediatric burns. *Journal of Craniofacial Surgery, 14*(5), 713–718.

Pearlman, L. A., & Saakvitne, K. W. (1995). Treating therapists with vicarious traumatization and secondary traumatic stress disorders. In C.R. Figley (Ed.), *Compassion fatigue: Coping with secondary traumatic stress disorder in those who treat the traumatized* (pp. 150–177). New York: Brunner/Mazel Publishers.

Power, T., DuPaul, G., Shapiro, E., & Kazak, A. E. (2003). *Promoting children's health: Integrating school, family and community.* New York: Guilford.

Rusch, M. D., Grunert, B. K., Sanger, J. R., Dzwierzynski, W. W., & Matloub, H. S. (2000). Psychological adjustment in children after traumatic disfiguring injuries: A 12-month follow-up study. *Plastic Reconstructive Surgery, 106,* 1451–1460.

Saxe, G. N., Stoddard, F. J., Hall, E., Chawla, N., Lopez, C., Sheridan, R., King, D., King, L., & Yehuda, R. (2005). Pathways to PTSD, Part I: Children with burns. *American Journal of Psychiatry, 162*(7), 1299–1304.

Schreier, H., Ladakakos, C., Morabito, D., Chapman, L., & Knudson, M. M. (2005). Posttraumatic stress symptoms in children after mild to moderate pediatric trauma: A longitudinal examination of symptom prevalence, correlates, and parent-child symptom reporting. *Journal of Trauma Injury, Infection, and Critical Care, 58*(2), 353–363.

Seng, J. S., Graham-Bermann, S. A., Clark, K., McCarthy, A. M., & Ronis, D. L. (2005). Posttraumatic stress disorder and physical comorbidity among female children and adolescents: Results from service-use data. *Pediatrics, 116,* 767–776.

Sexson, S. B. (2004). Religious and spiritual assessment of the child and adolescent. *Child and Adolescent Psychiatric Clinics of North America, 13*(1), 35–47.

Stallard, P., & Smith, E. (2007). Appraisals and cognitive coping styles associated with chronic post-traumatic symptoms in child road traffic accident survivors. *Journal of Child Psychology and Psychiatry, 48*(2), 194–201.

Stallard, P., Salter, E., & Velleman, R. (2004). Posttraumatic stress disorder following road traffic accidents. *European Child and Adolescent Psychiatry, 13,* 172–178.

Stallard, P., Velleman, R., & Baldwin, S. (1999). Psychological screening of children for posttraumatic stress disorder. *Journal of Child Psychology and Psychiatry and Allied Disciplines, 40,* 1075–1082.

Stoddard, F. J., & Saxe, G. N. (2001). Ten-year research review of physical injuries. *Journal of the American Academy of Child and Adolescent Psychiatry, 40,* 1128–1145.

Stoddard, F. J., Saxe, G., Ronfeld, H., Drake, J. E., Burns, J., Edgren, C., & Sheridan, R. (2006). Acute stress symptoms in young children with burns. *Journal of the American Academy of Child and Adolescent Psychiatry, 45*, 87–93.

Stuber, M. L., Kazak, A. E., Meeske, K., Barakat, L., Guthrie, D., Garnier, H., et al. (1997). Predictors of posttraumatic stress in childhood cancer survivors. *Pediatrics, 100*, 958–964.

Stuber, M. L., Schneider, S., Kassam-Adams, N., Kazak, A. E., & Saxe, G. (2006). The Medical Traumatic Stress Toolkit. *CNS Spectrum, 11*(2), 137–142.

Studdert, D., Burns, J., Mello, M., Puopolo, A., Troug, R., & Brennan, T. (2003). Nature of conflict in the care of pediatric intensive care patients with prolonged stay. *Pediatrics, 112*, 553–558.

Walsh-Kelly, C. M., & Strait, R. (1998). Impact of violence and the emergency department response to victims and perpetrator: Issues and protocols. *Pediatric Clinics of North America, 45*(2), 449–457.

Wells, P. J. (1993). Preparing for sudden death: Social work in the emergency room. *Social Work, 38*(3), 339–342.

Winston, F. K., Baxt, C., Kassam-Adams, N., Elliott, M. R., & Kallan, M. J. (2005). Acute traumatic stress symptoms in child occupants and their parent drivers after crash involvement. *Archives of Pediatric and Adolescent Medicine, 159*, 1074–1079.

Winston, F. K., Kassam-Adams, N., Garcia-España, F., Ittenbach, R., & Cnaan, A. (2003). Screening for risk of persistent posttraumatic stress in injured children and their parents. *Journal of the American Medical Association, 290*(5), 643–649.

Winston, F. K., Kassam-Adams, N., & Marks, A. (2008). Screening and secondary prevention of posttraumatic stress after injury. A brief report: Current best practices and practical tools for health-care providers. Retrieved May 15, 2008, from http://stokes.chop.edu/programs/injury/files/Traumatic_Stress/screening_prevent_posttraumatic_stress.pdf.

Winston, F. K., Kassam-Adams, N., Vivarello-O'Neill, C., Ford, J., Newman, E., Baxt, C., Stafford, P., & Cnaan, A. (2002). Acute stress disorder symptoms in children and their parents after pediatric traffic injury. *Pediatrics, 109*(6), 1163–1169. Retrieved July 7, 2008, from http://www.pediatrics.org/cgi/content/full/109/6/e90.

Challenges and Guidelines for Helping

Part

The Challenge of Maintaining Hope and Fostering Resiliency

Implications for Youth, Families, and Practitioners

Nancy Boyd Webb

18

Chapter

Is the glass half empty or half full? The various chapters in this book describe in detail the multiple challenges associated with living with acute and chronic health conditions. Because of differences in human nature and in family dynamics, some young people tend to minimize the impact of their medical situations, whereas others magnify the influence and become preoccupied and depressed with fears about how the condition will derail or even destroy their lives. The reactions of families when learning about a diagnosis also may reflect these two extremes of either despair or optimism. Of course, it would be unrealistic to deny that a diagnosis of a serious medical condition will require certain lifestyle adjustments. The question is, to what extent does this diagnosis take control and become the centerpiece of the entire family's present and future day-to-day existence?

Practitioners and writers, like patients, also convey different perspectives when communicating about children and families with either medically *challenging* conditions or medically *compromising* circumstances. Both adjectives could be considered accurate in describing situations of chronic illness, but the language and terminology carry hidden messages. A *compromise* implies that something has been forfeited, whereas a *challenge* conveys the sense of an ongoing struggle. Although both terms may be correct, when applied to medical situations, one suggests that if the challenge is met successfully a positive outcome may be possible.

The purpose of this book is to demonstrate a variety of helping methods to assist the many children, youth, and families who must find a way to deal with the life-altering medical conditions that sometimes seem to take control of their lives. This chapter reviews some of the main points enunciated by the book's authors for helping medically challenged youth and families, emphasizing the importance of resiliency and positive expectations. The chapter concludes with a discussion about how this work can impact the helping professional, who must learn and practice principles of self-care in order to maintain the positive emotional energy to inspire and care for others who are struggling to cope.

Children and Youth in Family and Community Context

As we emphasize repeatedly in this book, an ecological perspective serves as the foundation for practice with children and youth because of their susceptibility to the influences of family members, peers, the school, and their community environments. Thus, while it is *the child* who is diagnosed with cystic fibrosis, it is *the parents* who must make the necessary adjustments in their own schedules to provide caretaking, arrange schooling, and help the child understand the restrictions and the possibilities associated with the disease. Because the parents' attitudes have such a significant influence on the medically ill child, it behooves professionals involved with the child's medical care to *always* pay attention to the parents' emotional states and to their corresponding ability to assist their ill youngster and other family members with the challenges imposed by the medical condition.

Professionals also should be open to answering questions and to recommending services for the parents pertaining to the child's diagnosis. The medical social worker or child life practitioner can also help the parents figure out and plan questions to ask the physician. Many parents are intimidated by physicians, and their anxiety may interfere with recall of important recommendations. The health care professional can help by sitting in on parent-and-physician meetings and by taking notes to review later with the parents. Other useful interventions include, for example, giving informational pamphlets about the child's illness and making a referral to a support group of parents whose children have similar conditions. Ideally, family-oriented psychoeducational or support groups emphasize family strengths and the development of positive coping and problem-solving skills (Gonzales & Steinglass, 2002). Support groups for siblings also serve to meet the needs of these family members, who sometimes feel neglected when all the attention is focused on the designated patient. These types of consultation and referrals are especially critical soon after diagnosis, but professionals should also make it a point to check with parents and siblings periodically about their feelings as time goes on and avoid focusing exclusively on the child or youth who is the designated patient.

A liaison with the school is also very important and, of course, should be done only with the parents' full knowledge, permission, and occasional participation. Often, it is helpful for the professional with medical knowledge to accompany the parent to the school for a conference focused on the child's educational needs. Interdisciplinary collaboration is essential to meet the various requirements of children with medical conditions and their families. Since school is such an integral part of a child's life, the medical professional can play an important role in helping the teacher understand the impact of the condition on the child's ability to concentrate and about any medically related restrictions on the youth's activities. However, as mentioned in other chapters, this sharing must be done with respect to the parent and child's comfort level and following the guidelines of HIPPA that protect the parent and child from having sensitive medical information disclosed to others without their permission (Openshaw, 2007).

These various forms of support for families of children and youth with chronic or acute health conditions combine methods of crisis intervention, psychological first aid, support groups, parent mentoring, and individual counseling that encourage the development of coping, resilience, reframing, and the positive dynamics of optimism and hope (Morison, Bromfield, & Cameron, 2003).

A Trauma/Crisis Perspective on Acute and Chronic Illness

Several chapter authors pointed out how the diagnosis of a serious illness can qualify as a traumatic event for parents and also for children and youth, especially when painful medical procedures have to be implemented (see, especially, Chapter 4). The degree of the traumatic response can vary from full-blown PTSD to partial traumatic anxiety reactions or, in some fortunate circumstances, to posttraumatic growth (Peterson, Park, & Seligman, 2008; Bonanno, 2004). These three different types of responses are discussed here.

Severe and Exaggerated Responses

The traumatic event of the diagnosis causes some parents to deny its reality and to ask for a second and third opinion. Later, when confirmation occurs, the parents may repeatedly verbalize the question, "Why?" When the illness has a genetic component, parents may be overcome with guilt feelings that can seriously disrupt their ability to focus on their children's needs. As a result, ill or injured children sense that something is terribly wrong and that their current and future life now has a black cloud over it. Their sense of identity may be affected, with the consequence that instead of thinking of themselves as "a child with an illness," they begin to feel as if they are "an ill child." In other words, the illness begins to occupy center stage and to dominate their self-image. This viewpoint, in turn, can make young people question their abilities and cause them to pull back from activities rather than attempting to carry on with whatever modifications might be necessary. Once the parents' fears have been communicated to their child, the child's reduced willingness to engage with the world further confirms the parents' worst expectations. It is a vicious, self-perpetuating cycle of negativity.

Minimizing Responses

In contrast, optimistic parents may emphasize how their child can "beat" or "overcome" the illness, and they may encourage the youth to proceed with school and other activities without focusing on the medical condition. This can be helpful as long as it does not cross the boundary into denial and lack of sensitivity to the youth's needs. The trick is to find the right balance between expecting *everything* to change drastically due to the medical condition and expecting *some* things to change, with willingness to make the necessary accommodations in order to permit life to proceed on course.

Transformative Responses

The situations of the resilient youth and their families who experience positive character transformations as a result of the medical condition will be described further below after considering some cognitive methods to help with either magnifying or minimizing responses.

Using Cognitive Methods to Enhance Self-Esteem and Improve Coping

The health professional can help the parents and the young person learn to reframe and restructure their thinking about the illness so that it becomes more manageable. This may involve the use of cognitive-behavioral strategies that encourage expectations of positive outcomes (Clay, 2004; Nader, 2001). The rationale behind cognitive-behavioral interventions is that thoughts influence feelings and then those feelings influence behaviors. For example, a young boy who wakes up and starts the day with the *thought* "I'm never going to feel better, there is no point to going to school" will probably begin to *feel* depressed and hopeless as he eats his breakfast, and this may lead to his developing a headache and a stomachache (*behavior*), which convinces his mother that he should stay home from school. However, if the mother has been instructed by the health professional to encourage the child to think positive thoughts, it may be possible for her to help the boy change his negative self-talk to positive statements that lead to more optimistic feelings and behaviors. For example, the mother might suggest that the boy say to himself, "The bad feelings will go away very soon and then I'll start to feel better." Another version of this positive self-talk that appeals to many children is to have them repeat the statement "I'm the boss of *me!*" This kind of response is very self-affirming and tends to increase self-esteem and resilience.

Readers who want more examples of positive reframing such as this may consult a practical guidebook that includes some very useful worksheets with exercises illustrating various methods for helping children deal with stress and improve their coping (Clay, 2004). Chapter 10 in this book also discusses the use of a number of cognitive methods to reduce anxiety and enhance coping. Of course, this positive reframing does not take the place of regular medical assessment to monitor the youth's condition.

Dealing with Stigma and Bullying

It can be difficult for children to retain positive self-images when their peers say hurtful and negative things about them, either directly or behind their backs. Children who are stigmatized or bullied because they look or act differently can experience reactions ranging from extreme anxiety to depression. Unfortunately, school-age children have quite circumscribed and rigid expectations about how their peers should appear and behave. A child with mobility or speech problems due to disability does not fit the mold. These children may be teased because they look or move differently from their peers, and this may take the form of ridiculing or of ignoring those who have a chronic illness that affects their appearance or behavior. According to Englander and Lawson (2007), who cite Olweus (1993), "Bullying can be either direct, such as physical or verbal aggression, or indirect, such as insults, threats, name calling, spreading rumors, or encouraging exclusion from a peer group." The aftereffects are serious for children who are bullied. They are five time more likely to become depressed; boys are four times more likely to be suicidal; and girls who are bullied are eight times more likely to be suicidal (Fox et al., 2003).

In view of the possibilities of these severe consequences, bullying should be taken very seriously, with interventions aimed at the entire school community to educate and sensitize all students, teachers, support staff, and administrators regarding peers who appear to be different from the norm (Englander & Lawson, 2007). It is *not* appropriate to ignore bullying. Rather, a social justice approach to this behavior is recommended that engages members of the entire school community and aims to work through the problems created by the offender's behavior without humiliation or stigma (Ahmed & Brathwaite, 2006; Braithwaite, 1999). This approach rests on the principles that bullying will not be tolerated and that methods to increase empathy and forgiveness will reduce insensitive and harmful behaviors (Harris, Petrie & Willoughby, 2002). Clearly, when a school sponsors programs that emphasize respect for all people, *everyone* will benefit, not only the medically challenged youth.

Another form of stigma that surrounds some medically compromised youth and that must be confronted is the *social taboo* associated with certain illnesses such as HIV/AIDS (see Chapter 15). Although we know that there is no danger of transmission through casual contact (Mangione, Landau, & Pryor, 1998) and that children with the diagnosis of HIV can participate in most school events without danger to themselves or others (Clay, 2004), many people still have fears about the possibility of contamination in situations of close contact with an infected person. Several decades ago, cancer also was a stigmatized illness because it was perceived as incurable and was associated with certain death. Now, with improved medications and improved longevity, this stigma no longer persists about cancer. We can only hope that HIV/AIDS will experience a similar acceptance over time. Clearly, young people with this diagnosis must be educated about how to protect themselves and others by avoiding unprotected sexual activity, shared needles, and uncovered bloody wounds. However, youth with HIV who behave responsibly can expect to live happily into adulthood, since the diagnosis no longer is a death sentence. While they may be subject to numerous infections, these can usually be managed with appropriate medications. Health professionals and counselors can help these young people develop and retain a positive view of their futures, despite their illness.

A Transformative View of Trauma and Crisis: Building on the Resilience of Youth and Families

The diagnosis of an acute or chronic illness, while always a shock, does not necessarily lead to the development of enduring traumatic symptoms. Typically, families experience a multitude of emotions that may wax and wane sequentially over time. Different families and youth respond differently, including the possibility that for some, the life-threatening experience can actually shape their character and lead to growth (Peterson, Park, D'Andrea, & Seligman, 2008). The positive psychological changes that can occur following a potentially traumatic event include improved relationships with others, openness to new possibilities, greater appreciation of life, enhanced personal strengths, and spiritual development (Tedeschi & Calhoun, 1995). Although the research confirming these associations was conducted on adults, we have many anecdotal examples of children who have flourished emotionally and spiritually despite chronic, and even fatal, illnesses. Several of these were cited in Chapters 1 and 10 and include Grollman (1988), Stepanek (2001), and children discussed in Krementz (1989 and 1992). The personal accounts of these children are extremely moving and inspirational, as is evident in the following poem by 10-year-old Mattie J. T. Stepanek (2001, p. 2), who was dealing with a rare form of muscular dystrophy that had resulted in the deaths of several of his siblings (used with permission, from *Journey Through Heartsongs* by J.T. Stepanek. Copyright © 2001. Mattie J.T. Stepanek. Reprinted by permission of Hyperion. All rights reserved.):

> I am Mattie J.T. Stepanek
> My body has light skin
> Red blood, blue eyes and blond hair.
> Since I have mitochondrial myopathy

I even have a trach, a ventilator, and oxygen.
Very poetic, I am, and very smart, too.
I am always brainstorming ideas and stories.
I am a survivor, but some day, I will see
My two brothers and one sister in Heaven.
When I grow up, I plan to become
A father, a writer, a public speaker,
And most of all, a peacemaker.
Whoever I am, and whatever happens,
I will always love my body and mind,
Even if it has different abilities
Than other people's bodies and minds.
I will always be happy, because
I will always be me.
May 2001

Maintaining Hope

We marvel at how some individuals not only survive, but even *thrive* despite the many restrictions and painful medical procedures associated with their medical conditions. Because I have taught a course on the topic of death and dying for the past 20 years, and because of my own interest in this subject, I habitually read the obituary notices in newspapers. I pay special attention when the death involves a relatively young person with a complicated medical history. In the course, we use the term *untimely* to describe deaths that occur to a person who is not elderly and who, according to insurance statistics, would be expected to live for several more decades. In most instances, the families of those who die young try to present the heroic characteristics of their beloved family member in the obituary. Sometimes, the account of the person's life reviews the numerous medical procedures that had to be endured, and usually the obituary concludes with a tribute to the spirit and bravery of the person. Sometimes these details seem to exceed the realm of possibility; yet facts are facts.

The following summary of the obituary of a 42-year-old man diagnosed with a rare form of kidney cancer is presented here with the permission of his mother, who feels honored that the story of her son's life and death could be useful in sensitizing health practitioners to the possibility of positive and transformative responses to chronic illness.

The obituary begins by stating that the man's extraordinary spirit and enthusiasm for life were qualities that he shared freely and lovingly with everyone he met. It continues by commenting that his life was defined by his refusal to succumb to his disease, despite a succession of operations, beginning with brain surgery at age 10, followed by multiple spinal cord surgeries, radiation treatments to his head and spine, the removal of his spleen, adrenal gland, and most of his pancreas, the development of diabetes, and later, the loss of hearing due to an inoperable tumor.

The account continues by detailing his adventures and accomplishments, including graduating from community college, being employed for two years, traveling, playing poker, building miniature furniture, and collecting *Star Trek* memorabilia and comic books. He even coauthored a book about the positive effects of the Beatles and their music on several generations. He had a number of pets, including a parrot whose favorite saying (copied from his owner) was, "Live long and prosper."

This obituary reflects both denial and transformation, insofar as the man, as a youth and into his adulthood, refused to let his serious medical condition define or defeat him, and, in fact, managed to maintain a positive, hopeful, and loving attitude toward his family and friends.

The concept of hope, in this situation and in many others where full recovery is impossible, evolves from the initial hope for a cure, to later hope of being able to carry on daily activities, to hope to be able to spend time with family and friends, and, in some instances, to hope for a pain-free, peaceful death. Thus the downsizing and reframing of the concept of hope makes it possible to continue to rely on it as a source of strength. Chapter 11 refers to an understanding of hope that is "functional, rather than outcome-based" (Lester, 1995). It has been said that "people need to have hope regardless of their life circumstances. Hope builds resilience and provides a window to the future" (Morison et al., 2003, p. 129). For many, it also connects with the concept of spirituality, which underlies the very meaning of existence. When medical conditions threaten to take away *physical* abilities, then emotional and spiritual needs seek and find a higher realm of expression.

Preventive Interventions to Assist the Practitioner in Avoiding Vicarious Traumatization

Sensitive readers who think about the many heartbreaking case examples in this book can feel overwhelmed and drained by the descriptions of the emotionally laden work with medically challenged youth and families. Practitioners in the medical field who face the pain and even death of young people every day sometimes come to dread their inevitable encounters with these difficult, life-altering cases. Young children and youth, in the best of all worlds, should not have to endure such painful medical challenges, and practitioners who encounter these circumstances on a daily basis may begin to question the purpose of life and their faith in its essential goodness. They may dread going to work, and when they are there they may avoid eye contact with patients and their families, and they may reduce the amount of time they spend with some of their more difficult cases. Other practitioners may find themselves obsessively thinking about a particular patient's situation and may even have difficulty sleeping because of an overwhelming sense of anxiety and/or worry about the outcome.

All of these reactions constitute serious cause for concern, both because they suggest that the mental health of the practitioner has been affected and because, under these circumstances, the medical worker may not be able to function adequately. The possibility of *vicarious traumatization* should be considered and appropriate treatment initiated.

Vicarious Traumatization: Definition

The concept of "vicarious traumatization" was developed in 1990 by McCann and Pearlman to describe the impact on therapists whose work with traumatized individuals becomes dangerous to them because of the therapists' empathic engagement with their clients. The medical professional who observes and hears firsthand the pain and trauma associated with a child's medical procedures may begin to secondarily feel some of the same hurt, and this experience can actually traumatize the professional. It may cause the helping person to feel helpless about protecting the child from pain, and, as a self-protective measure, he or she may withdraw, or become detached, from situations where more stressful experiences are likely. On a professional visit to a pediatric oncology ward of a children's hospital, I heard a young child screaming behind closed doors as he received a treatment that involved strapping him down and inserting a tube for his chemotherapy. As soon as this procedure ended, the child emerged from the room smiling and holding a stuffed toy and his mother's hand. A few minutes later, the nurse came out of the room and I commented that her job must be very difficult. She looked at me and said, "I am used to it: I spend *all* my mornings torturing children!" Although I was later reassured by other staff that this nurse was a very competent and upbeat practitioner, her comment made me think about the phenomenon of medical humor and how it serves the function of dealing with the anxiety-producing stress of the job. I also wondered how many hospitals are aware of the concept of vicarious traumatization and how many implement staff training to help professionals deal with their traumatic experiences in providing medical care.

Reasons Health Professionals May Experience Vicarious Traumatization

The basic reason for traumatization of the helping professional is the fact that the helper has empathy and wants to alleviate the child's pain, but cannot do so. People go into the fields of counseling and therapy (and even nursing and medicine) because they want to help others. Confrontation with situations beyond their control stimulates feelings of anger and helplessness. Also, uncertainty about a patient's prognosis increases the professionals' doubts about the future and reduces the possibility of offering reassurance to the patient and the family that things will improve. When there is no certain outcome, or when the outcome is negative, practitioners understandably find it difficult to offer the encouragement and inspiration their patients and families want and need.

Furthermore, when children and youth have conditions that are incurable, and when their deaths are inevitable, practitioners have to cope, not only with the family's grief, but also their own. After a child's death, staff members at some hospitals follow a ritual to help them process the death. Because staff members have developed close relationships with the critically ill child, they feel the loss deeply and must have an opportunity to process that loss.

Example of a Hospital's Response to the Death of a Child

Some hospitals hold a "remembrance gathering" for any of the staff who knew the child who died and who wish to attend. Family are not invited, which allows staff members to freely share their memories of the patient if they so choose. A "memory note box" is placed on the unit so that staff members who are not working on the day of the gathering can share their memories in writing. The service is designed to reflect the patient's particular spiritual beliefs. For example, when a young boy from India died, a *puja* (an offering of fruit and flowers) was included in the ceremony. The child was especially faithful, and this was a way of honoring him. Many staff members believe that the service helps them acknowledge their feelings of grief and that this, in turn, helps them feel the strength to move on and help other families and other children in their care.

Medical workers must learn to cope with their own stressful feelings in order to help their patients and families develop more positive outlooks. This process can be compared to being in an airplane when there is a drop in altitude and the pilot instructs passengers to put on their air masks; parents are told to put on their *own* masks first and then assist their children. Similarly, health workers need to deal with their own feelings of traumatic anxiety in order to be able to assist the youth and families who have been traumatized by various medical procedures and who are struggling to carry on with their lives.

Strategies for Health Care Professionals

This section is drawn from Ryan and Cunningham (2007) and Gamble (2002), who wrote about all clinicians who work with traumatized clients. Here, this content will be applied specifically to health care professionals dealing with medically traumatized children and youth.

The first step is for medical professionals to acknowledge that their work is taking an emotional toll on them and that it is affecting them both personally and professionally. Then the following guidelines can prove to be helpful for the purpose of learning to maintain a sense of personal well-being and competence.

Guidelines for Health Care Workers
- Create boundaries between home and work, and maintain a *personal* (as opposed to only a professional) identity.

- Seek out rejuvenating relationships and experiences.
- Engage in activities that promote a sense of efficacy and self-worth (these may include physical exercise, meditation, or any activities that are personally gratifying).
- Locate professional colleagues who understand the stress and trauma of hospital work and who can meet together periodically to support one another. (This mutual debriefing process helps normalize and universalize reactions of sadness and anger about a child's pain and decline.)
- Seek supervision from professionals who understand the stresses of medical work with children and their families.
- Spend time with children who are not medically challenged to maintain a perspective on typical child and youth behavior and the scope of normative development.
- Accept the fact of one's personal limitations. It is not possible to protect everyone from pain and death. Be comforted by the important fact that the child and family received the benefit of the team's best efforts.

These suggestions all support the concept of maintaining a balance between personal and professional identities. Professionals must give themselves permission and make a commitment to take care of themselves in order to be effective in their professional lives. Because medical work places such a great strain on an individual's emotional and spiritual resources, professionals must utilize some of these self-help strategies on a regular basis in order to restore and maintain a sense of well-being. The resulting positive energy will revive the self, so that compassionate attention once again can be focused on young people with acute and chronic health conditions and their families.

References

Ahmed, E., & Brathwaite, V. (2006). Forgiveness, reconciliation, and sharing: Three key variables in reducing school bullying. *Journal of Social Issues, 62*(2), 347–370.

Bonanno, G. A. (2004). Loss, trauma, and human violence: Have we underestimated the human capacity to thrive after extremely aversive events? *American Psychology, 59*, 20–28.

Braithwaite, J. (1999). Restorative justice: Assessing optimistic and pessimistic accounts. *Criminal Justice. A. Review of Research, 25*, 1–127.

Clay, D. L. (2004). *Helping schoolchildren with chronic health conditions: A practical guide.* New York: Guilford Press.

Englander, E. K., & Lawson, C. (2007). New approaches to preventing peer abuse among children. In N. B. Webb (Ed.), *Play therapy with children in crisis: Individual, group, and family treatment* (3rd ed., pp. 251–269). New York: Guilford Press.

Fox, J. A., Elliott, D. S., Kerlikowske, R. G., Newman, S. A., & Christeson, W. (2003). *Bullying prevention is crime prevention.* Washington, DC: Fight Crime: Invest in Kids.

Gamble, S. J. (2002). Self-care for bereavement counselors. In N. B. Webb (Ed.), *Helping bereaved children: A handbook for practitioners* (2nd ed., pp. 346–362). New York: Guilford Press.

Grollman, S. (1988). *Shira: A legacy of courage.* New York: Doubleday.

Gonzales, S., & Steinglass, P. (2002). Application of multifamily discussion groups in chronic medical disorders. In W. R. McFarlane (Ed.), *Multifamily groups in the treatment of severe psychiatric disorders* (pp. 315–340). New York: Guilford Press.

Harris, S., Petrie, G., & Willoughby, W.(March 2002). Bullying among 9th graders: An exploratory study. *National Association of Secondary School Principals Bulletin, 86*(630).

Krementz, J. (1989). *How it feels to fight for your life.* New York: Simon & Schuster.

Krementz, J. (1992). *How it feels to live with a physical disability.* New York: Simon & Schuster.

Lester, A. (1995). *Hope in pastoral care and counseling.* Louisville, KY: Westminster John Knox Press.

Mangione, C., Landau, S., & Pryor, J. B. (1998). HIV and AIDS (pediatric and adolescent). In L. A. Phelps (Ed.), *Health-related disorders in children and adolescents: A guidebook for understanding and educating* (pp. 328–336). Washington, DC: American Psychological Association.

McCann, L. A., & Pearlman, L. (1990). Vicarious traumatization A framework for understanding the psychological effects of working with victims. *Journal of Traumatic Stress, 3*(1), 131–149.

Morison, J. E., Bromfield, L. M., & Cameron, H. J. (2003). A therapeutic model for supporting families of children with a chronic illness or disability. *Child and Adolescent Mental Health, 8*(3), 125–130.

Nader, K. (2001). Treatment methods for childhood trauma. In J. P. Wilson, M. Friedman, & J. Lindy (Eds.), *Treating psychological trauma and PTSD* (pp. 278–334). New York: Guilford Press.

Olweus, D. (1993). *Bullying at school: What we know and what we can do.* Cambridge, MA: Blackwell.

Openshaw, L. (2008). *Social work in schools: Principles and practice.* New York: Guilford Press.

Pearlman, L. A., & Saakvutne, K. (1995). *Trauma and the therapist: Counter-transference and vicarious traumatization in psychotherapy with incest survivors.* New York: Norton.

Peterson, C., Park, N., D'Andrea, W., & Seligman, M. E. (2008). Strengths of character and posttraumatic growth. *Journal of Traumatic Stress, 21*(2), 214–217.

Ryan, K., & Cunningham, M. (2007). Helping the helpers: Vicarious traumatization of play therapists working with traumatized children. In N. B. Webb (Ed.), *Play therapy with children in crisis: Individual, group, and family treatment* (3rd ed., pp. 443–460). New York: Guilford Press.

Stepanek, M. J. T. (2001). *Journey through heartsongs.* New York: Hyperion.

Tedeschi, R. G., & Calhoun, L. G. (1996). The posttraumatic growth inventory: Measuring the positive legacy of trauma. *Journal of Traumatic Stress, 9*, 455–471.

Child-, Youth-, and Family-Health-Related Professional Organizations

Many of these organizations have national and regional conferences at which presentations feature current research, policy, and practice. Some also offer specialized training and certifications (see next section).

American Academy of Pediatrics
141 Northwest Point Boulevard
Elk Grove Village, IL 60007-1098
Phone: 847-434-4000
http://www.aap.org

American Art Therapy Association
11160-C1 South Lakes Drive, Suite 813
Reston, VA 20191
Phone: 888-290-0878
info@arttherapy.org
www.arttherapy.org

American Cancer Society
1599 Clifton Road NE
Atlanta, GA 30329
Phone: 800-ACS-2345, 404-320-3333
http://www.cancer.org

American Medical Association
515 North State Street
Chicago, IL 60610
Phone: 312-464-5000
http://www.ama-assn.org

American Music Therapy Association
8455 Colesville Road, Suite 1000
Silver Spring, MD 20910
Phone: 301-589-3300
info@musictherapy.org
www.musictherapy.org

American Professional Society on
   the Abuse of Children
350 Poplar Avenue
Elmhurst, IL 60126
Phone: 630-941-1235, 877-402-7722
http://www.apsac.org

American Psychiatric Association
1000 Wilson Boulevard, Suite 1825
Arlington, VA 22209-3901
Phone: 703-907-7300
http://www.psych.org

American Psychological Association
750 First Street NE
Washington, DC 20002-4242
Phone: 800-374-2721, 202-336-5510
http://www.apa.org

Association for Play Therapy, Inc.
3198 Willow Ave
Suite 110
Clovis, CA 93612
Phone: 559-294-2128
www.a4pt.org

Association of Pediatric Oncology Social Workers
No permanent mailing address or phone; see web site.
http://www.aposw.org

Asthma and Allergy Foundation of America
1125 15th Street, NW, Suite 502
Washington, DC 20005
Phone: 800-727-8462, 202-466-7643
info@aafa.org
http://www.aafa.org

Brain Injury Association
105 North Alfred Street
Alexandria, VA 22314
Phone: 703-236-6000, 800- 444-6443
FamilyHelpline@biausa.org
http://www.biausa.org

Child Welfare League of America
2345 Crystal Drive, Suite 250
Arlington, VA 22202
Phone: 703-412-2400
www.cwla.org

Children's Group Therapy Association
P.O. Box 521
Watertown, MA 02172
Phone: 617-894-4307, 617-646-7571

EMDR International Association
5806 Mesa Drive, Suite 360
Austin, TX 78731-3785
Phone: 512-451-5200
info@emdira.org
www.emdira.org

International Society for Traumatic Stress Studies
111 Deer Lake Road, Suite 100

Deerfield, IL 60015
Phone: 847-480-9028
http://www.istss.org

Juvenile Diabetes Association
120 Wall Street
New York, NY 10005
Phone: 800-223-1138, 212- 785-9500
http://www.jdfcure.com

National Association of Social Workers
750 First Street, NE, Suite 100
Washington, DC 20002-4241
Phone: 800-638-8799, 202-408-8600
http:www.naswdc.org

National Association of Perinatal Social Workers
http://www.www.napsw.org

The National Childhood Cancer Foundation
440 East Huntington Drive
P.O. Box 60012
Phone: 800-458-6223, 626-447-1674
http://www.nccf.org

National Adolescent Health Information Center
3333 California Street, Suite 245
San Francisco, CA 94118
Phone: 415-502-4856
http://www.nahic@ucsf.edu

Starlight Starbright Children's Foundation
5757 Wilshire Boulevard, Suite M-100
Los Angeles, CA 90036
www.starbrightworld.org

Training Programs and Certifications Related to Helping Medically Challenged Youth and Families

Play Therapy

A comprehensive directory of play therapy training programs may be obtained for a fee from the Center for Play Therapy, Denton, TX 76203. The programs listed here represent a small selection of those available in different parts of the United States.

Boston University
Advanced Child and Adolescent Psychotherapy
Betty J. Ruth, Director Professional Education Programs
School of Social Work
264 Bay State Road
Boston, MA 02215
Phone: 617-353-3756
www.bu.edu/ssw/pep

California School of Professional Psychology
Dr. Kevin O'Connor
5130 East Clinton Way
Fresno, CA 93721-2014
Phone: 559-456-2777

Center for Play Therapy
Dr. Sue Bratton, Director
P.O. Box 311337
University of North Texas
Denton, TX 76203
Phone: 940-565-3864

Lesley University
Advanced Professional Certificate in Play Therapy
29 Everett St.
Cambridge, MA 02138
Phone: 800-999-1959, 617-349-8544
www.lesley.edu/info/play

The Play Therapy Training Institute
Dr. Charles Schaefer and Dr. Heidi Kaduson, codirectors
P.O. Box 1435
Hightstown, NJ 08520
Phone: 609-448-2145

Postmaster's Certificate Program in Child and Family Therapy
Dr. Nancy Boyd Webb and Dr. Judith Siegel, codirectors
NYU Silver School of Social Work
Sparkill, NY 10976-1050
Phone: 845-398-4129
ssw.rockland@nyu.edu
www.socialwork.nyu.edu

Reiss-Davis Child Study Center
Director of Training
3200 Motor Avenue
Los Angeles, CA 90034
Phone: 310-836-1223

Art Therapy

See www.gradschools.com/Subject/Art-Therapy.

Music Therapy

See www.uscollegesearch.org/music-therapy-colleges.

Sandplay Therapy

The Center for Culture and Sandplay
P.O. Box 1064
College Park, MD 20740
www.cultureplay.com

Center for Sandplay Studies
Upper Grandview, NY
ljcarey@optonline1.net
Phone: 845-358-2318

Animal-Assisted Therapy

Delta Society
580 Naches Avenue SW
Suite 101
Renton, WA 98055-2297
Phone: 425-226-7357

Mercy College
555 Broadway
Dobbs Ferry, NY 10522
Phone: 914-693-7600
Special program in animal-assisted therapy.

People, Animals, Nature, Inc.
1820 Princeton Circle
Napierville, IL 60565
Phone: 630-369-8328
www.pan-inc.org
E-learning course in animal-assisted therapy.

EMDR and Trauma Treatment

Child Trauma Institute
P.O. Box 544
Greenfield, MA 01302
Phone: 413-774-2340
www.childtrauma.com

Andrew M. Leeds, PhD
1049 Fourth Street, Suite G
Santa Rosa, CA 95404
Phone: 707-579-9457
Fax: 707-579-9415
indo@AndrewLeeds.net

EMDR Institute, Inc.
P.O. Box 750
Watsonville, CA 95077

Phone: 831-761-1040

Fax: 831-761-1204

inst@emdr.com

Grief/Bereavement Counseling

Association for Death Education and Counseling

111 Deer Lake Road Suite 100

Deerfield, IL 60015

Phone: 847-509-0403

adec@adec.org
Certification courses for grief counselors and death educators. Offered during the two days preceding the annual National Conference in March or April of each year. Contact ADEC Central Office for details.

National Center for Death Education

Mount Ida College

777 Dedham Street

Newton Centre, MA 02459

Phone: 617-928-4649
Offers one-day workshops (spring) and weeklong institutes (summer) to train professional caregivers. A Certificate of Thanatology will be awarded following completion of necessary requirements.

Parent Training

National Parent Network on Disabilities

1130 17th Street NW, Suite 400

Washington, DC 20036

Phone: 202-463-2299

npnd@cs.com

http://www.npnd.org

Child-, Youth-, and Family-Health-Related Professional Journals

Art Therapy: Journal of the American Art Therapy Association

Mount Mary College

2900 N. Menomonee River Parkway

Milwaukee, WI 53222

Phone: 414-256-1215
atj@mtmary.edu

American Journal of Medicine
1840 East River Road
Suite E120
Tucson, AZ 85718
Phone: 800- 654-2452
JournalsOnlineSupport-usa@elsevier.com

American Journal of Public Health
APHA Books/AJPH
800 I Street, NW
Washington, DC 20001
Phone: 202-777-2464
ajph.production@apha.org

Child Abuse and Neglect
Elsevier Science, Inc.
360 Park Avenue South
New York, NY 10010-1710
Phone: 212-989-5800
www.elsevier.com

Child and Adolescent Social Work Journal
Kluwer Academic Publishers
P.O. Box 358
Accord Station
Hingham, MA 02018-0358
Phone: 781-871-6600
www.kluweronline.com

Child and Family Behavior
Haworth Press, Inc.
10 Alice Street
Binghamton, NY 13904
Phone: 800-429-6784
www.haworthpressinc.com

Child: Care, Health and Development
Blackwell Publishing
350 Main Street
Malden, MA 02148
Phone: 781-388-8200
www.blackwellpublishing.com

Child Development
c/o Society for Research in Child Development
3131 South State Street, Suite 202
Ann Arbor, MI 48108-1623
Phone: 734-998-6524
www.scrd.org

Child Psychiatry and Human Development
Kluwer Academic Publishers
P.O. Box 358
Accord Station
Hingham, MA 02108-0358
Phone: 781-871-6600
www.kluweronline.com

Child Study Journal
State University of New York College at Buffalo
Educational Foundations Department
Bacon Hall 306
1300 Elmwood Avenue
Buffalo, NY 14222-1095
Phone: 716-878-5302
www.buffalostate.edu/~edf/csj.htm

Child Welfare (formerly *Child Welfare Quarterly*)
P.O. Box 2019
Annapolis Junction, MD 20797-0118
Phone: 800-407-6273
www.cwla.org

Children and Youth Care Forum
Human Sciences Press, Inc.

233 Spring Street
New York, NY 10013-1578
Phone: 212-807-1047
www.cyc-net.org

Children and Youth Services Review
Elsevier Science, Inc.
360 Park Avenue South
New York, NY 10010-1710
Phone: 212-633-3730
www.elsevier.com

Children's Health Care
Lawrence Erlbaum Associates
10 Industrial Avenue
Mahwah, NJ 07430
Phone: 201-258-2200
www.erlbaum.com

Diabetes Care
6925 East Tenth Street
Indianapolis, IN 46219
Phone: 317-354-1508
http://diabetes.manuscriptcentral.com

Early Child Research Quarterly
Ablex Publishing Corp.
355 Chestnut Street
Norwood, NJ 07648
Phone: 201-767-8450

Gifted Child Quarterly
National Association for Gifted Children
1707 L Street NW, Suite 550
Washington, DC 20036
Phone: 202-785-4268
www.nagc.org

Health and Social Work
Taylor & Francis Group

325 Chestnut St, Suite 800
Philadelphia, PA 19108
Phone: 800-354-14
www.haworthpress@taylorfrancis.com

Infant Mental Health Journal
John Wiley & Sons
111 River Street
Hoboken, NJ 07030-5774
Phone: 201.748.6000
info@wiley.com

Journal of Abnormal Child Psychology
Kluwer Academic Publishers
P.O. Box 358
Accord Station
Hingham, MA 02108-0358
Phone: 781-871-6600
www.kluweronline.com

Journal of the American Academy of Child and Adolescent Psychiatry
Williams & Wilkins
351 West Camden Street
Baltimore, MD 21201
Phone: 410-528-4000
www.jaacap.com

Journal of Child and Adolescent Group Therapy
Kluwer Academic Publishers
P.O. Box 358
Accord Station
Hingham, MA 02108-0358
Phone: 781-871-6600
www.kluweronline.com

Journal of Child Psychology and Psychiatry
and Allied Disciplines
Blackwell Publishing
350 Main Street
Malden, MA 02148

Phone: 781-388-8200
www.blackwellpublishing.com

Journal of Clinical Child Psychology
Lawrence Erlbaum Associates
10 Industrial Avenue
Mahwah, NJ 07430
Phone: 201-258-2200
www.jccap.net

Journal of the American Hospital Association
P.O. Box 10946
Chicago, IL 60610-0946
Phone: 800-262-2350, 312-670-7827
e-mail: ama-subs@ama-assn.org
www.ama-assn.org/

Journal of Family Violence
Kluwer Academic Publishers
P.O. Box 358
Accord Station
Hingham, MA 02018-0358
Phone: 781-871-660
http://www.kluweronline.com

Journal of Traumatic Stress
Kluwer Academic Publishers
P.O. Box 358
Accord Station
Hingham, MA 02018-0358
Phone: 781-871-6600
http://www.kluweronline.com

Psychoanalytic Study of the Child
Yale University Press
P.O. Box 209040
New Haven, CT 06520-9040
Phone: 203-432-0960
www.yale.edu/yup/books/083718.htm

Social Work in Health Care
Haworth Press
Phone: 800-722-5857
http://swhchaworthpress.com *Trauma and Loss: Research and Interventions*

National Institute for Trauma and Loss in Children
900 Cook Road
Grosse Pointe Woods, MI 48236
Phone: 313-885-0390, 877-306-5256
http://www.tlcinst.org

Trauma, Violence and Abuse
Sage Publications Ltd.
6 Bonhill Street
London, EC2A 4PU, UK
Phone: +44 (0)20 7374 0645
http://www.sagepub.co.uk

Additional Health-Related Resources for Youth and Families

Foundations and Web Sites

For Children

Children's Hopes and Dreams Foundation www.childrenswishes.org
Educational booklets for terminally and chronically ill children who suffer any kind of illness, such as cancer, cystic fibrosis, AIDS, Hodgkin's disease, leukemia, muscular dystrophy, and sickle cell disease (706-482-2248).

For Teens

Online: www.grouploop.org. Web-based teen support groups.
Starlight Starbright Children's Foundation
5757 Wilshire Boulevard, Suite M100
Los Angeles, CA 90036
Phone: 800-315-2580, 323.556.3324
www.starlight.org

Starlight has launched *My Life*, an extension of the *Starbright World* online social network for seriously ill teens and teen siblings. *My Life* was developed specifically to help teens with life-threatening illnesses acknowledge and cope with the possibility of death (see www.myspace.com/starlightfriends).

Gilda's Club offers in-person support groups for teens who have cancer and/or who have a family member or friend with cancer (see www.gildasclub.org).

For Siblings

Supersibs!

5055 Newport Drive, Suite 502

Rolling Meadows, IL 60008

www.supersibs.org

Camp Make A Dream has a weeklong camp for siblings ages 6-17 (see www.campdream.org).

A national directory can be found at http://imtooyoungforthis.org/community/12y-camps.html.

For Parents and Teachers

www.ldonline.com (parenting tips, activities for kids, and current research).

CureSearch National Childhood Cancer Foundation www.CureSearch.org.

Nessim, S., & Katz, E. R. (1995). Cansurvive. *Teachers' guide for kids with cancer.* Los Angeles: Children's Center for Hematology-Oncology. http://www.cancervive.org/sfbv.html.

Two 15-minute videos and a 50-page teacher's guide.

For Medically Challenged Youth

www.kissyourcancergoodbye.com

bvholston@yahoo.com

I'm Too Young For This!

A national survivor-led support, research, and advocacy organization working exclusively on behalf of
[survivors and care providers under the age of 40].
http://imtooyoungforthis.org/community/i2y-camps.shtml
linkedin: http://linkedin.i2y.com
facebook: http://facebook.i2y.com
myspace: http://myspace.i2y.com

Sickle Cell
www.starlight.org/sicklecell

Miscellaneous

Adapting Motor Vehicles for People with Disabilities
Phone: 888-327-4236
www.nhtsa.dot.gov/cars/rules/adaptive/brochure/index.html

Books and Workbooks

Alexander-Azlin, M. L. (2000). *Beyond the rainbow*. Enumclaw, WA: Wine Press Publishing.
   A mother's story of her son's deadly battle with leukemia.

Best, C. (2002). *Goose's story*. New York: Farrar, Straus and Giroux. [Grades K-5] www.any-book-in-print.com.
   One of the geese is different.

Brown, B. S. (1997). *Oliver's high five*, Health Press.
   Octopus who has five arms instead of eight learns about discrimination and prejudice. Grades 2 to 5.

Brown, L. K., & Brown, M. (1996). *When dinosaurs die: A guide to understanding death*. New York: Little, Brown Young Readers.
   Ages 4 to 10.

Carion, H. S. (2008). *Sixty-five roses. A sister's memoir*. Toronto: McArthur & Co. (Teens).

Foss, K. S. (1996). *The problem with hair*. Omaha, NB: Centering Corporation.

Heegaard, M. E. (2003). *Living well with my serious illness*. Lanham, MD: Fairview Press.

Gerner, M. (1990). *For bereaved grandparents*. Omaha, NB: Centering Corporation.

Gordan, M. A. (1999). *Let's talk about sickle cell anemia*. New York: Rosen Publishing.

Gouss, D. J., & Leeds, E. M. *Tool box of hope*. Atlanta, GA: Healing Hearts Communications.
   An interactive workbook to develop coping skills when the body does not feel good.

Keane, N., Hobbie, W., & Ruccione, K. (2006) *Childhood cancer survivors: A practical guide to your future* (2nd ed.). Sebastopol, CA: O'Reilly.

The back of this book has a tear-out cancer treatment summary card that can be completed by oncology team or patient to use as a portable medical history.

Keene, N. (2003). *Chemo, craziness, and comfort.* Kensington, MD: Candlelighters.

Klein, S. D., & Schive, K. (2001). *You will dream new dreams: Inspiring personal stories by parents of children with disabilities.* New York: Kensington Books.

Krishner, T., Levine, A., & Westcott. B. (1992). *Kathy's hats: A story of hope.* Atlanta, GA: Whitman & Co.
    Ages 4 to 8.

McCue, K. (1996). *How to help children through a parent's serious illness.* New York: St Martin's Press.

Miles, B. S., & Wong, N. (2006). *Imagine a rainbow: A child's guide to soothing pain.* Washington, DC: Magination Press.

Mills, J. C. (1992, 2003). *Little tree: A story for children with serious medical problems.* Washington, DC: Magination Press.
    Grades kindergarten through third, www.anybookinprint.com

North, S. (200). *My brand new leg* LLC, Lithonia: Northstar Entertainment Group.
    Grades prekindergarten through third, www.anybookinprint.com.

O'Toole, D. (1995). *Facing change: Falling apart and coming together again in the teen years.* Burnsville, NC: Compassion Press.
    For teen siblings.

O'Toole, D., & Corr, J. (2004). *Helping children grieve and grow: A guide for those who care.* Omaha, NB: Centering Corporation.
    For parents.

Platt, A. (2003). *Hope and destiny: A patient's and parent's guide to sickle cell disease.* www.hiltonpub.com.

Sacerdote, A., Platt, A., & Sacerdote, A. (2002). *Hope and destiny: The patient and parent's guide to sickle cell disease and sickle cell trait.* Munster, IL: Hilton Publishing Company.

Salloum, A. (1998). *Reactions: A workbook to help young people who are experiencing trauma and grief.* Omaha, NB: Centering Corporation.

Samuel-Trailsman, E. (1992). *Fire in my heart, ice in my veins: A journal for teens experiencing loss.* Omaha, NB; Centering Corporation.

Scherago, M. G. (1987). *Sibling grief.* Redmond, WA: Medic Publishing Co.
    For parents.

Schmidt, R. C. (2003). *My book about cancer: A workbook to help children deal with the diagnosis and treatment of a father with cancer.* Oncology Nursing Society.

Schultz, C. M. (2002). *Why, Charlie Brown, why? A story about what happens when a friend is very ill.* New York: Ballantine Books.

Schwiebert, P., & DeKlyen, C. (1999). *Tear soup*. Bel Air, CA: Grief Watch.

Shavatt, D. & Shavatt, E. (2002). *My grieving journey book*. Mahwah, NJ: Paulist Press.
　　Ages 9 to 12.

Silverman, J. (1999). *Help me say good-bye*. Lanham, MD: Fairview Press.
　　Art therapy activity book.

Sonnenblick, J. (2006). *Drums, girls, and dangerous pie*. New York: Scholastic, Inc.
　　Junior high school to young adult; sibling issues in a family when a child is diagnosed with cancer.

Temes, R. (1992). *The empty place*. A child's guide through grief. Far Hills, NJ: New Horizon Press.
　　For young siblings.

Videos

Why Charlie Brown, Why? (1990). Leukemia & Lymphoma Society.

Making the Grade
　　For high school kids.

With a Little Help from My Friends
　　For middle school.

Dr. Nancy Boyd Webb, DSW, LICSW, RPT-S, was on the faculty of Fordham University's Graduate School of Social Service for 30 years, where she taught in the clinical practice area and developed and directed a Post-Master's Certificate Program in Child and Adolescent Therapy for 22 years. Dr. Webb holds the title of Distinguished Professor of Social Work Emerita at Fordham and formerly occupied the James R. Dumpson Chair in Child Welfare Studies. Dr. Webb is a leading authority on social work and play therapy with children who have experienced trauma, various kinds of losses, and bereavement. She is a prolific author and editor, with several texts on these topics. She currently is working on the third edition of *Helping Bereaved Children*. She has also been featured in a video demonstration of play therapy techniques and in several audio training tapes. Dr. Webb presents frequently as a keynote speaker and workshop leader at conferences nationally and internationally as well as fulfilling her varied writing commitments. She provides consultation and training to agencies and individuals related to play therapy and traumatic bereavement. She now divides her time between Massachusetts and Vermont, in close proximity to her two children and four grandchildren.

Jennifer Baggerly, PhD, LMHC-S, RPT-S, is an associate professor in the Counselor Education program at the University of South Florida. She holds a doctorate in counseling education with a specialization in play therapy. Baggerly is a Licensed Mental Health Counselor, a Registered Play Therapist Supervisor, and a Field Traumatologist. She has more than 14 years of clinical experience in play therapy and counseling children and families who have experienced trauma and disabilities. Baggerly's research projects and publications include the effectiveness of play therapy with children who are homeless and counseling interventions for traumatized children.

Rose A. Bartone, MSW, LCSW-R, is a medical social worker specializing in pediatric hematology and oncology. She provides long-term counseling and psychosocial and emotional support to children diagnosed with cancer and their families. Bartone has taught undergraduate courses in Early Childhood Development, Marriage and Family, Stress, and Self-Management and has facilitated grief/bereavement support groups. She earned a Master of Social Work degree from Fordham University, with a specialization in Children and their Families. She is currently a candidate for certification in Heart-Centered Hypnotherapy.

Ariel Allena Botta, MSW, LICSW, is the director of Group Psychotherapy for the Department of Psychiatry at Children's Hospital in Boston, Massachusetts. In this role as a teaching associate in Psychiatry at Harvard Medical School, she created and directs the group therapy program in the outpatient department and provides group work supervision, consultation, and training to the staff and trainees in the inpatient and community- and school-based programs within Psychiatry. She also has a private practice that includes group work and school consultation.

Roxia B. Bullock PhD, LCSW, ACSW, has a Post Master's Certificate from New York School Psychoanalytic Psychotherapy. She has taught at the Graduate School of Social Service and served as the Assistant Director for the Post Master's Certificate Program in Child and Adolescent Therapy at Fordham University. She served many years at the Department of Education in New York City. Currently, she has a private practice in Ossining, New York.

Cindy Dell Clark, PhD, MA, is an associate of the Center for Children and Childhood Studies at Rutgers University in Camden, New Jersey, where she currently teaches. Clark has published extensively on children's health issues, including *In Sickness and In Play: Children Coping with Chronic Illness*. She has also written about family rituals of childhood in *Flights of Fancy, Leaps of Faith: Children's Myths in Contemporary America*. She has done qualitative inquiry with children and families, both in academia and in applied research, and has been named a fellow of the Society for Applied

Anthropology. Clark is preparing a state-of-the-art book on child-centered qualitative research.

Douglas Davies, MSW, PhD, is lecturer at the School of Social Work, University of Michigan, Ann Arbor. His clinical articles focus on intervention with toddlers and parents, traumatized children, and child cancer survivors. His book *Child Development: A Practitioner's Guide* (2004) demonstrates how to apply child development principles to clinical practice. His current practice is devoted to reflective supervision of infant mental health clinicians and child care consultants. In 2005, the National Academies of Practice, Washington, DC, named Davies as Distinguished Social Work Practitioner, and in 2007 he received the Michigan Association for Infant Mental Health's Selma Fraiberg Award.

Rosemary Doyle, PsD, is a school counselor at Northwood School District in Minong, Wisconsin, where she has worked with students in kindergarten through twelfth grade for 20 years. She is also a senior lecturer at the University of Wisconsin, Superior, where she has taught in the graduate program in Counseling Professions for 10 years. Doyle is also a licensed professional counselor working with traumatized children and adults in outpatient and in-home settings. Her related research and presentations cover resiliency, abuse and neglect issues, play therapy, and school counseling.

M. Carlean Gilbert, DSW, LCSW, is an associate professor at the School of Social Work, Loyola University, Chicago. Gilbert joined the faculty in 1999 after practicing for 17 years as a pediatric social worker at the University of North Carolina at Chapel Hill and Duke University hospitals. She teaches clinical social work practice in health care, group work, psychopathology, and time-limited psychotherapy. Her scholarship focuses on health issues of children, clinical supervision, group therapy, and spirituality. She is editor of *The Clinical Supervisor: An Interdisciplinary Journal of Theory, Research, and Practice* and editorial board member of *Social Work in Health Care*.

Suzanne C. Griffith, PhD, is a professor of Counseling at the University of Wisconsin, Superior, where she has taught in the graduate program in Counseling Professions for 18 years. She specializes in school counseling and working with children and adolescents. Griffith has also worked as a middle and secondary school teacher and counselor, a district school psychologist, a community agency counselor working with adolescents and their parents in-home, and as a developmental disabilities specialist. Her related research and presentations cover ethnicity, gender, and class issues; women and violence; and promoting child and adolescent healthy development and assets.

Virginia Rondero Hernandez, PhD, is an associate professor in the Department of Social Work Education at California State the University, Fresno and a faculty researcher/evaluator for the Central California Social Welfare Evaluation, Research and Training Center at Fresno State University. She has taught at the university level for 16 years, and her social work career includes service in clinics, hospitals, schools, and community-based agencies. She has published research related to child health disparities, children's mental health, and substance abuse.

Joan Lovett, MD, FAAP, is a behavioral pediatrician in private practice in Berkeley, California. She graduated from Wellesley College and the University of California San Francisco School of Medicine. She completed pediatric internship and residency at Montreal Children's Hospital, after which she was a Robert Wood Johnson Clinical Scholar at Stanford University. Currently, Lovett is an EMDRIA Approved Consultant and EMDR Institute Facilitator. She has given presentations on treating childhood trauma at Menninger's Clinic, EMDRIA conferences in the United States, Canada, and Europe, and trainings in the United States, Europe, and Costa Rica. Lovett is the author of *Small Wonders: Healing Childhood Trauma with EMDR*.

Elaine C. Meyer, PhD, RN, a nurse and clinical psychologist, has provided many years of direct clinical service, consultation, and staff education in neonatal and pediatric intensive care settings. Her areas of clinical research include patient and family perspectives of critical care and end-of-life care, innovative family-centered psychosocial service delivery models, and interdisciplinary experiential training for holding difficult conversations in health care. Presently, she is director of the Institute for Professionalism & Ethical Practice at Children's Hospital Boston and associate professor of Psychology at Harvard Medical School.

Linda Openshaw, DSW, ACSW, is associate professor of Social Work and MSW program director, Texas A&M University, Commerce. Her interests include school social work, child and adolescent welfare, clinical practice, and the role of spirituality in social work. Openshaw practiced as a school social worker for 14 years in Utah and Texas and worked for three years in community mental health in Utah and California. She is the author of *Social Work in Schools: Principles and Practice*.

Patrick Shannon, PhD, currently an assistant professor in the School of Social Work at the University of Buffalo, will be an associate professor in the Department of Social Work at the University of New Hampshire in the fall of 2009. Shannon has been involved in the lives of individuals with developmental disabilities in various capacities for more than 20 years. He has published numerous journal articles and book chapters focusing on making service delivery systems more accessible for individuals with developmental disabilities.

Barbara Sourkes, PhD, is the first John Kriewall and Elizabeth Haehl Director of the Pediatric Palliative Care Program at Lucile Packard Children's Hospital at Stanford and associate professor of Pediatrics at Stanford University.

Paul Thayer, MDiv, DMin, is an associate professor of Education and Child Life and chair of the Child Life Department at Wheelock College in Boston. He teaches courses on Children and Illness, Bereavement Care, and Program Development. He has a Master of Arts degree from Assumption College, a Master of Divinity from Yale University, and a Doctor of Ministry from Boston College. He has held leadership positions in pediatric hospice and palliative care.

Deborah Vilas, MS, CCLS, LMSW, is a faculty adviser and instructor at the Bank Street College of Education in New York City, teaching graduate students in Education and Child Life. She teaches courses in Child Development and Therapeutic Play Techniques. Vilas has worked with children, adolescents, and families as a child life specialist in several New York hospitals, as well as in private practice. On a consulting basis, she provides clinical supervision to child life specialists and facilitates a peer support group for the Clown Care Unit of the Big Apple Circus.

Leslie H. Wind, PhD, is a clinical associate professor at the University of Southern California School of Social Work. She is also director of the Massachusetts Coalition of Child and Family Disaster Mental Health Education, a multidisciplinary team of professionals engaged in disaster research, and a member of the research and consulting team at the Terrorism and Disaster Center of the National Child Traumatic Stress Network. As a professional social worker for more than 20 years, Wind has extensive postgraduate training in the field of trauma. She has devoted most of her direct practice to trauma survivors and their families.

Author Index

Note: Page numbers in *italic* refer to authors listed in the reference lists.

Heisler, A., 122, *134*
Helfaer, M., 286, 287, *298*
Heller, D., 174, *185*
Hendricks, C. O., 258, *264*
Heyman, R., 107, *119*
Hiatt-Michael, D. B., 205, 213, *223*
Hibbard, R. A., 196, *203*
Hicks, B. A., *283*
Hicks, C. L., 289, *299*
High Noon Communications, 45, *53*
Hilden, J. M., *283*
Hobbie, W. L., 29, *33*, 244, *265*
Hoff, A., *118*
Hoffman, E. D., 40, 41, *53*
Holberg, C. J., *239*
Holbrook, T. L., 286, *299*
Holden, J. J. A., 193, *203*
Hollidge, C., 32, *33*
Holmes, A., 269, *283*
Holroyd, J., 93, *103*
Hom, C., 16, *19*
Horner, R. H., 195, *202*
Horwitz, S. M., 237, *239*
Hover, M., 172, *185*
Howe, N., 253, *264*
Hoyt, D. B., 286, *299*
Huegel, K., 108, *119*
Hughes, R. C., 196, *203*
Hull, G. H., Jr., 129, 130, *134*
Hunt, C., 191, *203*
Hwang, W-T., *265*

I

Ickowicz, A., 192, 193, *203*
Individuals with Disabilities Act, 200
Individuals with Disabilities Education Act (IDEA), 107, *119*
Individuals with Disabilities Education Improvement Act (IDEIA), 107, *119*, 124, *134*

Irvin, C., *54*
Ittenbach, R., 295, *301*

J

Jaaniste, T., *239*
Jansen, M. T., 274, *283*
Janssens, J. M. A. M., *204*
Jerrett, M., 23, *33*
Jimerson, S. R., *223*
Joe, T., 123, *134*
Johnson, A. M., 48, 50, *53*
Johnson, B. H., 48, *53*
Johnson, C., *118*
Johnson, L. S., 99, *103*, 107, 108, *119*
Johnston, C. C., *265*, *284*
Joiner, K., 95, *104*
Joint Committee on Infant Hearing, *223*
Jones, E., 100, *103*
Jones, H., 139, 140, *154*
Jones, K., *54*
Jones, L., 95, *102*, *264*
Jones, S. M., 270, *283*
Josephson, A. M., 287, 291, *300*

K

Kabat-Zinn, J., 164, *168*
Kaffenberger, C. J., 91, *103*, 105–111, *119*
Kahan, M. W., 276, *283*
Kain, Z. N., 61, 62, *72*
Kaiser Family Foundation, 40, 43, *53*
Kallan, M. J., *301*
Kanaan, S., *284*
Kassam-Adams, N., *265*, *282*, 285–289, 291, 295, 296, *298*, *299*, *301*
Katz, E. R., *264*, *266*
Kaufman, F., *240*
Kawachi, I., 45, *53*
Kazak, A., 21, *33*, *265*, 286, 287, *298*

Kazak, A. E., 14, *18*, 245–246, 253, *265–266*, 285, 286, 288, 295, 296, *299–301*
Keens, T. G., *283*
Kellam, T., 95, *102*
Kenardy, J. A., 290, *299*
Kennard, B. D., *239*
Kennedy, D., *240*
Keppel-Benson, J. M., 286, *299*
Kerlikowske, R. G., *316*
Kerry, S., 270, *282*
Kieckhefer, G. M., 50, *55*
Kincaid, D., 200, *202*
King, D., 287, *300*
King, L., 287, *300*
Kirby, D., *134*
Kirst-Ashman, K., 129, 130, *134*
Kish, V., 287, *299*
Kivimae Krimgold, B., 51, *55*
Klees, B. S., 40, *53*
Kleiber, C., 276, 278, *283*
Kleinman, A., 30, *33*
Kliebenstein, M. A., 105–109, *119*
Klingbeil, K. S., 296, *298*
Klingensmith, G., *240*
Knell, S. M., 167, *169*
Knittel-Keren, 192, 193, *203*
Knoblock, P., 208, *223*
Knudson, M. M., *300*
Knutson, J. F., 196, *204*
Koclas, L., *202*
Koenig, H., 172, *185*
Koepfer, S. R., 291, *299*
Kohlberg, L., *185*
Kolk, A. M., *267*
Kolodny, R., 139, 140, *154*
Kolterman, O. G., 234, *239*
Koocher, G. P., 269, 272–274, *282–284*
Koopman, H. M., *267*
Koren, G., 192, 193, *203*
Kotchick, B. A., 257, *263*
Kovacs, M., 93, *103*, 234, *239*
Kramer, E., 156, *169*

Subject Index

In vitro tests, 229
Isolation:
    and health care, 45–46
    social, 195
I Spy books, 78
ISRC (Immediate Stress
    Response Checklist),
    290

J
Joint Committee on Infant
    Hearing, 217
*Journal of Autism and
    Developmental Disorders*,
    211
Journey through Heartsongs
    (Mattie J. T. Stepanek),
    163, 310
Juvenile rheumatoid
    arthritis, 5

K
Katie Beckett Waiver, 48

L
Language:
    and autism, 211
    literal interpretation of, 64
    of medical conditions, 8–9
    person-first, 175
    and Spina Bifida, 194
Language barriers, 46
Large print, 220
Latex allergy, 15–16
Laxatives, 236, 237
Learning disabilities, 100
Legacy, 176
Legal considerations
    (in school-based
    interventions), 106–108
Legal rights, 90
Leukemia, 246–247, 251
LFTU (long-term follow up),
    114
Life review, 176
Life support, 84
Life threat, 288

"limbo" stage, 23–26
Limitations, 6
Long-term follow up (LFTU),
    114
Long-term perspective,
    247–248
Losses, 27–29

M
Magnetic resonance imaging
    (MRI) scan, 213
Mainstreaming, 217–219
Major depressive disorder, 234
Maltreatment, 195–196
Managed care, 43–44
Management:
    of pain and distress, 83
    of time, 92
Mandala drawing series, 159
Manual perspective, 217
Maternal and Child Health
    Bureau, 37, 42
Maternal serum screening,
    199
MCC model, *see* Medical crisis
    counseling model
Meaning-making, 22–23, 27,
    175
Medicaid, 39, 40–41, 123, 130
Medical conditions, 190–194
Medical crisis counseling
    (MCC) model, 272–273
Medical equipment, 75
Medical home, 48–49
Medical play, 75, 79, 158–159
Medical procedures:
    and child life practice,
        74–78
    and play therapy, 159
Medical social workers, 137–
    138
Medical trauma, 59–71
    and behavioral
        pediatricians, 68–69
    case study, 69–70
    and childhood cancer,
        245–246

and clinician knowledge,
    67–68
cognitive methods for,
    310–311
complicating factors of, 64
degrees of, 307–308
and normal child
    development, 65–67
and other trauma, 60–61
potential factors leading to,
    61–63
special considerations for,
    63–64
as term, 60
Medicare, 39
Medications:
    for asthma, 228–230
    for epilepsy, 26
    and hospital treatment,
        270
    for pain, 84
    for seizure disorders,
        213–214
    for sickle cell disease, 221
    and stress, 90–91
Memory boxes, 84, 181, 314
The Memory Keeper's Daughter
    (K. Edwards), 10
Meningitis, bacterial, 5
Mental Health Amendments,
    48
Mental retardation, 193
Military health care, 39, 40, 42
Mindfulness, 164–165
Mobility, 246
Modalities of treatment, 17
Model of spiritual care,
    178–182
Models of service, 122–124
Mood disorders, 36
Mothers, teen, 123
Motor disorders, 191
Motor movements, 211
MRI (magnetic resonance
    imaging) scan, 213
Multisensory deprivation
    (MSD), 216–217